ANALYZING QUANTITATIVE DATA

ANALYZING QUANTITATIVE DATA

An Introduction for Social Researchers

Debra Wetcher-Hendricks

Sociology Department
Moravian College
Bethlehem, Pennsylvania

A JOHN WILEY & SONS, INC., PUBLICATION

Published by John Wiley & Sons, Inc., Hoboken, New Jersey.
Published simultaneously in Canada.

For general information on our other products and services or for technical support, please contact our
Customer Care Department within the United States at (800) 762-2974, outside the United States at
(317) 572-3993 or fax (317) 572-4002.

Wiley also publishes its books in a variety of electronic formats. Some content that appears in print may
not be available in electronic formats. For more information about Wiley products, visit our web site at
www.wiley.com.

Library of Congress Cataloging-in-Publication Data:

Wetcher-Hendricks, Debra, 1970–
   Analyzing quantitative data: an introduction for social researchers / Debra Wetcher-Hendricks.
      p. cm.
   Includes bibliographical references and index.
   ISBN 978-0-470-52683-5 (cloth)
   1. Social sciences–Statistical methods.   2. Quantitative research.   I. Title.
   HA32.W48 2011
   001.4'2–dc22

                                                                    2010039497

Printed in Singapore.

10 9 8 7 6 5 4 3 2 1

CONTENTS

PREFACE

Until I reached graduate school, I never pictured myself as a social researcher, much less one who focuses on quantitative analysis. I took my first applied statistics course in graduate school only because the program's faculty recommended it. Little by little, though, the concepts of significance, linear relationships, and other statistical analyses became interesting and, even, appealing. Applied statistics allows me to use both my mathematics and writing skills. I have tried to convince many, including my students, that social research and data analysis is the best of all academic worlds, sometimes more successfully than others.

Those new to data analysis, I've noticed, fret over its mathematical component. After spending some time teaching data analysis, trying to find the most effective way to explain the meaning of a significant difference, and playing with numbers to develop perfect examples for my students, I realized that I had a book. The only problem was that the book existed in my mind and in my sloppily scribbled lecture notes. During a 2008 sabbatical, though, I decided to organize my thoughts and notes, rationalizing that, if I considered them worthy of my students, others might find them useful as well.

This book began as a short, "bare bones" guide to data analysis. In fact, its original title was *A Bare-Bones Guide to Data Analysis in the Social Science*. In my original vision, students and those needing to do research for their occupations could use the book as a resource for understanding what tests to perform and how to analyze the results. It contained as little mathematics as possible. A portion of the book description first sent to publishers touted it as presenting a "less math-focused approach to data analysis" than other data analysis texts do and that, "even those plagued by the commonly referenced "math anxiety" should find the explanations in *A Bare-Bones Guide to Data Analysis in the Social Sciences* easy to understand and apply.

As you leaf through this book, however, you can easily see that this vision changed. With encouragement from my publisher, I drastically expanded the book to include basic theoretical explanations for distributions, background information regarding formulas, and instructions for using SPSS® (Statistical Package for the Social Sciences, proprietary to SPSS, Inc.) to perform each of the analyses presented in the chapters. Thus, readers who just want to learn how to obtain a particular statistic can focus on the sections and examples related to these processes, focusing either on their own calculations or SPSS protocol. Information about the principles behind these statistics, however, is also available for those interested in such matters.

In its present form, the book can be used in a variety of contexts. Faculty teaching undergraduate and graduate courses may choose to use it in their data analysis courses. Although the title suggests that the topics covered in the book relate only to social science issues, faculty teaching research courses in related disciplines, such as communications and medicine, may find that the book suits their purposes as well. Faculty who use the book in their courses can consider it as a reference book, instructing students to locate particular topics if and when they become relevant to course assignments, or a text, assigning consecutive reading assignments as the semester progresses. Outside the academic realm, those involved in public service industries, including medicine, communications, government, marketing, and education professions, would find the book's information useful in understanding the research of others in their fields and in evaluating their own research projects. For these individuals, the book would most likely serve as a reference for particular analyses and interpretations as necessary.

The main portion of the book consists of three parts. The first part, entitled "Summarizing Data," describes methods of organizing data, including suggestions for coding and entry into spreadsheets or databases. In addition, Part I introduces readers to commonly used descriptive statistics, clarifying their roles in data analysis. The bulk of the chapters fall into Part II, entitled, "Statistical Tests," which addresses inferential statistics, and presents explanations of and instructions for performing chi-square tests, t tests, analyses of variance, correlation and regression analyses, and some advanced statistical procedures. Each of these chapters contains explanations for when to use the tests in question, relevant formulas, and sample computations. The final part of the book, "Applying Data," provides direction on eliciting meaningful conclusions from statistical tests and on writing research reports that describe procedures and analyses.

Each chapter ends with practice problems and, when relevant, statistical resources for SPSS. The "Statistical Resources" sections provide fundamental instruction for using SPSS to obtain the statistics discussed in the chapters. Companion websites for these chapters, found at **www.moravian.edu/aqd**, contain additional details about these processes. Other features of these websites include derivations of the formulas and some formulas mentioned, but not discussed fully, in the chapters.

The aspect of the book that likely caught your attention first, however, is its cover. At the risk of seeming philosophical, I find the photograph on the cover of this book analogous to the process of social research. With each level building on the level that came before, a social researcher moves closer to the answers that he or she seeks. This search inevitably becomes a never-ending process as each one prompts more questions and, thus, calls for more research. The building that reaches toward an endless sky, therefore, seemed a perfect fit for the cover of this book, and I thank Margaret Hunter Quigley, a wonderfully talented photographer, for allowing me to use it.

Many others deserve acknowledgment for their help during the process of writing this book as well. Steve Quigley, Associate Publisher at John Wiley & Sons, Inc., has served as a mentor throughout the course of writing and publication, and Jacqueline Palmieri, Assistant Editor at John Wiley & Sons, Inc. has shown great patience as I worked my way through the publication process. My colleagues, especially Dr. Bettie Smolansky and Dr. Dana Dunn, and family have given me much needed moral support.

I must also thank the directors of statsoft.com for allowing me to use the distribution and critical value tables from their website as a basis for creating those found in the appendixes of this book. An additional note of gratitude is extended to Gary D. Miner, who assisted me in obtaining these permissions. Finally, Andrew Watson has my sincere appreciation for his work in designing the book's supplementary website.

The cooperation of these individuals, along with my own tedious writing and revising, has produced a final product that I hope encourages the appreciation for and excitement about data analysis that I have.

PART I

SUMMARIZING DATA

1

DATA ORGANIZATION

1.1 INTRODUCTION

High school math teachers must cringe when they hear the age-old question "When am I ever going to need to know this?" Social scientists learn the answer to this question during their first attempts at social research. Early stages of research, including developing a research hypothesis, performing a literature review, creating data-gathering instruments, and actually gathering data certainly challenge novice researchers like you. However, the greatest anxiety seems to surround the anticipation of data analysis.

Those who have become familiar with data analysis, though, would tell you to relax. The challenges posed by data analysis pale in comparison to those already encountered by one who has designed and implemented a means of gathering data. Statistical analysis follows a relatively structured plan that, once recognized, provides a basis for evaluating data in any form. In fact, at the point of statistical analysis, the topic of one's study becomes somewhat irrelevant. The same protocols and techniques apply to all data, regardless of the issues to which the data pertain or the method used to collect them.

Analyzing Quantitative Data: An Introduction for Social Researchers, First Edition. Debra Wetcher-Hendricks.
© 2011 John Wiley & Sons, Inc. Published 2011 by John Wiley & Sons, Inc.

1.2   CONSIDERATION OF VARIABLES

You can refer to anything that changes as a *variable*. In the research context, a variable is an entity about which you gather data. These entities can change over time, for different people, in different situations, and for many other reasons. In your analysis, you attempt to determine whether these changes follow any particular pattern.

1.2.1   Units of Analysis

Before beginning the analysis process, you must acknowledge the origin points of your data, called the *units of analysis*. Each data point describes a particular unit of analysis. For social research, the units of analysis are most often human beings. Data indicating the responses to survey questions, behaviors observed during field studies, and performances on pretests and posttests of experiments all pertain to individuals. Social researchers refer to these individuals as *subjects* and to the compilation of their subjects as a *sample*. Proper ways to select your sample are discussed in Chapter 4.

Example 1.1: Human Units of Analysis A researcher who wishes to determine whether a relationship exists between the placement of one's tattoo on one's body and the cost of the tattoo, for example, would gather information about individuals who have tattoos. By speaking with these individuals or by observing them while they receive and pay for the tattoos, the researcher would obtain the information that he or she needs. Each data point originates with one individual person and, after data collection the researcher can associate each person with a tattoo placement and cost. Thus, people serve as the unit of analysis.

Like many other aspects of the social sciences, however, the identification of analysis units does not always remain so straightforward. Rather than evaluating individuals, some social research compares and contrasts social institutions or settings. Data points in these situations do not correspond to people. The origin of the data and, thus, the units of analysis, reflect the nonhuman entity that the data describe.

Example 1.2: Nonhuman Units of Analysis Slightly changing the focus of the study described in Example 1.1 to one that compares the prices of tattoo parlors in urban and in rural areas provides an example of nonhuman units of analysis. A researcher conducting this study would obtain prices from various randomly selected tattoo parlors and would characterize each as located in an urban or a rural area. In this case, the data pertain to locations of and prices at tattoo parlors, making these establishments the units of analysis.

1.2.2   Variables

Data analysis begins with the recognition of variables. In a general sense, the term *variable* describes anything that changes. This definition provides a foundation for understanding the concept of variables for social research. In this context *variables* are issues that the researcher measures. Each piece of data (datum) collected by a researcher provides information about a particular unit of analysis. The term *variable* applies because the information gathered generally addresses behaviors, attitudes, and characteristics that change from subject to subject.

Example 1.3: Variables For example, a researcher pursuing the study proposed in Example 1.1 would, at the very least, need to note the part of the body on which each individual receives a tattoo as well as the cost for receiving the tattoo. The information recorded about placement of tattoos on the body and cost of tattoos changes with each individual who provides information. These two aspects, then, are variables.

Some studies use more than two variables. The complexity of your study and your intentions determine the number of variables that you need to consider. Some scenarios involving more than two variables receive attention in Section 1.4 and in Chapters 8 and 10 of this book. However, developing an understanding of these situations rests on your recognition and description of the two main variables.

Roles of Variables. Even if you didn't realize it, you were likely aware of your study's independent and dependent variable(s) even before collecting data. However, you must formally address the distinction between the independent and dependent variables at the data analysis stage. When first introduced to the concept of research, you may have learned to regard the independent variable as the causal factor and the dependent variable as the effect of that causal factor. Although these associations may hold true for research in the natural sciences, social scientists should avoid causal terms when describing the roles of the independent and dependent variables. The section of this chapter entitled "Variable Relationships" further explains the importance of doing so.

You should think of the *independent variables* as a predictor of behaviors, attitudes, and characteristics. The independent variable describes a given condition, either already existing or created by the researcher before the start of data gathering. The *dependent variable*, then, refers to the behaviors, attitudes, and characteristics predicted by the independent variable.

With this understanding and previous identification of the two main variables for a study, you can simply insert variable names into the sentence, "Data about _____ predict data about _____." Placing the variable names into the incorrect positions leads to an illogical statement. Once the sentence accurately portrays the researcher's goal in the study, you know that the variable inserted into the first blank is the independent variable and the variable inserted into the second blank is the dependent variable.

Example 1.4: Independent and Dependent Variables This technique works well with the tattoo example. To determine whether tattoos cost more in urban or rural areas, the researcher wishes to investigate whether "data about location predict data about cost" and thus, will designate location as the independent variable and cost as the dependent variable.

Researchers who mistakenly placed the variable names in the wrong blanks would immediately notice the discrepancy between the statement and their intentions. Statements such as "data about cost predict data about location" do not depict the focus of a study investigating differences in cost as they relate to locations of tattoo parlors.

Variable Relationships. Even with a full understanding of Example 1.4, you may wonder why you can't simply claim that changes in the independent variable cause changes in the dependent variable, as depicted in the Figure 1.1.

Stated simply, social researchers can do no more than determine how well the independent variable predicts the dependent variable. The possibility that changes in dependent-variable data do not result directly from changes in the independent-variable data always exists. Such complexity may reflect issues of causal time order and intervening variables.

CAUSAL TIME ORDER. The possibility that a given relationship could reflect the influence of a dependent variable on the independent variable often exists. Thus, the order of causation, or *causal time order*, does not follow the assumed path. The causal diagram shown in Figure 1.2 appropriately illustrates this situation. This diagram displays the possible mutual influence of the variables on each other.

Example 1.5: Causal Time Order   It may be clear, for example, that artists at tattoo parlors in urban areas charge more than do those in rural areas. However, one cannot determine whether the location determines the price or the price determines the location. The generally higher prices in cities than in rural areas may explain the difference in cost, suggesting that difference with regard to the independent variable of location actually does cause differences with regard to the dependent variable of cost. But the researcher must also consider the possibility that location reflects cost. Perhaps, tattoo artists who insist on charging high prices find more wealthy clientele—who can afford expensive tattoos—in urban than in rural areas. Thus, they tend to open their parlors in cities, leaving those who charge low prices to open parlors in rural areas. (See Fig. 1.3.)

Independent variable ⟶ Dependent variable

Figure 1.1. Assumed causal diagram. The direction of causality, as indicated in the diagram, flows from the independent variable to the dependent variable. Although this progression may seem logical, it does not always characterize the relationship between the variables.

Independent variable ⟷ Dependent variable

Figure 1.2. Causal time order diagram. The arrows pointing in both directions suggest uncertainty as to whether independent-variable data influence the dependent-variable data or vice versa, whether the dependent-variable data influence the independent-variable data.

Figure 1.3. Causal time order causal diagram. The arrows pointing in both directions suggest uncertainty about the direction of causality. Although a clear relationship between location of tattoo parlors and the cost for receiving tattoos exists, one cannot conclusively determine whether location determines cost or cost influences determines.

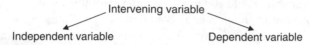

Figure 1.4. Basic intervening-variable causal diagram. A pattern between the independent variable and the dependent variable does not reflect one's influence on the other. Rather, a third, intervening, variable causes changes in both the independent and the dependent variables.

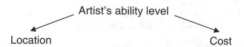

Figure 1.5. Intervening-variable causal diagram. The causal diagram including artist's ability level as an intervening variable suggests the lack of a direct causal relationship between location of tattoo parlors and the cost to receive tattoos.

INTERVENING VARIABLES. The potential presence of a third factor, called an *intervening variable*, can also dismiss the assumption that independent-variable scores cause dependent-variable scores. You rarely can claim with certainty that no intervening variable affects the relationship between the independent the dependent variables. The causal diagram (see Fig. 1.4) for such a situation identifies the intervening variable as the cause of changes in both the independent and dependent variables.

Example 1.6: Intervening Variable A tattoo artist's levels of ability might serve as an intervening variable in the relationship between location of tattoo parlors and price of tattoos. Very talented tattoo artists may tend to operate their tattoo parlors in urban areas, possibly because of the demand for high-quality work in cities where customers can choose from many tattoo parlors. Also, good tattoo artists can charge more for their work than can those who do poor-quality or mediocre work. This situation would lead to the presence of high-priced tattoo parlors in urban areas and comparatively low-priced tattoo parlors in rural areas.

The consistent relationship between location and cost (see Fig. 1.5) may make it seem as though one variable causes the other. However, no such causal path exists. The consistency results from the fact that the artist's ability level affects them both.

You should not make the mistake of thinking that a relationship between variables cannot reflect causal time order and intervening variables. These two issues can, and regularly do, coexist within a single relationship.

Example 1.7: Causal Time Order and Intervening Variable   The most obvious example of such a circumstance involves a combination of the scenarios presented in Examples 1.5 and 1.6. One could contend that the artist's cost of receiving a tattoo reflects both the location of the tattoo parlor and the ability of the tattoo artist. Further, the amount that tattoo artists wishes to charge for their work may determine the locations where they chooses to open their tattoo parlors.

Additional variables could add to the complexity of this relationship. For instance, the placement of a tattoo on one's body could play a role. Tattooing some parts of the body, possibly the neck or face, may require more skill than tattooing other parts of the body does. In fact, only very talented artists may be comfortable in placing tattoos on the face and neck. Clearly, then, a relationship exists between the ability of the tattoo artist and the placement of the tattoo. Also, because of the difficulty involved in drawing tattoos on clients' faces and necks, artists willing to do so may charge more for these tattoos than for others. The causal diagram in Figure 1.6 represents the relationship between location of the

Causal time order and intervening-variable issues prevent you from making concrete statements about causality. Some likelihood that the independent variable does serve as the "cause" and the dependent variable does serve as the "effect" in a relationship always exists. However, unless you can eliminate all ambiguity in time order as well as all intervening variables while gathering data, you can go no further than to acknowledge a general, nondirectional, relationship between the independent and dependent variables.

The Nature of Data.   The issue addressed by each variable dictates its nature. Some variables, for example, seek to group *subjects*, those who supplied data, according to shared features. Other variables seek to characterize subjects according to amounts of some measurable element. Therein lies the distinction between categorical and continuous variables.

CATEGORICAL VARIABLES.   *Categorical variables* sort subjects according to common characteristics. Essentially, they indicate the relevant category (hence the name) to which a subject belongs. These designations range from very straightforward everyday descriptions, such as identifying an individual as left-handed or right-handed, to rather complex, such as distinguishing between those in different tax brackets.

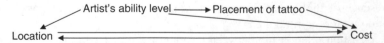

Figure 1.6. Causal time order and intervening-variable causal diagram. The causal diagram indicates interwoven relationships between the four variables. Intervening variables of the artist's ability level and placement of tattoo variable suggests the lack of a direct causal relationship between location of tattoo parlors and the cost of receiving tattoos. Further, the arrows pointing in both directions between location and cost suggest uncertainty about the direction of causality.

Most often, categorical variables address *qualitative data*, which provide nonnumerical descriptions of people or conditions. The simplest forms of categorical variables reflect qualitative data in the form of preexisting groups, often addressing personal characteristics such as area of residence, marital status, and eye color. Naturally existing categorical variables can also pertain to behaviors, situations, or beliefs.

Example 1.8: Naturally Existing Categorical Variables   The researcher who wishes to focus on the part of the body that people choose to tattoo, for instance, may visit many randomly selected tattoo parlors and make note of the area of the body on which each observed customer receives his or her tattoo. This information automatically creates categories into which the researcher can place each subject. Researchers can make the categories as detailed as necessary to serve their purposes. However, most prefer to use specific, detailed categories with the understanding that they can collapse the categories if necessary. Therefore, the researcher may use the categories of lower leg, upper leg, lower arm, upper arm, lower back, upper back, neck, and other parts of the body. Combining these categories into more general groupings, such as "torso" or "extremities," always remains an option.

Researchers may also impose categories on continuous data. Doing so generally begins with the creation of operational definitions to clarify the boundaries of each category. Using these definitions, the researcher can determine the appropriate group placement for each unit of analysis.

Example 1.9: Researcher-Developed Categorical Variable   Researcher-developed categories may help the individual described in Example 1.1 if that researcher wishes to consider the location of tattoo parlors. Because different people have different ideas about what constitutes an urban area and a rural area, the researcher must determine an operational definition for each.

Many alternatives for operationalizing categories in this context exist. On the basis of the US Census Bureau 2000 Urban and Rural Classification, the researcher may designate areas with population densities of at least 500 people per square mile as urban areas and those with less than 500 people per square mile as rural areas. Thus, the researcher can create a rubric for assigning tattoo parlors into categories based on their locations.

If you develop your own categories, you should record the name of each category and the qualifications for data to fall into it. This record becomes the beginning of a coding scheme, which receives further attention in Section 1.3.

CONTINUOUS VARIABLES.   Rather than indicating group affiliation, as categorical variables do, *continuous variables* describe subjects according to their positions along a sliding scale of values. A data point can fall anywhere along the continuum (hence the term *continuous*) of possible values. The progression of values indicates a consistent change in intensity or amounts. Mathematical operations, when applied to these values, can identify concrete relationships between data points. The typical person uses continuous variables every day when considering such things as temperature, prices of items to purchase, and calories consumed.

Example 1.10: Continuous Variable   The cost of tattoos, which served as the dependent variable in previous examples, is a continuous variable. Each data point for this variable exists along a sliding scale. Rather than indicating group placement, this variable seeks to identify placement within a range of amounts.

It would seem, given the association between categorical variables and qualitative data, that continuous variables always produce *quantitative data*, which uses numerical values to describe subjects. The arrangement, however, is not so straightforward. Quantitative data *do* reflect continuous variables. However, some of you may choose to adjust qualitative data in such a way as to characterize the relevant variable as continuous. Teachers, for example, assess students' performance on a writing assignment according to a variety of subjective factors, such as the clarity of a main-idea sentence and effective use of supporting details, which lend themselves to verbal, qualitative description. However, each teacher eventually develops an operationalized system of determining a numerical grade for each students' performance on writing assignments, thus quantifying the originally qualitative data. The resulting data points lie on a scale of values, giving the variable of "grade" a continuous nature.

Some survey formats can provide subject responses that further complicate the distinction between continuous and categorical variables. Likert-scale-type questions, for example, require subjects to indicate their levels of agreement to statements provided by the researchers (e.g., 1 = strongly disagree; 2 = disagree; 3 = indifferent; 4 = agree; 5 = strongly agree). The context of the question determines whether the researcher wishes to consider the relevant variable continuous or categorical. If she or he wishes to use the subject's levels of agreement as a basis for assigning them to groups for comparison on another factor, then the variable has a categorical nature. Comparing the levels of agreement for those in previously defined groups, however, makes the variable continuous.

Example 1.11: Implications of Context   Likert scale reponses to the statement "I've always wanted to get a tattoo," posed to subjects as they enter the tattoo parlor, can provide a good example of this ambiguity. The variable might take a categorical form for an investigation into whether those who have different degrees of desire for tattoos receive different sizes of tattoos. Assuming that the researcher uses the subjects' responses to the statement to create five groups, the independent variable of desire serves as a basis for tattoo size comparison, making it a categorical variable. Analysis would involve comparing the sizes of tattoos received by those placed into each category to determine whether those in one category stand out from the others. Although, in some cases, the researcher may expect to find that those in the "strongly agree" and "agree" categories received larger tattoos than did those in "strongly disagree" and "disagree" categories, other motives for such an investigation may exist as well. The researcher, for example, may wish to determine whether those with no strong feelings about getting tattoos (those in the "indifferent" category) received larger or smaller tattoos than did those with preexisting opinions, positive or negative, about tattoos.

Desire for a tattoo, however, does not always exist as a continuous variable. For an investigation into the possibility of a relationship between whether one's parents have tattoos and one's own level of desire for a tattoo, desire becomes a continuous dependent variable. The researcher would compare the levels of desire, which increases with the Likert scale numerical designation, for those whose parents do have tattoos to the levels of desire for those whose parents do not have tattoos.

Levels of Measurement. You have likely considered the natures of the independent and dependent variables before beginning to collect data. However, in the excitement of planning and conducting a study, many researchers give little thought to methods of efficiently arranging data until the task of data analysis looms before them. Although, ideally, researchers consider levels of measurement before the collection of data, attention to this issue often serves as the first step in the analysis process.

The *level of measurement* describes associations between measures of a variable and dictates the degree of precision with which the researcher can report findings. A variable's level of measurement depends, to a great degree, on its nature. When the issue of variable's nature (or characteristics) receives attention before data collection, it can influence the levels of measurement in the which researchers request or record data. After data collection, an understanding of the variable's nature helps you determine the appropriate descriptive and inferential statistics to apply in analyses. Statisticians have basically accepted and implemented Stanley Smith Steven's definitions of four levels of measurement. In 1946, Stevens presented the levels by distinguishing between the inferences that researchers can draw with each. As the level of measurement rises, increasingly sophisticated analyses become possible.

The lowest level of measurement simply categorizes. The name of this level of measurement, *nominal*, reflects the use of names (or, more formally, nomenclature) to distinguish between categories. Data measured at this level permit very few inferences. With its categorical qualitative nature, nominal data have no numerical value.

Example 1.12: Nominal Level of Measurement   Because of the categorical nature of the data regarding the location of tattoo parlors, as determined in Section 1.2.2, a researcher would use a nominal level of measurement to assess this variable. The designations of "urban" or "rural" do not insinuate any sort of value. They merely use category names to classify data.

Ordinal data's use of meaningful numbers places these date at a higher level than that produced by nominal measures. *Ordinal* measures produce numbers that specify rankings. These numbers permit the organization of data with respect to increasing or decreasing degrees of the measured behavior, attitude, or characteristic. Essentially, ordinal measures, as the name indicates, can place subjects into an order.

The presence of numbers in ordinal data makes it tempting to characterize the relevant variables as continuous. However, ordinal measures simply provide means to compare the categories established by nominal levels of measurement. They cannot indicate the amount of difference between the ranked elements. The difference between the highest-ranked subject and the next-highest-ranked subject may not be the same as that between any other two consecutively ranked subjects. The lack of consistent distances between data points renders calculations using ordinal data impossible. Variables that require ordinal measures, therefore, do not qualify as truly continuous.

Example 1.13: Ordinal Level of Measurement An extension of the tattoo study to address customer preferences for tattoo parlors may utilize an ordinal level of measurement. Researchers may ask tattoo artists, as a group, to indicate the most popular themes of tattoos (e.g., love, animals, patriotism, cartoon characters), the next-most-popular theme, the third-most-popular theme, and so on. Researchers would assign a ranking of "1" to the theme identified as the most popular and continue systematically with the assignment of values until reaching the least-popular theme.

These values only place the tattoo themes in order of ascending or descending popularity. The ordinal data do not indicate the amount of popularity that one theme has over another. For example, one cannot tell whether one more customer requests tattoos with the most popular theme than with the next-most popular theme or if 10 times as many customers do so. Further, one cannot apply mathematical principles to data collected using ordinal measures. A statement such as, "The theme ranked as '5' has only one-fifth the popularity of the theme ranked as '1'" has no validity in this context. The researcher can only conclude that, to some degree, more customers receive tattoos with the theme ranked with low numbers than with comparatively high numbers.

You can acknowledge degrees of differences between units of analysis only when data result from an *interval* or *ratio* measure. These measures produce data points that have consistent, known distances from one another. Therefore, they generally pertain to continuous variables. Because of the similarities in the types of data obtained by using these measures, many researchers refer to them collectively as the *interval-ratio level* of measurement. The particulars of the distinction between the two lie in the presence of an absolute-zero point.

Number sets without an absolute zero do not have a definite starting point. Negative values can exist, and the value of 0 does not necessarily represent the absence of a behavior, attitude, or characteristic. Such data, including temperatures and historical time (don't forget that years can have B.C. or A.D. designations), emerge from the use of an interval level of measurement. Although you can make sense of the distance between data points obtained through interval measures, you must use caution when making comparisons between values. Because data can extend into the range of negative numbers, interval measures do not always provide a clear understanding of relative amounts.

Example 1.14: Interval Level of Measurement The variables discussed thus far in the tattoo study do not require the use of an interval measure. Therefore, consider the issue of temperature. Degrees represent consistent units of measurement. So, contrasting 10° from 30° or −40° from −20° implies the same amount of difference in temperature. However, one could not express 30° as three times as warm as 10° or −20° as half as cold as −40° because such relative descriptions change with the values placement in the range of values.

As a result of the presence of an absolute zero point, ratio levels of measurement allow you to make the relative comparisons not permissible when using an interval measure. Ratio measures produce data points that differ by known, consistent amounts and that lend themselves to descriptions of one value as a portion of another.

Example 1.15: Ratio Level of Measurement   The costs of tattoos would use a ratio measure based on dollar units. The size of each unit and the difference between units forms a consistent, predictable system of values. Further, in this context, a value of 0 indicates no cost. This value serves as the starting point for data points, allowing for comparative statements regarding one value in relation to another. One could, for instance, describe a $300 tattoo as three times as expensive as a $100 tattoo.

A lack of understanding about the capabilities of each level of measurement can lead to invalid analyses and conclusions. Table 1.1 provides a quick reference to the four levels of measurement and the information available from each. You can use the table to help determine the appropriate level of measurement, based on expectations for data analysis.

When in doubt about the appropriate measure to use, you should gather data using the highest level of measurement possible. You can always simplify interval and ratio data into ordinal data and ordinal data into nominal data. However, data cannot become more advanced that its original form.

1.2.3   Attributes

Having identified a study's independent and dependent variables and considered the nature and measurement levels of each, you face the task of determining exactly how

TABLE 1.1. Measurement–Level Summary[a]

Capability	Nominal	Ordinal	Interval	Ratio
Allows for recognition of subjects' distinguishing factors	√	√	√	√
Allows for ranking of subjects	—	√	√	√
Allows for understandings of differences between subjects	—	—	√	√
Allows for relative comparisons between subjects	—	—	—	√

[a]Columns represent each of the four levels of measurement, progressing from the weakest level, on the left, to the most powerful level, on the right. The checkmarks below each column title indicate the extent to which the relevant measure allows researchers to describe data.

to obtain the data that you need. Most variables have a variety of *attributes*, or elements that provide the relevant data. The attributes indicate the values that the researcher desires, thus leading some social researchers to call them *indicators*.

Example 1.16: Attributes   For example, a researcher can obtain data about the costs for tattoos in a variety of ways. Listings of hourly rates for the tattoo artist's work, posted in tattoo parlors visited by the researcher, may appear the most obvious source. Using this method of obtaining data, the actual monetary values that appear on the price board (not the board, itself) constitute the attribute. Alternately, attributes can take the forms of tattoo artists' answers to questions about the prices of different tattoos. Answers from those leaving tattoo parlors with new tattoos about the amount that they paid the artist can also serve as attributes.

Clearly, you have options regarding the attribute to use. The attributes that prove the simplest to access often become the ones on which researchers choose to focus. However, because some attributes provide unreliable and inaccurate data, you must take into account the practicality and validity of the possible attributes to determine the most appropriate one or ones.

Example 1.17: Choosing Attributes   Giving this sort of attention to the attributes mentioned in Example 1.16 would likely lead to the recognition of some as substandard. On investigating the possible attributes, the researcher may determine that prices posted in tattoo parlors provide only estimates about the overall cost of tattoos. These prices may not include additional expenses such as tax or tip and various issues (e.g., number of colors used, deals for return customers) may alter the final cost of the tattoo. Thus, information gained this way may not accurately represent the total amounts that people pay for their tattoos. General answers given by tattoo artists about prices may pose the same problem. The researcher, therefore, would determine that answers from customers leaving the tattoo parlor about the prices they paid for the tattoos that they just received serve as the best attribute for the variable of cost.

Although appropriate in this case, researchers should not always rely on questioning subjects as a certain means of obtaining appropriate attributes. Questions about the amount that one paid for a tattoo have little chance of offending or embarrassing the subjects. So, only a very small likelihood of dishonest answers to this question exists. However, subjects may lie or provide limited information in their responses to questions about other topics. A researcher concerned about the legitimacy of information provided by subjects should gather data using some other attribute.

Gathering information from multiple attributes can provide you with some assurance that you receive correct information about a variable. If two or more indicators for the same variable provide very similar data, then you can feel relatively comfortable with the validity of the data. You can even combine these attributes to create a comprehensive representation of the variable. Blatant differences in data provided by multiple attributes signal at least one flawed attribute. In this situation, you must contemplate your choice of attributes.

1.3   CODING

Qualitative data easily become cumbersome during data analysis. For this reason, as well as to accommodate the requirements of statistical software programs that cannot interpret words, researchers develop *coding systems* to replace verbal data with numbers. Doing so does not make the data quantitative. The codes merely serve as symbols used to describe subjects.

Researchers most often use codes to represent subjects' categories or rank-order placements. However, even nonresearchers have encountered codes in their everyday lives. One evident example of codes in the nonresearch world involves baseball. Those familiar with the sport know that each defensive position has a numerical designation (1 = pitcher, 2 = catcher, 3 = first baseman, etc.). These designations simplify the process of recording and reporting plays. If, for example, with a runner at first base, the shortstop catches a fly ball and then throws it to the second baseman, who then throws the ball to the first baseman, sportscasters might refer to a "6–4–3 double play."

1.3.1   Coding Categorical Data

As presented thus far in the chapter, the nominal levels of measurement simply group subjects with similar behaviors, attitudes, or characteristics. A descriptive term for each division of a categorical variable, such as the "urban" and "rural" designations used in Example 1.9, usually suffice while collecting data. However, for analysis, numbers replace these verbal titles. The numbers are assigned arbitrarily and lack arithmetic value. They serve only as labels for the variable categories, maintaining the nominal characteristic of the data. Researchers call such numbers *dummy variables*.

Example 1.18: Codes for Categories   A simple system of codes can apply to the categories used to identify tattoo parlor locations. The researcher could code the parlors located in urban areas as "1" and those located in rural areas as "2." The dummy variables do not imply any value or ranking to the types of tattoo parlors. One cannot assume superiority of tattoo parlors located in urban areas due to its designation of "1," or that the designation of "2" for rurally located parlors implies that these parlors have more of something than do the urban parlors.

Because numerical dummy variables do not provide obvious descriptions of categories, as terms such as "urban" and "rural" do, you should create a coding frame. The *coding frame* serves as a key, listing the dummy values for a particular variable along with their meanings. Although you might believe that you will remember the meanings of the codes used, especially for variables with very few categories, you may not remember as much as you thought you would after collecting data for many other variables. Thus, you should purposefully record the coding scheme for each variable during data collection so that you have a reference for interpreting the dummy variables during analysis.

You can arrange the coding frame in any way that you see fit. Many, though, find it useful to use tables.

TABLE 1.2. Location and Placement Codes[a]

Variable	Code	Meaning
Location	1	Urban
	2	Rural
Placement	1	Arm
	2	Leg
	3	Shoulder
	4	Back
	5	Chest/stomach
	4	Neck
	6	Hands/feet
	7	Other

[a]Codes used to record data about the location of tattoo parlors and the placement of tattoos on subjects' bodies appear in the center column of the coding frame, and code meanings appear in the right column. Of course, the researcher may choose to make his or her categories more specific, requiring a greater number of dummy variables, or less specific, requiring fewer dummy variables, than those listed in the table.

Example 1.19: Coding Frame   Table 1.2 provides a sample arrangement for the variables of location of tattoo parlors and tattoo placement on the body.

Beyond the necessity of creating a coding frame, few rules govern the use of dummy variables. Although you have freedom to choose any numbers that you wish to use to represent the relevant categories, you must make sure that your coding scheme is logical and inclusive. The following suggestions help to create logical, inclusive coding schemes:

1. Dummy variables should remain as small as possible. To avoid unnecessary awkwardness, the researcher should keep the number of digits in the dummy variables to a minimum.
2. Generally, the number "0" represents a lack of category placement. This sort of situation likely wouldn't exist with respect to the scenario presented in Example 1.15. But a researcher who asks tattoo artists about the means with which they received training in tattoo artistry may have a need for this dummy variable, and could refer to a tattoo artist who indicates no formal training with a "0."
3. You should ensure mutual exclusiveness. Coded categories may not overlap. Each individual should fit clearly into one and only one category. The following codes for responses about tattoo artists' training are *not* mutually exclusive:

    0 = no training
    1 = apprenticeship

2 = tattoo artist school

3 = medical school

A tattoo artist may have received training through more than one of these means. One who attended tattoo artist school and worked as an apprentice under a licensed tattoo artist would not know whether to choose code 1 or code 2. To avoid such a problem, you should develop very specific categories or use individual "yes or no" questions to determine whether the subject has received training through each of the possible means.

4. You should ensure inclusiveness. The coding scheme should designate a number to represent data that do not fall into the established categories. Often, these data receives the designation "other." Failing to create such a dummy variable could result in the omission of important data, thus threatening the study's external validity.

5. Researchers should designate a number to represent missing data. A standout value that does not have a place in the coding scheme, such as "9" for Example 1.19, might suitably serve this purpose.

1.3.2   Coding Ordinal Data

Many of the issues relevant to coding schemes for categorical data apply to ordinal data as well. The fact that ordinal measures incorporate a ranking system, however, confines you somewhat in your assignment of codes. With ordinal data, you cannot arbitrarily assign dummy variables, as you can for categorical data. The numbers used to code ordinal data have a bit more meaning than dummy variables do because they follow a prescribed course with increases in numbers usually corresponding to consistent changes in ranks.

Data measured with formal scales may contain intrinsic coding systems. For example, Likert scales ask subjects to indicate their levels of agreement with a given statement by choosing a value from one to five (or, sometimes, from one to seven.) Responses of one suggest low levels of agreement, and values increase as levels of agreement increase. These values become the codes. If you do not have the convenience of a preexisting rank-ordered scale, however, you must develop a coding frame. Doing so generally poses little challenge as long as you remember to define your codes in a logical manner.

Example 1.20: Coding of Ordinal Data   A researcher may code the ordinal data regarding the popularity of tattoo themes, introduced in Example 1.13, by assigning a "1" to the theme identified as the most popular, a "2" to the next-most-popular theme, and so on until addressing all themes mentioned by tattoo artists. Data regarding individuals who receive tattoos could, then, identify the themes of their tattoos with these codes. The number assigned to each person would indicate the theme of that person's tattoo as well as its comparative degree of popularity. True to the definition of ordinal measures, the codes do not indicate the amount of difference in the popularity between the themes, but simply place them in descending order of popularity.

A modified version of this investigation may prompt the researcher to separate tattoo themes into three categories, coding very popular tattoos as "1," moderately popular tattoo themes as "2," and unpopular tattoo themes as "3." Then, each tattoo theme would receive a numerical designation, based on information provided during discussions with tattoo artists and predetermined operational definitions, to indicate its level of popularity.

1.4 DATA MANIPULATIONS

For the most basic of studies, you may be able to use your data in their raw form. The demands of a particular study, however, may force you to manipulate the data in preparation for analysis. Some analyses may pertain only to a subset of subjects or may consider each subset of subjects separately, requiring the separation of subjects according to the relevant categories. Other research scenarios might involve data not directly available to the researcher, but obtainable through computations using existing data. Filtering or splitting datasets and performing basic calculations with data before analysis begins can organize data as needed in preparation for the subsequent analysis.

1.4.1 Filtering Subjects

Filtering allows for the omission of certain subjects from an analysis. You may need to filter the subject's dataset if the analysis pertains only to a subset of subjects. Analogous to a coffee filter, which collects the unwanted grinds and allows the desired liquid to pass, a data filter withholds data from subjects who do not meet the desired standard. Thus, the data that pass through the filter correspond to subjects suitable for the analysis at hand.

With a relatively small dataset, filtering does not pose much of a challenge. You simply need to perform necessary computations (discussed at appropriate times in other chapters of this book) using data from the chosen subset of the population.

Example 1.21: Filtered Dataset   For example, suppose that the researcher performing the tattoo study wishes to investigate the responses that those with tattoos receive regarding their body art from the general public in everyday situations and creates a variable called "reaction." To gather information for this variable, the researcher may ask subjects to estimate the number of positive and negative comments that they receive about their tattoos on a monthly basis. But, because, in most everyday situations, one does not expose one's torso, the researcher may decide to exclude responses provided by individuals who have tattoos only on their backs, chests, or stomachs.

To do so, the researcher using the categories presented in Example 1.19 must filter data from those in the back and chest/stomach categories. The researcher, thus, only inserts data provided by individuals who have tattoos on their arms, legs, shoulders, feet, hands, and necks into the relevant statistical formulas.

1.4.2   Splitting Datasets

Unlike a filtered dataset, which allows for analysis of only selected subjects, a split dataset does not omit data from the analysis. Rather, it allows for separate analyses of subjects within each independent-variable category. The act of *splitting* a dataset, in and of itself, simply involves creating an individual listing of subjects that fit into each independent-variable category. Doing so allows for the evaluation of dependent-variable data within each independent-variable group. You would most often perform this task with the intent of obtaining descriptive statistics (explained in Chapters 2 and 3) for each category.

Example 1.22: Split Dataset   A researcher who wish to compare the responses received by those who have tattoos on different parts of their bodies would find it helpful to split the dataset. A split dataset would the enable researcher to distinguish between the number of comments received by those with tattoos on each part of their bodies rather than obtaining an overall summary for the entire sample.

1.4.3   Calculations with Data

Statistical analysis often involves the use of values that do not exist in the raw data. You can use calculations to merge data from different but related variables and to convert raw frequencies into percentages somewhat regularly. Such practices lead to the creation of new, calculated, variables.

Basic Operations. The basic mathematical operations of adding, subtracting, multiplying, and dividing account for most of the calculations performed on raw data. The rationales for using each of these strategies are obvious. Adding can produce a new variable to represent the total of multiple existing variables; subtraction can produce a new variable to represent the difference between values for two existing variables; and division, in conjunction with multiplying by 100, can produce a new variable to represent the percentage of one existing variable within another.

Example 1.23: Sum, Difference, and Percentage   Modification of data regarding the number of positive comments and the number of negative comments that subjects have received about their tattoos might involve any of these operations. Adding the values for the positive-comments and the negative-comments variables provides a value for the total number of comments received by each person. One who wishes to determine how many more positive comments than negative comments (or vice versa) that subjects receive would subtract the values for these variables. To determine the percentage of all comments received that were positive or that were negative, the researcher would divide the relevant variable by the total obtained through addition and then multiply each of the resulting proportions by 100.

Combining Multiple Indicators. Another motive for performing calculations with raw data stems from the use of multiple indicators or attributes, as described in Section 1.2.3 of this chapter. If you have used more than one attribute to supply data points, you may wish to combine the data points from the attributes to create a new collective indicator of the variable. As explained in Section 1.2.3, when only slight differences exist between data from attributes that pertain to the same variable, you can consider the measure a reliable one. Given this situations, you may choose to select only one dataset to use for your analysis. However, some researchers, loathe to ignore the minor differences that may exist in the data provided by the multiple indicators, prefer to incorporate all of the data gathered into a comprehensive representation of the issue at hand.

Many techniques for combining multiple indicators into a single all-inclusive value exist. The most straightforward method requires calculating the sum of each attributes values. The rationale for adding values in this context differs from the rationale for calculating sums discussed earlier. With regard to multiple attributes, the summed value can indicate fluctuations in values pertaining to a particular variable. If a subject's values for all attributes pertaining to a variable remain low, then that subject's overall summed score remains low. The corresponding logic applies to a subject with high values for all attributes. However, when attributes provide inconsistent values, the researcher benefits by using the sum to "balance out" the low and high values.

A technique slightly more advanced than adding values from multiple indicators involves the calculation of averages or, more specifically, means. Chapter 3 describes the role of means as output statistical analysis and provides instructions for interpreting these values as such. However, the use of averages as a tool in data manipulation requires only a very basic explanation. In fact, the mean really just serves as an alternate way of representing the sum. To obtain the mean, you would divide the sum by the number of addends used to obtain that sum. Means, like sums, account for fluctuations in the values provided by multiple attributes. But the values of means often prove more manageable to analyze than do the sometimes extremely large sums.

1.5   CONCLUSION

Clearly, based on the vast range of information presented in this chapter, data organization involves more than merely creating lists of information. The process of organizing data involves both conceptual and material elements.

Organization begins even before data collection begins. Identifying the independent and dependent variables and determining appropriate attributes and levels of measurement for each provides the a framework for understanding the managing the data collected. Further, the decisions made during these beginning steps essentially determine the focus of the entire study and the types of conclusions that can emerge.

These early steps generally prove the most challenging because they involve abstract entities. In comparison to contemplating as-yet intangible variables and levels of measurement, most novice researchers find the actual arrangement and manipulation of data easy. At this point, they can see the results of their previous efforts, generally promoting a sense of at least moderate self-satisfaction.

Many consider data manipulations coding, sorting, filtering, splitting, data files, and computing new variables as the conclusion of data organization and the beginning of data analysis. However, in truth, data organization rarely ends when analysis begins. You may find that you need to return to your raw data for further manipulations on the basis of the results of ongoing statistical analysis. Some reasons for doing so include reorganizing subject groups, comparing statistics for particular subsets of those who supplied data to each other or to the entire sample, and merging the values for two or more continuous variables. Thus, the procedures described in this chapter have relevance throughout the research process.

STATISTICAL RESOURCES FOR SPSS®

The data manipulations described in Section 1.4 of this chapter require minimal computations. You can easily handle them with a pencil, sheet of paper, and a calculator. However, social research projects often involve many subjects and many variables, making computations very cumbersome to perform without the help of a computer. Statistical software programs are most often used to help with the types of statistical analyses described in later chapters of this book. However, methods of basic data input and arrangement provide a good point of introduction into using such programs.

You may already have experience with spreadsheets, which resemble statistical software programs in basic appearance. Spreadsheets can organize data, perform basic analyses, and produce summary graphics of data. But they can perform only cursory assessments of data, providing a standard set of analysis options used most often by novice researchers. Statistical software programs provide more advanced statistical tests and more options for evaluation than spreadsheets do. Therefore, in the interest of maximizing the analysis capabilities, subsequent descriptions of software-based analyses refer to statistical software programs rather than spreadsheets.

Many statistical software programs exist, and each has its own benefits. One of the most popular programs used by social scientists, the Statistical Package for Social Science (SPSS), has a wide range of functions, including organizing data, obtaining and displaying descriptive statistics, and, as discussed later in the book, performing inferential statistical tests.

SPSS Screens

SPSS shows its users three screens at various points during an analysis. You input raw data in the "Data View" screen, which resembles a spreadsheet (Table 1.3).

By clicking the "Variable View" tab at the bottom of the "Data View" screen, you can access the "Variable View" screen, in which you supply SPSS with information about your variables (Table 1.4).

On this screen, you can

- Identify a name for each variable in the column entitled "Name"
- Inform SPSS of any special units of measurements or characteristics of the data in the column entitled "Type"

TABLE 1.3. SPSS "Data View" Screen[a]

	Name	Type	Width	Decimals	Label	Values	Missing	Columns	Align	Measure
1										
2										
3										
4										
5										

[a]The highlighted "Data View" tab at the bottom of the screen identifies the contents of the worksheet. Each column represents an individual variable. The numbers on the left of the screen refer to subjects. Thus, reading across a row, one can see a particular subject's scores on all variables for which data exist.

TABLE 1.4. SPSS "Variable View" Screen[a]

	Name	Type	Width	Decimals	Label	Values	Missing	Columns	Align	Measure
1										
2										
3										
4										
5										

[a]The highlighted "Variable View" tab at the bottom of the screen identifies the information that the page contains. On this screen, users can supply names and information for the data supplied by each variable.

- Increase or decrease the number of digits visible for a value in the column entitled "Width"
- Adjust the appearances of numerical values in the column entitled "Decimals"
- Provide a description of each variable in the column entitled "Label"
- Provide a coding scheme for qualitative data in the column entitled "Values"

A third SPSS screen appears when you request statistics or illustrations from the program. This "Output" screen varies greatly in appearance depending on the functions that you ask SPSS to perform. Chapters 2–9 contain examples of tables from output for the summaries and tests that they address.

Entering Data

Although the "Data View" screen greets you when you enter SPSS, you may find it easier to define the characteristics of your data in the "Variable View" screen first. Working in this screen first permits the SPSS program to correctly interpret the data as you enter them on the "Data View" screen.

TABLE 1.5. "Variable View" Screen with Data Information[a]

File	Edit	View	Data	Transform	Analyze	Graphs	Utilities	Window	Help

	Name	Type	Width	Decimals	Label	Values	Missing	Columns	Align	Measure
1	location	Numeric	8	0		{1, urban}...	None	8	Right	Nominal
2	placement	Numeric	8	0		{1, arm}...	None	8	Right	Nominal

[a]The names of all variables involved in the analysis appear in the leftmost column. The other columns contain information about the variables.

Example 1.24: Defining Data in SPSS   Table 1.5 shows a "Variable View" screen that provides SPSS with all necessary information about the variables described in Example 1.19.

All except three of the columns to the right of the "Name" column in Table 1.5 contain the SPSS default settings. Changes to the "Decimals" and "Measure" columns reflect the fact that both variables produced whole-number nominal data. Most importantly, though, the "Values" column contains a coding scheme for each variable.

The column headings on the "Variable View" screen refer to characteristics of your variables and the appearance of data on the "Data View" screen. You use the "Name," "Type," "Labels," and "Values" columns to input information about your variables, themselves.

In the "Name" column, you can list the names of your variables. After you enter them in the "Variable View" screen, the names of the variable should appear at the top of a column on the "Data View" screen. For variable names that do not clearly indicate what the variable measures, you may wish to input short descriptions in the column entitled "Label."

By default, SPSS identifies all variables as numeric. However, clicking on a cell in the "Type" column and then choosing the correct data type from those listed can change the default setting to indicate specified values (e.g., dates, money). To enter a word or name, such as to identify subjects by initials, you should identify that variable as a string. Be aware, however, that SPSS cannot interpret these strings; they have meaning only for users.

If your study involves categorical variables that you have coded, you can list codes and their meanings in the "Values" column. To enter the coding frame, you must click on a cell in this column. A window entitled "Value Labels" should appear (Fig. 1.7).

In this window, you can input the code for each category as a value and the names for each category as a label.

Other column titles on the "Variable View" screen refer to the appearance of data on the "Data View" screen. By entering information into these columns, you can change SPSS's default settings for the number of decimal places shown, the width of the screen's cells, and similar features.

Having input the specifications for your variables, you can refer to the "Data View" screen, where you simply need to enter the data for each variable in the cells below the appropriate variable name. Because SPSS understands only numbers, all data must take numerical form.

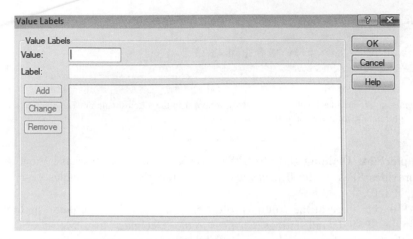

Figure 1.7. "Value Labels" window. The user provides codes for categorical data by typing the dummy variables and their meanings respectively into the value and label spaces. With this information entered, SPSS refers to the categories by name rather than by their numerical dummy-variable designations.

TABLE 1.6. "Data View" Screen with Data[a]

	location	placement
1	1	2
2	2	3
3	2	2
4	1	1
5	2	7
6	1	3
7	1	4
8	1	4

[a]Each variable name appears in the gray area at the top of the column that contains its values. Each row contains the data for a particular tattoo shop.

Example 1.25: Entering Data in SPSS   The data defined in Table 1.5 do not include any variables that need to be defined as strings. However, coding frames for the location and placement variables should appear on the "Variable View" screen. Doing so allows one to easily interpret the numerical values entered on the "Data View" screen. Data for 8 mock subjects appear in Table 1.6.

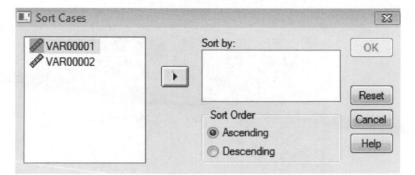

Figure 1.8. SPSS "Sort Cases" window. The user sorts data by selecting the appropriate variable from those listed in the box above. The designation in the "Sort Order" portion of the window instructs SPSS whether to arrange the values in increasing or decreasing order.

Formatting Data

The data in Example 1.6 appear as the user entered them. Various SPSS utilities, however, allow the user to manipulate inputted data. Options within the program's "Data" and "Transform" pulldown menus perform tasks such as sorting data, filtering cases, and performing computations.

Sorting Data. You can access the command to sort selecting "Data" from the options at the top of the SPSS "Data View" or "Variable View" screen; a pulldown menu should then appear. This pulldown menu contains a "Sort Cases" prompt and a "Select Cases" prompt. Each of these prompts leads to a window in which you input specific instructions.

An untitled box in the "Sort Cases" window (Fig. 1.8) contains the names of all variables for which data exist in the file. You can indicate the variable that should serve as the basis for sorting by clicking on its name and clicking on the arrow to the right of the box.

The "Data View" screen should change only in terms of the order in which it lists subjects. If you chose an ascending order, all information about the subject with the lowest score on the selected variable appears first and the information about the subject with the highest score on the selected variable appears last. If you chose a descending order, all information about the subject with the highest score on the selected variable appears first and the information about the subject with the lowest score on the selected variable appears last.

Example 1.26: Sorted Data Table 1.7 shows the data from Example 1.6 rearranged into ascending order according to placement.

Filtering Data. To filter data, you begin by selecting the "Data" menu from the options at the top of "Data View" or "Variable View" screen, just as you do to sort data. For this function, though, you need to use a "Select Cases" window (Fig. 1.9). The

TABLE 1.7. Sorted Data[a]

	location	placement
1	1	1
2	1	2
3	2	2
4	2	3
5	1	3
6	1	4
7	1	4
8	2	7

[a]As opposed to the arrangement of data in Table 1.6, the values in this table appear in numerical order of the placement variable's values. Although, in this context, these numbers have no numerical meaning, sorting still allows for distinctions between the variable's categories. Sorting based on an ordinal, interval, or ratio variable allows the user to see the progression from greatest to least or from least to greatest.

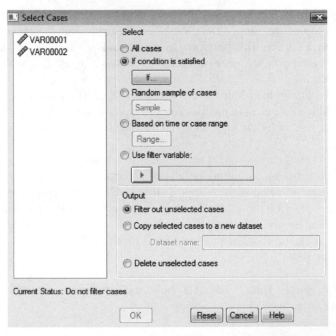

Figure 1.9. SPSS "Select Cases" window. The filtering process begins with the user informing SPSS that she or he will describe the data that should remain viable for future analyses. Selecting the "If condition is satisfied" option accomplishes this task.

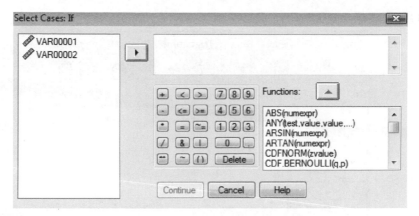

Figure 1.10. SPSS "Select Cases: if" window. The user filters data by selecting the appropriate variable from those listed in the box above and then defining the conditions for inclusion in the subsequent analysis. Until the user removes the filter, SPSS ignores all other data points.

"Select Cases" window, like the "Sort Cases" window, lists all of the variables for which SPSS has data in a box on the left.

The "If" button located in the "Select" portion of the window allows you to specify the guidelines that you would like SPSS to use when filtering a particular variable's data. Clicking on this button leads to another window, entitled "Select Cases: If," appears (Fig. 1.10).

Then, you can select a variable name from those listed in the box on the left and use the keypad located in the center of the window to describe the values of the selected variable that should remain in your analysis.

Example 1.27: Filtered Data   For example, using the data from Example 1.6, one who wishes to omit subjects coded with a "2" for the location variable of tattoo data from subsequent analyses would need to specify "location > 1." To do so, one would click on the variable name in the box on the left of the "Select Cases" window, then the ">" and the "1" buttons (e.g., location > 1).

The researcher would know that the dataset was filtered because the "Data View" screen would show diagonal lines through the numbers of all subjects not considered in future analyses (see Table 1.8).

To remove the filter, you need only choose the "All Cases" option from the "Select" portion of the "Select Cases" window.

Computing Variables.   The process for instructing SPSS to compute new values from the data that you have input begins differently than the process for sorting or filtering data does. The "Transform" option at the top of the SPSS "Data View" or "Variable View" screen contains the prompt for computations. From the "Transform" pulldown menu, you should select "Compute Variable." A new window entitled "Compute Variable" should appear (Fig. 1.11).

TABLE 1.8. Filtered Data[a]

		File	Edit	View	Data	Transform	Analyze	Graphs

	location	placement	filter_$
1	1	2	1
2	2	3	0
3	2	2	0
4	1	1	1
5	2	7	0
6	1	3	1
7	1	4	1
8	1	4	1

[a]One who wishes to focus only on tattoo shops located in urban areas for a part of the study would filter out shops with a code of "2" for the location variable. With this filter applied, the "Data View" screen contains an additional variable entitled "filter_$," which identifies the shops that remain in the analysis with a 1 and the shops omitted from the analysis with a 0. SPSS also displays a diagonal line through the subject numbers of omitted shops.

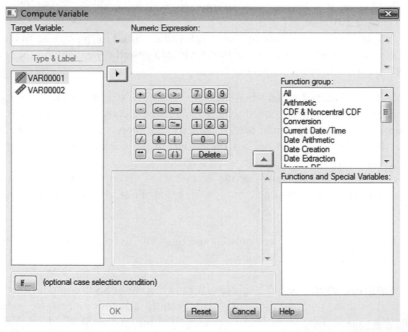

Figure 1.11. SPSS "Compute Variable" window. The user calculates a new variable from the existing values by first creating a name for the new variable and then inputting a formula to compute the new variable. The "Function Group" box contains commands for mathematical operations more advanced than those available from the keypad in the center of the window.

In this screen, you must identify the variable that SPSS will calculate, called the *target variable*, with a new name. By entering variable names from the box on the left of the window and operators for the middle of the window to the "Numeric Expression" box, you can instruct SPSS to perform the calculations that you desire.

The tattoo data do not lend themselves to an example for computing variables. The dataset contains only nominal values, so calculations would have little meaning. However, with a ratio measure, such as the cost for a tattoo, one might find the SPSS "Compute" function useful. You can see an example of a "Data View" screen that contains a computed variable on this chapter's companion website.

www.moravian.edu/aqd

REVIEW QUESTIONS

1.1. Identify the units of analysis for each of the following studies:

    (A) an investigation into whether a relationship exists between the number of acres on a college campus and the number of students enrolled at the college.

    (B) an investigation into whether a direct relationship exists between coffee consumption and blood pressure levels.

    (C) an investigation into whether boys or girls spend more time playing videogames.

    (D) an investigation into whether identical twins finish each others' sentences more often than do fraternal twins.

1.2. Identify the independent and the dependent variable for each of the research topics presented in Question 1.1.

1.3. Identify an appropriate attribute for each independent and dependent variable identified for Question 1.2.

For Questions 1.4 and 1.5, suppose that a researcher wishes to determine whether a direct relationship exists between the amount of violence that children see on television and their levels of aggression. The researcher's data indicate that increases in the amount of violence viewed on television correspond to increases in aggression.

1.4. (A) Provide a sample scenario to explain why the possibility of a causaltimeorder issue prevents the researcher from claiming that watching violence on television causes aggressive behavior.

    (B) Draw a causal diagram to show this relationship.

1.5. (A) Provide a sample scenario explain why the possible presence of an intervening variable prevents the researcher from claiming that watching violence on television causes aggressive behavior.

    (B) Draw a causal diagram to show this relationship.

1.6. Suppose that the results of a study indicate that students in advanced reading classes like to read more than do those in grade-level or remedial reading classes. On investigating this finding, though, researchers learn that a rather complex relationship between the variables exists. Explain this relationship in terms of the following causal diagram:

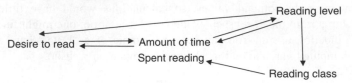

1.7. Identify the data described in Question 1.6 as most likely qualitative or quantitative.

(A) pages in a book.

(B) political party.

(C) food ordered at a restaurant.

(D) weeks of gestation.

(E) shipping costs.

1.8. (A) Give an example of a context in which the variable of "voting behavior" produces naturally existing categorical data.

(B) Give an example of a context in which the variable of "voting behavior" produces continuous data.

1.9. Give a real-life example of data that exist naturally in continuous form, but are regularly placed into categories.

1.10. Identify the level of measurement used to assess each of the following variables:

(A) distance.

(B) class rank.

(C) bank account balance.

(D) marital status.

(E) economic class.

(F) area code.

1.11. Identify each of the following statements as true or false. Explain your reasoning in terms of measurement levels.

(A) An apple orchard with 1000 trees has 500 fewer trees than does an apple orchard with 1500 trees.

(B) At Daily Grind High School, the homeroom class in room 309 contains 6 more students than the homeroom class in room 303 does.

(C) The second-place finisher in a swim race completed the race faster than the fourth-place finisher did.

(D) A person standing at 50 feet above sea level is 10 times as high as a person standing 5 feet above sea level is.

(E) The coding of private roads as "1," local roads as "2," state highways as "3," and national highways as "4" suggests that national highways are the biggest and private roads are the smallest.

1.12. Identify the problem with each of the following coding frames, used to notate the most time-consuming activity of each patron observed at a fitness/workout center on a particular day:

(A) 0 = activities other than exercise

   1 = arm and shoulder exercises

   2 = leg exercises

(B) 0 = activities other than exercise

   1 = aerobic exercise

   2 = nonaerobic exercise

   3 = exercise class

   4 = independent exercise

(C) 1 = aerobic exercise

   2 = nonaerobic exercise

1.13. Create a coding scheme for both independent and dependent variables in a study investigating whether a relationship exists between the weather and people's moods.

For Questions 1.14–1.16 consider a study for which a researcher asks a random sample of subjects about their most recent vacations. The researcher gathers information about the method of transportation used to reach the vacation destination, the number of nights spent at the destination, and the total amount of money spent during the vacation.

1.14. (A) Why might the researcher choose to filter his or her data?

   (B) Based on the response to part A (above), what categories of subjects would the researcher omit?

1.15. Why might the researcher choose to split her or his data file?

1.16. (A) Why might the researcher choose to perform a computation using the data that he or she has collected?

   (B) Based on the response to part A (above), what calculation(s) would provide the desired value?

2

DESCRIPTIVE STATISTICS FOR CATEGORICAL DATA

2.1 INTRODUCTION

Most figures reported by news sources, contained in speeches, and used in school reports take the form of descriptive statistics. These values simply summarize data. They *describe* (hence the name) the subjects in the sample that supplied data for the study at hand. This description often serves as the first step for a detailed analysis in which a researcher wishes to determine whether conditions present in the sample exist in the general population. As a researcher, you have an obligation, before actually performing any inferential statistics, to provide descriptive statistics for subjects' scores or category placement on the basis of the variables measured.

Admittedly, though, this explanation oversimplifies the matter. With numerous descriptive statistics available, you must give some thought to the most appropriate procedures to use. You should begin by considering the nature of your data because categorical and continuous variables require different methods of assessment. Knowledge of the variable's nature, however, does not, in and of itself, determine the appropriate statistic. Other differences, including the number of categories used for a categorical variable, the detail with which the data need to be presented, and the audience for the research report, must receive attention as well.

Analyzing Quantitative Data: An Introduction for Social Researchers, First Edition. Debra Wetcher-Hendricks.
© 2011 John Wiley & Sons, Inc. Published 2011 by John Wiley & Sons, Inc.

Descriptive statistics for categorical data generally involve measures of frequency. The "type of circus act" variable lends itself well to such measures. You can easily count the number of subjects in each established act category. In some cases, you may choose to code continuous data, such as those pertaining to weekly salary, into categories to make measures of frequency appropriate. If you separate weekly salary into categories that include ranges of values, you can determine the frequency for each category. Regardless of whether categories occur naturally or artificially, you can choose from a variety of frequency measures to describe the data.

The following mock data, based on a very small sample for purposes of demonstration, serves as a basis for descriptions and examples of these measures of frequency presented in this chapter. It characterizes each of 40 performers in The Other Brothers' Circus as part of a stunt act, a clown act, an acrobatics/strength act, an animal act, a sideshow act, or some other type of act. The dataset also includes weekly salaries (to the nearest $50) for each individual.

Subject	Type of Act	Weekly Salary
1	Acrobatics/strength	$800
2	Animal	$700
3	Animal	$750
4	Clown	$600
5	Sideshow	$550
6	Clown	$650
7	Sideshow	$450
8	Clown	$650
9	Other	$550
10	Animal	$700
11	Acrobatics/strength	$750
12	Acrobatics/strength	$600
13	Sideshow	$500
14	Sideshow	$500
15	Stunt	$800
16	Clown	$700
17	Acrobatics/strength	$650
18	Stunt	$750
19	Acrobatics/strength	$750
20	Sideshow	$350
21	Acrobatics/strength	$600
22	Stunt	$850
23	Other	$950
24	Sideshow	$450
25	Acrobatics/strength	$700
26	Acrobatics/strength	$750
27	Animal	$700
28	Clown	$500

Subject	Type of Act	Weekly Salary
29	Stunt	$650
30	Clown	$400
31	Animal	$800
32	Sideshow	$400
33	Sideshow	$500
34	Clown	$600
35	Stunt	$850
36	Clown	$550
37	Clown	$600
38	Sideshow	$450
39	Stunt	$700
40	Acrobatics/strength	$750

2.2 FREQUENCY TABLES

2.2.1 Using Existing Categories

The simplest way to report frequencies for categorical data involves simply providing the numbers pertaining to each category. Frequency tables do so by listing the categories on the left and the corresponding frequencies on the right with the sum (Σ) of the values at the bottom of the chart.

Example 2.1: Frequency Table for Categorical Data   The process of creating a frequency table remains quite straightforward when tending to a variable such as type of act. As well as displaying frequencies, Table 2.1 contains percentages of the entire population encompassed in each group. The researcher can determine whether to include or omit this additional column.

By viewing the frequency table, one can easily discern the category into which the most subjects fall and the category into which the least subjects fall. For this example, a three-way tie exists for the most popular category. Statisticians refer to this situation as *trimodal*, with the term *mode* referring to the most common populous. With categorical data, as in the circus example, the mode's value refers to the code assigned to the relevant category or categories. So, in this case, assuming a coding scheme of 1 = stunt, 2 = clown, 3 = acrobatics/strength, 4 = animal, 5 = sideshow, and 6 = other, the modes would be 2, 3, and 5. However, these values have no meaning unless the researcher further explains that they specify clown acts, acrobatics/strength acts, and sideshow acts respectively.

2.2.2 Creating Categories

A frequency table based on the dependent variable requires an additional step. Because the variable of weekly salary exists on a continuous scale, you must begin by defining categories. Doing so involves a number of steps:

TABLE 2.1. Frequency Table for Circus Act[a]

Act	Frequency	Percentage (%)
Stunt	6	15
Clown	9	22.5
Acrobatics/strength	9	22.5
Animal	5	12.5
Sideshow	9	22.5
Other	2	5
Σ	40	100

[a]Categories for the variable of type of act appear in the left column of the table, and frequencies for each category appear in the right column.

1. Determine the desired number of categories or *classes*. When making this decision, you should consider the specificity with which you need to report information. As the number of classes increases, the amount of detail available about the data increases.

2. According to the number of categories chosen, establish the class width. The *class width* refers to the range of the categories. The easiest way to determine this value involves dividing the difference between the dataset's maximum and minimum values by the number of categories. If this calculation does not produce a whole number (which isn't absolutely necessary, but helps to limit the complexity of later operations), you can use values slightly higher than the maximum or slightly lower than the minimum values to produce the difference.

3. Identify the *class limits*. The smaller of the two numbers used to calculate the class width becomes the lower class limit of the first category. Obtain lower class limits for subsequent categories by repeatedly adding the value of the class width. Upper class limits should lie just below the following class' lower limits or, in the case of the limit for the last class, just below the value of the imaginary next category. With very specific values, you may choose to end these values in .9 or .99.

4. Obtain frequencies for each class and produce the frequency table. Using tallymarks often helps with this task.

Example 2.2: Frequency Table for Continuous Variable Divided into Classes   The following four steps, when applied to the continuous variable of weekly salary, permit the creation of a frequency table that appears very similar to that provided for the categorical variable of circus act:

1. Given the minimum value of 350 and the maximum value of 950 for the variable of weekly salary, a researcher who needs to report relatively general descriptions may choose to use five categories.

TABLE 2.2. Frequency Table for Weekly Salary[a]

Weekly Salary ($)	Tallies	Frequency	Percentage (%)
300–449	III	3	7.5
450–599	IIIIIIIIII	10	25
600–749	IIIIIIIIIIIIII	14	35
750–899	IIIIIIIIIIII	12	30
900–1050	I	1	2.5
Σ		40	100

[a]Class limits appear in the left column of the table and frequencies for each category appear in the right column. The center column, consisting of tallymarks, allows the researcher to keep track of the number of elements in each class while reviewing the data, but the chart does not need to contain this feature.

2. Many options for extending the range of values in the dataset exist. In the interest of maintaining simplicity, one may wish to use the values of 300 and 1050. Subtracting these values and dividing the difference by 5, one obtains the number of classes chosen, which produces a class width of 150.

3. The lower class limits for the weekly salary data become 300, 450, 600, 750, and 900. Although upper class limits can specify to the nearest tenth or hundredth of a value, weekly salaries rounded to the nearest $50 do not require such particularity. Upper class limits of 449, 599, 749, 899, and 1050 suffice.

4. The resulting frequency table appears as shown in Table 2.2.

2.3 CROSSTABULATIONS

Each of the frequency tables presented in Section 2.2 addresses a single variable. If you have frequencies for a combination of two or more variables' categories, a crosstabulation becomes necessary. A *crosstabulation* is essentially a table that presents each variable as a row, column, or, in the case of complex crosstabulations, a layer. The intersection of each row, column, and layer produces a cell that contains the number of subjects who have the relevant combination of characteristics. *Marginal values* provide sums of all cells in a particular row, column, or layer.

2.3.1 Basic (Single-Layer) Crosstabulations

A simple example of a crosstabulation involves two categorical variables, such as circus performers' sexes and types of acts, and uses only rows and columns.

Example 2.3: Basic Two-Variable Crosstabulation   A researcher who happens to know that—of the 40 subjects who provide the sample circus data—subjects 1–20 are male and subjects 21–40 are female could combine this information with circus act frequencies to produce the crosstabulation in Table 2.3. Although the arrangement of this crosstabulation designates circus act as columns and sex as rows, these placements are arbitrary. The researcher can assign the variables to rows and columns as desired.

TABLE 2.3. Frequency Crosstabulation for Act and Sex[a]

| | Act | | | | | | |
Sex	Stunt	Clown	Acrobatics/strength	Animal	Sideshow	Other	Σ
Female	2	4	5	3	5	1	20
Male	4	5	4	2	4	1	20
Σ	6	9	9	5	9	2	40

[a]Each cell in the crosstabulation contains the frequency for the combination of circus act and sex or as a marginal value. The total number of subjects who perform each type of act appear in the row labeled Σ, which represents the process of summing values. Similarly, the column labeled Σ contains the total number of males and females in the sample.

TABLE 2.4. Row Percentage and Frequency Crosstabulation for Act and Sex[a]

| | Act | | | | | | |
Sex	Stunt	Clown	Acrobatics/strength	Animal	Sideshow	Other	Σ
Female	2 (10%)	4 (20%)	5 (25%)	3 (15%)	5 (25%)	1 (5%)	20 (100%)
Male	4 (20%)	5 (25%)	4 (20%)	2 (10%)	4 (20%)	1 (5%)	20 (100%)
Σ	6 (15%)	9 (22.5%)	9 (22.5%)	5 (12.5%)	9 (22.5%)	2 (5%)	40 (100%)

[a]Along with the frequencies, each cell of the crosstabulation contains the row percentage. This value conveys the percentages of males or females who perform each type of act. Marginal row values indicate a sum of 100% within the categories of male and female. Marginal row values provide the sums of frequencies and percentages for males and females within each act category.

In some cases, you wish to display percentages along with frequencies. The percentages can indicate each group's proportion within row or column of the crosstabulation or among the entire sample.

Example 2.4: Two-Variable Crosstabulation with Row Percentages Table 2.4 displays percentages within each row of the basic crosstabulation presented in Table 2.3.

Example 2.5: Two-Variable Crosstabulation with Column Percentages Table 2.5 displays percentages within each column of the basic crosstabulation presented in Table 2.3.

Example 2.6: Two-Variable Crosstabulation with Total Percentages Table 2.6 displays percentages within the entire sample for the basic crosstabulation presented in Table 2.3.

Example 2.7: Two-Variable Crosstabulation with All Percentages Researchers who wish to view row, column, and total percentages simultaneously may create a crosstabulation that displays all percentages along with the frequencies, as shown in Table 2.7.

TABLE 2.5. Column Percentage and Frequency Crosstabulation for Act and Sex[a]

			Act				
Sex	Stunt	Clown	Acrobatics/ Strength	Animal	Sideshow	Other	Σ
Female	2 (33.3%)	4 (44.4%)	5 (55.6%)	3 (60%)	5 (55.6%)	1 (50%)	20 (50%)
Male	4 (66.7%)	5 (55.6%)	4 (44.4%)	2 (40%)	4 (44.4%)	1 (50%)	20 (50%)
Σ	6 (100%)	9 (100%)	9 (100%)	5 (100%)	9 (100%)	2 (100%)	40 (100%)

[a]Along with the frequencies, each cell of the crosstabulation contains the column percentage. This value conveys the percentages those performing each type of act who are male or female. Marginal column values indicate a sum of 100% within each act category. Marginal row values provide the sums of frequencies and percentages males and for females that perform each type of act.

TABLE 2.6. Total Percentage and Frequency Crosstabulation for Act and Sex[a]

			Act				
Sex	Stunt	Clown	Acrobatics/ Strength	Animal	Sideshow	Other	Σ
Female	2 (5%)	4 (10%)	5 (12.5%)	3 (7.5%)	5 (12.5%)	1 (2.5%)	20 (50%)
Male	4 (10%)	5 (12.5%)	4 (10%)	2 (5%)	4 (10%)	1 (2.5%)	20 (50%)
Σ	6 (15%)	9 (22.5%)	9 (22.5%)	5 (12.5%)	9 (22.5%)	2 (5%)	40 (100%)

[a]Along with the frequencies, each cell of the crosstabulation contains the total percentage. This value conveys the percentage of the entire sample who fall into each combination of gender and act category. Marginal column values indicate the frequency and percentage of all subjects who perform each type of act. Marginal row values provide the sums of frequencies of all males and all females.

2.3.2 Multilayer Crosstabulations

A crosstabulation that includes more than two variables uses layers in addition to rows and columns. The visual representation of a crosstabulation including layers is a three-dimensional table.

Example 2.8: Three-Dimensional Crosstabulation For example, Figure 2.1 would display frequencies for the combinations of circus performers' sexes, acts, and the artificially created weekly salary categories.

Although this arrangement provides a cell for all combinations of act, sex, and weekly salary, it does not make all cells visible, leaving some cell frequencies unknown. To remedy this issue, you can choose between two methods of displaying layers. One method involves producing a split crosstabulation with separate charts for each layer of the third variable. The second method involves nesting layers of the third variable within categories of one of the others.

TABLE 2.7. Full Percentage and Frequency Crossabulation for Act and Sex[a]

	Act						
	Stunt	Clown	Acrobatics/ Strength	Animal	Sideshow	Other	Σ
Female	2	4	5	3	5	1	20
	10%	20%	25%	15%	25%	5%	100%
	33.3%	44.4%	55.6%	60%	55.6%	50%	50%
	5%	10%	12.5%	7.5%	12.5%	2.5%	60%
Male	4	5	4	2	4	1	20
	20%	25%	20%	10%	20%	5%	100%
	66.7%	55.6%	44.4%	40%	44.4%	50%	50%
	10%	12.5%	10%	5%	10%	2.5%	50%
Σ	6	9	9	5	9	2	40
	15%	22.5%	22.5%	12.5%	22.5%	5%	100%
	100%	100%	100%	100%	100%	100%	100%
	15%	22.5%	22.5%	12.5%	22.5%	5%	100%

[a]Each cell contains four values. The first value provides the frequency for the cell. The second value, refers to the particular cell's percentage within that row (sex). The third value refers to the particular cell's percentage within that column (act). The last value refers to that particular cell's percentage within the entire sample.

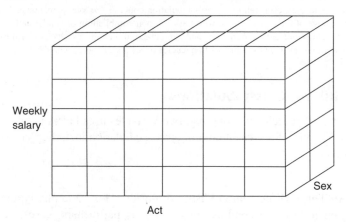

Figure 2.1. Three-Variable Crosstabulation. A crosstabulation involving three variables takes the form of a cube. Rows correspond to weekly salary categories. Columns correspond to act categories. Layers correspond to sex categories.

Split Crosstabulations. A *split* crosstabulation uses multiple tables. Each table corresponds to a layer of the three-dimensional illustration. When creating crosstabulations with a split design, the variable with the fewest categories usually becomes the layers.

TABLE 2.8. Crosstabulations for Act and Weekly Salary Split by Sex[a]

Weekly Salary ($)	Act						Σ
	Stunt	Clown	Acrobatics/Strength	Animal	Sideshow	Other	
(a) Layer: Male							
300–449	0	0	0	0	1	0	1
450–599	0	0	1	0	3	1	5
600–749	0	4	2	2	0	0	8
750–899	2	0	2	1	1	0	6
900–1050	0	0	0	0	0	0	0
Σ	2	4	5	3	5	1	20
(b) Layer: Female							
300–449	0	1	0	0	1	0	2
450–599	0	2	0	0	3	0	5
600–749	2	2	2	0	0	0	6
750–899	2	0	2	2	0	0	6
900–1050	0	0	0	0	0	1	1
Σ	4	5	4	2	4	1	20

[a]Part (a) of the table presents the frequencies for all combinations of act and weekly salary categories for females; part (b) does the same for males. Adding the marginal values for the corresponding act column or weekly salary row in both parts the table of produces the overall marginal value for that category.

Example 2.9: Split Crosstabulation Following this logic for the circus data, then, layers represent subjects' sex. Males and females have their own subtables, including cell and marginal frequencies for weekly salary and act categories, as shown in parts (a) and (b) of Table 2.8.

The number of categories within the layer variable determines the number of crosstabulation tables produced. Because the variable of gender, which produced the layers in this demonstration, contains two categories, two crosstabulations result. This technique works well for one who wishes to acknowledge patterns among just male or just female subjects or who wishes to compare particular cells of the two subgroups.

However, with the data split between two crosstabulations, obtaining marginal values becomes tricky. The marginal values in Table 2.8 do not characterize the entire sample, but, rather, refer only to those subjects, male or female, to which that particular crosstabulation refers. To obtain overall marginal values, you must add the marginal value for one row or column of one crosstabulation to the corresponding value of the other crosstabulation.

Example 2.10: Split Crosstabulation Marginal Values Calculation For instance, determining the number of subjects who perform clown acts entails finding the sum of the men and the women who do so. The marginal values in Table 2.8(a) indicate that four males perform clown acts, and the marginal values in Table 2.8(b) indicate that five females perform clown acts, thus producing an overall marginal value of 9. The same process applies to determining marginal values for rows. The knowledge that 12

subjects earn between \$750 and \$899 per week comes from adding the marginal values in the two crosstabulations.

Nested Crosstabulations. Those who wish to avoid the extra step of computing overall marginal values may favor the *nested design*, which displays all data within a single crosstabulation. The nested design uses layers that repeat themselves within each row category. (In fact, for this reason, some refer to the nested design as a *repeated-measures design*, especially in the context of inferential statistics.) For this technique, unlike the situation involving split crosstabulations, the arrangement of the variables into rows, columns, and layers depends on your intentions. The variable for which the category distinctions hold the most value generally becomes the levels.

Example 2.11: Nested Crosstabulation In keeping with the circus example, a researcher with a special interest in comparing the acts and weekly incomes of males and females would arrange the nested crosstabulation as shown in Table 2.9.

This crosstabulation, unquestionably, looks more complicated than the split cross-tabulation does, especially when crosstabulation cells include percentages. For this reason, you may prefer to use the split crosstabulation. However, the nested crosstabulation does have some advantages over the separate split crosstabulations.

First, with the nested design the researcher can nest as many variables within other variables as necessary.

TABLE 2.9. Crosstabulations for Act and Weekly Salary Nested by Sex[a]

Weekly Salary (\$)	Sex	Act						
		Stunt	Clown	Acrobatics/Strength	Animal	Sideshow	Other	Σ
300–449	Male	0	0	0	0	1	0	1
	Female	0	1	0	0	1	0	2
450–599	Male	0	0	1	0	3	1	5
	Female	0	2	0	0	3	0	5
600–749	Male	0	4	2	2	0	0	8
	Female	2	2	2	0	0	0	6
750–899	Male	2	0	2	1	1	0	6
	Female	2	0	2	2	0	0	6
900–1050	Male	0	0	0	0	0	0	0
	Female	0	0	0	0	0	1	1
Σ		6	9	9	5	9	2	40

[a]Categories of "male" and "female" appear as nested elements within each weekly salary category in the rows of the crosstabulation. Marginal values for each act category appear at the end of the respective column. The sum of male and female values at the end of each row constitute the marginal values for the weekly salary categories. Adding the values at the end of all rows marked "female" or "male" produces the marginal values for the respective sex category.

TABLE 2.10. Crosstabulations for Weekly Salary Nested by Sex and Act Nested by Audience Participation Context[a]

Weekly Salary ($)	Sex A/P	Act												Σ
		Stunt		Clown		A/S		Animal		Sideshow		Other		
		Y	N	Y	N	Y	N	Y	N	Y	N	Y	N	
300–449	Female													
	Male													
450–599	Female													
	Male													
600–749	Female													
	Male													
750–899	Female													
	Male													
900–1050	Female													
	Male													
	Σ													

[a]This crosstabulation (where A/P = audience participation; A/S = acrobatics/strength; N = no; Y = yes) includes the nested categories of "male" and "female" within each weekly salary category as well as the nested categories according to whether the act involves audience participation within each act category.

Example 2.12: Double-Nested Crosstabulation For example, a fourth variable, that of distinguishing acts that involve audience participation from those that don't involve audience participation might appear as a nested variable within the columns of the crosstabulation (Table 2.10).

Some researchers even nest variables within nested variables. In some situations, nesting one variable into rows and another into columns simply doesn't make sense, given your logic or the goal of the study. The "nested within nested variable" design proves useful for situations involving many independent variables that create fine distinctions between subjects and the need to assess these subjects with regard to a single dependent variable.

Example 2.13: Nested Variable within Nested-Variable Crosstabulation This design could apply to an analysis of the circus data for which the researcher wishes to compare circus performers' salaries, based on a combination of their sexes, types of acts, and audience participation context. Rearrangement of the variables in Example 2.11 could nest sex within weekly salary and then nest each audience participation context within sex to create a total of four subcategories for each row (Table 2.11).

Overall, in the case of many variables and many categories, a nested design provides a more concise summary of data than does a split crosstabulation. You should, however, consider the complexity of the nested design's appearance when deciding which of the two methods most appropriately provides information.

TABLE 2.11. Crosstabulation of Act and Weekly Salary Nested within Sex and Audience Participation Context[a]

Weekly Salary ($)	Sex	A/P	Stunt	Clown	A/S	Animal	Sideshow	Other	Σ within Context	Σ within Sex	Σ
					Act						
300–449	Female	Y									
		N									
	Male	Y									
		N									
450–599	Female	Y									
		N									
	Male	Y									
		N									
600–749	Female	Y									
		N									
	Male	Y									
		N									
750–899	Female	Y									
		N									
	Male	Y									
		N									
900–1050	Female	Y									
		N									
	Male	Y									
		N									
	Σ										

[a]This crosstabulation depicts the categories of audience participation context nested within the categories of "male" and "female"; further, "male" and "female" appear as nested categories within the weekly salary designations (abbreviations are same as those in Table 2.10).

The proximity of values in nested designs also allows for easy comparisons of patterns among subjects in different categories of a particular variable. To compare males and females who earn between $750 and $899 per week using the split crosstabulation, you must simultaneously look at the two tables. However, with the relevant values lying right next to each other in the nested design, the comparison takes little effort.

2.4 GRAPHS AND CHARTS

The frequency table and the crosstabulation clearly present the counts for all variables, yet do not have much aesthetic quality. Bar graphs and pie charts, which add a visual element to the presentation of frequencies, can make information appear more interesting than it does when presented in tabular form. Your rationale and audience, in combination with the number of variables involved, should help you determine whether a bar graph or a pie chart, and what version of the chosen illustration, best depicts the data.

2.4.1 Bar Graphs

The presence of axes qualifies this illustration as a graph rather than a chart. The bar graph consists of an x axis (abscissa), along which the names of variables' categories, such as circus act, appear; and a y axis (ordinate), which displays a scale for frequencies. The bar that appears above each category label on the x axis rises to the value on the y axis that indicates the frequency for that category. The basic bar graph, like the frequency table, addresses only one variable. However, complex versions of the bar graph, namely, the clustered and the stacked graphs, can indicate frequencies for combinations of variables, as the crosstabulation does.

Basic Bar Graphs. As early as elementary school, children learn to create basic bar graphs. These graphs summarize frequencies for categories of a single variable.

Example 2.14: Basic Bar Graph Information from a frequency table presented in Table 2.1 easily transfers onto an X axis and a Y axis, as shown in Figure 2.2.

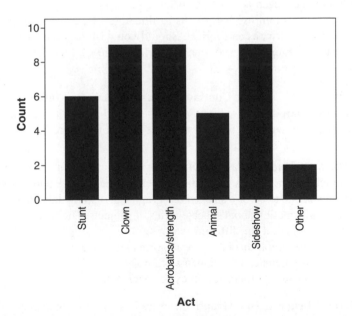

Figure 2.2. Bar graph for circus act. The graph presents the frequencies for each type of act on the basis of the sample data provided in Section 2.1.

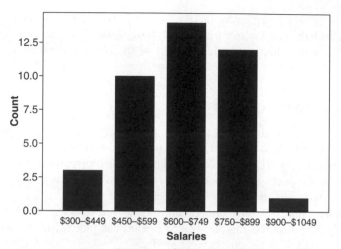

Figure 2.3. Bar graph for weekly salaries. This chart presents the frequencies for each salary category on the basis of the sample data from Section 2.1 and the class limits provided in Section 2.2.2.

Figure 2.2 not only effectively conveys the frequencies for each act category but also allows for a quick comparison of these frequencies. Thus, with a little work, one viewing the table can determine, for example, that fewer subjects fall into the "other" acts category and that the data have three modes, with clown acts, acrobatic/strength acts, and sideshow acts each accounting for nine subjects.

Researchers most often use bar graphs to illustrate frequencies for variables that exist, in their original form, as categorical. Should you wish to produce a bar graph for artificially created categories of a continuous variable, the *x*-axis labels identifies class limits.

Example 2.15: Bar Graph for Continuous Variable Divided into Classes   Using the same categories introduced used for the comparable frequency table (see Table 2.2.), we obtain a bar graph depicting weekly salary as shown in Figure 2.3.

Clustered and Stacked Bar Graphs.   Bar graphs can become more complicated than the ones pictured in Figures 2.2 and 2.3 when they address groups based on more than one variable. A clustered or a stacked bar graph can display data from a crosstabulation, providing information about subcategories of subjects. The two graphs, however, do so in different ways and for different reasons.

The clustered bar graph displays subcategories side by side, allowing for an easy comparison of the frequencies for segments of subjects within categories. However, it does not clearly indicate the total frequency for each category.

Example 2.16: Clustered Bar Graph   Bars representing frequencies for each act category of the circus data, separated according to the sexes of those performing the acts, appear in the clustered bar graph in Figure 2.4.

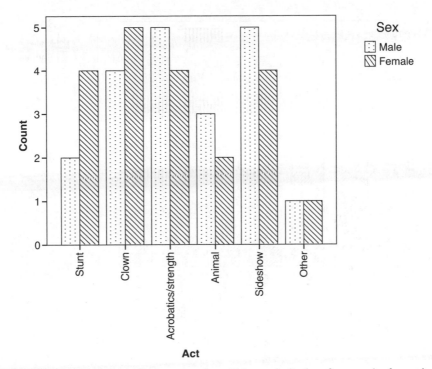

Figure 2.4. Clustered bar graph for type of act. This graph displays frequencies for each sex. Side-by-side bars indicate frequency of each car color for males and for females. The sum of the two frequencies corresponding to each color equals the values shown in Figure 2.2.

Although the stacked bar graph also displays subcategories, it resembles the basic bar graph with the exception of the division of each bar according to its subcategories. It takes a bit more effort to determine and compare the frequencies for each subcategory using a stacked bar graph than using a clustered bar graph. However, the stacked graph provides a clearer indication of the portion of each category composed of each subcategory than the clustered graph does.

Example 2.17: Stacked Bar Graph   The same gender-specific frequencies shown in Figure 2.4 could appear in a stacked bar graph as shown in Figure 2.5.

It is easy to see the heights of the bars in Tables 2.2–2.6. However, looking at a bar, you can easily tell the exact frequency for the respective category. The ability to do so, though, reflects the small sample size used for this example. Often, the y axis has a rather large scale, making the determination of exact frequencies difficult. If you wish to present a detailed description of frequencies, you may find other measures of frequency more useful than bar graphs.

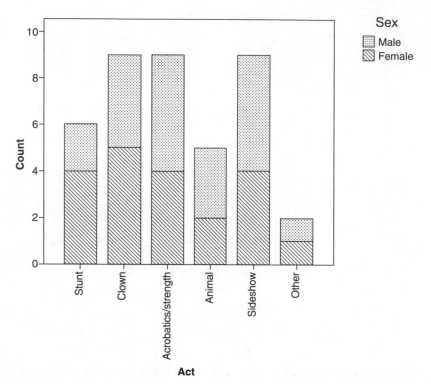

Figure 2.5. Stacked bar graph for type of act. The overall shape of this graph is the same as that of the basic bar graph. However, the division of each bar into frequencies according to sex allows for recognition of the balance between males and females within each act category.

2.4.2 Pie Charts

Because the pie chart has no axes, you must consider it a chart rather than a graph. A pie chart uses the analogy of a circle to display category frequencies as portions of the entire sample. It provides a visual representation of the sample's distribution into the different categories. Like the bar graph, the pie chart can take very basic or rather complex forms.

Basic Pie Chart. Generally, the same data used to create the basic bar graph can also lend themselves to a pie chart.

Example 2.18: Basic Pie Chart   The pie chart shown in Figure 2.6 presents the same circus act frequencies that appear in Figure 2.2. Each bar from Figure 2.2 simply becomes a piece of the pie.

Paneled Pie Charts. The layout of a pie chart makes a stacked and clustered versions difficult to produce and read. Rather than stacked and clustered pie charts, you should try to use paneled pie charts, which show a separate frequency distribution for each relevant category,

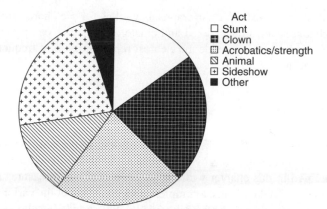

Figure 2.6. Pie chart for type of circus act. Wedges of the pie in the above chart show the amount of the entire sample composed of subjects who perform each type of act. The values that appear outside the wedges indicate the exact percentage of the sample falling into each category. The researcher can choose whether to include these percentages, to replace them with frequencies, or to omit numbers from the chart altogether.

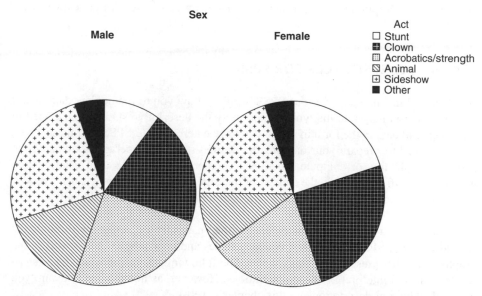

Figure 2.7. Paneled pie chart for circus act. The circle on the left pertains to male circus performers, and the circle on the right pertains to female circus performers in the sample. Wedges of each circle show the amount of individuals of the respective sex who perform each type of act.

Example 2.19: Paneled Pie Chart Figure 2.7 depicts a paneled pie chart, distinguishing males from females, for the circus act data.

Paneled illustrations exist for bar graphs as well as for pie charts. However, other forms of pie charts, such as the stacked and clustered versions, can provide data efficiently. For pie charts, panels provide the clearest representation of frequency distributions within categories.

2.5   CONCLUSION

Measures of frequency qualify as the only types of descriptive statistic appropriate for summarizing categorical data. Moreover, because of the ability to categorize continuous data, as exemplified in this chapter with the variable of salary, measures of frequency are useful for all types of data. Thus, a complete understanding of the various approaches to conveying frequencies serves a researcher well. Such knowledge allows you to select the most effective way to describe data.

Regardless of the number of variables involved or the method chosen to display frequencies, the summary statistics presented in this chapter provide the basis for a number of important inferential statistics. The chi-square test, discussed in Chapter 5, always relies on frequencies. Correlation and regression analysis, discussed in Chapter 8, may utilize frequencies as well. For this reason, novice researchers should form the good habit of computing and reporting frequencies for categorical variables whenever possible.

STATISTICAL RESOURCES FOR SPSS

As explained in Chapter 1, various SPSS utilities allow you to manipulate data to suit your needs. You may find that you cannot apply the descriptive statistics described in this chapter to data in the form in which you have entered it into SPSS. For these cases, you may need to prepare your data for the desired statistical operations by using the sort, filter, split file, or compute functions. Another type of SPSS data manipulation worthy of specific mention in the context of measurements of frequency is the "recode" function, which can separate values from a continuous variable into artificially created categories.

Once you have identified categories, either naturally occurring or through the recode function, SPSS can create frequency tables and crosstabulations as well as the graphs and charts presented in this chapter. The following sections provide basic steps for creating and interpreting these illustrations. However, as noted when relevant, you can find additional descriptions on this chapter's website.

www.moravian.edu/aqd

Frequency Tables in SPSS

SPSS can create tables displaying category names, frequencies, and percentages. For proper category names to appear in the output, you need to have entered the raw data

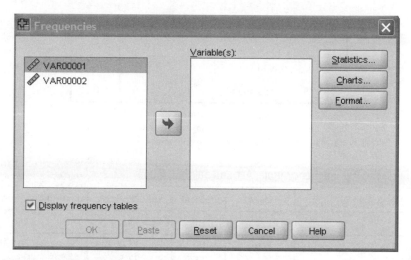

Figure 2.8. SPSS "Frequencies" window. The user creates frequency tables by selecting appropriate variables from those listed in the window above. The "statistics," "charts," and "format" buttons provide options regarding the information included in the table and alternative forms of presenting the data.

into a column on the "Data View" screen, input a coding frame, and recoded if necessary. (See Chapter 1's companion website for help with these tasks.)

www.moravian.edu/aqd

The process of creating frequency tables begins with the analyze pulldown menu, which contains an option for "Descriptive Statistics." When you select this option, SPSS lists the types of descriptive statistics available. You should select "Frequencies" from the list. A window entitled "Frequencies" should appear (Fig. 2.8).

Frequency table output contains a small chart entitled "Statistics" as well as one frequency table for each variable placed into the "Variable(s)" box in the "Frequencies" window. The statistics chart states the number of subjects who contributed data and the number with missing data for the analysis. Along with the frequencies, themselves, the frequency tables contain three percentage values. The *percent*, itself, refers to the proportion all subjects who fall into a particular category. However, the other two percentage values often provide more useful data than the values in the "Percent" column do. The *valid percent* considers only the subjects who supplied data for the relevant variable in determining the proportion of subjects within each category. The *cumulative percent* expresses an ongoing sum of the valid percentages.

Example 2.20: Frequency Table in SPSS   All of these values appear in the output expressed in tabular format in Tables 2.12 and 2.13. The first frequency table [Table 2.13(a)] uses the categorical circus act data. The second table [Table 2.13(b)] uses the artificially categorized salary groups.

TABLE 2.12. SPSS Frequency Table: Statistics[a]

		Act	Salary
N	Valid	40	40
	Missing	0	0

[a]Frequency table output always includes a statistics summary table (this table), indicating the number of values included in the analysis and the number of missing values.

TABLE 2.13. SPSS Frequency Table: Act and Salary Group[a]

Act or Salary Group	Frequency	Percent	Valid Percent	Cumulative Percent
(a) Act				
Valid Stunt	6	15.0	15.0	15.0
Clown	9	22.5	22.5	37.5
Acrobatics/strength	9	22.5	22.5	60.0
Animal	5	12.5	12.5	72.5
Sideshow	9	22.5	22.5	95.0
Other	2	5.0	5.0	100.0
Total	40	100.0	100.0	
(b) Salaries				
Valid $300–$449	3	7.5	7.5	7.5
$450–$599	10	25.0	25.0	32.5
$600–$749	14	35.0	35.0	67.5
$750–$899	12	30.0	30.0	97.5
$900–$1049	1	2.5	2.5	100.0
Total	40	100.0	100.0	

[a]Parts (a) and (b) of this table appear as a result of the user requesting frequency tables for "act" and "salaries." The category names, appearing in the leftmost column of this table, use the terms entered into the "values" on the "Variable View" screen.

Because of the arbitrary order of the categories in Table 2.13(a), pertaining to circus act, the values in the cumulative percent column have little importance. However, the ascending order of categories in Table 2.13(b), pertaining to salaries, makes the cumulative percentages noteworthy. Using the cumulative percent column, one can easily determine the percent of subjects who earn less than those in a particular salary category and, by simply subtracting that value from 100%, the percent of subject who earn more than those in that category.

Crosstabulations in SPSS

Crosstabulations essentially divide values from a frequency table according to a second variable. So, the process of creating a crosstabulation in SPSS begins with the same steps as the process of creating a frequency table does. However, you should not choose the "Frequencies" option from the "Analyze" menu. Instead, the "Descriptive Statistics" option in the pulldown menu contains the prompt for crosstabulations. When you select the crosstabulations prompt, a window entitled "Crosstabs" appears.

An untitled box in the "Crosstabs" window contains the names of all variables in the file. Indicate the variable for which the categories should appear as rows in the crosstabulation by clicking on its name and then clicking on the arrow to the left of the box marked "Rows." Indicate the variable for which the categories should appear as columns by clicking on its name and then clicking on the arrow to the left of the box marked "Columns."

Designating variables into the row and column boxes instructs SPSS to produce a two-variable crosstabulation with each cell containing the frequency for the appropriate combination of categories.

Example 2.21: Basic Crosstabulation in SPSS   Instructing SPSS to create a cross-tabulation based on circus performers' acts and sexes, including row, column, and total percentages, results in Table 2.14 which displays the SPSS version of Table 2.3.

Cells do not contain percentages unless you request these values. To include per-centages along with frequencies in the crosstabulation, you must click the "cells" button at the bottom of the "Crosstabs" window. The companion website for this chapter explains the percentage selections available to you.

www.moravian.edu/aqd

For crosstabulations involving three of more variables, you must enter a variable name into the box within the "Layers" section of Figure 2.9. SPSS nests rows of the crosstabulation within the layers. Once again, each cell contains the frequency for the appropriate combination of categories unless you request percentages.

TABLE 2.14. SPSS Two-Variable (Sex vs. Act) Crosstabulation[a]

Sex		Act						
		Stunt	Clown	Acrobatics/Strength	Animal	Sideshow	Other	Total
Male	Count	2	4	5	3	5	1	20
Female	Count	4	5	4	2	4	1	20
Total	Count	6	9	9	5	9	2	40

[a]Each cell contains four values. The first value provides the frequency for the cell. The second value refers to the particular cell's percentage within that row (sex). The third value refers to the particular cell's percentage within that column (act). The last value refers to that particular cell's percentage within the entire sample.

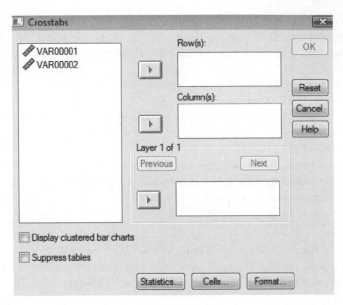

Figure 2.9. SPSS "Crosstabulations" window. The user creates a crosstabulation by selecting appropriate variables from those listed in the box above. The "statistics," "cells," and "format" buttons provide options regarding the information included in the crosstabulation and alternative forms of presenting the data.

Example 2.22: Nested Crosstabulation in SPSS The nested crosstabulation in Table 2.15 utilizes the same variables as and, accordingly, provides the same information as contained in Table 2.9. Interestingly, though, unlike the crosstabulation in Table 2.9, the crosstabulation created by SPSS does not display rows or columns that have frequencies of 0. Thus, no row appears for the income category of $900–$1049 in the male layer of Table 2.14.

Graphs and Charts in SPSS

More than one way to create bar graphs and charts in SPSS exist. One of the easiest ways is to use the "Graphs" option at the top of the "Data View" and "Variable View" screens. The "Graphs" menu provides you with two prompts from which to choose.

Basic Bar Graphs. The "Legacy Dialogues" prompt is the simpler of the two to use when creating bar graphs. From the "Legacy Dialogues" menu, you should select "Bar." A window entitled "Bar Charts" should appear. Unless you instruct SPSS otherwise in this window, it creates a simple bar graph. Assuming you request a simple graph, clicking on "Define" brings a new window, entitled "Define Simple Bar: Summaries for Groups of Cases" to the screen (see Fig. 2.10). In this window, you can indicate the variable for which to create the bar graph by clicking on its name and then clicking on the arrow to the left of the box marked "Category Axis."

TABLE 2.15. Salaries–Act–Sex Crosstabulation[a]

Sex	Weekly Salary ($)	Stunt	Clown	Acrobatics/ Strength	Animal	Sideshow	Other	Total Stunt
Male	300–449	0	0	0	0	1	0	1
	450–599	0	0	1	0	3	1	5
	600–749	0	4	2	2	0	0	8
	750–899	2	0	2	1	1	0	6
	Total	2	4	5	3	5	1	20
Female	300–449	0	1	0	0	1	0	2
	450–599	0	2	0	0	3	0	5
	600–749	2	2	2	0	0	0	6
	750–899	2	0	2	2	0	0	6
	900–1049	0	0	0	0	0	1	1
	Total	4	5	4	2	4	1	20

[a]Categories of "male" and "female" appear as nested elements within each weekly salary category in the rows of the crosstabulation. Marginal values for each act category appear at the end of the respective column. Adding the values at the end of all rows marked "female" or "male" produces the marginal values for the respective sex category.

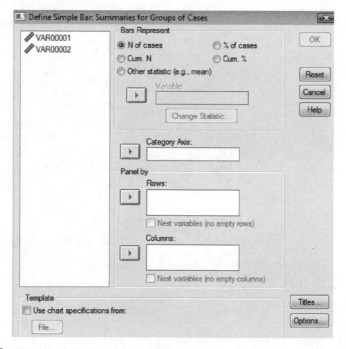

Figure 2.10. SPSS simple bar graph window. The user creates one-variable bar graph by selecting the appropriate variable from those listed in the box above. The designation in the "Bars Represent" portion of the window identifies the comparison factor used for the graph.

If you change the default setting from "simple" to "clustered" or "stacked" in the "Bar Charts" window, you will not see the "Define Simple Bar: Summaries for Groups of Cases" window. Instead, a window entitled "Define Clustered Bar: Summaries for Groups of Cases or Define Stacked Bar: Summaries for Groups of Cases" appears. The companion website for this chapter describes the process of instructing SPSS how to arrange variables for these graphs.

www.moravian.edu/aqd

Section 2.4 contains examples of SPSS-generated graphs and charts. Basic bar charts pertaining to the circus act and to salary category appear as Figures 2.2 and 2.3, respectively.

Basic Pie Charts. The options in the "Legacy Dialogues" menu include a prompt for pie charts. After you click on the prompt, SPSS asks you to how you would like it to consider your data. You should select "Summaries for Groups of Cases," and a window entitled "Define Pie: Summaries for Groups of Cases" appears (see Fig. 2.11).

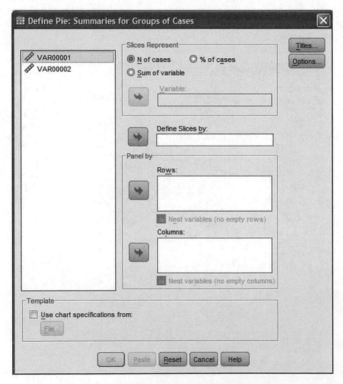

Figure 2.11. "Define Pie: Summaries for Groups of Cases" window. The user creates one-variable pie chart by selecting the appropriate variable name from those listed in the box on the left of the window and moving it to the "Define Slices by" box in the center of the window.

You can indicate the variable for which to create the pie chart by moving its name from the box on the left to the box marked "Define Slices by."

Figure 2.6 contains the SPSS-created pie chart based on the circus act. Ordinarily, SPSS uses different colors to distinguish between pie slices. However, Figure 2.6 utilizes patterns rather than colors to visually exaggerate the distinction.

Clustered, Stacked, and Paneled Illustrations. SPSS can also produce clustered and stacked bar graphs as well as paneled pie charts. To create clustered or stacked bar graphs, you do not request the "Simple" option from the "Legacy Dialogues" prompt. Rather, you select the "Clustered" or "Stacked" option. Creating a paneled pie chart requires only that you identify the grouping variable in the "Define Panels by" portion of the "Define Pie: Summaries for Groups of Cases" window. For details on these processes, please see this chapter's companion website.

www.moravian.edu/aqd

Examples of the clustered, stacks, and paneled illustrations appear in Section 2.4. For the bar graphs, circus act determines the category axis and sex serves as the variable by which to define the clusters or stacks, producing Figures 2.4 and 2.5. Similarly, defining slices of the pie chart by circus act and paneling the data according to sex produces Figure 2.7. Once again, SPSS ordinarily distinguishes between clusters, stacks, or categories by using different colors. However, the illustrations in Section 2.4 use patterns rather than colors to show distinctions in this black/white-print book.

REVIEW QUESTIONS

Use the data below for Questions 2.1–2.4 where (work status = 0 = no job/not retired/ not a student; 1—full-time; 2—part-time; 3—student; 4—retired).

Subject	Work Status
1	2
2	1
3	1
4	4
5	0
6	1
7	4
8	1
9	2
10	2
11	1

Subject	Work Status
12	2
13	0
14	3
15	1
16	1
17	2
18	3
19	1
20	2
21	2
22	4
23	1
24	0
25	1

2.1. Create a frequency table, including percentages, for work status.

2.2. Find the mode for work status. Explain what this value means.

2.3. Create a bar graph for work status.

2.4. Create a pie graph for work status.

Use the data below for Questions 2.5–2.8.

Transmission: 1 = automatic   Color: 1 = blue
                2 = standard   2 = tan
                                             3 = white
                                             4 = red
                                             5 = black
                                             6 = green

Subject	Car Color	Miles Driven in A Typical Week	Transmission
1	1	51	1
2	1	10	2
3	2	10	2
4	3	24	2
5	4	78	1
6	5	68	2
7	3	50	1
8	2	15	1
9	3	3	1
10	3	47	1
11	1	14	1

Subject	Car Color	Miles Driven in A Typical Week	Transmission
12	6	83	1
13	4	60	2
14	5	46	2
15	3	30	1
16	4	41	1
17	1	65	1
18	2	76	1
19	3	90	1
20	2	36	1
21	2	33	2
22	1	10	1
23	6	8	1
24	5	10	2
25	4	75	1
26	1	10	1
27	3	25	1
28	1	26	1
29	3	50	1
30	6	28	1
31	4	25	2
32	2	15	1
33	3	28	1
34	1	34	1
35	5	19	2
36	2	82	1
37	5	64	1
38	1	28	1
39	3	75	1
40	2	5	1

2.5. Create a frequency table for miles driven using five categories and with the first class having a lower limit of 1.

2.6. Create a clustered bar graph for car color separated by transmission.

2.7. Create a stacked bar graph for car color separated by transmission.

2.8. Create a paneled pie chart for car color separated by transmission.

Use the data below for Questions 2.9–2.13.

Sex: 1 = male	Crime: 1 = misdemeanor	Outcome: 1 = suspect pleaded guilty
2 = female	2 = felony	2 = suspect found innocent
		3 = suspect found guilty

Subject	Sex	Type of Crime Committed	Outcome
1	1	2	2
2	1	1	1
3	1	2	3
4	2	1	3
5	1	1	2
6	2	1	1
7	1	1	2
8	1	1	3
9	2	2	1
10	2	1	2
11	1	2	1
12	1	1	2
13	1	2	1
14	1	2	3
15	1	1	1
16	1	1	2
17	1	1	1
18	2	2	2
19	1	1	1
20	2	1	3
21	1	1	3
22	1	1	1
23	2	1	3
24	2	1	2
25	1	2	2

2.9. Create a crosstabulation, including frequencies and total percentages for type of crime committed (rows) and outcome (columns).

2.10. Find column percentages for the crosstabulation created for Question 2.9.

2.11. Find row percentages for the crosstabulation created for Question 2.9.

2.12. Split the crosstabulation created for Question 2.8 into layers according to sex. Display frequencies only.

2.13. Nest the variable of sex into the crosstabulation created for Question 2.9. Display frequencies only.

Use the crosstabulation below for Questions 2.14–2.21.

Guest Affiliation	Overnight Accommodations	Entrée			Marginal Values Within Guest Affiliation	Marginal Values
		Beef	Fish	Vegetarian		
Groom	No	23	25	12	60	—
		38.3%	41.7%	20.0%	100%	—
		85.2%	83.3%	80.0%	83.3%	—
		31.9%	34.7%	16.7%	83.3%	72
		14.7%	16.1%	7.7%	38.5%	100%
	Yes	4	5	3	12	100%
		33.3%	41.7%	25.0%	100%	46.2%
		14.8%	16.7%	20.0%	16.7%	—
		5.6%	6.9%	4.2%	16.7%	—
		2.6%	3.2%	1.9%	7.7%	—
Bride	No	32	39	8	79	—
		40.5%	49.4%	10.1%	100%	84
		94.1%	97.5%	80.0%	94.0%	100%
		38.1%	46.4%	9.5%	94.0%	100%
		20.5%	25%	5.1%	50.6%	53.8%
	Yes	2	1	2	5	—
		14.8%	20%	40.0%	100%	—
		5.6%	2.5%	20.0%	6.0%	—
		40.0%	1.2%	2.4%	6.0%	—
		1.3%	0.6%	1.3%	3.2%	—
Σ		61	70	25	—	156
		39.1%	44.9%	16.0%	—	100%
		100%	100%	100%	—	100%
		39.1%	44.9%	16.0%	—	100%

2.14. Find the percentage of subjects in the sample who ate fish entrées.

2.15. Find the percentage of subjects in the sample who were guests of the groom.

2.16. Find the percentage of subjects in the sample who had overnight accommodations for the wedding.

2.17. Find the percentage of subjects who were guests of the bride and ate vegetarian entrées.

2.18. Find the percentage of the groom's guests who did not have overnight accommodations.

2.19. Find the percentage of subjects in the sample who did not have overnight accommodations and ate vegetarian entrées.

2.20. Find the percentage of the bride's guests who ate vegetarian entrées and did not have overnight accommodations.

2.21. Find the percentage of guests with overnight accommodations who ate beef entrees.

3

DESCRIPTIVE STATISTICS FOR CONTINUOUS DATA

3.1 INTRODUCTION

The types of descriptive statistics presented in Chapter 2 focused on categorical variables, arranging subjects into groups and then using frequencies to summarize data in various ways. In your study, however, you may wish to do more than place subjects into groups. Your study may require you to gather continuous data instead of categorical data. *Continuous data* exist within a range of real numbers. Unlike categorical data, which tend to use whole numbers only as dummy variables to indicate subjects' group placement, continuous data points have numerical value. As a result, you have many more options for descriptive analyses of categorical data than for continuous data.

You will likely understand these analyses best by considering them in terms of a hypothetical dataset. To this end, you could consider the following tabulation of mock data. This list contains information provided by 30 hypothetical third-graders about the number of baby teeth that they have lost and their estimates of the number of times per day that they wiggled their loose teeth.

Analyzing Quantitative Data: An Introduction for Social Researchers, First Edition. Debra Wetcher-Hendricks.
© 2011 John Wiley & Sons, Inc. Published 2011 by John Wiley & Sons, Inc.

Subject	Lost Teeth	Wiggles	Subject	Lost Teeth	Wiggles
1	6	14	16	7	35
2	7	26	17	7	8
3	2	10	18	2	12
4	6	14	19	1	15
5	2	20	20	3	35
6	5	14	21	5	5
7	10	55	22	2	4
8	7	45	23	3	16
9	0	0	24	6	36
10	8	9	25	8	29
11	9	29	26	3	16
12	4	8	27	7	31
13	0	0	28	5	11
14	4	42	29	4	18
15	5	30	30	10	25

In some cases, you may wish to create artificial categories based on class limits that you impose on your continuous data. Section 2.2.2 explains how to do so. You can then apply any of the descriptive statistics explained in Chapter 2 to the newly created categorical data. However, the descriptive statistics explained in this chapter can be applied to continuous data in their natural form and usually provide more detailed information than analyses of categorical data do.

3.2 FREQUENCIES

Measures of frequency can apply to continuous data in much the same way that they apply to categorical data. However, rather than measuring the number of subjects that fall into each category, the frequency analyses for continuous data measures the number of subjects with each particular numerical score. Although you could create a frequency table to show these values, such a table would be very cumbersome. Researchers most commonly display frequencies for continuous-variable scores with graphs and diagrams. The frequency histogram and the stem-and-leaf chart display frequencies for continuous data both efficiently and understandably. Further, these illustrations allow you to notice patterns among data frequencies more easily than you would with a frequency table.

3.2.1 Frequency Histograms

A *frequency histogram* uses an *x* axis and a *y* axis to show subject counts for data points using rectangles (bars). At first glance, a frequency histogram looks much like a bar graph. The two, however, differ in two ways: (1) values along the *x* axis of a histogram represent continuous-data scores—they have numerical value, unlike the nominal dummy values that may appear along the *x* axis of the bar graph; and (2) because of the data's continuity, there is generally no space left between bars on a histogram, as there is between the bars on a bar graph.

The height of each bar, measured along the *y* axis, indicates the number of subjects with a particular *x*-axis score. Thus, you can often quickly determine the x value(s) with the highest frequency, the x value(s) with the lowest frequency, and make comparisons between frequencies for different x values.

Example 3.1: Basic Frequency Histogram   A frequency histogram showing the number of teeth lost by subjects from the dataset in Section 3.1 would situate "teeth lost" values along the *x* axis. The height of the bar corresponding to each *x* value, then, indicates the number of children who lost that amount of teeth.

It is easy to see from Figure 3.1 that the highest number of subjects, a total of five, have lost seven teeth. The graph also shows a lower frequencies at the extremes of than toward the middle of the range.

The histogram (Fig. 3.1) in Example 3.1 is based on a single variable. However, variations of this histogram can incorporate additional variables. Any added variable would most likely be categorical, included with the intent of finding frequencies for each score within groups of subjects as opposed to within the entire sample. Separating the basic histogram into panels or using a stacked histogram allows you to see the portions of the overall frequencies associated with each category.

Paneled Histograms.   A *paneled histogram* consists of a set of graphs, each pertaining to one category. The histogram in each panel has bars that show to the number of subjects just within that panel's category that have each *x*-value score.

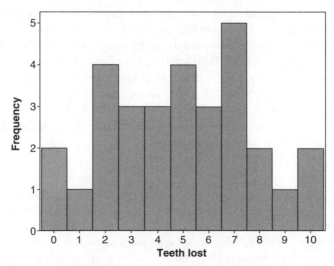

Figure 3.1. Frequency histogram for teeth lost. The numbers of teeth lost listed in Example 3.1 appear along the *x* axis. Frequencies appear along the *y* axis. The height of the bar above each *x* value indicates the numbers of subjects who have lost that particular number of teeth.

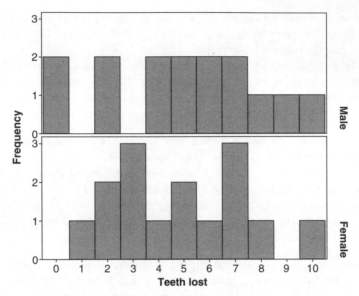

Figure 3.2. Paneled histogram. The top panel displays frequencies for teeth lost among males and the bottom panel displays frequencies for teeth lost among females. The sum of the corresponding frequencies in the two graphs equals the values shown in Figure 3.1.

Example 3.2: Paneled Histogram   If the researcher conducting the tooth-loss study happens to know that subjects 1–15 are males and subjects 16–30 are females, she or he could include the variable of sex in the investigation. The overall histogram from Example 3.1 can be separated into two separate panels, one corresponding to the sample's 15 males and one corresponding to the sample's 15 females.

Figure 3.2 allows a researcher to make many comparisons between the numbers of teeth lost by male and female third-graders. One can easily see, for instance, that females have more varied rates of tooth loss than males do. Also, given the frequencies of 0 on the paneled histograms, one could reason that all males or all females must have accounted for some of the frequencies shown in Figure 3.1. A researcher investigating a possible relationship between gender and the rate at which children lose baby teeth may find this sort of information valuable.

For very large datasets or when you wish to address frequencies across many categories of subjects, a paneled histogram works well. It obviously provides more detailed information than a basic histogram does. Also, with each panel representing frequencies of only a portion of subjects, the paneled histogram tends to have a smaller maximum y value than the basic histogram or the stacked histogram does. Thus, you can often see exact frequencies for a category most easily on a paneled histogram.

Paneled histograms, however, may not easily show total frequencies. To determine the total frequency for a particular x value, you must add the y values at the tops of that x score's bars on all panels. With other versions of the histogram, however, you can avoid this task.

Stacked Histograms. Dividing the bars of a histogram according to a categorical variable's groups, as a *stacked histogram* does, allows you to see both group and overall frequencies on one graph. The stacked histogram works in very much the same way that a stacked bar graph (described in Chapter 2) does. These graphs are most useful when you or your audience wishes to focus on overall frequencies, but have a secondary interest in each category's contribution to these values.

In a stacked histogram, the height of each bar indicates the overall frequency, as Figure 3.1 does. However, the different colors or patterns within each bar of the stacked histogram represent the different categories of subjects. Thus, this single graph not only shows each x-value frequency within the entire sample, but gives a rough idea of frequencies by subject group.

Example 3.3: Stacked Histogram   The stacked histogram in Figure 3.3 shows the same information available from the paneled histogram in Example 3.2. However, the stacked histogram incorporates the frequencies for both males and females into a single graph.

Although Figure 3.3 provides the same data as that available from Figure 3.2, the two graphs draw attention to different aspects of the data. The stacked histogram makes the proportion of each frequency comprised of males and females more evident than the paneled histogram does.

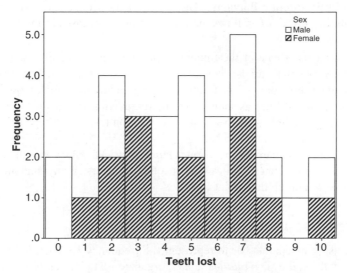

Figure 3.3. Stacked histogram. The bars on this histogram have the same shapes as those in Figure 3.1 do. However, the division of each bar into frequencies according to sex allows for recognition of the balance between males and females with each tooth-loss value.

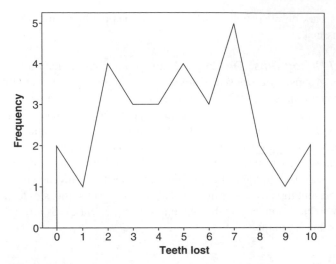

Figure 3.4. Frequency polygon for teeth lost. The height of the polygon's upper boundary at any point along the *x* axis shows the number of third-graders in the sample who have lost that particular number of teeth.

Frequency Polygons. To highlight the differences between frequencies for consecutive independent-variable values, researchers may draw lines connecting the tops of the bars on a frequency histogram. They refer to the resulting shape as a *frequency polygon*.

Example 3.4: Frequency Polygon   The shape of the frequency polygon, based on the histogram in Figure 3.1, follows the increases and decreases in the bars.

The very jagged shape of the frequency polygon shown in Figure 3.4 results, in part, from the very small sample size used to create it. On the basis of the central limit theorem, the upper boundary of the frequency polygon begins to look more like a curve than a series of jagged lines as sample size increases. Statisticians presume that, with an extremely large sample size, the frequency polygon takes the shape of a symmetric curve with a high middle and low ends.

They refer to this shape as the *normal curve* (Fig. 3.5). As you will see in subsequent sections of this chapter as well as in other chapters, many statistical analyses assume normality among data points.

3.2.2   Stem-and-Leaf Charts

Rather than using a separate bar to represent the frequency for each individual value, as a histogram does, the *stem-and-leaf chart*, organzies data into classes. This chart has characteristics of both the frequency table with created categories (explained in Section 2.2.2) and the histogram. It takes a bit more effort to read a stem-and-leaf plot than it does to read either of these other two illustrations. But researchers have good reasons

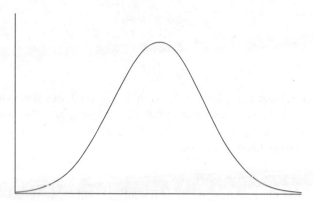

Figure 3.5. Normal curve. Theoretically, with very large samples, the greatest numbers of subjects should have scores toward the middle portion of the series of data values. Frequencies decrease as scores near the extremes.

for preferring stem-and-leaf charts. They provide more detailed information than a frequency table can and can display data more compactly than a histogram can.

A stem-and-leaf chart shows classes (discussed in Chapter 2) as the "stem" and individual values within the classes as the "leaves." The classes are generally defined by the first digit in the data points' values. These numbers appear on the left of the chart. Each row, then, represents a class of data. Individual values within each class appears to the right. The length of a row indicates the class' frequency.

Example 3.5: Stem-and-Leaf Chart　　Although histograms nicely show frequencies for the number of baby teeth lost, they would not do so as nicely for the number of times that children estimate that they wiggle their loose teeth. With so many values for the "wiggle" variable, a histogram would look cluttered. A stem-and-leaf chart (Fig. 3.6) can present these data much more neatly than a histogram can.

For the wiggle variable, the tens digits define the classes. Each value, then, appears with its ones digit to the right of the tens digit in the appropriate row.

To identify particular data points, one must combine the stem values on the left with the leaf values on the right. For instance, the "3" stem pertains to wiggle values in the 30s. Combining the stem value with the leaf values indicates that one student estimated that he or she wiggled loose teeth 30 times per day, one student estimated 31 wiggles, two students estimated 35 wiggles, and one student estimated 36 wiggles. This class, then, has a total frequency of five.

While considering Figure 3.6, you may have realized that the outline of stem-and-leaf chart looks very much like a bar graph turned on its side. In fact, if you drew boxes around the numbers in the leaves, you would create a bar graph based on classes with widths of ten. This bar graph may suit your purposes if you need only to determine frequencies for each artificially created category of data, as described in Chapter 2. The stem-and-leaf chart, however, provides the details of these class frequencies by supplying you with the actual data values that compose them.

```
0  |  0045889
1  |  01123445668
2  |  05699
3  |  01556
4  |  25
```

Figure 3.6. Stem-and-leaf chart. Tens digits, which define the classes of data in this example, appear on the left side of each row, forming the stems of the graph. The ones digits on the right form the leaves of the graph. The number of digits in each leaf indicates the frequency of values within its corresponding classes.

You should also know that stem-and-leaf charts do not necessarily need to use tens and ones digits, as Figure 3.6 does. You can easily adjust a stem-and-leaf chart for different ranges of data. Values measured to the tenths place, for instance, may be arranged with whole numbers serving as the stems and tenths digits serving as the leaves. In contrast, for values larger than those used in Figure 3.6, you may need to define the stems as hundreds and define the leaves as tens digits. You might even create leaves within leaves to show hundreds, tens, and ones digits.

3.3   MEASURES OF CENTRAL TENDENCY

Frequency histograms and stem-and-leaf graphs address each data point separately, making them useful in seeing distributions of data. However, such detailed information is not always necessary. More concise than frequency histograms and stem-and-leaf graphs are references to values in the data range that describe the "typical" subject in the sample. These values generally summarize the dataset with a central value, leading to their designations as *measures of central tendency*.

The fact that you can define the center of the dataset in many ways results in more than one measure of central tendency. The choice of which measures of central tendency to use for your analysis depends on the research situation and your own research goals. Subsequent portions of this section present and explain the three most commonly used measures of central tendency: the mean, the median, and the mode.

3.3.1   Mean

The mean differs from the other two measures of central tendency because it factors in sample size when describing a dataset's values. For this reason, researchers refer to the mean more often than to the median or mode. You have likely encountered the mean, described generically as the average, in elementary-level mathematics classes, defined as the average. In the statistical world, though, all of the measures of central tendency can be considered averages. Statisticians consider the *mean*, in particular, as the *arithmetic* average of a dataset. You can find this value by using the following equation 1:

$$\bar{X} = \frac{\Sigma x}{N}$$

(3.1)

In this equation, Σ instructs you to add the values represented by the variable that follows it. So, according to this equation, calculating the mean requires you to divide the sum of all values in the dataset by the sample size.

Example 3.6: Mean Determining the mean number of teeth lost by the hypothetical third-grade students from the dataset in Section 3.1, then, involves the following calculations.

$$\bar{X} = \frac{\Sigma x}{n} = \frac{\begin{array}{c}6+7+2+6+2+5+10+7+0+8+9+4+0+4+5+ \\ 7+7+2+1+3+5+2+3+6+8+3+7+5+4+10\end{array}}{30} = 4.93$$

3.3.2 Median

The *median* lies at the midpoint of the dataset. To find the median, you must order all data points from smallest to greatest (or, for the sake of argument, from greatest to smallest). The median value has the same number of data points smaller than it and larger than it. When the dataset contains an odd number of values, the median is obvious. However, when the dataset contains an even number of values, no true midpoint exists. In this situation, the median is the mean of the middle two numbers.

Example 3.7: Median The data from Section 3.1 contain an even number of values, providing the basis for a good example of this process. The first step in determining the median for the "tooth-loss" variable involves placing the values in ascending or decending order. With a total sample size of 30, the mode becomes the mean of the 15th and 16th values in the list, which, in this case, are both 5. So, the tooth-loss variable has a median of 5 because

$$\bar{X} = \frac{\Sigma x}{N} = \frac{5+5}{2} = 5$$

3.3.3 Mode

The most frequently occurring value in a dataset is the *mode*. To find the mode given a raw dataset, you must simply count the number of times each score appears in the dataset to determine the value(s) with the highest frequency. The mode does not necessarily refer to a single number as the other measures of central tendency do. If multiple values share the distinction of having the highest frequency, then the dataset has multiple modes.

Example 3.8: Mode According to the data presented in Section 3.1, five children in the sample have lost seven teeth. No other tooth-loss amount has a higher frequency, making seven the sole mode of the dataset.

You can also determine the mode of a dataset from its raw data or from the illustrations described in Section 3.2. Assembling separate stem-and-leaf digits from a stem-and-leaf chart provides the same values that appear in the list of raw data. You can, then, count to find the frequency of each score. The mode also corresponds to the data point(s) with the highest bar(s) on a frequency histogram. For a stem-and-leaf chart, assembling the digits on the right and left provides the same values that appear in the list of raw data. You can then count to find the frequency of each score.

3.3.4   Deciding between Measures of Central Tendency

Any or all of the measures of central tendency can describe a continuous dataset. The mode, in addition, can describe categorical data. When using dummy variables, the *mode* refers to the value corresponding to the category containing the greatest number of subjects. But because dummy variables have no numerical values, the mean and median have no use. It would make little sense to discuss a central value or an arithmetic average of categories.

The mean and median, however, get their fair share of use when describing continuous data. Although you can use the mode to indicate the particular score that occurs most frequently, this information generally serves more as a point of interest than a valuable descriptor. Your main decision, then, likely becomes whether the mean or the median best represents the dataset.

There is, unfortunately, no standard rule by which to make this decision. Both the mean and the median's abilities to accurately describe data vary with the expanse of the dataset and the distribution of points within that expanse. Considering a dataset with extreme values, those that differ drastically from the majority of data points, can clarify the merits of each.

Example 3.9: Mean versus Median   The dataset from Section 3.1. does not have any drastically extreme values. But in the dataset

$$\{16, 19, 2, 19, 3, 17, 15, 17, 18\}$$

the data points of 2 and 3 lie at the extreme low end of the series of values. Because such a large gap exists between the values of 2 and 3 and the rest of the data, they can be considered outliers. These outliers can radically affect the value of the mean. However, without access to access to the raw data, one does not realize that seven of the nine points in the dataset exceed the mean of 14. The inclination to consider the mean as a central value could easily lead one to assume that that the dataset contains more low values than it actually does.

The opposite problem can occur when focusing on the median. With the values in ascending or descending order, 17 lies at the midpoint, making it the median. This value focuses attention on the higher values in the dataset. One who does not see the raw data may not realize that a much greater difference exists between the median and the dataset's lowest value than between the median and the dataset's highest value.

Your own judgment, based on the values themselves and your intent for performing a particular analysis, should help you determine whether to report the mean or the median. Should you believe that either value, alone, cannot present a complete picture of the dataset, you should not hesitate to report both.

3.4 MEASURES OF DISPERSION

Information about differences between data points often helps to describe a dataset. For instance, an infinite number of three-point data sets could have a mean of 10. Values such as 9, 10, and 11, however, lie much closer together than values such as 5, 10, 15 do. If you described these datasets using only the measures of central tendency, you would mislead your audience into believing that they are identical. Mentioning the variability of the data points avoids this situation. The family of descriptive statistics known as *measures of dispersion* use various approaches to describe how far apart the values in a dataset lie from one another.

3.4.1 Maximum and Minimum

A very simple way to describe your data is to identify the largest data point, formally called the *maximum*, and the smallest data point, formally called the *minimum*. The minimum and maximum identify the extreme values of the dataset. These values provide two important pieces of information about your dataset: (1) when considered together, they serve as a measure of dispersion, indirectly indicating the amount of values spanned by the data; and (2) they specify the position of data points on a numerical scale. One can tell, from the maximum and minimum values, the data points' locations among all rational numbers.

Example 3.10: Maximum and Minimum For example, among the 30 hypothetical third-graders who provided tooth-loss data, the lowest number of teeth lost is 0 and the greatest number of teeth lost is 10. So, the dataset has a minimum of 0 and a maximum of 10. These numbers indicate the amount of disparity in the number of teeth lost by the children as well as the series of numbers encompassed within the dataset.

3.4.2 Range

The distance of the interval between the maximum and minimum values called the *range*, describes how expansive the dataset is. To find a dataset's range, you must simply subtract the minimum value from the maximum value. The *resulting value* refers to the same units as the data, themselves, do. You may wish to report the range rather than maximum and minimum because it provides a direct measure of dispersion, saving your audience the trouble of subtracting the minimum value from the maximum value.

The range is actually one of the lesser-preferred measures of dispersion for statisticians. It does not indicate the position of data points, as the maximum and minimum values do. Also, extreme values greatly affect the range. However, an audience of nonstatisticians can usually easily understand the concept of a range, making it a widely used measure of dispersion.

Example 3.11: Range   Subtracting the maximum and minimum values obtained in Example 3.10 provides the range of teeth lost by subjects. The maximum of 10 and the minimum of 0 suggest a range of 10. Thus, one could state that the number of teeth lost by third-graders varies by no more than 10 teeth.

You do not always need to refer to the range of an entire dataset. Sometimes, you may wish to focus on a particular range of values within the dataset. Researchers do so most often with the *interquartile range*, which refers to the middle 50% of values. To obtain the interquartile range, you must have a basic understanding of percentiles.

A data point's *percentile* tells you where the point falls in the overall range of values by indicating the percentage of scores in the dataset that it exceeds. A score at the 3rd percentile exceeds only 3 percent of scores in the dataset. A score at the 75th percentile exceeds 75% of scores in the dataset. You may have already figured out that the score at the 50th percentile is also the median of the dataset.

You have likely seen percentiles used in nonresearch contexts. Pediatricians use them to characterize young children's weights and heights in comparison to those of other children of the same age. Also, students often receive their scores on standardized tests in terms of percentiles, comparing their performance to the performances of their cohorts. Rather than ranking a particular subject, as these types of percentiles do, statisticians generally use percentiles to describe the distribution of values in a dataset. They most often note the values of evenly spaced percentiles (e.g., 10th, 20th, 30th). The difference between consecutive percentiles tells you how dispersed scores are in that particular portion of the dataset. If a cluster of scores exists somewhere, percentile values in this segment of the range lie very close to one another. Large differences between percentile values exist when scores within a particular portion of the dataset have a wide spread.

A specific form of percentiles, quartiles, divide the dataset into four equal segments. The 25th percentile value identifies the score under which 25% of data points fall; the 50th percentile value identifies the score under which 50% of data points fall; the 75th percentile indentifies the score under which 75% of data points fall; and the 100th percentile value, the maximum in the dataset, identifies the score under which all data points fall. Values in the second and third quartiles fall within the interquartile range.

Your knowledge of how to find the median of a dataset (see Section 3.3.2) makes finding the interquartile range relatively easy. You should first determine the median, or the 50th percentile, of the entire dataset. Then, you must simply find the median of each half of the dataset. The median for the lower half of the dataset is the 25th percentile value, and the median for the upper half of the dataset is the 75th percentile value. Subtracting the 25th percentile value from the 75th percentile value provides the interquartile range value.

Example 3.12: Interquartile Range   The data regarding lost teeth, presented in Section 3.1, have an interquartile range of 4. Calculations in Example 3.7 identified the 50th percentile (median) as 5. The half of the values below the 50th percentile have a midpoint of 3 and the half of the values above the 50th percentile have a midpoint of 7. Thus, 3 is the 25th percentile value and 7 is the 75th percentile value. The difference between these values is the interquartile range.

A *box-and-whisker plot* provides a visual representation of all the measures of dispersion discussed thus far in the section. A box surrounds the second and third quartiles, with a line inside indicating the median. Subtracting the values at the upper and lower ends of the box provide you with the interquartile range. The "whiskers", lines on either side of the box, extend to the minimum and maximum values. The difference between these values is the overall range.

Example 3.13: Box-and-Whisker Plot   Figure 3.7, the box-and-whisker plot for the tooth-loss data, therefore, shows a box between the values of 3 and 7 with whiskers extending to 0 and 10.

All of the information first presented in Examples 3.9–3.12 appears on this box-and-whisker plot. The left whisker on this box extends from the minimum to the first quartile value, indicating that 25% of subjects have lost between 0 and 3 teeth. The right whisker begins as the third quartile value, indicating that 25% of subjects have lost between 7 and 10 teeth. The most apparent aspect of this illustration, the box itself, encloses the second and third quartiles, which represents the middle 50% of subjects. The length of this box, 4, is the interquartile range. Within this box, a vertical line appears as the 50th percentile value (median), separating the second and third quartiles at 5.

From Figure 3.7, you can see that a box-and-whisker plot presents a dataset's maximum, minimum, median, range, quartiles, and interquartile range more consisely than verbal descriptions can. Thus, you may find box-and-whisker plots useful in reporting basic measures of dispersion. You should not be surprised, though, if your scatterplots do not have the symmetry that Figure 3.7 does. This example uses a rather small and evenly distributed dataset. Your own data will likely produce a box-and-whisker plot with an off-center median and one whisker longer than the other.

3.4.3 Variance and Standard Deviation

To avoid the potential problems caused by extreme values within a dataset (see Section 3.4.2), many researchers prefer to report the variance and standard deviation rather than the range. The variance and standard deviation (Section 3.4.3) address the way in which data points are scattered throughout the range as well as the range, itself. As the amount of dispersion in the data increases, the extent of the variance and standard deviation increases. The variance and standard deviation values do not represent the same units as the raw-score measures do. But they play important roles in standardizing values

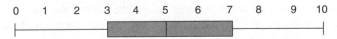

Figure 3.7. Box-and-whisker plot. The width of the entire plot indicates the data's range, and the width of the shaded box indicates the interquartile range. The 25th percentile value appears at the lower boundary of the box, the 50th percentile value (median) appears within the box, and the 75th percentile value appears at the upper boundary of the box.

(see Section 3.5), which provides the basis for many statistical tests. Researchers tend to favor the variance and standard deviation over the range. A variable's range reflects the units used to measure the variables. However, the standard deviation and range use common units, allowing for easy comparisons.

Both of these values rely upon the differences between each individual data point and the mean for the entire dataset. The mean of these values constitutes the *variance*. The *standard deviation* is simply the square root of the variance. Consequently, statisticians notate the variance as σ^2 and the standard deviation as σ.

Basic Formulas. The most common version of the variance formula reflects these definitions:

$$\sigma^2 = \frac{\sum (X_i - \bar{X})^2}{N} \tag{3.2}$$

The numerator of this formula consists of the sum of squared differences between each data point and the sample mean.[1] The denominator is the sample size.

It follows, then, that the formula for the standard deviation resembles the formula for the variance with the addition of a radical sign:

$$\sigma = \sqrt{\frac{\sum (X_i - \bar{X})^2}{N}} \tag{3.3}$$

Important variations of Equations (3.2) and (3.3), which are appropriate when analyzing data from a sample, replace the N in the denominators with $N-1$. The adjustment accounts for any inaccuracies that may exist because of the use of sample statistics rather than population parameters. Because the resulting value is a sample statistic rather than a population parameter, you should notate the sample variance as s^2 and the standard deviation as s:

$$s^2 = \frac{\sum (X_i - \bar{X})^2}{N-1} \tag{3.4}$$

$$s = \sqrt{\frac{\sum (X_i - \bar{X})^2}{N-1}} \tag{3.5}$$

You can imagine that inserting each individual score into the numerator of either of these formulas would make for a very long calculation process. Therefore, it may help to calculate the squared difference between individual scores and the mean in column form first. Then, you can simply add the values in the column to produce the sum of squared values needed for the numerator.

---

[1] If you did not square the differences, the value of the numerator would always equal zero.

Example 3.14: Variance and Standard Deviation Using Basic Formulas This procedure works well to find the variance and standard deviation of tooth-loss values for third-graders. From the raw-data values presented in Section 3.1 and the mean of 4.93 obtained in Example 3.7, calculations begin as shown below:

Teeth Lost	Teeth Lost $- \bar{X}_{teeth\ lost}$	(Teeth Lost $- \bar{X}_{teeth\ lost})^2$
6	1.07	1.1449
7	2.07	4.2849
2	-2.93	8.5849
6	1.07	1.1449
2	-2.93	8.5849
5	0.07	0.0049
10	5.07	25.7049
7	2.07	4.2849
0	-4.93	24.3049
8	3.07	9.4249
9	4.07	16.5649
4	-0.93	0.8649
0	-4.93	24.3049
4	-0.93	0.8649
5	0.07	0.0049
7	2.07	4.2849
7	2.07	4.2849
2	-2.93	8.5849
1	-3.93	15.4449
3	-1.93	3.7249
5	0.07	0.0049
2	-2.93	8.5849
3	-1.93	3.7249
6	1.07	1.1449
8	3.07	9.4249
3	-1.93	3.7249
7	2.07	4.2849
5	0.07	0.0049
4	-0.93	0.8649
10	5.07	25.7049
		$\Sigma = 223.867$

The sum of squared differences, 223.867, appears at the bottom of the row on the right. Inserting this value, along with the sample size of 30, into Equation (3.4) produces a variance of 7.72:

$$s^2 = \frac{223.867}{30-1} = 7.72$$

The simple step of taking the square root of this value produces the standard deviation.

$$s = \sqrt{s^2} = \sqrt{7.72} = 2.78$$

Raw-Score Formulas. Often researchers find other versions of the variance and standard deviation formulas more useful than the basic formulas are. One popular alternative, the raw-score method, does not require you to find the differences between the mean and each individual data point, which can become a very tedious task with a large dataset. The derivation of the raw-score variance formula from Equation (3.2) appears on this book's companion website.

www.moravian.edu/aqd

The following formula emerges from this derivation:

$$\sigma^2 = \frac{\sum x_i^2 - \left(\sum x_i\right)^2 / N}{N} \tag{3.6}$$

To transform Equation (3.6) into the raw-score formula for the standard deviation, you must take the square root of both sides of the equation.

$$\sigma = \sqrt{\frac{\sum x_i^2 - \left(\sum x_i\right)^2 / N}{N}} \tag{3.7}$$

Equations (3.8) and (3.9) show the raw-score method's formulas for calculating the variance and standard deviation for a sample:

$$s^2 = \frac{\sum x_i^2 - \left(\sum x_i\right)^2 / N}{N-1} \tag{3.8}$$

$$s = \sqrt{\frac{\sum x_i^2 - \left(\sum x_i\right)^2 / N}{N-1}} \tag{3.9}$$

To begin the actual calculations of the variance and standard deviation using the raw-score formula, you should focus on the numerator. The numerator of the first term, $\sum x_i^2$, requires you to square each individual value and then add the squared values. (You can do these computations most easily in column form.) For the numerator of the second term, $\left(\sum x_i\right)^2$, you must first add all values and then square the sum.

Example 3.15: Variance and Standard Deviation Using Raw-Score Formulas These initial computations, when applied to the data regarding teeth lost by third-graders, produces the following values:

Teeth Lost	(Teeth Lost)^2
6	36
7	49
2	4
6	36
2	4
5	25
10	100

Teeth Lost	(Teeth Lost)^2
7	49
0	0
8	64
9	81
4	16
0	0
4	16
5	25
7	49
7	49
2	4
1	1
3	9
5	25
2	4
3	9
6	36
8	64
3	9
7	49
5	25
4	16
10	100
$\Sigma x = 148$	$\Sigma x^2 = 954$

Inserting the values of Σx and Σx^2, calculated above, and the sample size of 30 into Equation (3.8), followed by arithmetic simplification, produces the same variance obtained using the basic variance formula in Example 3.14:

$$s^2 = \frac{954 - 148^2/30}{30 - 1}$$

$$s^2 = \frac{954 - 730.13}{29} = \frac{223.87}{29} = 7.72$$

Because the standard deviation is always the square root of the variance, s equals 2.78, as it did in Example 3.14.

3.5   STANDARDIZED SCORES

The "standard" in the term *standard deviation* implies that the value represents some fundamental element of statistical analysis. In fact, it serves as the basis for *standardized scores*, or *z scores*, which allow you to compare data points from variables measured using different units. When you standardize scores, you change their values to represent generic units rather than the units used to measure them in raw-score form. Section 3.4 notes that the range describes dispersion in terms of the units used to measure the variable, but the standard deviation does not. As a result, you cannot really compare the ranges of two datasets measured with different scales. Comparisons of the standard deviation, however, are possible.

Example 3.16: Comparisons Using Measures of Dispersion   One would expect greater variation in the number of times per day that children wiggle a loose tooth than in the number of teeth that they have lost because they have only a limited number of teeth to lose, but can wiggle their teeth an infinite number of times. Section 3.1 identifies the range of tooth wiggles as 45, which greatly exceeds the range of teeth lost, 10. But one cannot say that children differ more in terms of their tooth-wiggling behavior than in terms of their tooth loss. The two variables refer to incomparable entities.

Standardizing the measure of dispersion, however, accommodates differences in units to enable you to compare scores for variables evaluated using different scales. The standard deviation does so by referring to the disparity within a dataset in terms of the distance that scores lie from the mean of that dataset. Using the standard deviation, you can change raw scores into standardized scores. Standardized values have consistent meanings regardless of the scales originally used to measure the variables. The mean, regardless of its raw-score value, always has a standardized score of 0. Values less than the mean have negative standardized scores, and values greater than the mean have positive standardized scores.

3.5.1   Computing Standardized Scores

The number of standard deviations that a score lies above or below the mean is its standardized (z) score. Given a normal distribution, about 68.3% of data fall within one standard deviation of the mean, 95.4% fall within two standard deviations of the mean, and 99.7% fall within three standard deviations of the mean. Figure 3.8 shows these relationships.

You should remember that the normal curve shown in Figure 3.8 merely serves as an approximation of what you can expect given the assumption of normality. It should not surprise you if the frequency histogram for your data does not form a perfect, or even near-perfect, normal curve. The assumption of normality is based more on a general resemblance to the normal curve than an identical image of Figure 3.11.

Example 3.17: Whole-Number Standard Deviations   The frequency polygon for tooth-loss data (Fig. 3.4), for example, has the general shape of the normal curve, with high scores in the middle and low scores toward the ends of the range. Interestingly, some of the raw-score values suggested by the normal distribution do not exist. With a minimum value of 0 and a relatively small range, the raw-score values that correspond to $\mu-2\sigma$ and $\mu-3\sigma$ lie below 0.

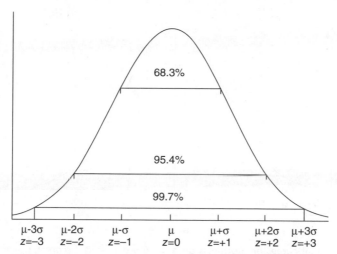

Figure 3.8. Normal curve with standard deviations. The number of standard deviations away from the mean that a raw score lies determines its *z* score. A raw-score value one standard deviation less than the mean has a *z* score of −1, a raw-score value one standard deviation greater than the mean has a *z* score of +1, a raw-score value two standard deviations less than the mean has a *z* score of −2, and so on. The mean *z* score is always 0.

In some situations, raw score values *can* be negative. But for the tooth-loss data, all raw values remain positive. (A child can't lose a negative number of teeth.) The raw-score values for this example, do not perfectly follow the theoretical path predicted by the normal curve. Still, the overall shape of the polygon resembles the normal curve enough to make the assumption of normality reasonable.

Figure 3.9 shows how to associate raw-score values with whole-number *z* scores. The raw-score values that you need to analyze, however, may not necessarily fall exactly one, two, or three standard deviations away from the mean. Most often, they lie in between whole standard deviations. For this situation, the method used to obtain *z* scores in Example 3.17 will not work. Equation (3.10), however, can provide you with the *z* score for any raw-score value:

$$z = \frac{x - \mu}{\sigma} \tag{3.10}$$

The numerator denotes the raw-score value's distance from the mean and the direction of this difference. Subtracting the mean from a raw score produces the negative *z* scores that reflect values less than the mean and the positive *z* scores that reflect values greater than the mean. The denominator does the actual job of standardization. Dividing by the standard deviation puts the numerator's difference in terms of the disparity within the sample from which the data came. The *z* scores produced by Equation (3.10) allow you to compare scores relative to the means of their own datasets.

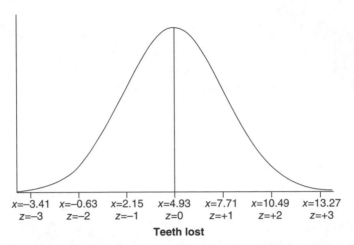

x=−3.41 x=−0.63 x=2.15 x=4.93 x=7.71 x=10.49 x=13.27
  z=−3   z=−2   z=−1   z=0   z=+1   z=+2   z=+3

Teeth lost

Figure 3.9. Normal curve for tooth-loss data. Raw scores and z scores appear along the x axis of the graph. The z scores that appear on the illustration reflect the number of standard deviations above or below the mean that their corresponding raw scores lie.

Example 3.18: Calculation of z Score   One might use z scores for a preliminary investigation into whether some relationship exists between wiggling loose teeth and actually losing teeth. If, for example, the investigation focuses on subject 1 (see the data in Section 3.1), who has lost six teeth, Equation (3.10) would produce a z-score of +0.38:

$$z = \frac{6 - 4.93}{2.78} = \frac{1.07}{2.78} = 0.38$$

According to the z score, the raw-score value of 6 lies .038 standard deviations above the mean. This explanation makes sense because the 6 value lies between the mean and the raw-score value of 7.71, which lies a full standard deviation above the mean, as shown in Figure 3.12.

3.5.2   Using Standardized Scores

Earlier portions of this chapter explain that you can compare data points from different datasets if you first transform raw scores into z scores. This sort of comparison becomes useful if you must characterize a particular subject with regards to that individual's counterparts in a sample.

Example 3.19: z Scores for Multiple Variables   In addition to having lost six teeth, as addressed in Example 3.18, subject 1 reports having wiggled loose teeth about 14 times per day. This raw score corresponds to a z score of −0.40 (based on the mean of 18.9 and standard deviation of 12.35 for the "wiggles" data in Section 3.1).

A quick look at the raw-score value compared to the mean would have indicated that this student wiggles his or her loose teeth less often than the typical third-grader does and has lost more teeth than the typical third-grader has. However, the scales of these variables can distort the extent of the differences between the raw scores and the means. For this subject, the difference between the raw score and the mean for the wiggles variable is much greater than the comparable difference for the tooth loss variable is. However, in terms of z scores, this subject's values differ from the mean by nearly the same amount, although in different directions. Standardization makes it clear that the subject's scores don't differ much from the mean scores for either variable.

Even more often than the type of comparison shown in Example 3.19, though, researchers use z scores to determine percentages of data within a single sample that falls above or below a given raw score. This process uses formula (3.16) as well as a z score table, also called a *standard normal distribution table* because it relies on the assumption of normality. A z score table appears in Appendix A of this book. Various versions of this sort of table exist. Some provide percentages of scores in the sample that lie above or below a particular z score. The values in Appendix A, however, indicate the percentage of scores in a particular z score lie between a negative z value and $z = 0$ (see Fig. 3.10). With this information, you can determine the percentage of data that lie between any raw score and the mean, between any two raw scores, below any raw score, or above any raw score.

The simplest of these values to find, the percentage of data between any raw score and the mean, involves only two steps. First, you must change the raw score into a z score using Equation (3.10). Then, you use the z score table to obtain the corresponding probability. To locate a probability in the table, you must find the row corresponding

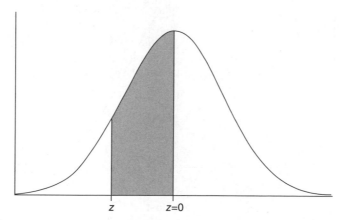

Figure 3.10. Percentage of scores between a given z score and $z = 0$. The shaded portion shows the frequencies of data points between a negative z value and $z = 0$. A similar portion of the graph, symmetric to the one shown, would highlight the frequencies of data points between the comparable positive z value and $z = 0$. A z-score table indicates the proportion of z scores that lie within the shaded region.

to the absolute value of the z score's ones and tenths digits (using the absolute value because of the normal curve's symmetry; the same amount of scores lies between the mean and z as between the mean and $-z$) and the column corresponding to the z score's hundredths digit. The value at the intersection of this row and column tells you the probability that any data point will lie between the raw-score value and the mean.

In some situations, the probability may serve your purpose. But, most often, you need to add a third step to explain the relative position of a data point in terms of percentages, not probabilities. By moving the decimal point two positions to the right, you change the probability from the table into a percentage value.

Example 3.20: Percentage of Scores between $\bar{x}$ and x For a basic example, consider the raw-score value of 6 for the tooth-loss data. The calculations in Example 3.18 have already determined that this value has a z score of 0.38. The shaded area in Figure 3.11 shows the portion under the normal curve that lies between $z = 0$ and $z = 0.38$.

The value at the intersection of the row labeled "0.3" and the column labeled ".08" indicates the probability that any z score lies between the values of 0 and 0.38. In this case, this probability is .1430. In other words, a z score has a 14.30% chance of falling between 0 and .36. In practical terms, a third grader has a 14.30% chance of having lost between 4.93 and 6 teeth.

With an adjustment to this method, you can find the percentage of values that lie above or below any z score. This process is based on the understanding that, in the normal distribution, the mean and the median are the same. So, 50% of scores lie to the right of the mean and 50% of scores lie to the left of the mean. Depending on the

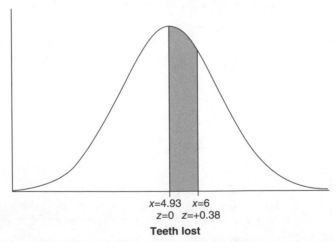

x=4.93   x=6
z=0   z=+0.38
Teeth lost

Figure 3.11. z Scores between $z = 0$ and $z = +0.38$ under normal curve. Raw-score values between 4.93 ($z = 0$) and 6 ($z = +0.38$) lie in the shaded portion under the normal curve. Because 6 exceeds the mean in this case, the shaded portion lies to the right of the mean. Values in Appendix A's z-score table indicate the probability that any subject's score will lie within the shaded area.

placement of the z score that you wish to analyze, then, you either subtract its proportion (from the z score table) from .50 or add it to .50.

If the area for which you need to determine the proportion lies entirely on one-half of the normal distribution, then the z score table provides you with the proportion of values that do *not* meet your criteria. You must subtract this proportion from .05 to obtain the value that you desire.

Example 3.21: Percentage of Scores Greater or Less than x (Not Including $\bar{x}$)   A diagram of the scores included in this type of analysis, as it pertains to the percentage of tooth-loss scores greater than 6, can help to clarify this process (Fig. 3.12).

The shaded portion of scores lies entirely within the right half of the normal curve. Any score has a .50 probability of falling under the entirety of this half of the curve, and, as shown in Example 3.20, a score has a .1430 probability of lying within the unshaded portion of this half of the curve. Therefore, the remainder of the area under the curve on the right half of the diagram, the shaded portion, must equal .50 −.1430. So, a .3570 probability, or a 35.7% chance, that a child in third grade has lost more than 6 teeth exists.

Subtracting the percentage of third-graders who have lost at least 6 teeth out of a total of 100 provides the percentage of third-graders who have lost fewer than six teeth. However, if you have not yet performed the computations from Example 3.21, a more direct method exists. Unlike the previously described situation, these students' tooth-loss values lie on both sides of the mean. On a normal curve, an area on both sides of

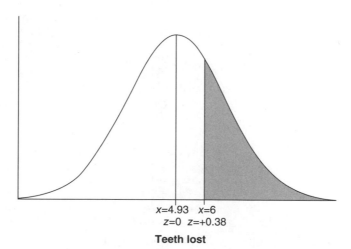

$x=4.93$ $x=6$
$z=0$ $z=+0.38$

Teeth lost

Figure 3.12. Scores greater than $z = +0.38$ under normal curve. Raw-score values greater than 6 ($z = +0.38$) lie in the shaded portion under the normal curve. Values in the z-score table indicate the probability that a score that a score lies in the unshaded area to the right of the mean. Subtracting this value from .50 provides the probability of a score falling into the shaded area.

the mean contains all the scores that lie on the fully shaded side of the mean in addition to the portion of the curve in the shaded area on the other side of the mean. To obtain the proportion, you must use the z score table to find the proportion of scores that lie between $z = 0$ and the z score that forms the boundary of the shaded area. Then, you can add this value to .50, which corresponds to the proportion of all scores lying on the fully shaded side of the mean.

Example 3.22: Percentage of Scores Greater or Less than x (Including $\bar{x}$)   Figure 3.13 provides a visual representation of the tooth-loss scores less than 6. The shaded area covers the entire left side of the graph as well as the area under the graph between the raw-score mean ($z = 0$) and $x = 6$ ($z = +0.38$).

Computing the probability that a third-grade child has lost fewer than six teeth, then, involves adding the probability that a score lies under the curve on the left side of the graph to the probability that a score lies under the curve between $z = 0$ and $z = .038$. The symmetry of the normal curve defines the first of these value as .50. The second, as determined in Example 3.20, is .1430. Their sum, .6430, suggests that a child has a 64.30% chance of losing fewer than 6 teeth by third grade.

The decision about whether to add or subtract in Examples 3.21 and 3.22 depends on the shaded portion of the diagram, not the description of values greater or less than an x value. When the shaded portion of the diagram lies only on one side of the mean, you should subtract the proportion from the z-score table from .50. When the shaded portion of the diagram spans both sides of the mean, you should add the proportion from the z-score table to .50.

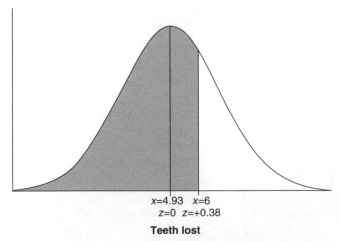

x=4.93   x=6
z=0   z=+0.38

Teeth lost

Figure 3.13. Scores less than $z = +0.38$ under normal curve. Raw-score values less than 6 ($z = +0.38$) lie in the shaded portion under the normal curve. Values in the z-score table indicate the probability that a score lies only in the shaded area to the right of the mean. Adding this value to .50, representing the area under the entire left side of the curve, provides the probability of a score falling into the entire shaded area.

A similar logic can help you to find the percentage of scores that lie between any two values. When the two values lie on the same side of the mean, producing both positive or both negative z scores, you must subtract the percentages that you obtain from the z score table. When the two values lie on opposite sides of the mean, producing one positive and one negative z score, you must add the percentages that you obtain from the z-score table.

Example 3.23: Percentage of Scores between x_1 and x_2 (Not Including $\bar{x}$)   Finding the percentage of third-graders from the date in Section 3.1 who have lost between six and nine teeth, therefore, requires subtraction. Both of these values fall above the mean. The shaded portion under the normal curve, therefore, lies between the z scores that correspond to the raw scores of 6 and 9 and +0.38 and +1.46 (Fig. 3.14), respectively, lies entirely on the right side of the graph.

According to the z-score chart in Appendix A, any score has a .4279 probability of falling between $x = 9$ and the mean. This probability encompasses both the shaded and unshaded portions of between these values in Figure 3.14. Subtracting the probability of a score falling into the unshaded portion between the mean and $x = 3$ results in a value that describes the probability of a score falling between $x = 6$ and $x = 9$. Knowing, from Example 3.20, that a .1430 probability of a score falling between the mean and $x = 3$ exists, we find that the probability of a score falling between $x = 6$ and $x = 9$ becomes .4269 − .1430, or .2839. There is a 28.49% chance that a third grader has lost between 6 and 9 teeth.

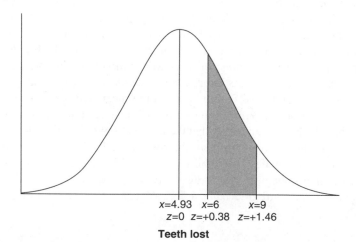

$x=4.93$ $x=6$ $x=9$
$z=0$ $z=+0.38$ $z=+1.46$

Teeth lost

Figure 3.14. Scores between $z = +0.38$ and $z = +1.46$ under normal curve. Raw-score values greater than 6 ($z = +0.38$), but less than 9 ($z = +1.46$), lie in the shaded portion under the normal curve. Values in the z-score table can indicate the probability that a score lies between each of these boundaries and the mean. Subtracting the smaller from the larger value provides the probability of a score falling into the shaded area.

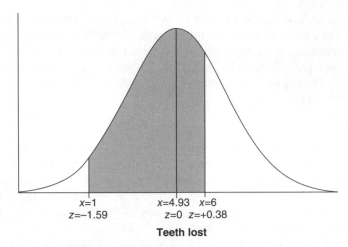

x=1   x=4.93 x=6
z=−1.59   z=0 z=+0.38

Teeth lost

<u>Figure 3.15.</u> Scores between $z = -1.59$ and $z = +0.38$ under normal curve. Raw-score values greater than 1 ($z = -1.59$), but less than 6 ($z = +0.38$), lie in the shaded portion under the normal curve. Values in the z-score table can indicate the probability that a score lies between each of these boundaries and the mean. Adding these values provides the probability of a score falling into the entire shaded area.

Example 3.24: Percentage of Scores between x_1 and x_2 (Including $\bar{x}$) A researcher who wants to determine the percentage of third-graders who have lost between one and six teeth needs encounters a slightly different scenario than described in Example 3.23. The raw scores of 1 and 6 lie on opposite sides of the mean and, therefore, the shaded portion under the curve includes the mean (see Fig. 3.15).

To find the percentage of scores between these values, one must consider the shaded portions under the curve on each side of the mean separately. Using the z score table to find the percentage of scores between each of the values and the mean and then adding these percentages produces the desired value. As shown in Example 3.20, any score has a .1430 probability of falling between the mean and the raw-score value of 6. The comparable probability for a raw score of 1 can be found in the z-score table using the z score of −1.59. (Remember that the table contains absolute values of z scores due to the normal curve's symmetry; so, the row labeled 1.5 and the column labeled .09 suffice.) The table provides a probability of .4441. The sum of the two probabilities, .5871, describes the probability that a raw score lies between 1 and 6. Consequently, the data suggest that a third-grader has a 58.71% chance of having lost between one and six teeth.

3.6 CONCLUSION

Throughout this chapter, you have encountered many of the values and procedures that serve as bases for the statistical analyses described in later chapters of this book. Tests of significance, discussed in the majority of the following chapters, rely on the assumption of normality. Measures of central tendency, measures of dispersion, and probabilities also play strong roles in the inferential statistical procedures that test for significance.

Tests of significance compare two or more groups of subjects according to some descriptive representation of them, such as the mean. Obviously, before you can perform such an analysis, you must understand and be able to compute the means, making the information presented in Section 3.3 especially important. You can often tell, with a nonstatistical comparison, whether these means differ extensively. However, you probably will not consider issues such as sample size and the dispersion of data in this judgment. The formulas presented in Chapter 5 (which actually compare frequencies, not means) through Chapter 8 incorporate both sample size and standard deviation, presented in Section 3.4, to determine whether a particular difference qualifies as statistically significant.

Your familiarity with probabilities also plays an important role in significance testing. The decision as to whether a difference qualifies as significant relies on judgments about probabilities. Explanations of statistical significance presented in Chapter 4 focus on the likelihood that the difference in means could reflect random variation rather than a true distinction between the groups examined. The tests of significance indicate the probability of a difference between descriptive values occurring arbitrarily. You can illustrate these probabilities on graphs similar to the ones shown in Section 3.5.

In short, all statistical analyses should contain these descriptive statistics. Presented alone, they provide your audience with a general understanding of the distribution of subjects into categories, estimates of subjects' scores on a continuum of values, and ranges within which their scores fall. But they also provide a foundation for the inferential statistics that most researchers must perform to properly test their hypotheses.

STATISTICAL RESOURCES FOR SPSS

The creation of descriptive illustrations and the calculation of descriptive statistics is manageable with the relatively small model dataset presented in Section 3.1. For small datasets, you can create relevant graphs and charts or perform calculations on your own. It may become challenging, however, to do the necessary organization and calculations for large datasets. Many calculators can perform basic statistical functions, providing you with values such as the mean and standard deviation. However, if you need to perform an analysis that involves more than these sorts of descriptors, you should use a software program. SPSS can create most descriptive graphs and charts and calculate all frequencies, measures of central tendency, and measures of dispersion.

The SPSS "Explore" screen can supply most of the descriptive statistics and graphs discussed thus far in the chapter. To access this screen, you must select "Descriptive Statistics," and then "Explore" from the "Analyze" pulldown menu (Fig. 3.16).

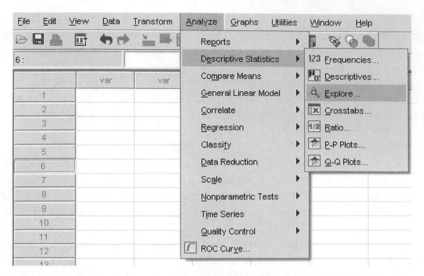

<u>Figure 3.16.</u> "Explore" prompt in SPSS. The "Descriptive Statistics" option in the SPSS "Analyze" pulldown menu contains a prompt for the "Explore" screen. This screen provides measures of central tendency, measures of dispersion, and descriptive graphs for individual datasets.

Frequency Histograms in SPSS

Default output from the "Explore" screen does not include a histogram. However, you can request that SPSS produces a histogram (as well as a stem-and-leaf plot) by clicking on the screen's "Plots" button (Fig. 3.17).

SPSS produced the frequency histograms and the frequency polygon that appear in Section 3.2 of this chapter. Actually, in their original forms, these illustrations also display the dataset's mean, standard deviation, and sample size. But these values were removed from the figures in Section 3.2 so as to avoid confusion. (Information about other ways to obtain measures of central tendency and measures of dispersion appears in the next section, entitled "Measures of Central Tendency and Measures of Dispersion in SPSS.")

Once the histogram appears on the output screen, double-clicking on it produces a "Chart Editor," similar to the ones available for bar graphs and pie charts as described in Chapter 2. The "Chart Editor" allows you to alter the graph's appearance by changing colors or patterns, axis scales, and other qualities. With the "Chart Editor," you can also superimpose a frequency polygon or a normal curve over your histogram. Directions for producing these and similar illustrations can be found in this chapter's companion website.

Example 3.25: Frequency Histogram and Polygon with Normal Curve for Tooth-Loss Data Figure 3.18 puts together the frequency histogram and the frequency

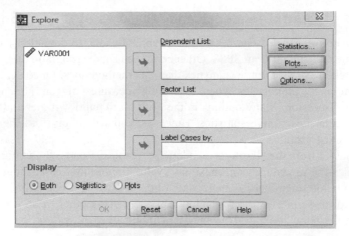

Figure 3.17. "Explore" window in SPSS. The name of the variable involved in the analysis should be moved from the box on the right to the box labeled "Dependent List:" The "Plots" button, on the right of the window, allows the user to include a histogram and a stem-and-leaf graph in the output.

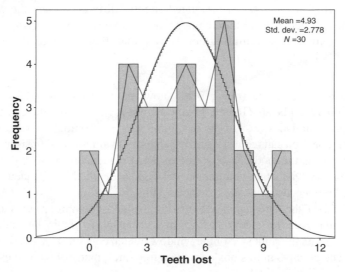

Figure 3.18. Frequency histogram with polygon and normal curve. The upper boundary of the frequency polygon follows increases and decreases in actual frequencies for data points. The shape of the normal curve shows the expected frequencies for data points.

polygon for the tooth-loss data, shown in Section 3.2. The normal curve also appears on the graph.

Having both the frequency polygon and the normal curve on the same graph allows you to visually compare the differences between the actual distribution of frequencies and the theoretical distribution of frequencies.

Measures of Central Tendency and Measures of Dispersion in SPSS

You already know that you can obtain the mean and standard deviation for a dataset by requesting a histogram from SPSS. Other commands in the program, though, provide more comprehensive descriptive statistics than this method does. Once again, you can choose from many approaches when requesting measures of central tendency and measures of dispersion. Many options in the "Analyze" pulldown menu allow you to request particular descriptive statistics. However, you will likely find the "Explore" window the most useful.

Basic output from the "Explore" window (see Table 3.1 and 3.2 and Figs. 3.19 and 3.20) includes the median, mean, maximum value, minimum value, range, variance, standard deviation, interquartile range, and a box-and-whisker chart. It is possible to obtain each of these pieces of information separately using other SPSS functions. But the "Explore" window has the advantage of including all of these descriptors in a single output.

Example 3.26: "Explore" Window Basic Output for Tooth-Loss Data   Between the four parts of the output, you can obtain much of the information presented in examples throughout this chapter. Although, the stem-and-leaf graph (Fig. 3.19) and the box-and-whisker plot area are arranged slightly differently than the ones shown earlier in the chapter, But a quick comparison between the non-SPSS versions and the SPSS versions of the illustrations shows that they provide the exact same information.

The box-and-whisker chart (Fig. 3.20) shows the approximate values of the quartiles, but you may not be able to determine their exact values from the chart. Likewise, the "Descriptive Statistics" box in the "Explore" window's output does not provide the value of the mode. You can request quartile values and values for all measures of central tendency, including the mode, through the SPSS "Frequencies: Statistics" window.

Selecting the "Statistics" button on the right side of the "Frequencies" screen produces a "Frequencies: Statistics" window (Fig. 3.21).

The left side of the "Frequencies: Statistics" window contains prompts to determine the quartile and percentile values discussed in Section 3.4. To obtain the mode, however, you should focus on the right side of the window, which contains a box entitled "Central Tendency." The prompts in this box allow you to request many of the values also avail-

TABLE 3.1. "Explore" Window Output: Case-Processing Summary[a]

	Cases					
	Valid		Missing		Total	
	N	Percent	N	Percent	N	Percent
Teeth lost	30	100.0%	0	.0%	30	100.0%

[a]This table provides details on the number of and the percentage of the total sample that provided the data.

TABLE 3.2. "Explore" window Output: Descriptives[a]

Teeth Lost		Statistic	Standard Error
Mean		4.93	.507
95% confidence	lower bound	3.90	—
Interval for mean	upper bound	5.97	—
5% trimmed mean		4.93	—
Median		5.00	—
Variance		7.720	—
Standard deviation		2.778	—
Minimum		0	—
Maximum		10.000	—
Range		10	—
Interquartile range		4	—
Skewness		.012	.427
Kurtosis		−.755	.833

[a]This table presents values for most of the descriptive statistics.

```
                teethlost
                Stem-and-Leaf Plot

            Frequency    Stem & Leaf

                3.00     0.001
                7.00     0.2222333
                7.00     0.4445555
                8.00     0.66677777
                3.00     0.889
                2.00     1.00

            Stem width:       10
            Each leaf:    1 case(s)
```

Figure 3.19. "Explore" window output: stem-and-leaf chart.

able through the "Explore" window or other SPSS functions. For the purposes of obtaining quartile values, however, you should focus on the portion of the window labeled "Percentile Values," and to obtain the mode, you should focus on the portion of the window labeled "Central Tendency." The resulting output contains a table labeled "Statistics" that appears before the frequencies.

Example 3.27: Quartiles and Mode for Tooth-Loss Data   Table 3.3 shows the "Statistics" table that contains quartile values and the mode for the tooth-loss data.

Table 3.3 contains only quartile values and the mode because only these statistics were chosen from the options provided in SPSS's "Frequencies: Statistics" window. One can obtain other measures of central tendency or percentile values, as well as measures of dispersion by selecting these prompts in the window.

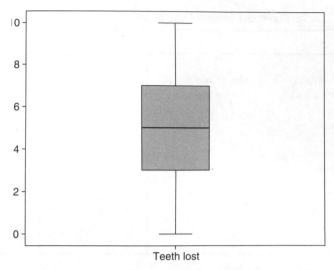

Figure 3.20. "Explore" window output: box-and-whisker chart.

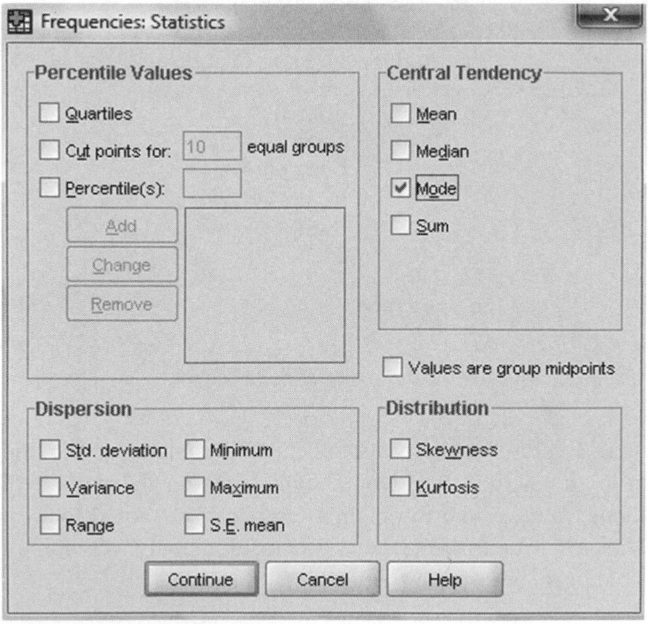

Figure 3.21. SPSS "Frequencies: Statistics" window. Through this window, one can instruct SPSS to calculate specific measures of central tendency, specific measures of dispersion, and percentile or quartile values. The requested output appears along with a frequency table.

TABLE 3.3. SPSS "Statistics" Output Table[a]

Teeth lost		
N	Valid	30.00
	Missing	0
Mode		7
Percentiles	25	2.75
	50	5.00
	75	7.00

[a]The "Statistics" table contains information missing from the output in Example 3.26. To obtain this particular output, the user specifically requested the mode from the variety of measures of central tendency and specified quartile values from the types of percentile values available through the SPSS "Frequencies: Statistics" window.

Other methods of obtaining the desired descriptive statistics exist as well. SPSS offers many groupings of commonly-used descriptive statistics. For example, the "Descriptives" option in the "Analyze" menu "Descriptive Statistics" option provides the sample size, maximum value, minimum value, mean, and standard deviation. Researchers who wish to focus on these values can obtain them without having to search through the "Explore" window's output. Details about functions that you may find useful for obtaining descriptive statistics and illustrations appear on this chapter's companion website.

www.moravian.edu/aqd

REVIEW QUESTIONS

Use the data below for Questions 3.1–3.8. The "homes viewed" data refer to the number of homes that each of 40 home buyers viewed before making a purchase. The "purchase type" data indicate whether they used a real estate company (coded as "1") or purchased the home privately (coded as "2").

Subject	Homes Viewed	Purchase Type	Subject	Homes Viewed	Purchase Type
1	6	1	21	5	1
2	12	1	22	8	1
3	3	1	23	10	2
4	7	2	24	8	1
5	6	1	25	13	1
6	9	2	26	7	2
7	14	2	27	4	2

Subject	Homes Viewed	Purchase Type	Subject	Homes Viewed	Purchase Type
8	3	1	28	9	1
9	8	1	29	9	1
10	6	1	30	15	1
11	6	1	31	16	1
12	2	2	32	7	1
13	18	1	33	3	1
14	9	2	34	10	1
15	12	2	35	8	1
16	14	1	36	3	2
17	18	1	37	5	1
18	4	1	38	11	1
19	6	1	39	5	1
20	11	1	40	8	2

3.1. Create a frequency histogram for the number of homes viewed.

3.2. Create a stacked histogram for the number of homes viewed, separated by purchase type.

3.3. Create a paneled histogram for the number of homes viewed, separated by purchase type.

3.4. Find the maximum and minimum number of homes viewed.

3.5. Find the range for the number of homes viewed.

3.6. Find the mean for the number of homes viewed.

3.7. Find the mode for the number of homes viewed.

3.8. Find the median for the number of homes viewed.

Use the data below, indicating the lengths in seconds of 24 randomly selected television commercials, for Question 3.9–3.12

Commercial	Seconds	Commercial	Seconds
1	48	21	65
2	39	22	41
3	62	23	32
4	74	24	36
5	74	25	35
6	52	26	45
7	70	27	62
8	32	28	72
9	91	29	83
10	42	30	65
11	19	31	74
12	73	32	67

Commercial	Seconds	Commercial	Seconds
13	54	33	47
14	25	34	56
15	68	35	87
16	26	36	22
17	44	37	58
18	85	38	17
19	63	39	68
20	65	40	40

3.9. Create a stem-and-leaf graph based on the data.

3.10. Find the quartile values for the data.

3.11. Find the interquartile range of the data

3.12. Create a box-and-whisker plot for the data.

For Questions 3.13 and 3.14, consider the values {6.7, 4.3, 8.1, 5.6, 6.4, 5.1}.

3.13. Find the variance.

3.14. Find the standard deviation.

3.15. Explain the advantage of using standardized scores over raw scores.

3.16. Explain the relationship between the standard deviation and standardized scores.

For Questions 3.17–3.19, consider a dataset with a mean of 88 and a standard deviation of 21.

3.17. Find the standardized score (z) that corresponds to each of the following raw scores (x):
  (A) $x = 109$
  (B) $x = 25$
  (C) $x = 70$
  (D) $x = 134$

3.18. Find the raw score (z) that corresponds to each of the following standardized scores (z):
  (A) $z = +2$
  (B) $z = +0.6$
  (C) $z = -2.8$

3.19. What percentage of the population could be expected to have scores between
  (A) 46 and 130?
  (B) 67 and 109?
  (C) 25 and 151?
  (D) 130 and 151?

3.20. Find the standardized score (z) that corresponds to each of the following raw scores (x):

(A) $x = 78$

(B) $x = 41$

(C) $x = 95$

(D) $x = 124$

3.21. Draw a normal curve, indicating where each of the raw scores and standardized scores from Question 3.20 lies on the distribution.

3.22. Draw and shade the normal curve to show the portion that illustrates scores

(A) between 78 and 88.

(B) between 88 and 124

(C) less than 41

(D) greater than 95

(E) between 78 and 124

(F) between 41 and 78

3.23. Use the standardized scores from obtained from Question 3.20 and the z-score table in Appendix A to find the percentage of the population that can be expected to have a scores

(A) between 78 and 88

(B) between 88 and 124

(C) less than 41

(D) greater than 95

(E) between 78 and 124

(F) between 41 and 78

Use the following scenario for Questions 3.24–3.31. Researchers observed 200 subjects type a given script and recorded their typing speeds. The subjects had a mean typing speed of 31 words per minute with a standard deviation of 5.5.

3.24. Find the percentage of the population that can be expected to have a typing speed between 14.5 and 31 words per minute.

3.25. Find the percentage of the population that can be expected to have a typing speed between 25.5 and 42 words per minute.

3.26. Find the percentage of the population that can be expected to have a typing speed between 31 and 40 words per minute.

3.27. Find the percentage of the population that can be expected to have a typing speed between 18 and 31 words per minute.

3.28. Find the percentage of the population that can be expected to have a typing speed greater than 40 words per minute.

3.29. Find the percentage of the population that can be expected to have a typing speed less than 18 words per minute.

3.30. Find the percentage of the population that can be expected to have a typing speed between 18 and 40 words per minute.

3.31. Find the percentage of the population that can be expected to have a typing speed between 36 and 40 words per minute.

PART II

STATISTICAL TESTS

4

EVALUATING STATISTICAL SIGNIFICANCE

4.1 INTRODUCTION

A common exercise for preschoolers involves presenting them with two (or more) pictures of items and asking the children to characterize the items as "same" or "different." The children simply describe the items identical to those that are the same and the non-identical items as those that are different. Later in life, though, most realize that all comparisons do not fit so neatly into these dichotomous categories.

Suppose, for example, that Worthalots department store has a mean daily revenue of $31,000 and Dandys department store has a mean daily revenue of $30,000. These values, although clearly not identical, are similar. In fact, had one of Worthalots' dedicated free-spending customers chosen to shop at another store instead, Worthalots' revenues may have fallen below those of Dandys. Similarly, just one individual choosing to purchase big-ticket items at Dandys rather than at another store may have increased Dandys' revenues above $31,000. Is it appropriate to characterize these stores' revenues as different when even one customer gained or lost from either store could change the relationship between the values? The procedure for deciding whether the $1000 discrepancy suffices to justify labeling Worthalots as the more profitable store lies in the issue of statistical significance.

Analyzing Quantitative Data: An Introduction for Social Researchers, First Edition. Debra Wetcher-Hendricks.
© 2011 John Wiley & Sons, Inc. Published 2011 by John Wiley & Sons, Inc.

4.2 CENTRAL LIMIT THEOREM

The normal curve serves as the basis for tests of statistical significance. Chapter 3 should have provided you with an understanding of the curve with respect to individual scores within a sample. The normal curve, however, describes the distribution of values from multiple samples as well. The *central limit theorem* explains this relationship. Luckily, statisticians regard the central limit theorem, as both an amazing and vital component of probability theory. Appreciation of the theorem begins with the acknowledgment that values from any one particular sample may or may not distribute themselves normally. The normal curve described in Chapter 3 really represents an expected distribution. Data that you gather from a single sample would very rarely distribute themselves perfectly along the normal curve. They will likely produce a curve that skews to the right or left, is platokurtic or leptokurtic, or has more than one mode. Data for the same variable gathered from a different sample by another individual, or at another time, will also produce a distribution that differs from the normal curve. But it likely won't differ in the same way as the original dataset does.

4.2.1 Definition of the Central Limit Theorem

It would seem that placing the distributions for multiple datasets on a single set of axis would produce a haphazard jumble of curves. However, you should not encounter such chaos. In 1733 Abraham deMoivre explained that, when considered in total, the scores produced by multiple datasets tend to approximate the normal curve. In other words, the distribution of all values from the sum of samples or, even, of the means for a collection of samples, approaches normality.

Example 4.1: Combination of Distributions A visual representation sometimes helps to clarify this idea. Consider the following three distributions of data, obtained from three separate samples of subjects that provide data for the same variable.

The curves in Figure 4.1 indicate differences between the samples that produced them. However, one who combines data from the three samples finds that the skewness of Figures 4.1(a) and 4.1(c) offset one another. Mean probabilities, thus, remain rather low at the ends of the combined distribution. The highest mean probabilities appear in the middle of the combined distribution, where values remained relatively high in each of the individual distributions. The resulting distribution very closely resembles the normal curve.

The three individual datasets used for this example make their relationship to the mean probability distribution (Fig. 4.2) relatively easy to see. Even in situations that involve individual distributions more varied than those used for this example, the resulting mean probability distribution tends to resemble the normal curve.

As the size of n increases, the shape of the distributions approximation of the normal curve improves. Eventually, this idea, originally proposed by deMoivre (1733), became known as the *central limit theorem*. After many iterations, others later formally defined it as

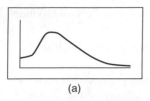 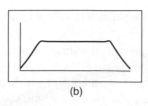 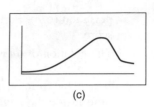

(a)   (b)   (c)

Figure 4.1. Probability Distributions from Individual Samples. Data gathered from any one sample rarely follow the predicted path of normality. Accordingly, none of these curves resembles the normal distribution.

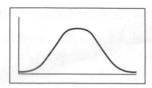

Figure 4.2. Mean Probability Distribution. A distribution of mean probabilities from Figure 4.1 approximates the normal curve. Large probabilities from Figure 4.1(a) compensate for small probabilities from Figure 4.1(c) and vice versa. Thus, neither of the very high values in these figures appear in the mean probability distribution.

$$\lim_{n\to\infty} P\left(\frac{\sqrt{n}(\bar{X}_n -)}{\sigma} \le x\right) = \Phi(x) \tag{4.1}$$

This equation probably looks scary. Two points should put your mind at ease. First, it describes a theoretical relationship; thus, you do not have to apply the formula to perform statistical analyses. Still, understanding the formula's components helps to clarify the pattern of change that the distribution undergoes, which leads to the second point. Although the formula may seem intimidating, it actually tells a rather straight-forward story.

In fact, with a close look at Equation (4.1), you'll notice that much of the formula actually consists of the equation to compute z scores presented in Chapter 3. This portion of the equation reflects the fact that the normal curve associates raw scores with standardized (z) scores. The remainder of Equation (4.1)'s components represent the process and results of increasing the number of samples involved in the analysis:

- The beginning of the formula, $\lim_{n\to\infty}$, explains that the number of samples and, thus, data points can increase with no limit.
- The P that appears below the large parenthetical expression indicates that you should consider the probability of the situation inside the parentheses occurring.
- The expression inside the large parentheses presents the ratio of the residual between sample means and the population mean to the population standard

deviation (σ/n). Further, it states that this ratio does not exceed each individual score.

- The notation of $\Phi(x)$ represents the standard normal distribution function.

Overall, then, the formula describes a situation in which increases in n lead to increases in the ratio inside the large parentheses. As a result, the probability of the inequality being true rises and the distribution gradually begins to follow the shape of the normal curve.

4.2.2 Demonstrating the Central Limit Theorem

Repeatedly tossing a coin presents a straightforward illustration of the central limit therem. The following exercise reveals the step-by-step convergence of data points around the population mean.

Example 4.2: Coin Flipping and the Central Limit Theorem   When tossing a fair coin, one expects the coin to land on "tails" 50% of the time. Sometimes two tosses results in two "heads" or in two "tails," but these results occur with equal probability. *Toss a coin two times and record the results.* In theory, you have only a 50% chance of obtaining one and only one result of "tails."

Toss the coin four more times, for a total of six tosses, which increases the number of possible combinations of landings. Although the possibility exists that all tosses have the same results, it is less likely with six tosses than with two tosses. Unlike the situation with two tosses, you have a much greater chance of obtaining values close to the mean, in this case, three, than of obtaining all "tails" (or all "heads") with your six tosses.

Further increasing the number of tosses raises the probability that the number of times the coin lands on "tails" lies near the mean. *Toss the coin four more times, for a total of 10 tosses.* Now, an extremely small chance of all tosses landing on "tails" (or all tosses landing on "heads") exists. But the number of times that the coin landed on "tails" is likely closer to the mean, in this case five, than it was when you tossed the coin six times.

If you need further convincing, *flip the coin an additional 20 times, for a total of 30 tosses.* This dataset has a mean of 15. The number of times that the coin lands on "tails" should fall proportionally closer to the mean (within the range of possible values) than when you tossed the coin twice, six times, or 10 times.

Of course, you cannot expect to obtain the exact mean in any of these situations. Most often, the coin lands on "tails" more than it lands on "heads" or lands on "heads" more than it lands on "tails," leading to values smaller or larger than the mean. However, according to the central limit theorem, if you consistently obtain values smaller than the mean, another individual who follows the same coin-tossing steps as you obtains the opposite results.

Find four other individuals to toss a coin 30 times and record the number of times that the coin lands on "tails." When combined with your results, you have five values to represent the number of "tails" results obtained from each of five samples. *Use a histogram to depict the frequency of each result.* (Given that each individual tosses the coin 30 times, the values on the x axis of the histogram should range from 1 to 30, with 15 identified as the mean. Label the y axis with frequency values.)

The shape of your histogram probably doesn't look much like the normal distribution. Just as when you tossed the coin only a few times yourself, you couldn't expect to obtain the mean number of "tails," you cannot expect a distribution based on only five samples of data to resemble the normal curve. *Find another 10 individuals to flip the coin 30 times and record the number of times that the coin lands on "tails."* Repeat this process a few more times, each time adjusting your histogram to include the results from the new samples. As you do so, the shape of the normal distribution should materialize, as predicted by the central limit theorem.

4.2.3 Limitations of the Central Limit Theorem

You have likely already realized that the central limit theorem has no value for categorical data. Categorical data do not have a mean or a variance and cannot form distributions, which is the focus of the central limit theorem. Within the realm of continuous data, though, the central limit theorem has widespread applicability. Only in higher-order statistical analyses would you encounter situations in which the central limit theorem does not apply to continuous data. These circumstances generally reflect special cases involving distributions that do not have means and variances.

Notwithstanding this limitation, the central limit theorem exists as a foundation of probability theory. The acknowledgment that, eventually, random sampling produces a normal curvelike distribution allows researchers to use this distribution to describe most datasets. The statistical tests described in later chapters of this book, therefore, assume normality and bases decisions regarding statistical significance on probabilities associated with the normal distribution.

4.3 STATISTICAL SIGNIFICANCE

Researchers generally need to know whether differences in data provided by subjects exist due to chance. A *significant difference* exists when values lie far enough apart that a very low likelihood of the disparity occurring randomly exists. Statistically, it involves the inference that a difference among sample values also occurs in the population.[1] Samples and *sampling*, selecting a portion of subjects to represent the entire population, receive attention in Section 4.3.1. In general, however, statisticians require very large differences in sample values because small differences in sample values may reflect

---

[1]Recall that a population includes all those to whom the data can apply. In most cases, it is impossible to gather data from all individuals in the population. Those in the sample, a representative subset of the population, actually supply the data.

something peculiar about the subjects in that particular sample. Had your sample consisted of different subjects, the same small difference may not have existed. For you to claim that a difference in a sample also exists in the population, the sample's values must differ by more than what such random factors could explain.

Methods to address this issue have received the fitting title of *inferential statistics*. Inferential statistical tests involve consideration of not only the numbers being compared but also sample size (n) and variance (s^2). Subsequent chapters of this book present methods for arranging these values into formulas to produce calculated statistics that indicate the significance level of the difference in category frequencies (Chapter 5), the difference between two means (Chapter 6), and the difference between three or more means (Chapter 7).

4.3.1   The Importance of Good Sampling

If you could somehow gather data from every single unit of analysis within the population, you would not need to use significance tests. A simple comparison of the data would tell you whether independent-variable conditions correspond to dependent-variable differences. Realistically, though, you do not have access to an entire population. Sampling, selecting a portion of subjects to represent the entire population, is the next-best option. Statistical tests characterize differences within a sample as indicative of differences within the population or as too trivial to have much meaning beyond that sample.

Example 4.3: Data from a Population   For example, those conducting the research regarding daily revenue of Worthalots and Dandys department stores may also show some interest in the amount of time that individuals spend shopping in these stores. The research pertains to every individual who ever shopped in either store, making them the population. Ideally, to conduct a study comparing the number of hours those in the population spend shopping in Worthalots and in Dandys department stores, the researcher would obtain information about how long these shoppers spent in the store during each of their visits. Then, having obtained information from all of these people, the researcher could compute the mean number of hours spent in each of these stores and compare the numbers to determine the extent to which they differ.

Anybody with an ounce of common sense would consider this plan ridiculous. It is impossible to locate every individual in this population, much less gather data from them! Thus, researchers resort to sampling. Gathering data from a subset of those who ever shopped at Worthalots or Dandys proves much more reasonable a task than does gathering data from the entire population.

The use of samples, although practical in one sense, creates some apprehension. Just because the sample is drawn from the population doesn't mean that those in the sample appropriately represent the entire population. A biased sample, one that includes units of analysis with only a particular characteristic or under certain conditions, may provide data that describe only a portion of the population.

Example 4.4: Biased Samples   Any number of issues can create bias within the study described in Example 4.3. An obvious potential source of bias relates to traditional gender roles, specifically those that distinguish between the demeanors and the shopping behaviors of males and females. According to gender roles, females tend to appear more "approachable" in public venues than men do. A researcher using an interview technique to gather data might, thus, tend to choose more females than males as subjects. However, gender roles also dictate that females spend more time shopping than men do. Thus, if a sample contains mostly women, then the data collected by the researcher likely overestimate the amount of time that the general population spends shopping. The researcher must make a conscious effort to include an equal number of males and females in the sample (or, if preferred, a proportion that reflect the correct proportion of the stores' populations of male to female shoppers).

Issues besides subject characteristics also deserve attention. For example, gathering data only during a certain time of day can create biased data. Individuals tend to spend less time shopping when they have children with them than when they are alone or with friends. So, data shouldn't be gathered only during weekday mornings or early afternoons when stay-at-home mothers or stay-at-home fathers have no choice but to bring their young children to the stores with them.[2] Data provided by the individuals in the stores at these times would likely underrepresent the amount of time that the general population spends shopping. To obtain generalizable data, the researcher must gather data from each store at various times on various days.

Statistical tests determine whether a difference evident within a sample also exists within the population and, therefore, rely on samples properly representing the population. The lack of a representative sample threatens *external validity*, the capacity to generalize results of a study to the population. Ensuring random selection of subjects and using large sample sizes helps to minimize this threat.

Random Sampling.   *Random sampling* relies entirely on probability. Each unit of analysis within the population has an equal chance of becoming a member of the sample. The researcher does not use any sort of subjective method to select subjects. So, using random sampling methods eliminates the possibility of any researcher bias toward or against particular individuals or conditions to affect the representativeness of the sample.

Many methods of obtaining a random sample exist. The purest form, simple random sampling, is based on the idea of "choosing names or numbers from a hat." However, other versions, such as systematic sampling, cluster sampling, stratified sampling, and probability proportionate to size sampling, exist as well. Additional information about these methods and the information that you must report if you use them is presented in Chapter 11.

Sample Size.   You already know that the normality of a statistical distribution, characterized by the central limit theorem, depends on large sample sizes. Small samples often produce skewed distributions because of the low probability that they produce the mean population value (μ). As demonstrated with the coin-flipping exercise, the dataset that contains only a few points has a reasonably good chance of producing extreme values. Increasing the number of trials increases the chance of "balancing out" these extremes, and eventually the shape of the distribution resembles that of the normal curve. This shifting of the distribution signifies a minimization of bias in the sample.

Example 4.5: Sample Size   For example, a single shopper from Worthalots department store and a single shopper from Dandys department store could not provide generalizable data for a comparison of the amount of time that individuals spend shopping each of the stores. The shopper selected to represent one of the stores may just happen to be an individual who simply needs to run in and out of the store on her lunch break. The data that this person supplies, then, would underrepresent the amount of time that the typical shopper spends in the store. Conversely, the subject may have be the person who is spending the whole day doing Christmas shopping at the store. In this case, the data provided by this subject would overrepresent the amount of time that the typical shopper spends in the store. However, if the sample includes both of these people, as well as many others who shop for varying amounts of time, the data that they provide balance out near the population mean.

Large datasets provide context for each individual data point. Given a single data point, you have no idea how well the value describes the sample or the population. It may, for all you know, be an extreme value. With a large dataset the most commonly occurring values and, thus, the extreme values, become evident. Adding data points to the sample amplifies this overall pattern, providing an increasingly accurate representation of the whole population. Thus, researchers should always strive for as large a sample as reasonably possible.

4.3.2   Identifying a Significant Difference

Even with very large samples, you cannot always assume that the data provided by subjects mimic the data you would have gathered from the population if such an exercise were feasible. Section 4.3.1 explains how minor changes in the constituency of the sample may change the relationship between data produced by each sample group. Thus, researchers rarely assume that small differences between sample groups reflect population differences.

The difference between sample groups must be sufficiently large to claim that same difference also exists in the population, referred to as a *significant difference*. Tests of significance allow you to determine whether a particular sample difference qualifies as large enough to indicate significance. These tests allow you to define your own criteria regarding how much you wish the sample values to differ before declaring them significant.

The particular test of significance used depends on the natures of the data involved in the analysis. Although each test requires the use of a separate formula, they all follow the same basic procedure—a mathematical comparison between two or more sample values produces a statistic that indicates the probability of a significant difference. If a significant difference exists, however, this value does not tell you the *way* in which values differ. It can only help you determine *whether* some sort of distinguishing trend in values exist.

A research hypothesis, symbolized as *H*, makes a prediction more specific than that related to the presence or absence of a trend. In your research hypothesis, you can identify the independent-variable group or situation associated with the highest (or lowest) dependent-variable scores. The statistics produced by significance tests cannot, in and of themselves, tell you whether your research hypothesis is correct. If the statistics indicate no significant difference, you know that you cannot accept the research hypothesis. But if a significant difference exists, it could reflect the difference that the research hypothesis suggests or another difference. Perhaps the group that you predicted to have a significantly higher score than the others actually has a significantly lower score than the others.

The only hypothesis for which a significance test can provide certain results is one that predicts absolutely no trend between scores on the independent and dependent variable. This statement is called the *null hypothesis*, denoted as H_0, because it suggests that independent-variable scores cannot predict dependent-variable scores. Researchers generally refer to the null hypothesis when discussing results of significance tests. An accepted null hypothesis indicates that no trend at all exists between independent-variable scores and dependent-variable scores. A rejected null hypothesis indicates that a significant difference exists. The researcher must further investigate this difference to determine whether the values differ in the way suggested by the research hypothesis. Section 10.2 further describes the support that the null hypothesis can receive from an accepted or a rejected null hypothesis.

Probability Values. The nature of your data (see Chapter 1) determines the statistics and, therefore, the formulas that you need to use to determine whether to accept or reject the null hypothesis. Regardless of the formulas used, *significance levels* refer to the probability that the difference between the entities being compared has occurred by chance. For this reason, significance level is symbolically represented as *p* (for *probability*). The value of $1 - p$ refers to the researcher's certainty that the difference between sample values actually has some meaning in terms of the population.

Researchers generally desire low *p* levels, indicating only a small probability that the difference evident in a sample reflects mere randomness rather than a true significant difference. A common standard defines *p* values greater than .05 as suggestive of significance because they indicate greater than a 5% chance that an existing difference may simply reflect a characteristic of the particular sample used, but not exist in the general population. Given this standard, a difference is considered significant only if $p < .05$, meaning that the researcher can be 95% certain that the same difference that exists in the sample also exists in the population. The largest *p* value that the researcher accepts as indication to reject the null hypothesis, in this case .05, is considered the alpha value, represented as α.

Alpha (α) and Critical Values. It is not always necessary to obtain an exact value for *p*. The researcher really only needs to know where *p* lies in relation to the α

value that he or she has decided to use. Mathematical formulas allow researchers without access to statistical software programs to obtain statistics called *calculated values*. The calculated values represent the extent of the difference between the number of individuals who fall into each subject group or between mean scores of subjects in each group. Because they refer only to the disparity in the sample, calculated values much be relatively high to suggest a difference in the population. A small calculated value would likely produce a *p* value greater than .05, meaning that you have more than a 5% chance of incorrectly stating that a significant difference exists. This mistake is called a *type I error* and receives additional attention later in this section. As calculated values increase, *p* values decrease, as does the chance of making a type I error. Fortunately, charts exist to help researchers determine exactly the point at which this chance crosses the $\alpha = .05$ threshold (or that of any other α value chosen by the researcher) by providing *critical values*. Calculated values that exceed critical values indicate such an extreme difference that the *p* value would fall below α. So, by simply comparing a calculated value to the appropriate critical values contained in the appropriate charts, the researcher can determine whether a significant difference exists and, thus, whether to accept or reject the null hypothesis.

Confidence Intervals and Distribution Tails. You can easily see the relationship between *p*, $1 - p$, α, the critical value, and the calculated value on a visual representation of the normal curve. Until this point, the term *normal curve* has been used to refer only to raw scores of data. However, similar distributions using calculated values for inferential statistics in place of raw scores resemble the normal curve to varying extents as well. (The similarities and differences between each statistic's distribution and the normal curve receive additional attention in Chapters 5 through 7 of this book.) The distribution can display frequencies of results from successive statistical tests, each using data from a separate sample, just as well as it can display frequencies of raw data points.

When referring to statistical values, the highest point on the normal distribution corresponds to the mean calculated value obtained from the many tests performed. The shape of the curve indicates that many values tend to conglomerate about this mean and that few points lie at the extremes, or "tails", of the distribution. Values in the tail have very low probabilities of occurring. In fact, these values occur by chance so infrequently that, when they do, the researcher must consider them indicative of a meaningful difference within the population. Therefore, a calculated value that lies within the tail of the distribution suggests a significant difference.

So, the question of exactly where the tail begins arises. Critical values form the boundaries for the tails (see Fig. 4.3). Because of the relationship between critical values and α values, placement of these boundaries depends on your choice of α. Large critical values reflect small α values, and small critical values reflect large α values.

The extreme calculated values that lie in the tails have a less than α probability of occurring ($p < \alpha$). These calculated values reflect differences between sample groups so large that they do not occur by chance, but rather indicate some difference within the population. The researcher, therefore, associates calculated values within the tails with significance. The area of the normal curve that lies between the tails encompasses

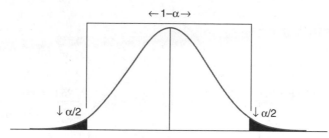

Figure 4.3. α and Tail Size. In a two-tailed distribution, calculated values have an $\alpha/2$ probability of falling into each tail. The size of the tails decreases as α decreases. Absolute values of critical values that fall into the darkened tails lie above the absolute values of their tests' critical values.

the remaining critical values and is called the *confidence interval*. You can think of a confidence interval as the percentage of the time that you can correctly claim a lack of significance. The sample data that produce critical values within the limits of the confidence interval occur by chance $100(1 - \alpha)$ percent of the time. As the size of the confidence interval grows, the researcher becomes increasingly comfortable about the decision to accept or reject the null hypothesis.

So, using the standard α of .05, the researcher uses a 95% critical value, meaning that all except 5% of calculated values lie between the tails. These values do not indicate a significant difference because they can occur by chance so often. In contrast, the calculated values that lie in the tails occur by chance no more than 5% of the time. Most likely, these calculated values result from differences that exist in the population as well as in the sample. You can describe this difference as significant at $\alpha = .05$. Using an α larger than .05 enlarges the sizes of the tails and, thus, allows you to declare significance more often than when using $\alpha = .05$. Using an α smaller than .05 reduces the sizes of the tails and thus does not allow you to declare significance as often as when using $\alpha = .05$. Figure 4.4 shows the relationships between the sizes of the tails (corresponding to calculated values that indicate significance) and for the area within the tails (corresponding to calculated values that indicate no significance) for $\alpha = .01$, $\alpha = .05$, and $\alpha = .10$.

Type I and Type II Errors. Because the possibility of a fluke, in which a sample produces data points that just happen to be the exception to the rule, always exists, the researchers always run some risk of incorrectly assuming that the difference between values in a sample also exists in the population. A researcher who does so makes a *type I error*. The standard of using a low α, such as .05, minimizes the possibility of making a type 1 error.

Of course, researchers can choose to stray from this standard α value. Those who feel uncomfortable knowing that a type I error may occur up to 5% of the time may decide to lower the α value to .01, .001, or any other value that satisfies them. Doing so, however, reduces the number of datasets with a significant difference. Suppose, for example, that the *p* value representing the difference in the mean number of times that

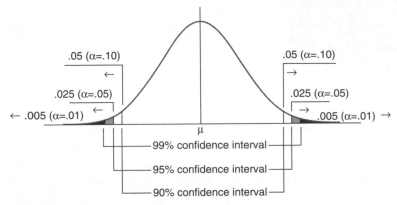

Figure 4.4. Tail Size and α. In a two tailed distribution, the confidence interval lies between the upper boundary of the left tail and the lower boundary of the right tail. Calculated values that lie within the confidence interval have a 1 − α probability or a 100(1 − α) percentage chance of correctly characterizing a difference as insignificant. So, as α decreases, the researcher becomes increasingly confident in his or her acceptance of the null hypothesis.

those who did and who didn't attend clown college can make people laugh within a minute is .03. The researcher could assume that such a difference would occur by chance in the sample only 3% of the time and, consequently, that the difference that exists in the sample exists in the population 97% of the time. A researcher using an α of .05 who is willing to accept as much as a 5% chance of incorrectly generalizing would declare a significant difference and reject the null hypothesis. A researcher who uses an α of .01, however, would not recognize a significant difference without 99% assurance that the difference evident in the sample also exists in the population. Therefore, this researcher would accept the null hypothesis and claim that no significant difference exists in the number of times that an individual who attends clown college and one who doesn't attend clown college can make people laugh. Although using a low α seems to "safeguard" the researcher from type I errors, she or he must acknowledge the fact that lowering the α value increases the possibility of making a *type II error*, in which the researcher fails to acknowledge a significant difference in the population (Table 4.1).

Values of α can be increased as well. Often, when the *p* value obtained by a researcher lies just above the standard of .05, researchers wish to acknowledge that the difference in their samples *almost* qualifies as significant. In these cases, the researcher may choose to increase the α to a higher value, such as .10 or .20, relaxing the criteria for significance. If, for example, the comparison between those who did and didn't attend clown college produced a *p* value of .06, the researcher could claim that a significant difference exists when using an α of .10, but not when using an α of .05. It is important to remember, though, that increasing the α value to make such claims possible has a large tradeoff in that it increases the possibility of making a type I error. A researcher who uses an α value greater than .05 must be willing to take more than a 5% chance that the differences evident in the sample do not exist in the population.

TABLE 4.1. Type I and Type II Errors[a]

	No Difference in Population	Difference in Population
No difference in sample	☺	Type II error
Difference in sample	Type I error	☺

[a]This table shows the various possibilities with regard to differences in a sample and differences within the population. No error exists when a difference exists in the dataset as well as in the sample or in which no difference exists in either. A type I error occurs when statistical tests incorrectly suggest that a difference evident in the sample dataset also exists in the population. A type II error occurs when a difference exists in the population, but is not evidenced by statistical tests performed on the sample dataset.

Using an α value of .10, as suggested in the example, means that claims of a significant difference will be correct only 90% of the time. Few researchers are willing to take such a chance and, thus, stick to α values of .05 and below.

4.4   THE ROLES OF HYPOTHESES

Your judgment about significant differences reflect your underlying objective for a particular project. On the basis of information obtained from your literature review, performed well before data collection begins, you should have formed an opinion about the relationship between the variables involved in your analysis.

If your logic for performing your investigation is based on the expectation that changes in the independent variable do not correspond to changes in the dependent variable, then you hope for a lack of significance.

Example 4.6: Desired Insignificance   Suppose that the motive for the comparison between shopping at Worthalots and Dandys department stores lies in determining whether having to use stairs, escalators, or elevators while shopping relates to the amount of time people spend shopping. Those involve in urban planning may undertake such a project in an attempt to convince store proprietors to build their new stores "up" rather than "out." The urban planning researcher hopes to show that the presence or absence of multiple floors makes no difference in the amount of time spent shopping at a particular store. Luckily, shoppers at Worthalots, with only one level, and at Dandys, with more than one level, can provide the necessary data. With the goal of proving that the number of floors in a store has no relationship to the amount of time that people spend shopping at that store, one would hope to find no significant difference between the mean shopping times of Worthalots and of Dandys customers.

However, a different objective for your study may change the expectations regarding significance. One who wishes to demonstrate that differences in the independent variable correspond to differences in the dependent variable hopes that the results of the relevant statistical test indicate significance.

Example 4.7: Desired Significance   Research regarding the amount of time that people spend shopping at Worthalots and Dandys may also be conducted by members of a "rights for the disabled" group. They may hope to convince store proprietors to build their new stores on only one level to accommodate those who have difficulty climbing stairs or, even, using elevators. These individuals would conduct a comparison of the time that individuals spend shopping at Worthalots and at Dandys, with one and more than one floor, respectively, similar to that conducted by the urban planners in Example 4.7. But the members of the rights-for the-disabled group would do so with the intent of finding that customers spend significantly more time at Worthalots than at Dandys so that they can use this information as evidence for their argument.

Clearly, no hard-and-fast rule regarding how to perceive the presence or the lack of a significant difference exists. You must consider your ultimate objective before characterizing the results of a study as "good" or "bad." Researchers explain their goals regarding the desire for significance or the lack of significance through their statements of hypotheses.

4.4.1   The Research and Null Hypotheses

The *research hypothesis* provides a clue regarding the researcher's expectations. Using their existing knowledge and information obtained from the literature, researchers make a prediction regarding the equality or inequality between entities that they wish to compare. This research hypothesis states the researchers' predictions of what they believe the outcome of the statistical analysis will be. For instance, a researcher who believes that Worthalots has a higher mean daily revenue than Dandys does would state the research hypothesis as

$$H: \mu_W > \mu_D$$

The researcher could use similar notation to represent a prediction that Dandys has a higher mean daily revenue than Worthalots does or that the two have equal mean daily revenues. Regardless of the researcher's prediction, however, she or he must translate the research hypothesis into a null hypothesis.

The need for defining a research hypothesis is dictated by the role of inferential statistics. The p values produced by inferential statistical tests simply indicate whether a significant difference exists. The researcher knows that a p value larger than α indicates no significant difference and a p value equal to or less than α indicates a significant difference. Should a significant difference exist, the statistical test cannot determine the "direction" of the difference. For example, given a p value lower than .05 (assuming $\alpha = .05$) or a calculated value that exceeds the critical value, the researcher can conclude that Worthalots and Dandys have significantly different mean daily revenues but cannot determine which of the two stores has the higher of the two revenues. Although the difference may exist in the manner predicted by the research hypothesis, it may also exist in the opposite direction. Inferential statistical tests, therefore, do not provide sufficient information to accept a research hypothesis that predicts inequality.

Unlike the research hypothesis, which represents the researchers' expectation, the *null hypothesis* always predicts equality between the compared values. Regardless of the appearance of the research hypothesis, the null hypothesis for the investigation into the mean amount of time spent shopping at Worthalots and at Dandys appears as

$$H_0: \mu_W = \mu_D$$

If the researcher actually believes that equality exists, the null hypothesis simply restates the research hypothesis. Most often, however, the researcher anticipates a difference between values, and thus the null hypothesis differs from the research hypothesis.

Because values can differ in many ways, but can be the same only one way, it makes sense to test the null hypothesis rather than the research hypothesis. An accepted null hypothesis often signifies the end of the statistical analysis cause that equality needs no further interpretation. A rejected null hypothesis, however, demands additional attention. At the very least, the researcher must examine the values being compared to determine which exceed(s) the others. Comparisons between multiple values can require additional testing to ascertain the exact source of the significant difference.

Only after establishing whether a significant difference exists and, if so, the direction of this difference, can a researcher determine whether said significant difference is good. The characterization of a difference as good or bad essentially depends on the relationship between the research hypothesis and the null hypothesis. The researcher whose research hypothesis proposes equality, such as one who truly believes that shoppers spend equal mean amounts of time at Worthalots and Dandys (so that the null hypothesis would mimic the research hypothesis), would happily accept the null hypothesis, rejoicing in the fact that no significant difference exists. One who, on the other hand, believes that mean time spent shopping at Worthalots is greater than mean time spent shopping at Dandys would prefer a rejected null hypothesis, indicating that a significant difference exists. This researcher must take caution, however, to avoid premature characterization of the significant difference as good, and must first ensure that Worthalots, not Dandys, has the higher mean shopping time.

Accepting the Null Hypothesis. You determined, earlier in the analysis, that you would not consider any sample difference meaningful for the population unless you had $100(1 - \alpha)\%$ assurance that it reflects more than chance. The standard α of .05 indicates your willingness to permit a $\leq 5\%$ chance of considering a difference within the sample significant when it really only reflects an arrangement of data points that just happened to occur within the sample. If you wish to have a a $< 5\%$ possibility of this situation occurring, then you choose an α lower than .05. If you are willing to accept a $> 5\%$ possibility of this situation occurring, then you chose an α greater than

.05. Your choice of α sets the standards for accepting the null hypothesis of equality between values.

The value of α that you choose determines the critical value used as a basis for comparison with the calculated statistical value that reflects the size of the difference between sample means or frequencies. When the critical value statistic exceeds the calculated value, the probability of the sample difference occurring by chance (p) remains below α. So, you accept the null hypothesis, indicating a lack of significant difference between the values that you have compared. An accepted null hypothesis requires little explanation. Essentially, by accepting a null hypothesis, you state that the sample values lie so close to one another that you regard them as equal.

An accepted null hypothesis tells you whether to reject the research hypothesis. Obviously, a null hypothesis that simply restates the research hypothesis, suggesting that you actually expected to find no difference in values, receives support from an accepted null hypothesis. However, if H_0 is accepted, you must reject a research hypothesis that predicts a difference between sample values. If the null hypothesis, predicting equality, is true, then you cannot accept a hypothesis predicting inequality between values.

Rejecting the Null Hypothesis. The decision to reject the hypothesis, itself, follows the same logic as the decision to accept the null hypothesis. The α value used for a particular study determines the critical value statistic. A computed value that exceeds the critical value indicates a difference in sample values so large that it occurs by chance less than $(100 - \alpha)\%$ of the time. One who uses the standard α of .05 thus acknowledges that the difference in sample data correctly characterizes the population at least 95% of the time. Those who would like more than 95% assurance can decrease the value of α, which increases the critical value and tightens the criteria for rejecting the null hypothesis. Those who need less than 95% assurance can increase the value of α, which decreases the critical value and loosens the criteria for rejecting the null hypothesis.

With identical research and null hypotheses, a rejected null hypothesis demands a rejected research hypothesis as they both predict equality. However, interpreting and explaining the presence of a significant difference when the research hypothesis predicts inequality between sample values can require careful reflection. A rejected null hypothesis does not necessarily demand the acceptance of such a research hypothesis.

When a significant difference exists, you must determine the direction of the existing difference. The mere fact that a significant difference exists does not mean that it exists in the way that the research hypothesis predicts. The difference may actually result from a situation opposite from the one that you expected. Before hastily accepting the research hypothesis of inequality, you must reexamine the sample values to determine whether the value you identified as larger actually *is* the larger one.

Example 4.8: Rejected Null and Research Hypotheses   The scenario introduced in Section 4.1.1, suggesting that people spend more time shopping at Worthalots than at Dandys, provides a good example of circumstances that require such consideration. An accepted null hypothesis (H_0) indicates that values do not differ and, thus, the researcher would reject the research hypothesis (H), which predicts inequality. However, one cannot assume the converse. A rejected null hypothesis does indicate that a significant difference exists. It may be that the mean amount of time that shoppers spend at Dandys significantly exceeds the mean amount of time that shoppers spend at Worthalots. This situation does not reflect the prediction made in H. It reflects the exact opposite! In this situation, the researcher would reject both the null and the research hypotheses. Accepting H, as stated in Section 4.11, thus has two criteria: (1) the researcher must reject the null hypothesis and (2) the researcher must confirm that Worthalots, not Dandys, has the higher mean.

4.4.2 Unexpected Results

Suppose that a researcher who proposes inequality in her or his research hypothesis does so because the Worthalots department store is frequented by well-to-do clientele, but Dandys caters to the average working-class citizen. In this situation, statistical results indicating that Worthalots' mean daily revenue significantly exceeds that of Dandys, would surprise few and the researcher would likely feel fulfilled in that her or his research supported what had previously been only suspected. The result suggesting that Dandys' mean daily revenues exceed those of Worthalots or an accepted null hypothesis, which indicates equality, however, would likely qualify as a revelation. The latter of these two scenarios would change individuals' understandings and perspectives of the situation, making these results more valuable information than those of the former scenario.

Few researchers wish to confirm well-accepted or logically inferred circumstances. They hope, instead, that the results of their data analyses support a research hypothesis unfamiliar to the general audience. Consequently, the rejection of a research hypothesis that seems to follow all lines of logic based on the researcher's literature review usually meets with more public interest and curiosity than does the acceptance of such a hypothesis. The lesson, simply, is that unexpected results provide novel information, which, by all accounts, fulfills the ultimate goal of social research.

4.5 CONCLUSION

The processes described in this chapter establish a routine for assessing statistical significance. The statistical analyses described in later chapters of this book all refer to the relationship between p and α. Those that address differences between groups of a categorical independent variable, specifically, the chi-square test, the t test, and the ANOVA, rely entirely on this relationship. Others, such as correlation analyses, use the p value to validate or invalidate trends between two continuous variables.

You should notice, as you progress through chapters of this book, that the procedure for determining significance remains the same regardless of which test you are using. Although each test uses a different formula and a different critical value table, all tests require the computation of a calculated statistic and the comparison of that value to the critical value. The same standards regarding the relationship between these numbers always apply. If the calculated value exceeds the critical value, then you know that the difference evident in the sample has less than an α probability of occurring by chance. You can then declare that a significant difference exists and reject the null hypothesis. Conversely, you should accept the null hypothesis of equality when the critical value exceeds the calculated value because this result indicates that any difference evident in the sample most likely occurred by chance and, thus, cannot describe the overall population.

Decisions regarding significance and insignificance eventually become a matter of routine. Most presentations of analysis simply require you to indicate whether a significant difference does or does not exist and to provide the computed statistic to substantiate your claim. The underlying principles of the decision regarding significance, however, are much more abstract than such a report suggests. Most evidently, the researcher faces the tasks of obtaining a representative sample and of determining the appropriate α level and understanding the potential threat of type I and type II errors associated with it. This chapter should help you understand the ramifications of using various α levels as they relate to the faith that you and others can put into your conclusions. Thus, you should constantly remain aware of the meanings of α, p, representativeness, and generalilzability during the course of conducting statistical tests and evaluating their results.

STATISTICAL RESOURCES FOR SPSS

Just as SPSS can help the researcher by performing computations and creating graphs for descriptive statistics, it can greatly minimize the "hands on" work required to test hypotheses. One using SPSS does not need to obtain calculated statistics and degrees of freedom using the formulas provided in the Chapters 5–8. SPSS output contains this information.

SPSS even simplifies the decisionmaking process regarding acceptance or rejection of the null hypothesis. Without SPSS, you must use the degrees of freedom and α values to locate the critical value on a critical value table. Then, you must compare the value from the table to the calculated statistic to determine whether the sample difference has occurred by chance or indicates some trend within the population. A critical value that exceeds the calculated value leads to an accepted null hypothesis because it indicates more than an α probability that any difference between groups in the sample reflects nothing more than chance. Only when the calculated value exceeds the critical value can you reject the null hypothesis because the probability of the difference between sample groups (p) lies below α. Thus, you can acknowledge a difference within the population with at least $100(1 - \alpha)$ certainty. In these cases, though, you don't really know the value of p. You can just determine whether it is larger or smaller than α. So, you may never really know the exact probability of simple chance accounting for the difference between sample groups.

SPSS output, however, provides the exact p value. This value generally appears in the output under the label of "significance."

TABLE 4.2. Signficance Value in SPSS Output[a]

Parameter	Value	df	Asymptote Significance (Two-Sided)
Pearson chi-square statistic	6.056^a	6	.417
Likelihood ratio	7.729	6	.259
Linear-by-linear association	.724	1	.395
Number of valid cases	19	—	—

[a]The chi-square test produced a p value .417. The table also provides values for the test's calculated statistic and the degrees of freedom. The other values in the table refer to tests that are more advanced or specified than those most often used in basic inferential analyses.

Example 4.9: Significance Values in SPSS　The sample SPSS output in Table 4.2 lists p values in the "Asymptote Significance (Two-Sided)" column. This table contains output from a chi-square test. (See Chapter 6 for information on chi-square tests.)

The p value in Table 4.2 indicates no significant difference between the values compared. With a p of .417, which lies well above any reasonable α value, the researcher must accept the null hypothesis. According to this output, a 41.7% chance of making a type 1 error exists. Given the fact that few researchers accept much more than the standard 5% chance (based on the standard $\alpha = -.05$) of incorrectly rejecting the null hypothesis, it certainly would not be rejected in this case.

SPSS produces an output table that contains a significance column for all inferential statistical tests, including the chi-square test that produced Table 4.2. As in the case of Table 4.2, some SPSS output tables contain more than one p value. When the table contains multiple p values, you should focus on the one labeled with the name of the appropriate test. The "Statistical Resources for SPSS" sections in Chapters 5–8 as well as this book's companion website contain instructions for finding and interpreting the appropriate values within the SPSS output for each inferential statistical test.

Inclusion of the p value in SPSS output benefits you in two ways:

1. It eliminates the need for using a critical value chart. The chart indirectly indicates whether p lies above or below α. However, with the actual p value, you can determine that for yourself.
2. This value indicates the exact probability of making a type I error.

The p value represents the possibility that chance, not a population trend, explains the difference between sample groups. A low p value results from differences so large that they likely reflect population differences and, thus, a low likelihood of making a type I error if you reject the null hypothesis. As p increases, the possibility of making a type I error increases. The α value serves as the boundary for determining which p values you will regard as indicative of significance and which reflect a lack of significance. Researchers simply need to compare the p value to the α that they have decided to use. One should reject the null hypothesis only when α exceeds p.

On the basis of the standard α value = .05, a p value greater than .05 indicates no significant difference in the values being compared, and a p value at or below .05 indicates a significant difference. Using earlier examples, a researcher who obtains a p value of .06 would not characterize any difference as significant because such a characterization would be incorrect 6% of the time. That researcher would, however, view a p value of .03 very differently because, in this situation, only a 3% chance of incorrectly characterizing a difference as significant exists. With the willingness to accept up to a 5% chance of making a type I error, the researcher acknowledges significance at p = .03, but not at p = .06 Once again, the researcher can adjust the α value as he or she sees fit to change the expectations for p values.

The fact that you can obtain these values from SPSS, though, should not imply that you can ignore the sections of the subsequent chapters that present and demonstrate the formulas. A full understanding of these values' meanings relies on familiarity with the procedures used to obtain them. This knowledge allows you to appreciate the actual extent of the differences between sample values needed to produce significant results. In addition, you can make educated decisions regarding changes to α rather than haphazardly adjusting the value to accommodate p. So, the availability of SPSS should not serve as a substitute for careful deliberation regarding procedures of descriptive and inferential analysis, but simply as a means of reducing the manual labor involved in performing the tests.

REVIEW QUESTIONS

4.1. (A) Explain the relationship between sample size and the shape of the sample distribution.

(B) What principle asserts this relationship?

For Questions 4.2 and 4.3, identify and explain the sampling bias.

4.2. To evaluate a new drug rehabilitation program, researchers decide to compare the number of relapses suffered by those who have undergone the new treatment to the number of relapses suffered by those who have undergone standard treatment. They obtain contact information for all those treated within the past 6 months at 300 randomly selected drug rehabilitation facilities around the nation, 150 of which use the new program and 150 of which use the standard treatment. The researchers gather information from these individuals regarding their success in avoiding drugs since leaving the facilities.

4.3. Family counselors conduct a study to determine whether the shift that people work (first, second, or third) has any relationship to the amount that they spend with their families. The counselors know of a particular restaurant chain that is open 24 hours. Randomly selected employees of this restaurant chain receive surveys on which they indicate the shift that they work and the amount of time that they spend with their families.

Use the following diagram to answer Questions 4.4–4.6:

4.4. What is the probability that a significant difference between sample values exists?

4.5. Above what value (or absolute value) must calculated values lie to indicate that a significant difference exists?

4.6. How would the value identified in the answer to Question 4.5 change if a smaller α value were used? Why?

4.7. Suppose that statistical computations produce a calculated F value of 15.76. The critical statistic, obtained from the appropriate chart, is 19.43. Can the researcher reject his or her null hypothesis? Why or why not?

Suppose that a school nurse who wishes to convince others that more students visit the nurses' offices on Monday than on any other day asks 100 randomly selected school nurses to record the number of students visiting the office on each day of a randomly selected week. The nurse conducting the study collects these data and obtains a calculated statistic of 8.36.

4.8. State a research hypothesis for the nurse's investigation.

4.9. State the null hypothesis for the nurse's investigation.

4.10. Does the nurse conducting the investigation hope to reject the null hypothesis? Why?

4.11. If the $\alpha = .01$ critical value obtained from the appropriate chart is 13.277, should the researcher reject the null hypothesis? Why?

4.12. If the $\alpha = .05$ critical value obtained from the appropriate chart is 11.143, should the researcher reject the null hypothesis? Why?

4.13. If the $\alpha = .10$ critical value obtained from the appropriate chart is 7.779, should the researcher reject the null hypothesis? Why?

4.14. Why does the researcher have the greatest chance of rejecting the null hypothesis when $\alpha = .10$? (See Questions 4.11–4.13.)

4.15. Why does the researcher have the greatest chance of committing a type I error when $\alpha = .10$? (See Questions 4.11–4.13.)

4.16. What incorrect inference would be made if the researcher commits a type I error?

4.17. Can a researcher who rejects the null hypothesis conclude that more students visit nurses' offices on Monday than on any other day of the week? Why or why not?

4.18. Why is it illogical for a researcher to make the possibility of committing a type 1 error infinitesimally small?

$$5$$

THE CHI-SQUARE TEST: COMPARING CATEGORY FREQUENCIES

5.1 INTRODUCTION

To determine the appropriate inferential statistical test for an analysis, you must first consider the nature of each of your variables. Some tests can analyze only continuous variables or only categorical variables. Other tests analyze combinations of categorical and continuous variables. As you learn the capabilities of each statistical test of significance, you should become able to immediately recognize the proper statistical test to use according to the nature of each variable.

Chapters 5–7 of this book present commonly used statistical analyses, identifying the types of variables relevant for each as well as procedures for conducting various versions of the tests. This chapter presents one of these tests, the chi-square test, which applies to situations involving only categorical variables. A chi-square (χ^2) test determines whether subjects break up into given categories as expected. With the chi-square statistic, you can determine how well the observed category frequencies fit your expectations. For this reason, the chi-square test is often referred to as a *goodness-of-fit test*.

In statistics terminology, the chi-square test assesses the hypothesis of equality between the frequencies produced by the data, known as *observed frequencies* (f_o), and

Analyzing Quantitative Data: An Introduction for Social Researchers, First Edition. Debra Wetcher-Hendricks.
© 2011 John Wiley & Sons, Inc. Published 2011 by John Wiley & Sons, Inc.

the anticipated or *expected frequencies* (f_e) for each category or, in the case of multiple variables, combination of categories,

$$H_0: f_o = f_e$$

For the simplest of chi-square scenarios, general experience or knowledge of your discipline tells you what to expect.

Example 5.1: One-Variable Chi-Squared Expected Values For example, the understanding that any baby born has a 50% chance of being male and 50% chance of being female will lead a researcher to expect, in a perfectly random sample of 600 subjects, a ratio of 300 males to 300 females. Most likely, though, the actual sample won't have an equal number of males and females. A chi-square test can compare the distribution of males and females in the actual sample to the expected distribution of 50% males and 50% females. Results of the test indicate whether the two differ significantly.

Example 5.1 involves a single variable. However, chi-square tests can also address multiple categorical variables, such as those that can be arranged into a crosstabulation. The chi-square test, in this case, determines whether the actual data produce cell frequencies that match the expected cell frequencies.

Example 5.2: Two-Variable Chi-Squared Expected Values Such an analysis might involve the the time of day at which they were born. Like the equal split between the sexes, equal numbers of subjects should, theoretically, have been born during the A.M. hours and during the P.M. hours. So, one would expect 50% of subjects to fall into each of these categories and half of those in each category to be male and half female. Then, 25% of the sample falls into each combination of categories. For a sample size of 600, each of the four groups has an expected frequency of 150. Table 5.1 presents the expected frequencies and percentages for this situation.

Once again, the observed frequencies and percentages generally differ from the expected frequencies and percentages. Most likely, 600 subjects would not break up neatly into four equal groups, as described by the expected values in Example 5.2. The chi-square test determines whether the difference between the expected and observed values qualifies as significant.

The example of sex and time of birth presents a rather simple scenario because of the equal expected values for each variable. As a result, it may seem that the chi-square test addresses the hypothesis that all categories have equal frequencies. However, the test has much wider applicability, and you need not limit use of the chi-square test to situations in that you expect equal-sized groups. The formulas provided in this chapter as well as the processes used by statistical software systems easily adapt to unequal expected values.

5.2   THE CHI-SQUARE DISTRIBUTION

Chapter 3 introduced the topic of distribution by explaining that randomly selected subjects generally produce data that form a bell-shaped histogram called the *normal*

TABLE 5.1. Expected Values[a]

| Sex | Time of Birth | | Σ |
	A.M.	P.M.	
Male	150	150	300
	(25%)	(25%)	(50%)
Female	150	150	300
	(25%)	(25%)	(50%)
Σ	300	300	600
	(50%)	(50%)	(100%)

[a]This crosstabulation contains frequencies and percentages for a random sample of 600 subjects as they would be expected to fall into categories of sex and time of birth.

curve. Among its many functions, this curve helps researchers estimate the probability of obtaining a particular score.

Chi-square values form a similar curve. The chi-square distribution shows the frequencies of the values obtained through the calculations described later in this chapter. A calculated value indicates the degree of the difference between expected and observed scores. You can, therefore, use the chi-square distribution to estimate the probability that observed values and expected values differ by chance. As explained in Chapter 4, probabilities that exceed α suggest insignificant differences and probabilities less than α suggest significant differences between the values.

5.2.1 The Chi-Square Distribution versus the Normal Distribution

Chi-square values from multiple analyses based on random selections of subjects, when combined into a histogram, produce an expected distribution of chi-square scores. The height of the curve at any point on this distribution indicates the probability of attaining a particular chi-square value.

The chi-square distribution emerges from modifications to the normal distribution. But the chi-square distribution is *nonparametric*, meaning that it does not necessarily follow the normal curve. The normal curve and a chi-square curve appear in Figure 5.1.

Unlike the scenario in the normal distribution, in the chi-square distribution all points lie to the right of the *y* axis and "trail off" only to the right. This distribution is one-tailed and has only positive coordinates because the chi-square formula consists of a fraction with a squared numerator [see Eq. (5.3)]. No squaring occurs when one constructs the normal curve, allowing for both positive and negative values.

5.2.2 Variations of the Chi-Square Distribution

Moreover, the number of degrees of freedom has a larger role in the shape that the chi-square distribution than for the normal distribution. The shape of the chi-square distribution varies according to the degrees of freedom, which, in this case, reflects the number of categories involved in the analysis [see Eqs. (5.4), (5.7), and (5.9)]. Changes

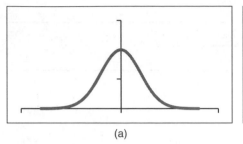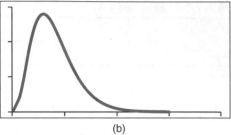

(a)	(b)

Figure 5.1. Normal (a) versus chi-square (b) distribution. As evident from the graphs, the normal distribution (a) differs from a chi-square distribution with df = 3 (b).

in the shape of the distribution can be explained by changes in the sizes of residuals possible with different numbers of categories. A *residual* indicates the size of the disparity between two values.

For the chi-square context, residuals increase with the number of categories involved in the analysis. The smallest number of degrees of freedom, one, corresponds to a dataset that includes two groups. In this situation, a particular element (person or item measured) either falls into the expected groups or doesn't. So, any observed value that differs from the expected value can do so in only one way, keeping the mean residual between the expected and the observed score rather small. As the number of categories increases, the number of possible differences between an element's expected group placement and observed group placement increases as well. Thus, the variables with many categories tend to produce larger residuals between the expected and the observed values than do variables with few categories.

Calculating the residual simply involves finding the difference between expected and observed frequencies:

$$\text{Residual} = f_\text{o} - f_\text{e} \tag{5.1}$$

The resulting value holds importance because, when squared, it forms the numerator of the chi-square formula. Mathematically speaking, given a constant denominator as the chi-square formula has, as the numerator of a fraction increases, the value of the fraction increases. Consequently, a large chi-square proportion results from a large residual, and a small chi-square proportion results from a small residual. Further, because of the relationship between the residual the number of categories involved in the analysis, increases in the number of categories become increases in the value of the chi-square statistic. Therefore, the shape of the chi-square distribution changes with respect to the degree-of-freedom value.

Figure 5.2 shows the changes in the distribution that accompany increases in degrees of freedom. In a one-degree-of-freedom (df = 1) situation, the chi-square distribution is leptokurtic and strongly skewed. Most of the chi-square values hover close to one because of the small residuals associated with this condition. As the degrees of freedom and, thus, residuals increase, however, the distribution appears less skewed and leptokurtic. Its shape eventually begins to resemble that of the normal curve.

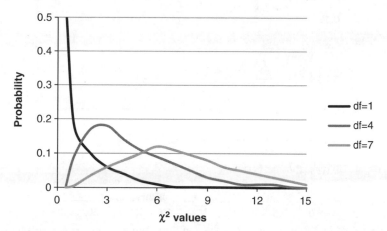

Figure 5.2. Chi-square Distributions. The graph shows probability curves for chi-square values with various degrees of freedom. The distribution begins to resemble the normal curve as degrees of freedom increase. The mean chi-square value for each curve equals the df value that serves as its basis.

5.2.3 Chi-Square Probabilities

The shapes of the distributions presented thus far in the chapter suggest that small chi-square values occur more frequently than large chi-square value do. Very large chi-square values result from drastic differences between expected and observed values, which occur relatively rarely. At a certain point, such differences become rare enough that you must consider them significant rather than assuming that they reflect random variation. The α value determines this point.

The role of α receives initial attention in Chapter 4 of this book. Its value establishes a boundary for determining whether a given inferential statistic does or does not suggest significance. The location of α on the distribution "cuts off" the right tail of the distribution, which contains the highest chi-square scores. Values that lie in the tail represent significant differences between expected and observed values, and those that lie to the left of the tail indicate a lack of significance.

Figure 5.3 highlights the highest 5% of chi-square values, based on the standard of $\alpha = .05$.

In this particular distribution, chi-square values equal to or greater than 20 constitute the highest 5% of possible scores. Such large values occur by chance no more than 5% of the time. Thus, you can assume with 95% certainty that the residuals responsible for creating these chi-square values reflect significant differences between observed and expected values. Statisticians refer to the value that distinguishes between nonsignificant and significant differences as the *critical value*. In this case, the critical chi-square value is 20. As indicated in Figure 5.3, chi-square values (computed using the formulas in Section 5.3) of at least 20 indicate significant differences between observed and expected frequencies. This critical value, however, changes with each investigation in response to the number of degrees of freedom and the α value used.

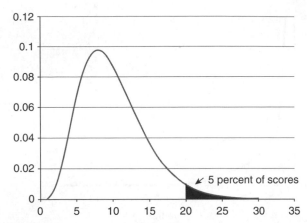

Figure 5.3. Chi-square distribution in right-tail area with α = .05. The darkened right-tail area of the distribution contains values that lie in the highest 5% of the range of all chi-square scores. The distinction between the highest 5% of scores and the remaining 95% of scores reflects the decision to use an α of .05.

To create a right tail area larger than that shown in Figure 5.3, you need to increase the value of α. Doing so lowers the critical value, which expands the range of calculated chi-square values that indicate significance. An α value of .10, for instance, characterizes the scores that fall into the highest 10% of the range of chi-square scores as rare enough to suggest significant differences between observed and expected values. This investigation would use a critical value lower than 20, making the right-tail area larger than that shown in Figure 5.3. The disadvantage in expanding the right-tail area this way lies in the greater chance of making a type I error as compared to use of small α values.

Those who wish to use stricter standards than α = .05 can lower the value of α to minimize the size of the right tail. Very small α values lead to very high critical values. Some of the calculated values that lie above the critical value in the α = .05 condition fall below the critical value in the α = .025 or α = .01 condition. Using such low α values can make it very difficult to obtain a significant difference. However, the possibility of making a type I error is small.

5.3 PERFORMING CHI-SQUARE TESTS

Various versions of the chi-square test exist. Although chi-square tests always pertain to categorical variables, these variables need not be dichotomous as in the male – female example above (Example 5.1). Variables such as geographic location, religion, or even favorite pizza topping, all of which contain more than two categories, also demand the chi-square test. In addition, as explained in Section 5.1, a chi-square test can assess differences between frequencies in cells of a crosstabulation that pertains to two or more variables.

To complicate the situation a bit further, although the presence of categories implies a nominal level of measurement, the chi-square test can also assess data obtained with higher levels of measurement.

Example 5.3: Categorizing Ordinal Data   For example, one may wish to consider ordinal data in categories rather than as rankings for an analysis using academic performance as the independent variable. Most schools use a grading system in which an A indicates superior performance and an F indicates complete inadequacy, with other grades indicating various levels in between. The grades lie on an ordinal scale in that they rank the students but do not indicate any of the students' percentage grades. An education researcher may wish to determine whether significantly more students in a particular sample received Cs than any other grade as the normal curve (often called the "bell curve" in educational contexts) suggests. In this case, the researcher considers those receiving each grade as a category without necessarily focusing on the level of concept mastery associated with each of these categories. He or she wishes to determine whether a higher percentage of students fall into the "C" category than into any other.

Continuous data, measured on an ordinal, interval, or ratio level, can even be converted into categorical form so that you can utilize a chi-square test.

Example 5.4: Categorizing Ratio Data   One situation in which this adjustment occurs involves medical tests such as cholesterol screenings. Many know that individuals with cholesterol levels of <200 mg/dL fall into the "low risk" for heart disease category, and those with levels of ≥200 mg/dL have at least a moderate risk of heart disease. Essentially, the existence of these categories relies on an operational definition to establish a cutoff point to transform the originally continuous data into categorical data.

Once categorized, data obtained with an ordinal, interval, or ratio level of measurement have the same characteristics as do data obtained with a nominal level of measurement. The chi-square test can determine whether the observed frequencies for categories differ significantly from the expected values. The remainder of this chapter describes the process of computing the chi-square statistic in one-variable and multivariable situations.

5.3.1   One-Variable Chi-Square Test

The rationale for using a chi-square test lies in the understanding that observed frequencies rarely equal expected frequencies. The one-variable chi-square test determines whether the actual number of elements in each category of a particular variable differs significantly from the expected number of elements in each category. The null hypothesis always predicts equality between the expected and the observed frequencies for each category. So, a rejected null hypothesis indicates a significant difference between these values, and an accepted null hypothesis indicates the lack of a significant difference between these values.

To compute the chi-square statistic, you must know the expected frequencies for each category of the variable. In the simplest of situations, expected frequencies reflect equal divisions among subjects by the number of levels of the variable. For example, as explained earlier in the chapter, if given no reason to believe otherwise, one would expect an equal division of subjects into "male" and the "female" categories. If, however,you know that, for some reason, one category should contain more subject than another or others, you can adjust the expected frequencies accordingly.

The One-Variable Chi-Square Formula. Equation (5.1)'s residual, which represents the difference between observed and expected frequencies, plays a prominent role in computing χ^2_{calc}. This residual becomes a factor because of the chi-square test's reliance on a standard normal distribution and, thus, the need to standardize scores (see Chapter 3). The numerator of the formula used to standardize scores [Eq. (5.2)] consists of a residual value:

$$z = \frac{X - \bar{X}}{s} \tag{5.2}$$

Statistical and mathematical equivalences convert Equation (5.2) into Equation (5.3). The steps of this process appear on this chapter's companion website. The resulting formula shows that the calculations involve simply dividing residuals by f_e for each group and then adding the quotients.

www.moravian.edu/aqd

$$\chi^2_{calc} = \Sigma \frac{(f_o - f_e)^2}{f_e} \tag{5.3}$$

The most straightforward application of Equation (5.3) uses equal expected distributions of subjects among categories of the independent variable. Example 5.5 demonstrates the calculation of χ^2_{calc} for this type of analysis.

Example 5.5: One-Variable Chi-Square Statistic Calculations (Equal Expected Values) Suppose that a media analyst may wish to investigate the differences between frequencies of those who watch the Superbowl on television with a focus on the commercials, with a focus on the actual game, and with a focus on both. It is reasonable to assume that the general public would expect an equal number of subjects (n) in each category. The resulting null hypothesis states that equal numbers of subjects prefer the commercials (C), prefer the game (G), and like both (B). This equivalence reflects the expectation of equal divisions of the subject group into the three categories. To investigate the null hypothesis, one compares the number of people who fall into each of three categories.

With a total sample size (N) of 60 (a rather small sample size for this type of study, but adequate for this basic example), one would expect that $n_C = 20$, $n_G = 20$, and $n_B = 20$. However, for this example, suppose that observations produce $n_C = 12$,

$n_G = 19$, and $n_B = 29$. These values clearly differ from the expected values. Determining whether this difference is large enough to qualify as significant begins with inserting the appropriate values into Equation (5.3) and performing the necessary arithmetic calculations, as shown below, to obtain the calculated chi-square value (χ^2_{calc}):

$$\chi^2_{calc} = \Sigma \frac{(f_o - f_e)^2}{f_e} = \frac{(12-20)^2}{20} + \frac{(19-20)^2}{20} + \frac{(29-20)^2}{20}$$

$$= \frac{64}{20} + \frac{1}{20} + \frac{81}{20} = \frac{146}{20} = 7.3$$

The value of 7.3, in and of itself, has little meaning. Only when paired with the degree-of-freedom (df) value and the critical chi-square value, described in later sections of this chapter, does the calculated chi-square value indicate whether the category sizes differ significantly.

Example 5.5 presents a rather simplistic scenario. By design, it involves equal expected scores for each group, which provides a common denominator. When expected values in each of the categories differ, you must pay special attention to the denominators of the fractions involved in your calculations.

Example 5.6: One-Variable Chi-Square Statistic Calculations (Unequal Expected Values) For instance, media moguls might claim that half of Superbowl viewers watch to see both the commercials and the game and that equal numbers of the remaining viewers watch to see one or the other. A researcher who wishes to address the validity of this claim with data from a sample of 60 would use expected values of $n_C = 15$, $n_G = 15$, and $n_B = 30$. One cannot base this analysis on the hypothesis of equal frequencies, as possible with Example 5.5. The null hypothesis for this investigation suggests equality between the observed frequencies and their respective expected frequencies.

Although the chi-square formula does not change, the unequal expected values lead to a lack of common denominators. The lack of consistency among the denominators makes calculations somewhat more difficult than they were with equal expected values. However, they still remain manageable, as shown below.

$$\chi^2_{calc} = \Sigma \frac{(f_o - f_e)^2}{f_e} = \frac{(12-15)^2}{15} + \frac{(19-15)^2}{15} + \frac{(29-30)^2}{30}$$

$$= \frac{8}{15} + \frac{16}{15} + \frac{1}{30}$$

$$= \frac{16}{30} + \frac{32}{30} + \frac{1}{30} = \frac{51}{30} = 1.7$$

Example 5.6's calculated chi-square value of 1.7 differs noticeably from Example 5.5's calculated value of 7.3 as a result of the change in expected values. Once again, though, the meaning of the calculated value does not become evident until it is interpreted with respect to the degrees of freedom and the critical chi-square value.

Interpreting the One-Variable Calculated Chi-Square Value. Chapter 4 and Section 5.3 explain that critical values provide means of comparison for calculated values. The meanings of the χ^2_{calc} produced in Examples 5.5 and 5.6 depend on their relationships with their respective the critical chi-square values (χ^2_{crit}) values.

Appendix B of this book contains a table of χ^2_{crit} values. To find the appropriate χ^2_{crit} in the chart. you must know the degree-of-freedom value. Degrees of freedom indicate the limitations on the distribution or values of data. Equation (5.4) defines *degrees of freedom* (df) as one less than the number of categories(K) into which an element might fall. This definition relies on the fact that, when choosing between categories, an individual needs to make one fewer decisions than the number of categories:

$$df = K - 1 \qquad\qquad (5.4)$$

Example 5.7: One-Variable Degree-of-Freedom Calculation   Equation (5.4) produces the same value for the scenarios presented in Examples 5.5 and 5.6. Both of these examples involve three categories. Thus, according to Equation (5.4), we obtain

$$df = K - 1 = 3 - 1 = 2$$

The χ^2_{crit} lies at the intersection of the df row and the selected α-value column in the table. A χ^2_{calc} smaller than χ^2_{crit} indicates more than an α (usually .05) probability that the actual frequencies differ from the expected frequencies by chance. This situation leads to an accepted null hypothesis. A χ^2_{calc} larger than χ^2_{crit} indicates less than an α probability that the difference between frequencies occurs by chance. In this situation, you should reject the null hypothesis, reasoning that some notable trend exists.

Example 5.8: Critical Value for One-Variable Chi-Square Statistic (Equal Expected Values)   For the situation described in Example 5.5, the χ^2_{crit} lies at the intersection of the row indicating two degrees of freedom (2 df) and the column marked with the chosen α. For the standard α value of .05, the chart provides a χ^2_{crit} of 5.99.

The χ^2_{calc} of 7.3 lies above the χ^2_{crit} of 5.99, indicating that $p < .05$. In other words, there is only a 5% probability that the difference between the observed and the expected frequencies occurs simply by chance. Given the 95% possibility that this difference reflects some underlying distinction, one rejects the null hypothesis, stating that a significant difference exists between the frequencies in each of the three categories.

A researcher who wishes to use an α value other than .05, simply chooses the appropriate column on the critical value chart. In some cases, researchers raise the α value to .10 in hopes of rejecting hypotheses when the calculated value lies just below the critical value at $\alpha = .05$. Chapter 4 and Section 5.2.3 explain that, as the value of α increases, critical values decrease, relaxing the requirement for the calculated value to exceed the critical value. As a result, rejection of the null hypotheses occurs more often with high α values than with low α values. Had the initial starting point of $\alpha = .05$ indicated a lack of significance, one might raise the α value. With an α value of .10, the critical value is 4.61. The calculated value 7.3 exceeds this critical value by more than it does in the $\alpha = .05$ condition. It is important to remember, however, that as α increases, so does the chance of making a type I error. Thus, before raising α, the researcher should consider the consequences of incorrectly labeling a difference as significant.

Lowering the α value has the opposite effect. An α value of .01 permits only a 1% chance of incorrectly claiming that a significant difference exists. So, null hypotheses are not rejected as freely as with α values of .05 or .025. For this example, $\alpha = .01$ produces a critical value of 9.21. The null hypothesis that was rejected at the .05 and .10 levels of significance values could not be rejected at $\alpha = .01$ because the calculated value of 7.3 does not exceed the critical value of 9.21. Using an α value of .01 would lead to the conclusion that no significant difference between observed and expected frequencies exists.

The procedure for interpreting the value is always the same. The steps followed to determine whether the χ^2_{calc} from Example 5.6 indicates significance, then, should be familiar.

Example 5.9: Critical Value for One-Variable Chi-Square Statistic (Unequal Expected Values) The scenario described in Example 5.6 also involves 2 df and thus also uses the critical value of 5.99 ($\alpha = .05$). This comparison, though, based on $\chi^2_{calc} = 1.7$, suggests no significant difference between expected and observed values. Because $\chi^2_{calc} < \chi^2_{crit}$, one cannot reject the null hypothesis. The same conclusion would be reached if $\alpha = .01$ as this α value imposes even harsher requirements for rejecting the null hypothesis than $\alpha = .05$ does.

A researcher motivated to reject a hypothesis may raise the α value to .10; however, in this example, doing so does not help. The calculated value still does not exceed the $\alpha = .10$ critical value of 4.61. Analyses at all three α values presented in this example, then, indicate that the numbers of subjects who fall into each of the three reason categories do not differ significantly from the expected frequencies for the categories.

If the chosen α value leads to a rejected null hypothesis, as it does for the $\alpha = .05$ and $\alpha = .10$ conditions in Example 5.8, you must explain the source of the significance. Tests performed with the intent of locating the source of a significant difference are called *post hoc* comparisons or post hoc tests. Section 5.7 contains information about post hoc tests.

5.3.2 Two-Variable Chi-Square Test

So far, discussions and examples have focused only on situations involving categories of a single variable. The single-variable chi, although a relatively good introduction to the chi-square concept, is generally not as useful as the multivariable χ^2 is. The multiple-chi-square test compares observed values for various combinations of categorical values to their respective expected values. The simplest form of this test, the two-variable chi-square test, usually analyzes categories of an independent variable and a dependent variable.

With two variables, you should organize observed data into a crosstabulation, sometimes called a *contingency table* in this context. When these data appear in a crosstabulation, the chi-square test compares the observed value and the expected value

TABLE 5.2. Mock Superbowl Data[a]

Gender	Game	Commercials	Both	Sum (Σ)
Males	5	8	11	24
Females	7	11	18	36
Sum (Σ)	12	19	29	60

[a]Cells of the crosstabulation display characterize subjects as male or female as well as according to the reason why they watch the Superbowl. Reason categories appear as columns, and the sex categories appear as rows, to clearly display the frequencies of subjects who fall into each combination of categories. The total frequencies for each reason category, identical to those used in Example 5.5, appear as marginal column values. The total frequencies for each gender category appear as marginal row values.

of each cell. The chi-square test determines whether the frequencies in each crosstabulation cell approximate the expected values so closely that you can accept the null hypothesis.

Example 5.10: Crosstabulation for Two-Variable Chi-Square Test   For instance, consider a version of the earlier hypothesis concerning individual preferences regarding the Superbowl broadcast. One who believes that males may have different reasons for watching the broadcast than females do may wish to include a variable that identifies subjects by their sexes.

In this design, data characterize subjects on the basis of two variables: gender and the reason for watching the Superbowl, likely with the intent of determining whether peoples' genders can predict their reasons for watching the broadcast (see Table 5.2). Suppose that the crosstabulation below provides mock data for observed values.

The chi-square investigation compares the observed frequencies for males who prefer the game (MG), females who prefer the game (FG), males who prefer the commercials (MC), females who prefer the commercials (FC), males who like both the games and commercials (MB), and females who like both (FB) their respective expected values.

The Two-Variable Chi-Square Formula.   Fortunately, you do not need to use different formulas to calculate chi-square values in one-variable and in multivariable situations. Equation (5.5) shows the chi-square formula used for the multivariable test as identical to Equation (5.3):

$$\chi^2_{calc} = \Sigma \frac{(f_o - f_e)^2}{f_e} \qquad (5.5)$$

The observed and expected frequencies in this equation refer to crosstabulation cell values. Thus, each combination of the two-variable categories produces its own ratio. The χ^2_{calc} value, then, is the sum of these ratios.

Interpreting the Two-Variable Calculated Chi-Square Value.   The χ^2_{calc} produced by using Equation (5.5) plays the same role as the comparable value for the one-variable chi-square test does. Still, computing the χ^2_{calc} value is more complex for the two-variable situation than for the one-variable situation, beginning with finding the expected values.

According to Equation (5.5), you must find the difference between the observed frequencies and the corresponding expected frequencies in each cell of the crosstabulation. However, expected frequencies are not as obvious in the two-variable situation as in the one-variable situation. The expected value for a particular cell consists of the product of the relevant marginal frequencies divided by the total number of subjects. The equation used to represent these calculations in a two-variable situation is as follows:.

$$f_{e=} \frac{(\text{row total})(\text{column total})}{n} \tag{5.6}$$

Theoretically, the expected value calculated by this method produces a mean because it is a summed score (albeit achieved by multiplying rather than repetitive addition) divided by the actual number of subjects. The psychometric principle that equates a mean to an expected value, characterizing it as the "best guess" for a data point (see Section 5.3.1), validates this process.

Example 5.11: Two-Variable Chi-Square Expected-Value Calculations. Combining the Σ values from Table 5.2 with Equation (5.6), used to obtain the expected frequencies for each cell, produces the computations shown in Table 5.3.

The fact that the observed-value crosstabulation (Table 5.2) and the expected-value crosstabulation (Table 5.3) have the same marginal values is no coincidence. Although expected values represent "best guesses," they do so within the constraints of the marginal totals. They do not change row and column frequencies, but, rather, redistribute cell frequencies *within* rows and columns. Each cell's expected value represents the proportion of the total number of subjects that *should*, theoretically, fall into that cell according to the observed relevant row and column sums.

Example 5.12: Marginal Frequencies and Expected Cell Values To demonstrate this point, consider the marginal frequencies for any cell, such as those associated with

TABLE 5.3. Superbowl Data Expected Values[a]

Gender	Game	Commercials	Both	Sum (Σ)
Males	$\frac{(24)(12)}{60} = 4.8$	$\frac{(24)(19)}{60} = 7.6$	$\frac{(24)(29)}{60} = 11.6$	24
Females	$\frac{(36)(12)}{60} = 7.2$	$\frac{(36)(19)}{60} = 11.4$	$\frac{(36)(29)}{60} = 17.4$	36
Sum (Σ)	12	19	29	60

[a]Calculations for determining expected values for each combination of sex and reason category, based on Equation (5.7), appear in the relevant cells.

males who watch the Superbowl with interest only in the game. The row total of 24 indicates that two-fifths (40%) of all subjects are male. If consistent among the three reason categories, then 40% of the 12 subjects who watch the Superbowl with primary interest in the game should be male. Two-fifths of 12 is 4.8, the value appearing in the identified cell. You can use the same process with respect to column totals. The marginal frequency for the "game" column indicates that one-fifth (20%) of subjects watch the Superbowl to see the game itself. The assumption that this 20% proportion applies to both males and females, means that 20% of the 24 males in the sample fit into the "game" category. Either way, 4.8 becomes the expected value for the cell.

After acquiring expected values for all cells, you can begin the actual computation of χ^2_{calc}. Expected and observed values fit into Equation (5.5).

Example 5.13: Two-Variable Chi-Square Statistic Calculations   Substitution of the appropriate values from Tables 5.2 and 5.3 into Equation (5.5) leads to the following calculations:

$$\chi^2_{calc} = \Sigma \frac{(f_o - f_e)^2}{f_e}$$

$$= \frac{(5-4.8)^2}{4.8} + \frac{(8-7.6)^2}{7.6} + \frac{(11-11.6)^2}{11.6} + \frac{(7-7.2)^2}{7.2} + \frac{(11-11.4)^2}{11.4} + \frac{(18-17.4)^2}{17.4}$$

$$\chi^2_{calc} = \frac{.04}{4.8} + \frac{.16}{7.6} + \frac{.36}{11.6} + \frac{.04}{4.8} + \frac{.16}{7.2} + \frac{.36}{11.4}$$
$$= .008 + .021 + .031 + .006 + .014 + .021 = .101$$

As with the single-variable situation, the next step of the process involves comparing the calculated value to the critical value. The chart in Appendix B contains χ^2_{crit} values. The formula for the degrees of freedom, however, expands to account for the multiple variables' categories. Equation (5.7) shows that calculating the degrees of freedom in a two-variable situation requires acknowledgment of both variables.

$$df = (R-1)(C-1) \tag{5.7}$$

Degrees of freedom still represent the number of category options for any one element. However, with two variables, this value indicates the number of row options available $(R - 1)$ among the available column options $(C-1)$.

Example 5.14: Two-Variable Degree-of-Freedom Calculation   The crosstabulations in Tables 5.2 and 5.3 consist of three columns, representing the three categories of the "reason" variable; and two rows, representing the two categories of the "gender" variable. Thus, according to Equation (5.7), two degrees of freedom (2 df) exist:

$$df = (R-1)(C-1) = (2-1)(3-1) = (1)(2) = 2$$

You can find the relevant critical value at the intersection of the df row and the chosen α column on the chi-square critical value table in Appendix B. A calculated value at or exceeding the critical value falls into the right-tail area of the distribution and, thus, suggests a significant difference between observed and expected values. In this case, you should reject the null hypothesis. You should accept the null hypothesis, indicating the lack of a significant difference, when you have a calculated value that is smaller than the critical value.

Example 5.15: Critical Value for Two-Variable Chi-Square Statistic   The chart in Appendix B shows a critical chi-square value of 5.99 with df = 2 and the standard α = .05. The calculated value of .101, obtained in Example 5.13, does not exceed the critical value. So, $p > .05$, meaning that there is greater than a 5% probability that the difference between expected and observed frequencies occurs purely by chance. A researcher who will accept no more than a 5% possibility of such a condition would accept the null hypothesis. By doing so, she or he indicates that the expected and observed differences in each of the crosstabulation's cells do not differ significantly.

Researchers can choose to use an α other than .05. Those concerned about making a type I error can lower the α value, but in this case, it makes little sense to decrease α. Doing so would only serve to raise the critical value, and, even at α = .05, the calculated value is smaller than the critical value, indicating a lack of significance. Using an α lower than .05 would merely verify this insiginificance.

One who wishes to reject the null hypothesis and is not concorned about type I error, however, may wish to explore α value higher than .05. At α = .10, $\chi^2_{crit} = 4.61$. Although, as expected, the critical value decreases somewhat from its value of 5.99 at α = .05, it still greatly exceeds the calculated value of .101. Continued efforts to raise α to a point at which the corresponding critical value falls below .101, with the goal of rejecting the null hypothesis, may occur. You would not find success in this particular endeavor, however, until α nears .95. A researcher willing to accept a 95% chance of falsely claiming that a significant difference exists could reject the null hypothesis. But good practice dictates that researchers do not take such chances of making a type I error. In fact, one would have difficulty finding a chi-square critical value chart that even acknowledges α values greater than .40.

5.3.3   Three-or-More-Variable Chi-Square

The type of crosstabulation used in Example 5.10 cannot accommodate more than two variables. To organize frequencies from more than two variables for a chi-square test, you must use a crosstabulation with layers. Chapter 2 introduces the idea of layers with Figure 1, which presents data from three variables within a single crosstabulation. The length, width, and depth of this crosstabulation cube each correspond to one of three variables involved in the analysis. You should use this design to arrange data for a chi-square test that involves more than two variables.

Example 5.16: Three-Dimensional Crosstabulation for Superbowl Data   A three-dimensional crosstabulation could be used to organize data if the researcher conducting the Superbowl study wishes to consider a third variable. Figure 5.4 includes columns

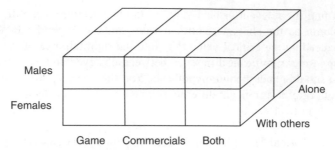

Figure 5.4. Three-Dimensional Crosstabulation. Situating three variables within a single crosstabulation requires rows, columns, and levels. In this case, rows distinguish between subjects' sexes, columns distinguish between subjects' reasons for watching the Superbowl, and levels distinguish between companionship categories.

TABLE 5.4. Nested Crosstabulation of Superbowl Data Observed Frequencies[a]

Gender	Alone or with Others	Game	Commercials	Both	Sum (Σ) within viewership	Sum (Σ)
Males	Alone	2	0	4	6	24
	With others	3	8	7	18	
Females	Alone	4	4	4	12	36
	With others	3	7	14	24	
Sum (Σ)		12	19	29	60	60

[a]Unlike the three-dimensional representation in Table 5.4, the nested crosstabulation allows all cell values to be visible. In this crosstabulation, columns represent categories of the reason variable, rows represent categories of the sex variable, and levels represent categories of the companionship variable.

to represent the reason for watching the game, rows to represent subjects' sexes, and layers to represent the additional variable of companionship while watching the game.

This arrangement accurately portrays the relationship between the three variables. Each cell represents a different combination of the three variables' categories. However, the inability to see all cell frequencies makes it impossible to obtain all of the needed values for substitution into the chi-square formula. In this situation, you should organize data into a nested or split crosstabulation, both described in Chapter 2.

Example 5.17: Nested Crosstabulation for Superbowl Data The crosstabulationin in Table 5.4 provides hypothetical raw data in a nested version of Figure 5.4. This arrangement shows the frequencies of all cells.

Although one can easily see cell frequencies, not all marginal frequencies are evident. Marginal frequencies for the "reason" categories appear at the end of the rows and marginal frequencies for the gender categories appear in the rightmost column of the crosstabulation. But acquiring the marginal values for viewership simply involves adding the "alone" and the "with other" sums for males and females to obtain values of 18 and 42, respectively.

Three-or-More-Variable Chi-Square Formulas. The same formula used for computing the chi-square statistic in one- and two-variable situations [shown in Eqs. (5.3) and (5.5)] produces the chi-square statistic in situations involving three or more variables. The formula for degrees of freedom, however, changes slightly in response to the number of variables involved. Fortunately, though, these changes follow a very predictable pattern. The df formula always requires subtracting one from the number of categories available for each variable. In a multivariable situation, the resulting values are combined by multiplication. So, to account for layers (L) in addition to rows (R) and columns (C), the formula for degrees of freedom in a three-variable situation takes the following form:

$$df = (R-1)(C-1)(L-1) \qquad (5.8)$$

To use the formula for χ^2_{calc}, you must know the expected values for each cell of the crosstabulation. The added variable of viewership also makes the process of calculating expected cell frequencies a bit more cumbersome than it was for the two-variable example. But, like the change in the degrees of freedom formula, changes in the expected-value formula follow a logical pattern as the number of variables increases. In the three-variable situation, multiplying the row, column, and layer marginal values produces the numerator for each cell's expected value. The denominator of the fraction requires the inclusion of n twice to accommodate the extra variable:

$$f_e = \frac{(\text{row total})(\text{column total})(\text{layer total})}{n^2} \qquad (5.9)$$

Example 5.18: Three-Variable Chi-Square Expected-Value Calculation Applying Equation (5.9) to the cell frequencies in Table 5.4 leads to the computations and expected values shown in Table 5.5.

Finally, you can apply the chi-square formula [see Eq. (5.3) or (5.5)]. You must simply substitute observed and expected values into the formula to obtain the chi-square statistic.

TABLE 5.5. Superbowl Data Expected Values Nested Crosstabulation[a]

Gender	Alone or with Others	Game	Commercials	Both	Sum (Σ) within Viewership	Sum (Σ)
Males	Alone With others	$\frac{(24)(12)(18)}{60^2}$ $= 1.44$	$\frac{(24)(19)(18)}{60^2}$ $= 2.28$	$\frac{(24)(29)(18)}{60^2}$ $= 3.48$	7.2	24
		$\frac{(24)(12)(42)}{60^2}$ $= 3.36$	$\frac{(24)(19)(42)}{60^2}$ $= 5.32$	$\frac{(24)(29)(42)}{60^2}$ $= 8.12$	16.8	

(Continued)

TABLE 5.5. (Continued)

Gender	Alone or with Others	Game	Commercials	Both	Sum (Σ) within Viewership	Sum (Σ)
Females	Alone With others	$\dfrac{(36)(12)(18)}{60^2}$ $= 2.16$	$\dfrac{(36)(19)(18)}{60^2}$ $= 3.42$	$\dfrac{(36)(29)(18)}{60^2}$ $= 5.22$	10.8	36
		$\dfrac{(36)(12)(42)}{60^2}$ $= 5.04$	$\dfrac{(36)(19)(42)}{60^2}$ 7.98	$\dfrac{(36)(29)(42)}{60^2}$ 12.18	25.2	
Sum (Σ)		12	19	29		60

^{a}Each cell contains the expected value for the relevant combination of variable categories. The calculations in the cells demonstrate the process of determining these expected values.

Example 5.19: Three-Variable Chi-Square Statistic Calculations   Table 5.4 contains observed frequencies for the three-variable Superbowl investigation, and Table 5.5 contains the comparable expected values. Substitution of these values into the chi-square formula and subsequent simplification take the following form:

$$\chi^2_{calc} = \Sigma \frac{(f_o - f_e)^2}{f_e}$$

$$= \frac{(2-1.44)^2}{1.44} + \frac{(0-2.28)^2}{2.28} + \frac{(4-3.48)^2}{3.48}$$

$$+ \frac{(3-3.36)^2}{3.36} + \frac{(8-5.32)^2}{5.32} + \frac{(7-8.12)^2}{8.12}$$

$$+ \frac{(4-2.16)^2}{2.16} + \frac{(4-3.42)^2}{3.42} + \frac{(4-2.55)^2}{5.22}$$

$$+ \frac{(3-5.04)^2}{5.04} + \frac{(7-7.98)^2}{7.98} + \frac{(14-12.18)^2}{12.98}$$

$$= \frac{.31}{1.44} + \frac{5.20}{2.28} + \frac{.27}{3.48} + \frac{.80}{3.36} + \frac{7.18}{5.32} + \frac{1.25}{8.12}$$

$$+ \frac{3.39}{2.16} + \frac{.34}{3.42} + \frac{2.10}{5.22} + \frac{4.16}{5.04} + \frac{.96}{7.98} + \frac{3.31}{12.98}$$

$$= .22 + 2.28 + .08 + .24 + 1.35 + .16 + 1.57 + .10 + .40 + .83 + .12 + .26 = 7.61$$

Once again, you need to find the value of χ^2_{crit} for the next step in the process. To use the critical value table, you must first obtain the degrees of freedom value by substituting marginal frequencies into Equation (5.9).

Example 5.20: Three-Variable Degree-of-Freedom Calculation   Tables 5.4 and 5.5 contain two rows, each pertaining to a category of the "gender" variable; three columns, each pertaining to a category of the "reason" variable; and two layers, each pertaining to a category of the "companionship" variable. Thus, two degrees of freedom exist, as shown in the following calculations, based on Equation (5.9):

$$df = (R-1)(C-1)(L-1) = (2-1)(3-1)(2-1) = (1)(2)(1) = 2$$

Using the values for the degrees of freedom and α, you can find the value for χ^2_{crit} in Appendix B. The critical value appears at the intersection of the row corresponding to the degrees of freedom and the column labeled with the chosen α value. You should reject the null hypothesis only when χ^2_{calc} exceeds χ^2_{crit}. A rejected null hypothesis allows you to declare that a significant difference between observed and expected cell frequencies exists. When $\chi^2_{crit} > \chi^2_{calc}$, no significant difference exists and, consequently, you cannot reject the null hypothesis.

Example 5.21: Critical Value for Three-Variable Chi-Square Statistic In continuing with the three-variable chi-square example, the critical value chart value corresponding to df $= 2$ and $\alpha = .05$ identifies a χ^2_{crit} of 5.99. The calculated value of 7.61, obtained in Example 5.19, exceeds this critical value. Because $\chi^2_{calc} > \chi^2_{crit}$, the null hypothesis must be rejected because observed values differ significantly from expected values.

One who feels uncomfortable with the 5% chance of making a type I error may choose to use an α value smaller than .05. Lowering α to .025 produces a critical value of 7.3, which still leads to the rejection of the null hypothesis, but, this time, with only a 2.5% chance of incorrectly doing so. The calculated value in this condition, though, only barely exceeds the critical value, indicating that the boundary for accepting and rejecting the null hypothesis lies just below .025. Not surprisingly, the critical value of 9.21 associated with $\alpha = .01$ (which appears as the next-lowest value after $\alpha = .025$ on most critical value tables) exceeds the calculated value of 7.61 and, thus, suggests equality between observed and expected frequencies.

This overall method doesn't change as the number of variables increases. For analyses that necessitate the use of four, five, or more variables, you may have some difficulty visualizing the data in a cohesive figure, such as the three-dimensional figure used to conceptually organize data for three variables. However, to avoid feeling overwhelmed, you can use split or nested crosstabulation charts to represent all levels of all variables. As demonstrated in the previous example, these designs make it relatively easy to view and, thus, account for all cell frequencies.

5.4 POST HOC TESTING

A post hoc test attempts to determine which observed values differ so drastically that they explain, or at least partly explain, the rejected null hypothesis. So, you need perform post hoc tests only if $\chi^2_{calc} > \chi^2_{crit}$.

A number of approaches to post hoc testing for significant chi-square test results exist. One of the simplest requires simply performing additional chi-square tests to assess the size of the difference between just two category frequencies. The first step in conducting this type of post hoc analysis involves reviewing the observed frequencies in search of likely reasons for the significant difference.

5.4.1   One-Variable Chi-Square Post Hoc Tests

If your variable contains only two categories, the source of the significant chi-square test results is evident, but if the variable contains more than two categories, you should begin by reviewing the category frequencies to determine whether any one of them lies far above or far below the others. You may suspect a particular extreme frequency as the source of significance. Performing post hoc chi-square tests to compare this frequency to another or to a combination of all others can verify your suspicion.

Example 5.22: Post Hoc Test for a One-Variable Chi-Square Statistic   The rejected null hypothesis that results from the chi-square test performed in Example 5.8, using the $\alpha = .05$ level of significance, demands post hoc testing. This example involves equal expected values. So, the rejected null hypothesis suggests inequality between the observed values.

This overall inequality could reflect a drastic difference between any two observed values or between any two combinations of observed values. For instance, the difference between the lowest- and highest-category frequencies, 12 and 29, respectively, may account for the significant chi-square results. A chi-square test based on two groups can assess the significance of this difference. Alternatively, might the overall significant difference reflect the difference between the observed frequency of 29 and the other frequencies. The comparison also involves two groups, but requires adjustment of the expected values. The two groups that do not seem to differ would be combined into a single group with an expected frequency of 40 for comparison with the remaining group, which has an expected frequency of 20. Many other possibilities exist as well. The post hoc tests assess each possible difference to determine which ones is (are) the driving force behind the rejected null hypothesis.

5.4.2   Two-Variable Chi-Square Post Hoc Tests

The same process of post hoc testing described in Section 5.3.1 of this chapter could be used for two-variable chi-square tests. However, the two-variable situation presents more possible sources of significance than the one-variable situation does.

The post hoc tests described in Section 5.4.1 contrasted each category with the others in the analysis. For the two-variable situation, this sort of investigation can compare the frequencies between categories of either variable. Further, you can compare the frequency of any individual cell with the frequency of any other individual cell or from a group of cells. You would use a one-variable chi-square test to perform any of these contrasts.

Example 5.23: Post Hoc Test for a Two-Variable Chi-Square Statistic   None of the tests discussed in Example 5.15 resulted in a rejected hypothesis. Therefore, you would not need to perform post hoc tests. However, had you obtained significant results, you could have contrasted frequencies for individual or combinations of reason categories, for individual or combinations of gender categories, or for particular cells in Table 5.2.

5.4.3 Three-or-More-Variable Chi-Square Post Hoc Tests

Because the possible sources of a significant difference increase with the number of variables involved in the original analysis, many post hoc comparisons may be needed following a chi-square test involving three or more independent variables. The source of a significant difference for a three-variable chi-square statistic may lie in distinctions between rows, columns, levels, or particular cells of the crosstabulation.

Example 5.24: Post Hoc Test for Three-Variable Chi-Square Statistic The rejected null hypothesis using $\alpha = .05$ in Example 5.21 indicates that a significant difference exists between the values in Table 5.5. The post hoc tests that follow the original chi-square test determine whether this result reflects differences between frequencies for the viewership categories, the gender categories, or the reason categories. The post hoc tests can also compare the frequency for a particular cell or group of cells to the frequencies of others in the crosstabulation.

To begin the post hoc analysis, most researchers review the observed values, looking for a blatant discrepancy between frequencies. The marginal values in Table 5.4 seem to differ somewhat, and a researcher may choose to begin the post hoc analysis by comparing the frequencies for the two viewership categories, for the two gender categories, or between one reason category and the other two. However, the most obvious disparity in the table exists between individual cells. The fact that no males watch the Superbowl alone and prefer the commercials, and that 14 females watch the game with others and like, the game and commercials equally, may explain the rejected original null hypothesis. Post hoc tests can begin with a comparison of these two cell frequencies. If the chi-square test comparing these two values indicates significance, then the researcher has found at least one reason for the rejected original hypothesis.

Many variations of cell comparisons exist. Rather than comparing the frequencies for two individual cells, one may wish to compare the frequency for a single cell, such as that for related males who watch the game alone with others and prefer the commercials to the frequencies for all other cells. In this case, the post hoc chi-square test would determine whether this cell's frequency of 0 stands out as being significantly different from the frequencies of the other cells. Another variation of cell comparison contrasts the frequencies for combinations of cells. For instance, one may wish to determine whether the combined number of males and females who watch the game alone and favor the commercials differs significantly from the combined number of males and females who watch the game with others and who like the game and the commercials equally. This analysis would involve a chi-square test to compare the frequency of 4, corresponding to the first of these groupings (obtained by adding 0 and 4, which pertain to the males and females in the "alone" and "commercials" cells in Table 5.4), to the frequency of 21 (obtained by adding 7 and 14, which pertain to the males and females in the "with others" and "both" cells in Table 5.4), corresponding to the second of these groupings.

Often, post hoc tests uncover more than one source for an overall significant difference. You must be careful, therefore, not to characterize the first source of difference that you find as *the* reason for the rejected null hypothesis. Continued post hoc testing would reveal other significant differences between categories in the analysis. Thus, you can claim only that the result of any post hoc test *helps to* explain the rejected null hypothesis.

5.5 CONFIDENCE INTERVALS

As explained in Chapter 4, confidence intervals indicate the limits within which a specified proportion of raw data lies. A confidence interval has the most relevance for continuous raw data because it identifies a range of values. For categorical raw data such as are used in the chi-square statistic, the confidence interval has little value.

Although algebraic manipulations of some statistical formulas can produce equations to obtain confidence intervals for raw-data values, they cannot apply to the chi-square statistic. Variations in the values of f_o and f_e make it impossible to determine confidence intervals for observed frequencies by algebraically manipulating the chi-square formula. Some statisticians take entirely different approaches to finding confidence intervals for categorical variables. Bayes (1763), for example, proposed a formula to determine the probability of an element falling into a particular combination of categories. This method, however, is relevant only for contexts involving two variables with two categories each. Thus, although worthy of mention and very valuable in some disciplines, such as medical research, Baysian theory has little relevance for situations that include more than two variables or more than two levels within any variable.

Others wish to consider confidence intervals with respect to probabilities instead of raw-data values. These confidence intervals identify ranges of statistical values that have more than an α probability of occurring. Recall that the α-value designates the highest probability of making a type I error (p) that you agree to take. Because the value of $1-\alpha$ represents the confidence with which you can claim that a significant difference exists, the confidence intervals are described in terms of $1-\alpha$.

Researchers most commonly refer to a 95% confidence interval, based on $\alpha = .05$. For a chi-square test, 95% of calculated chi-square values fall within the boundaries of this interval. Only the 5% of calculated values that exceed the critical value lie outside the confidence interval. Any of these values suggests less than a 5% probability ($p < .05$) that the difference between frequencies occurs by chance. So, if you consider χ^2_{calc} values outside the confidence interval as indicative of significance, you will be correct 95% of the time.

Example 5.25: 95% Confidence Interval   Example 5.8 establishes that an α value of .05 and two degrees of freedom corresponds to a critical value of 5.99. This confidence interval can be written as CI:$[0 < \chi^2 < 5.99]$. Figure 5.5 provides a visual representation of this interval in relation to the chi-square distribution.

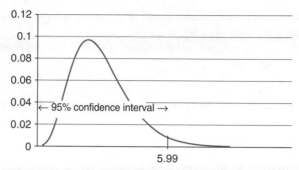

Figure 5.5. 95% confidence interval. The 95% confidence interval for df = 2 has a lower limit of 0 and an upper limit of 5.99. Calculated chi-square values within this interval indicate a lack of significance because $\chi^2_{calc} < \chi^2_{crit}$. The 5% of calculated chi-square values greater than 5.99 lie in the right-tail area and result in a rejected null hypothesis.

One can assume with 95% certainty that a calculated χ^2 value outside this confidence interval represents a significant difference between expected and observed values. The boundaries of this confidence interval support the decisions regarding the null hypotheses analyzed in Examples 5.5, 5.6, and 5.13. The calculated chi-square value of 7.3 from Example 5.5 does not fall into the 95% confidence interval. It lies in the right-tail area of Figure 5.5, which contains the values corresponding to a rejected null hypothesis. Examples 5.6 and 5.14, on the other hand, produce calculated values of 1.7 and 0.101, respectively. Both of these values fall within the confidence interval, confirming the claims of no significant differences.

If you desire more than 95% certainty that the values outside the designated range correspond to significant differences, you can widen the confidence interval. The confidence interval, based on an α value of .01 with two degrees of freedom (df = 2), is stated as CI:[$0 < \chi^2 < 9.21$]. This range includes more values than the 95% confidence interval does. So, you would not reject the null hypothesis as often as you would with only 95% confidence, decreasing the likelihood of a false rejection to only 1%.

On the other hand, if you need less than a 95% guarantee that a χ^2_{calc} outside the confidence interval correctly indicates an insignificant difference, you may choose to narrow the confidence interval. A 90% confidence interval with 2 df, CI:[$0 < \chi^2 < 4.61$], includes fewer calculated χ^2 values than a 95% confidence interval does. More calculated values lead to a rejected hypothesis when you accept a 10% chance of incorrectly claiming significance than when you accept only a 5% chance of doing so.

5.6 EXPLAINING RESULTS OF THE CHI-SQUARE TEST

Information about results of the χ^2 test should always accompany your claim of significance or insignificance. Most importantly, you should report the calculated χ^2 value and the degrees of freedom used for the analysis. If you have performed the χ^2 calculation yourself (without the use of SPSS or a similar program), you should also mention the chosen α value so that the audience knows the standards used to make the decision regarding significance.

Explaining the lack of a significant difference generally proves easier than explaining the presence of one.

Example 5.26: Summary of Insignificant Results   An appropriate summary of results for the two-variable example, used in this chapter, for which no significant difference exists, may appear as follows:

The χ^2 value of .101 suggests no significant difference with $\alpha = .05$, leading to an accepted null hypothesis. Therefore, the claims that no relationships exists between gender and reason for watching the game receives validation.

Of course, the presentation of this information can take a variety of forms. You can, for instance, present the statistical information in parenthetical context rather than within the main text.

Example 5.27: Summary of Insignificant Results Using Parentheses   Presentation of the values included in Example 5.22 can utilize parentheses in the following manner:

Results of chi-square test ($\chi^2 = .101; p > .05$) suggest that no significant difference exists. Subjects are equally distributed among the sex and reason groups. The null hypothesis, therefore, is accepted.

You may even choose to report some of the information in parenthetical form and to include other information within the framework of your sentence structure. Stylistic preferences should determine the most suitable way to present the results.

5.7   CONCLUSION

Chi-square tests are a good introduction to the principles related to significance. Although the test can address convoluted circumstances, such as the nested or split crosstabulation, researchers use it most often to characterize the significance between categories of one or two variables. So, calculation of the chi-square statistic seldom becomes much more complex than that shown in this chapter's early examples. Also, results of the test generally provide straightforward information regarding whether to accept or reject the null hypothesis. With the exception of possibly having to perform post hoc comparisons, the steps for performing chi-square tests and interpreting their results follows a very scripted procedure.

In addition to the simplicity of this test, its wide applicability makes it useful for many research situations. Obviously, situations involving only categorical data demand the test. However, as explained in Section 5.3, you can also make use of the chi-square test when given continuous raw data by grouping values. Researchers most often categorize continuous data with the intention of performing a chi-square test for one of two reasons:

1. On the basis of the standards presented in Chapter 2, urging collection of data at the highest level of measurement possible, many researcher gather data in more detail than needed. The immediate goal may involve comparing the numbers of data points that fall into particular ranges on an interval or ratio scale, such as the high and low cholesterol categories presented in Example 5.4. These researchers can keep the continuous values "in reserve" should they need to acknowledge specific data points at some point in their analyses.

2. The chi-square test may be useful for follow-up analyses to t tests, ANOVAs, and correlation analyses. The t test and ANOVA, respectively, described in Chapters 6 and 7, require categorical independent variables and continuous dependent-variable data. They compare mean dependent values for each independent-variable grouping. Sometimes, researchers who fail to obtain the significant results that they desire from the t test or ANOVA "downgrade" their analyses to chi-square tests. By doing so, they hope to find significance among general categories of data rather than between means of the original continuous variables. Researchers can also use this logic with respect to correlation and regression analysis, described in Chapter 8. These analyses use categorical independent and dependent variables. But the researcher who finds no significant patterns among the continuous values has the option of categorizing data from both variables to make a chi-square test appropriate.

You may find it comforting to know that the procedures used to calculate the chi-square statistic and evaluate its results greatly resemble comparable procedures for other statistical tests. All tests, for example, involve consideration of residuals, and most involve the same comparisons between calculated and critical values to determine whether to accept or reject the null hypothesis. Portions of Chapters 6–8, therefore, repeat many of the explanations and processes introduced in this chapter.

STATISTICAL RESOURCES FOR SPSS

The mathematical operations described in this chapter do not provide the researcher with the exact p value. The p value, as explained in Chapter 3, indicates the possibility of making a type I error. Most often, you simply need to know whether this probability lies above α. If more detailed information is desired, or needed, however, statistical software programs such as SPSS prove helpful.

The SPSS program contains two prompts for performing chi-square tests. Both are accessed by choosing the "Analyze" option from the main menu. With SPSS, performing a one-variable chi-square test using SPSS requires a different procedure than performing a multivariable test does.

One-Variable Chi-Square Test in SPSS

The prompt to conduct a one-variable chi-square test in SPSS appears under the program's "Analyze" heading within the "Nonparametric Tests" menu.

Values in the SPSS output for the one-variable differs bit from the values discussed in Examples 5.5–5.9. A table labeled with the relevant variable's name contains (Table 5.6) expected values, observed values, and residuals (Table 5.6). Another table presents the calculated chi-square value and the degrees of freedom. Neither table provides the critical value. Instead, SPSS determines the actual p value, otherwise known as the *asymptote significance level*, which appears in the second table of the output (Table 5.7).

A comparison of the asymptote significance level, of p value (for probability value) and the chosen α indicates whether the researcher should accept or reject the null hypothesis. Chapter 4 explains that researchers choose α according to their decision about the maximum chance of making a type I error that they wish to take. When $p < \alpha$, the probability of making a type I error is small enough to allow for rejection of the null hypothesis. With the most commonly used α value of .05, allowing only a 5% chance of incorrectly claiming that values differ significantly, a researcher rejects the null hypothesis only if $p \leq .05$. A p value greater than .05 indicates too large a possibility of making a type I error and results in an accepted null hypothesis. A researcher who wishes to use an α value other than .05 changes his or her requirements of p accordingly.

SPSS chi-square test output can appear quite intimidating at first. However, it provides information comparable to that produced by the manual calculation. An SPSS output table labeled with the relevant variable's name contains expected values, observed values, and residuals. Another table presents the calculated chi-square value, the degrees of freedom, and asymptote significance level. Although SPSS provides the

TABLE 5.6. SPSS Output Using Equal Expected Values: Reason[a]

Value	Observed N	Expected N	Residual
Game	12	20.0	-8.0
Commercials	19	20.0	-1.0
Game and commercials	29	20.0	9.0
Total	60		

[a]This table provides values used to compute chi-square statistics.

TABLE 5.7. SPSS Output Using Equal Expected Values: Test Statistics[a]

Value	Reason
Chi-square(a)	7.300
Degrees of Freedom	2
Asymptote significance	.026

[a]The decision as to whether to accept or reject the null hypothesis depends on the values presented in this table.

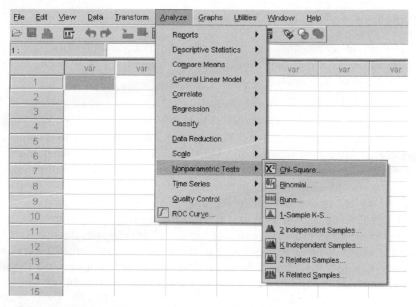

Figure 5.6. One-Variable Chi-Square Prompt in SPSS. The process of conducting a one-variable chi-square test in SPSS begins with the selection of "Chi-Square" from the "Nonparametric Tests" menu.

user with the calculated value, it does not provide the critical value. Instead, it determines the actual p value, otherwise known as the *asymptote significance level*. You can reject the null hypothesis only if $p < \alpha$.

Example 5.28: SPSS Output for One-Variable Chi-Square Test with Equal Expected Values Output produced by the data used for the one-variable chi-square test with equal expected values (see Example 5.5) appears as shown in Tables 5.6 and 5.7.

Tables 5.6 and 5.7 contain many familiar values. The values in Table 5.6 consist of the observed and expected values that constitute the chi-square formula. Table 5.7 tells you that χ^2_{calc}, itself, equals 7.3, the same value obtained through calculations earlier in the chapter, and that the test uses two degrees of freedom, also the same as the value obtained in the chapter. If you use the standard α value of .05, allowing up to a 5% chance of making a type I error, you would reject the null hypothesis because the p value (labeled "asymptote significance") of .026 does not exceed .05. However, if you do not accept a 5% chance of making a type I error, you may choose to compare the p value to an α of .01, which would result in an accepted hypothesis because .026 > .01. Again, these results are the same as those presented in Example 5.8.

Multivariable Chi-Square Test in SPSS

In SPSS, you can access the prompt to conduct any a chi-square test involving two or more variables by clicking the "Statistics" button in the "Crosstabs" window (Fig. 5.7).

(Information about SPSS in Chapter 2 describes how to find and use the "Crosstabs" window.)

This location reflects the fact that data for the multivariable chi-square test are often arranged into a crosstabulation. Further descriptions of how to conduct this test appear on this book's companion website.

www.moravian.edu/aqd

As in the one-variable situation, SPSS output for the multivariable chi-square test contains the calculated chi-square value, but not the critical value. Instead, the p value identifies the exact probability of making a type I error should the null hypothesis be rejected. You should reject the null hypothesis only if $p \leq \alpha$.

Output for chi-square tests involving more than two variables consists of three tables. A table called the "Case-Processing Summary" (Table 5.8) informs the user of any data that the SPSS program could not use in the analysis, usually due to missing values. The crosstabulation reminds you of the observed values that the researcher wishes to compare to the expected values. The output table contains the calculated chi-square and p values. Unlike the output resulting from a one-variable chi-square test,

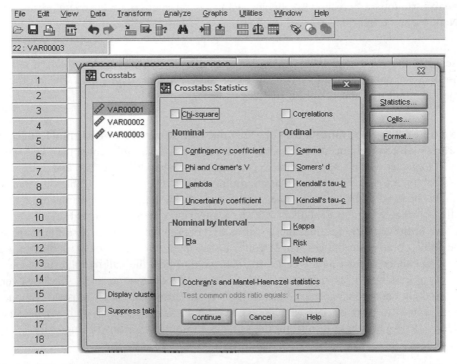

Figure 5.7. Two-variable chi-square prompt in SPSS. The process of conducting a multivariable chi-square test in SPSS begins with the selection of "Statistics" from the "Crosstabs" window. The new window that appears contains the chi-square prompt.

SPSS output for a chi-square test involving multiple variables does not include expected or residual values. All other important values appear in the chi-square table.

For a basic multivariable chi-square analysis, you should focus on the information in the first row of Table 5.10 labeled "Pearson Chi-Square." Here, you can obtain the degrees of freedom used for the test, the value of χ^2_{calc} and the asymptote significance (p) value.

Example 5.29: SPSS Output for Two-Variable Chi-Square   A chi-square test using the variables subjects' sexes and reasons for watching the Superbowl, as demonstrated by the calculations in Example 5.7, would generate the SPSS output presented in Table 5.8–5.10

SPSS produces the same calculated chi-square as obtained through the calculations presented in Example 5.13. Also, similar to the results of the analysis demonstrated in Example 5.15, the SPSS output indicates an accepted null hypothesis. The p value of .951 greatly exceeds any reasonable α value.

Explaining Results of an SPSS Chi-Square Analysis

Providing the χ^2_{crit} value to compare to χ^2_{calc}, as you do when you calculate t yourself, indicates whether the probability of making a type I error lies above or below α, but

TABLE 5.8. SPSS Output Using Two Variables: Case-Processing Summary[a]

	Cases					
	Valid		Missing		Total	
Value	N	Percent	N	Percent	N	Percent
Sex*reason	60	100.0%	0	.0%	60	100.0%

[a]The values in this table confirm that the chi-square test included data from all subject. n less than the total number of subjects and a corresponding percentage <100% indicate the omission of subjects, often as a result missing data.

TABLE 5.9. SPSS Output Using Two Variables: Sex*Reason Crosstabulation[a]

Sex	Reason (Count)			Total
	Game	Commercials	Game and Commercials	
Male	5	8	11	24
Female	7	11	18	36
Total	12	19	29	60

[a]This table provides values used to compute the chi-square statistics.

TABLE 5.10. SPSS Output Using Two Variables: Chi-Square Tests[a]

Factor	Value	Degrees of freedom	Asymptote Significance (Two-Sided)
Pearson χ^2-S	.101(α)	2	.951
Likelihood ratio	.101	2	.951
Linear-by-linear association	.072	1	.788
Number of valid cases	60		

[a]This table provides the values used to compute the chi-square statistics. The decision about whether to accept or reject the null hypothesis depends on the values in this table.

the audience does not know the exact value of this probability. Because SPSS supplies the exact probability of rejecting the null hypothesis when no significant difference really exists (in making a type I error), you can give this information to your audience. Examples 5.29 and 5.31 respectively show ways of doing so when $p < \alpha$, indicating a significant difference and when $p > \alpha$, indicating no significant difference between frequencies.

Example 5.30: Summary of Significant Chi-Square Results from SPSS One using the standard α of .05 as a comparison factor for the p value of .026, shown in Example 5.28, might explain one's results as follows:

No significant difference exists in the number of subjects who watch the Superbowl primarily to see the game ($\Sigma = 12$), primarily to see the commercials ($\Sigma = 19$), and to see both the game and the commercials ($\Sigma = 29$). A comparison of these frequencies produced a χ^2 value of 7.3 and a p value of .026. The null hypothesis of equality between frequencies cannot be rejected at $\alpha = .05$.

Like the explanation given in Example 5.30, a description of results that do not indicate a rejected hypothesis must contain category frequencies, the calculated χ^2 value and the p value.

Example 5.31: Summary of Insignificant Chi-Square Results from SPSS An explanation such as follows might describe the SPSS output shown in Example 5.29, which does not allow for a rejected null hypothesis:

Among the 24 males in the sample, 5 reported watching Superbowl to see the game, itself; 8 reported watching to see commercials; and 11 indicated that they watch to see both the game and the commercials. Among the 36 women in the subjects, 7 reported that they prefer watching the game over the commercials, 11 indicated that the prefer watching the commercials over the game, and 18 indicated that they like watching the game and the commercials equally. The null hypothesis of equality between the frequencies of males and females in each of the viewership categories was rejected at $\alpha = .05$ ($\chi^2 = .101$, $p = .951$), meaning that the frequencies differ significantly.

Although the descriptions in Examples 5.30 and 5.31 present the needed values in different orders, you can use either approach, or any other approach that contains the necessary information.

REVIEW QUESTIONS

5.1 Determine which of the following graphs depict a chi-square distribution with 1 df (degree of freedom), 5 df, and 10 df:

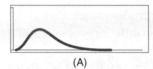   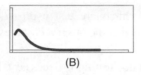   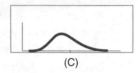

       (A)   (B)   (C)

5.2 Explain the relationship between the right-tail area of a chi-square distribution and the statistical significance.

Consider the following scenario for Questions 5.2–5.8:

Job market analysts wish to investigate whether more individuals are hired during one season of the year than in the others. They randomly select 100 companies across the country and ask human resource directors at the companies to report the number of hires made during the previous summer, winter, spring, and fall. The human resource directors collectively

reported a total of 1103 hires during the summer, 1096 hires during the fall, 998 hires during the winter, and 1051 hires during the spring.

5.3 State the null hypothesis for the relevant chi-square test.

5.4 Find the expected values for arrests during each season.

5.5 Find the calculated chi-square statistic.

5.6 Determine the number of degrees of freedom to use for this test.

5.7 Find the critical statistic at $\alpha = .01$; at $\alpha = .05$; at $\alpha = .1$.

5.8 Is the null hypothesis accepted at $\alpha = .05$; at $\alpha = .01$, or at $\alpha = .1$? If rejected, what is the source of the significant difference?

5.9 Write a short summary of the results for each of the significance values addressed in Question 5.8.

5.10 For a study investigating children's behavior on the playground, researchers spend time at random playgrounds observing children's choices and interactions. One of the issues of interest is the piece of playground equipment that children use first when they arrive at the playground. They expect that equal numbers of children will use each piece of equipment first. Of the 350 children observed, however, 78 first used the seesaw, 73 first used the monkey bars, 108 first used the swings, and 91 first used the sliding board. The chi-square test used to compare these values indicates significance at $\alpha = .05$. Perform post hoc tests to determine at least one source of this significance.

Consider the following scenario for Questions 5.11 and 5.12:

Each of 260 subjects draws a card from a separate standard 52-card deck. With the knowledge that each deck of 52 cards contains 12 face cards (four jacks, four queens, and four kings), one can expect that 60 of the subjects drew face cards and the remaining 200 drew numbered cards or aces. In reality, however, 72 subjects drew face cards.

5.11 Perform a one-variable chi-square test using $\alpha = .05$ to determine whether to reject the null hypothesis that the observed values do not differ significantly from the expected values.

5.12 Determine whether post hoc testing is necessary. If not, explain why. If so, determine at least one source of the significant difference.

For Questions 5.13–5.18, consider further division of the groups described for Questions 5.11 and 5.12 with respect to the suit of the card chosen as shown in the following observed-value crosstabulation:

Card type	Diamonds	Hearts	Spades	Clubs	Sum (Σ)
Face	17	13	25	17	72
Nonface	40	54	45	49	188
Sum (Σ)	57	67	70	66	260

5.13 Find the expected cell values.

5.14 Find the calculated chi-square statistic.

5.15 Determine the number of degrees of freedom to use for this test.

5.16 Find the critical statistic at $\alpha = .01$; at $\alpha = .05$; at $\alpha = .1$.

5.17 Is the null hypothesis accepted at $\alpha = .05$; at $\alpha = .01$, or at $\alpha = .1$? If rejected, what is the source of the significant difference?

5.18 Write a short summary of results for each of the α values addressed in Question 5.17.

5.19 A study to investigate the relationship between taking goodluck measures and finding success focuses on those auditioning for a prestigious choir. Researchers hypothesize that no relationship exists between the use of any sort of good-luck measure and being selected for the choir. Potential choir members are asked whether they took any measures to assure themselves of good luck during the audition and, if so, to specify whether they used a good-luck charm performed a good-luck ritual. After receiving a list of those selected for the choir, researchers arrange the data into the following crosstabulation:

		Good-luck measures			
		Nothing	Charm	Ritual	Sum (Σ)
Choir	Yes	30	9	15	54
	No	25	17	6	48
	Sum (Σ)	55	26	21	102

The chi-square test used to compare these values indicates significance at $\alpha = .05$. Perform post hoc tests to determine at least one source of this significance.

5.20 Creators of a new elementary-school reading series promise that teachers can accommodate the curriculum for use with advanced students, on-level students, and remedial students. Educational analysts who wish to confirm this assertion randomly choose 500 students to expose to the new reading curriculum. The analysts know that, in the general population, 15% of students qualify as advanced and another 15% qualify as remedial. So, they expect the same proportions in their random sample. They believe that, if the reading curriculum really is appropriate for those in each academic category, reading grades should be normally distributed within each, with 10% of students receiving As, 25% of students receiving Bs, 30% of students receiving Cs, 25% of students receiving Ds, and 10% of students receiving Fs.

(A) Perform a two-variable chi-square test using $\alpha = .05$ to address the null hypothesis that the following observed values do not differ significantly from the expected values:

	A	B	C	D	F	Sum (Σ)
Remedial	9	22	32	8	19	90
On-level	48	96	100	42	24	310
Advanced	12	30	32	20	6	100
Sum (Σ)	69	148	164	70	49	500

(B) Determine whether post hoc testing is necessary. If so, determine at least one source of the significant difference.

5.21 Suppose that educational researchers expand the scenario in Question 5.20 to distinguish between students enrolled in public schools and private schools. Fill in the expected values in the following nested crosstabulation.

Level	Public or Private	A	B	C	D	F	Σ (within School Type)	Σ (Total)
Remedial	Public		21.31	23.62	10.08		72.01	90
	Private	2.48	5.33		2.52	1.76		
On-level	Public	34.22			34.72	24.30	247.99	
	Private	8.56	18.35	20.34				
Advanced	Public	11.04	23.68	26.24		7.84	80	100
	Private	2.76	5.92		2.80	1.96	20	
Σ		69	148	164		49		500

5.22 (A) Find the range of standardized values within which a researcher could be 95% confident that the calculated chi-square value would fall given six degrees of freedom (6 df).

(B) Find the range of standardized values within which a researcher could be 90% confident that the calculated chi-square value would fall given 6 df.

(C) Why is the 95% confidence interval greater than the 90% confidence interval?

THE *t* TEST: COMPARING CONTINUOUS-VARIABLE DATA AMONG DICHOTOMOUS GROUPS

6.1 INTRODUCTION

A researcher who wishes to analyze data from at least one continuous variable must use a statistic other than chi-square, which accommodates only categorical data. One of the most basic circumstances involving continuous data requires the researcher to compare two mean values. Such situations require the use of a *t* test.

Although all *t* tests apply to situations involving two means, these means can have a variety of origins. In the simplest version of a *t* test, the one-sample *t* test, the researcher compares the mean of data collected from a sample to the known mean for the population.

One who wishes to determine whether the mean intelligence quotient (IQ) for a random sample of subjects differs significantly from the known population mean IQ of 100. Such an investigation rests on the null hypothesis that the sample mean $(\bar{X})$ does not differ significantly from the population mean (μ):

$$H_0: \bar{X} = \mu$$

The two-sample *t* test compares the mean score of subjects in one condition to the mean score of subjects in another condition, such as scores obtained from different types of

Analyzing Quantitative Data: An Introduction for Social Researchers, First Edition. Debra Wetcher-Hendricks.
© 2011 John Wiley & Sons, Inc. Published 2011 by John Wiley & Sons, Inc.

IQ tests. The data can reflect measures of the same subjects in each of the two conditions or a unique sample of subjects for each condition. Either way, the null hypothesis predicts equality between the means of the two datasets:

$$H_0: \overline{X}_1 = \overline{X}_2$$

6.2 THE *t* DISTRIBUTION

Acceptance or rejection of the null hypothesis depends on the *t* value or *t* score, obtained using the formulas in Section 6.3 of this chapter. Although the differences between means form the bases of these formulas, they also require knowledge of the sample sizes and standard deviations. Thus, even the same two means could produce different *t* values.

Sample size, in particular, has a large influence on the shape of the histograms that display the frequency with which different *t* values occur, often called the *density function*. References to a *t* distribution, therefore, often include identification of the degrees of freedom, which vary in relation to sample size. (See Section 6.3 for specific degree-of-freedom formulas.) The various versions of the distributions result from the fact that they represent data from randomly selected samples (not a single population, as the normal curve does), which can have different sizes. As illustrated by Student's *t* distribution (Fig. 6.1), developed by William S. Gossett[1] (1908), each sample size produces a distribution with a slightly different shape.

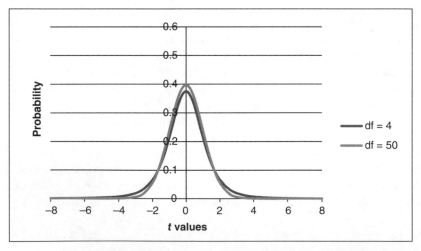

Figure 6.1. *t* distributions. The graph shows probability curves for *t* values with dF 4 and dF 50. As evident from these curves, the *t* distribution has the same basic shape as the normal distribution, and the resemblance between the two increases along with the degrees of freedom for *t*. The *t* distribution always has a mean of 0.

[1] Gossett published under the pseudonym of Student.

This shape provides some important facts about *t* values. Most obviously, the *t* distribution closely resembles the normal distribution. However, some differences, mostly related to sample size and, consequently, degrees of freedom, exist. The *t* distribution differs most from the normal distribution when degrees of freedom are low. In such situations the *t* distribution has a more platykurtic shape and a wider base than the normal distribution does. These differences decrease, however, as degrees of freedom for the *t* distribution increases. With very high sample sizes, the *t* distribution looks almost identical to the normal distribution.

Even given the slight differences evident with small sample sizes, the normal distribution and the *t* distribution share many qualities, including a mean of 0 and symmetry. As suggested by the mean of 0, both negative and positive *t* values exist. The sign of *t* simply refers to the "direction" of the difference between the compared means. A negative value indicates that the mean considered first by the researcher exceeds the mean considered second, and a positive sign indicates the opposite circumstance. Regardless of the way in which the researcher orders the means, however, the difference between them remains consistent. In fact, during tests of significance, you can ignore the signs of calculated *t* values, focusing on |*t*| (the absolute value of *t*) instead. Although the sign of *t* may have importance in later evaluations if means differ significantly, it has no role in the actual significance test.

Example 6.1: Signs of *t* Values   A researcher who wishes to compare the means of 10 and 12 could view the difference in terms of 10–12, which would produce a value of −2; or in terms of 12–10, which would produce a value of +2. Either version of this comparison indicates that the means differ by two units.

The assumption that the formula used to calculate *t* values produces an equal number of positive and negative values explains the symmetry of the *t* distribution. From its peak at 0, which always serves as the mean *t* value, the distribution tapers off on both the negative and positive sides of the *y* axis. This *two-tailed* distribution suggests that high *t* values occur less frequently than low *t* values do. This situation provides the basis of the logic behind establishing a critical value. The researcher chooses a critical value basis of the percentage of *t* values that she or he wishes to remain on the right (due to the use of absolute values) of its location on the distribution. This percentage, known in probability form as α, along with the degrees of freedom, dictates the lower limits for *t* values that indicate significance.

6.3   PERFORMING *t* TESTS

As suggested in Section 6.1, three main versions of the *t* test, one pertaining to single-sample situations and two pertaining to two-sample situations, exist. All versions, however, determine whether the difference between two means qualifies as statistically significant.

6.3.1   One-Sample *t* Tests

In some situations, the general public or, at least, the researcher, knows the mean value for a particular quality among members of the general population. A one-sample *t* test can compare this value to the analogous mean value for a randomly selected sample. This test, thus, allows the researcher to determine whether the sample differs significantly from the population with regard to the variable assessed. In notation form, the null hypothesis for a one-sample *t* test states

$$H_0: \overline{X} = \mu$$

Example 6.2:   One-Sample *t* Test Scenario   Suppose that a researcher who studies the sport of leisure fishing knows that anglers have a mean daily catch of 8.5 fish. A researcher who wishes to characterize fishermens' success at a particular fishing hole might wish to compare the mean number of fish caught at that location to the population mean of 8.5.

The following hypothetical raw data for 10 fishermen (very small sample size for a real study, but acceptable for the sake of example) has a mean of 3.9 and a standard deviation of 4.095.

Fisherman	Fish Caught
1	1
2	4
3	0
4	9
5	4
6	8
7	2
8	11
9	0
10	0

The one-sample *t* test determines whether the mean daily catch of 3.9 differs significantly from the population mean of 8.5.

One-Sample t-Test Formulas.   Reflective of the fact that the one-sample *t* test assesses the contrast between a sample mean and a population mean, this difference serves as the numerator of the formula used to calculate *t*. The denominator of the formula, however, contains the ratio of the sample's standard deviation to the square root of the sample size. Statisticians often refer to this ratio as the *standard error*. The inclusion of this value in the formula standardizes the size of the disparity between the sample mean and the population mean.

$$t_{calc} = \frac{\overline{X} - \mu}{s/\sqrt{n}} \qquad (6.1)$$

$$\text{df} = n - 1 \tag{6.2}$$

The formula for *t* does not require the researcher to square the numerator, as the formula for the chi-square values does. As a result, t_{calc} may have a negative value. A negative value indicates a lower sample mean than population mean, and a positive value indicates a higher sample mean than population mean. However, this issue has relevance only when significant differences between the values exist. Thus, the researcher should focus his or her immediate attention only on the value of t_{calc}.

Obtaining the degrees of freedom for a one-sample *t* test does not require as much calculation as computing the actual *t* value does. Equation (6.2) produces the degree-of-freedom (dF) value. Like the df formula for the chi-square situation, this formula involves subtracting 1 from the number of subjects contained in the sample (*n*). As explained in Chapter 2, the df value represents the number of limitations on data. Diminishing the number of entities by one exists as a regular pattern in computing degrees of freedom.

Example 6.3: One-Sample *t* Test Calculations   Example 6.2 provides all the values needed to use Equations (6.1) and (6.2):

$$t_{calc} = \frac{\bar{X} - \mu}{s/\sqrt{n}} = \frac{3.9 - 8.5}{4.095/\sqrt{10}} = \frac{-4.6}{1.295} = -3.55$$

$$\text{df} = n - 1 = 10 - 1 = 9$$

A negative t_{calc} exists because the population mean of 8.5 exceeds the sample mean of 3.9. At this point in the analysis, however, one need not worry about distinguishing between the higher and the lower means. The issue, now, is the size of the difference between the means. So, the absolute value of t_{calc}, 3.55, becomes the comparison factor for interpreting the results of the *t* test.

Interpreting the One-Sample Calculated t *Value.*   Knowledge of the degrees of freedom allows the researcher to determine the appropriate critical *t* value for comparison to t_{calc}. The *critical t value* (t_{crit}) has the same function in this context as χ^2_{crit} has for the chi-square test. A calculated *t* value with an absolute value that equals or exceeds the corresponding critical value signifies a significant difference between the means compared. Thus, the researcher rejects the null hypothesis, but otherwise accepts the null hypothesis, indicating no significant difference.

Critical *t*-value tables such as the one in Appendix C organize critical *t* values according to degrees of freedom and α values. The t_{crit} for a particular analysis appears at the intersection of the row representing the df value obtained with Equation (6.2) and the column representing the chosen α. Unless otherwise directed or without some other reasonable justification, most researchers begin by using the standard α of .05.

In addition to choosing the value α, you may also need to decide between a one-tailed or a two-tailed test. Researchers most commonly use a one-tailed rather than a two-tailed *t* test[2] because they need to consider only the absolute value of t_{calc} to determine whether the population mean and sample mean differ significantly. Doing so means that only the half of the *t* distribution to the right of the *x* axis remains relevant.

Example 6.4: One-Sample *t*-Test Critical Value   Using a one-tailed distribution (Fig. 6.2) and an α value of .05 to interpret the t_{calc} obtained in Example 6.3, one can locate t_{crit} in the critical *t*-value table. At the intersection of the chart's df = 9 row and the α = .05 column lies the critical value of 1.83. This outcome leads to the rejection of the null hypothesis and characterization of the difference between the sample mean and the population mean as significant.

When a significant difference exists, the researcher should describe the difference as much as possible. Given the *t*-test situation, which involves only two values, doing so simply involves identifying which one exceeds the other, usually determined by a quick look at the values of $\overline{X}$ and μ. If, for some reason, one does not have access to these values, the sign of t_{calc} can provide this information. A sample mean larger than the population mean produces a positive t_{calc} and, a population mean larger than sample mean produces a negative t_{calc} Acknowledgment of the negative value of t_{calc} in this example allows the researcher to claim with 95% certainty that those who fish at the particular location examined catch significantly fewer fish than do those in the population.

Of course, the results of the investigation described in Examples 6.2–6.4 could change if the researcher opts not to use the standard α value of .05. However, research-

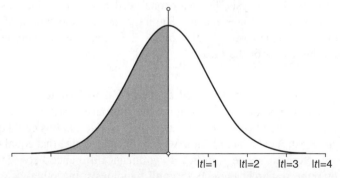

Figure 6.2. One-tailed *t* distribution. The symmetry of the *t* distribution allows researchers to consider the absolute value of the *t* statistic. Thus, They can focus on the half of the distribution to the right of the *y* axis. When doing so, the entire α proportion lies in the right tail, rather than being divided between two tails. A t_{calc} that lies to the right of t_{crit} indicates a significant difference between means.

---

[2] In some cases, a researcher may choose to perform a two-tailed *t* test. Unlike the one-tailed test, a two-tailed test does not specify the direction of difference between means.

ers should use care in selecting the value of α. Researchers who wish to identify significant differences may choose to use large α values, which produce small critical *t* values and, thus, maximize the possibility of rejecting the null hypothesis. However, increasing α also increases the chance of making a type I error, as explained in Chapter 2. Only those willing to accept more than a 5% possibility of incorrectly declaring a significant difference should use an α value larger than .05.

The social research community has a different opinion regarding α values smaller than .05. Those who wish to provide strong evidence of a significant difference often choose to report the smallest α value that they can. If t_{calc} remains larger than t_{crit} at $\alpha = .01$, then the researcher takes only a 1% chance of making a type I error, and this possibility continues to decrease with the value of α until $t_{calc} < t_{crit}$. For the case in Example 6.1, the researcher could use an α value as low as .0005, suggesting 99.95% certainty about the significant difference. The researcher would likely choose to report this value as it provides more impressive evidence of a significant difference than does $\alpha = .05$.

A researcher may also choose to lower the value of α to increase the likelihood of results that indicate the lack of a significant difference. For situations in which the researcher wishes to accept the null hypothesis, she or he expects the value of t_{calc} to exceed the value of t_{crit}. If such results do not occur using $\alpha = .05$, the researcher may raise the value of t_{calc} by decreasing α, hereby continually strengthening the requirements for claiming that a significant difference exists until results indicate a lack of significance. Researchers, however, should not use this practice haphazardly. Lowering the value of α as a means of forcing an accepted null hypothesis leads to the increased possibility of making a type II error, involving the failure to recognize a truly significant difference.

6.3.2 Paired (Dependent)-Samples *t* Test

All *t* tests involving two datasets result from situations involving a categorical independent variable and a continuous dependent variable. Most often, for a *t* test, the independent variable is *dichotomous*, meaning that it defines only two different conditions. However, researchers can also use such *t* tests to compare means for only two conditions from non-dichotomous variables (such as comparing the mean number of points scored by college basketball players during the first and last seasons played at their alma maters, singling out these seasons from all others played during their college careers). In both cases, however, the investigation focuses on two categories and compares two mean values. A situation in which each subject in one category has a counterpart in the other category requires a *paired-samples t test*.

The most obvious relationship between samples exists when the two groups contain the same subjects. Generally, in such a situation, the researcher wishes to compare the same subjects' scores in two different conditions or before and after the introduction of some stimulus. Doing so, however, requires acknowledgment of the dependence between the samples resulting from the logical connections between subjects. By using a paired-samples *t* test, the researcher integrates these connections into the comparison.

Example 6.5: Paired-Samples *t* Test Scenario   This type of matching would exist if the researcher from the examples in Section 6.3.1 altered her or his study, asking each of five subjects to fish in both a freshwater location and a saltwater location. This study could determine whether fishing in freshwater and fishing in saltwater yield different daily catches. So, location serves as the independent variable, and daily catch serves as the dependent variable. To gather the needed data, the researcher could have a random selection of subjects visit a freshwater location one day and a saltwater location another day, recording the daily catch for each person on each of the two days. The researcher could arrange the data similarly to the following hypothetical values, attributing the freshwater and saltwater values in a particular row to the same subject.

Fisherman	Fish Caught in Freshwater	Fish Caught in Saltwater
1	1	8
2	4	2
3	0	11
4	9	0
5	4	0

The same five subjects (again, a very small sample size, but suitable for an example) who provide data for the freshwater condition also provide data for the saltwater condition. Each subject in one condition serves as his or her own counterpart in the other condition, thus necessitating the use of a paired-samples *t* test. The test, itself, determines whether the mean daily catch of 3.6 in the freshwater location differs significantly from the mean daily catch of 4.2 in the saltwater location.

Paired-samples *t* tests may also apply to when the sample groups contain different individuals. The researcher must consider the structures of the groups to determine whether to use the paired-samples test or the independent-samples test, described in Section 6.1.3. Investigations that require comparisons of dependent-variable means for subject groups formed by dividing preexisting couples of subjects demand the paired-samples *t* test. In this situation, each sample group contains one partner of a pair of subjects such as husbands and wives or the winners and losers of a chess match. The paired-samples *t* test accounts for the association between particular subjects in the two groups.

Paired-Samples **t-Test Formulas.**   The one-to-one connections that exist between subjects in groups compared with a paired-samples *t* test allow for the computation of *difference scores* (*D*). These values, obtained simply by subtraction, represent the disparity between the dependent-variable value for subjects in one category and their counterparts in the other category. They form the foundation of the formula used to calculate the *t* statistic for the paired-samples test.

To use the formula for t_{calc} in the paired-samples test, you need to know the mean and the standard deviation of difference scores, $\overline{X}_D$ and s_D, respectively. So, you may find it useful to perform preliminary calculations to obtain these values. Chapter 3 describes the process for calculating mean and standard deviation values.

Example 6.6: Paired-Samples *t*-Test Difference Score Calculations   Subtracting each subject's scores from the two data sets presented in Example 6.5 produce the following difference scores:

Difference Scores
-7
2
-11
9
4

For this investigation, then, $\overline{X}_D = -0.60$ and $s_D = 8.20$.

The numerator of the t_{calc} formula consists only of $\overline{X}_D$, which represents the mean difference between corresponding values in the two datasets. The denominator contains the ratio of s_D to $\sqrt{n}$. As in the one-variable *t* test, this value is known as the *standard error*.

The formula for the degrees of freedom in the paired-samples situation looks similar to formula for the one-sample situation. The paired-samples formula takes into account the number of pairs of subjects (*P*) that provide data rather than the total number of subjects involved in the study. If the samples contain the same subjects measured in each of two conditions, the formula degenerates into $n - 1$. However, with different but logically connected subjects in each condition, one must take care to consider each grouped pair as a single entity; hence the distinction in the one-sample and paired-samples formulas.

$$t_{calc} = \frac{\overline{X}_D}{s_D/\sqrt{n}} \qquad\qquad (6.3)$$

$$df = n - 1 \qquad\qquad (6.4)$$

Example 6.7: Paired-Samples *t*-Test Calculations   Inserting the values from Example 6.6 into Equation (6.3) leads to the following calculations:

$$t_{calc} = \frac{\overline{X}_D}{s_D/\sqrt{n}} = \frac{-.60}{8.20/\sqrt{5}} = \frac{-.60}{3.67} = -0.16$$

For these computations, $n = 5$ because the raw data included five pairs of scores. This value is also used to compute the degrees of freedom:

$$df = n - 1 = 5 - 1 = 4$$

The $|t_{calc}|$ value indicates the extent of the difference between the scores obtained from subjects in the two conditions. The degree-of-freedom value allows you to find t_{crit}, which you must compare to t_{calc} to interpret this difference.

Interpreting the Paired-Samples Calculated t *Value.* You should use the same standards to determine whether means differ significantly for the paired-samples *t* test that you use for any test of significance. A significant difference exists when $t_{calc} < t_{crit}$. Otherwise, you must accept the null hypothesis of equality.

The t_{crit} for an analysis lies at the intersection of the row representing the degrees of freedom and the column representing α. For most cases, you should focus on the values associated with one-tailed *t* tests. (See Section 6.3.1 for further explanation of one-tailed vs. two-tailed tests.)

Example 6.8: Paired-Samples *t*-Test Critical Value The numbers of fish caught in the freshwater and in the saltwater locations differ significantly only if the t_{crit} value is less than the t_{calc} of 0.16 obtained in Example 6.7. However, with df = 4 and assuming that $\alpha = .05$, a critical *t*-value chart identifies the t_{crit} as 2.13. Because $t_{calc} < t_{crit}$, the researcher should accept the null hypothesis. No significant difference exists between mean number of fish caught by subjects in saltwater and in freshwater locations.

As always, one who wishes to claim that a significant difference exists can raise the value of α to produce a t_{calc} that exceeds t_{crit}. One should remember, however, that doing so increases the chances of making a type I error. In the case of Example 6.8, increasing α to the point necessary to obtain a low enough t_{crit} would be foolish as it would lead to an extremely high chance of incorrectly identifying a significant difference.

Although the context of the situation described in Example 6.5 involves one group of subjects that produced two sets of data, the same process could also pertain to matched subjects.

Example 6.9: Paired-Samples *t* Test with Different Subjects Scenario An investigation into whether fathers and sons who tend to fish together tend to catch the same number of fish in one day, for example, would also require a dependent-samples *t* test. Even though the two groups do not contain the same subjects, as in Examples 6.5–6.8, subjects have a one-to-one relationship with each other. The paired-samples *t* test factors in these implicit pairings when determining whether fathers' daily catches differ significantly from those of their sons.

So, the raw data in Example 6.5 could have easily referred to the daily catches of fathers and sons rather than the catches of the same set of individuals in two situations. Even with a different context to these data, the formulas, calculations, and outcome would not change. In this case, however, the researcher would explain that no significant difference exists between the number of fish caught in one day by fathers and their sons.

With different data points, however, calculations may have produced a t_{calc} greater than 2.13. The researcher could then reject the null hypothesis, explaining that a significant difference exists between the number of fish that people catch in freshwater locations and in saltwater locations. To determine which location results in the greater number of catches, the researcher must consider the means for the two datasets. The higher of the two means corresponds to the location where fishermen had greater success than the other.

6.3.3 Independent-Samples *t* Test

An *independent-samples t test* compares dependent variable means for groups containing different subjects that do not have logical connections to one another as the paired samples do. To apply an independent-samples *t* test, the researcher must have a categorical independent variable and a continuous dependent variable. As with the dependent-samples test, the independent variable often takes a dichotomous form, separating subjects into only two categories. But one may also use this test to highlight the distinction between only two categories of a nondichotomous independent variable (such as mean ages of Catholics to mean ages of Protestants, focusing on these two religious groups even though data from other religious categories may exist).

Example 6.10: Independent-Samples *t*-Test Scenario   The same data points used for the paired-samples *t*-test example can serve as an example for an independent-samples *t* test. The *t* test would, once again, determine whether a significant difference exists between the mean daily catch in the freshwater and saltwater locations. The context of the research scenario, however, differs. For the independent-samples test, one group of subjects supplies data from the freshwater location and another, unrelated, group of subjects supplies data from the saltwater location. Unlike the paired-variables situation, in which each subject provided data from both locations or logical pairs of subjects were split between the locations, subjects in one category do not have counterparts in the other category for an independent *t* test.

Independent-Samples t-Test Formulas.   The presence of two datasets from two distinct samples of subjects makes the process of calculating *t* and the degrees of freedom with independent-samples slightly more complicated than those for the one-sample or paired-samples situation. The formulas required knowledge of means, standard deviations, and sample sizes for both datasets. You may find it useful to obtain these values, using formulas from Chapter 3 first.

Example 6.11: Independent-Samples *t*-Test Preliminary Calculations   The five freshwater and the five saltwater raw scores, as well as their relevant descriptive statistics, are listed below.

Fish Caught in Freshwater	Fish Caught in Saltwater
1	8
4	2
0	11
9	0
4	0
$\bar{X}_F = 3.6$	$\bar{X}_S = 4.2$
$s_F = 3.51$	$s_S = 5.01$
$n_F = 5$	$n_s = 5$

Although both of the groups in Example 6.11 contain five subjects, groups being compared in an independent-samples *t* test need not have equal sample sizes. The preliminary calculations provide you with six values that appear in the formulas for computing t_{calc} and df.

The most commonly used formulas for independent-samples *t* tests rely on *homoscedasticity*, meaning that the variances of your datasets do not differ significantly. Most of the time, heteroscedasticity exists, allowing you to combine the variances of the datasets as shown in Equation (6.5) to create a *pooled variance*. This value, denoted as S_p, constitutes part of the equation for the independent-samples t_{calc}.

$$S_p = \sqrt{\frac{(n_1 - 1)s_1^2 + (n_2 - 1)s_2^2}{n_1 + n_2 - 2}} \tag{6.5}$$

With unequal variances, or *heteroscedasticity*, the pooled variance, cannot be used; thus, formulas vary slightly. Please see this book's companion website for further information about the formulas to compute *t* in such situations.

Example 6.12: Independent-Samples *t*-Test Pooled Variance Calculations To compute the pooled variance for the two groups in Example 6.11, group 1 can refer to the freshwater fishermen and group 2 can refer to the saltwater fishermen. In this case, the distinction between the sample size for group 1 (n_1) and the sample size for group 2 (n_2) has little importance because the two groups have an equal numbers of subjects. So, $n_1 = n_2$. Care must be taken to associate the correct *n* with the correct groups, though, when sample sizes differ.

Inserting the sample sizes and standard deviations obtained from preliminary calculations into Equation (6.5) produces a pooled variance of 4.32:

$$S_p = \sqrt{\frac{(n_1 - 1)s_1^2 + (n_2 - 1)s_2^2}{n_1 + n_2 - 2}} = \sqrt{\frac{(5-1)(3.51^2) + (5-1)(5.01^2)}{5+5-2}}$$

$$= \sqrt{\frac{49.28 + 100.40}{8}} = 4.32$$

Having computed the pooled variance, you have all of the values needed for substitution into the t_{calc} and df formulas.

$$t_{calc} = \frac{\bar{X}_1 - \bar{X}_2}{S_p \sqrt{(1/n_1) + (1/n_2)}} \tag{6.6}$$

$$df = n_1 + n_2 - 2 \tag{6.7}$$

These two equations actually present expanded versions of the formulas shown in Sections 6.1.1 and 6.1.2 of this chapter. Like all t_{calc} values, the independent-samples *t* standardizes the difference between *t* scores. The numerator contains the difference between mean scores, themselves, and the denominator contains the standard error. The complexity of this formula's standard error as opposed to those for the one-sample and the paired-samples tests results from the need to address each sample individually.

The formula used to compute the degrees of freedom also references each set of subjects separately. With the possibility of two different sample sizes, the researcher must distinguish between the n values from each sample group. After subtracting one from n_1 and from n_2, representing the sample sizes of each individual group, the researcher can add the resulting values together to account for all subjects. Of course, the researcher may also choose to use the mathematically simplified version of the formula, which involves subtracting two from the sum of the numbers of subjects from the two groups.

Example 6.13: Independent-Samples *t*-Test Calculations Substitution of the pooled variance, means, standard deviations, and sample sizes from Examples 6.11 and 6.12 into Equation (6.6) and subsequent arithmetic simplification produces the t_{calc} that represents the size of the difference between the mean number of fish caught in the freshwater and in the saltwater locations:

$$t_{calc} \frac{\bar{X}_1 - \bar{X}_2}{S_p \sqrt{(1/n_1)+(1/n_2)}} = \frac{3.6-4.2}{4.32\sqrt{\frac{1}{5}+\frac{1}{5}}} = \frac{-.60}{4.32(.63)} = -.220$$

Two interesting aspects of this particular example deserve mention. (1), the fact that both samples contain the same number of subjects makes simplification of the denominator rather easy—however, when the two n values differ, the researcher must find the least common denominator for the radical expressions; and (2), the negative value of the resulting t statistic should not cause concern. It simply reflects the order of the subtraction in the numerator. The researcher should use $|t_{calc}|$ as a basis for interpreting this test.

Of course, as in all tests of statistical significance, interpretation of the statistical value requires knowledge of the degrees of freedom. With sample sizes of 5 for both the freshwater and the saltwater groups, df becomes 8:

$$df = (n_1 - 1) + (n_2 - 1) = (5-1) + (5-1) = 4 + 4 = 8$$

Interpreting the Independent-Samples Calculated t *Value.* To obtain meaningful results from the independent-samples t test, one follows the familiar protocol of comparing the t_{calc} and t_{crit} values. Appendix C provides the critical t values needed to determine whether significant differences exist between the mean values for the two datasets analyzed. As always, you locate the appropriate t_{crit} using the degrees of freedom, calculated with Equation (6.7), and your chosen α.

Example 6.14: Independent-Samples *t*-Test Critical Value Interpreting the t_{calc} from Example 6.13, then, begins by locating the row that corresponds to 8 dF. The t_{crit} appears at the intersection of this row labeled and the column labeled with the appropriate α. Using a standard α value of .05, $t_{crit} = 1.86$. A comparison of this number to the $|t_{calc}|$ of .22 indicates no significant difference between the number of fish caught by those who fished in freshwater and those who fished in saltwater. The researcher cannot reject the null hypothesis of equality because t_{calc} does not exceed t_{crit}.

In some situations, the researcher without much concern about type I error can raise the value of α slightly to decrease the critical value enough to meet the criteria for rejecting the null hypothesis. This tactic would prove useless for this particular example, however, as the researcher would need to raise α to near .50, before rejecting the null hypothesis. Generally, this α value represents an unacceptable level as it communicates too high a likelihood of incorrectly characterizing the difference between population means as significant.

However, a researcher who obtains raw data different from those shown in Example 6.11 and thess data legitimately produce a t_{calc} that exceeds t_{crit}, could reject the null hypothesis in good faith. The rejected hypothesis indicates that a significant difference exists between the number of fish caught by fathers and their sons. The sign of the calculated t value indicates whether group 1 or group 2 provided the greater mean.

A positive t_{calc} specifies that $\bar{X}_1$ exceeds $\bar{X}_2$, and a negative t_{calc} specifies the opposite.

6.4 CONFIDENCE INTERVALS

Formulas used to calculate the upper and lower limits for mean difference scores vary according to the version of the t test used. For this reason, researchers often choose to consider confidence intervals for t_{calc}. Any t values that fall outside the boundaries of this confidence interval result in a rejected null hypothesis. As with the chi-square situation, the researcher can adjust the size of this range by changing the value of α. Small α values, which impose strict standards for rejecting the null hypothesis, produce larger confidence intervals than do large α values, which loosen the requirements for rejecting the null hypothesis. Using $\alpha = .01$, for example, allows fewer t values to fall outside the confidence intervals' boundaries than does the standard α value of .05; however, the researcher can claim with 99% certainty that these values correctly indicate significant differences. Conversely, one who wishes to increase the number of t values that fall outside the confidence interval might be wise to reduce the size of the confidence interval by using an α value such as .10, which signifies only a 90% chance of avoiding a type I error.

Regardless of the size of the confidence interval that the researcher prefers, she or he can establish the interval's limits with knowledge of the degree-of-freedom value and by using a critical t table. Although the critical t table contains only positive values, these numbers represent the absolute values of t scores, based on the symmetry of the t distribution. As explained in Section 6.2, the distinction between $-t$ and $+t$ merely reflects the order in which the researcher subtracts mean values. To account for the equal possibility of obtaining values that lie between $-t$ and 0 and between 0 and $+t$, the confidence interval includes values ranging from $-t_{crit}$ to $+t_{crit}$. So, when $-t_{crit} < t_{calc} < +t_{crit}$, the researcher accepts the null hypothesis.

Example 6.15: Confidence Interval   For example, one could obtain the 95% confidence interval (based on the standard α value of .05) for calculated t values resulting from the comparison used in Example 6.14 by considering the critical value of 1.86. The researcher knows that $|t_{calc}|$ values larger than 1.86 indicate a significant difference between means and that those smaller than 1.86 indicate no such difference. If the formula used to obtain t_{calc} produced only positive numbers, the researcher could establish the confidence interval as CI:$[0 < t < 1.89]$. However, in reality, the formula produces $-t$ just as often as it produces $+t$. To allow for the possibility of these inverse values, researchers define the confidence interval as CI:$[-1.89 < t < +1.89]$. A researcher who wishes to be 95% confident that any difference evident in the sample also exists in the population would not claim significance unless the calculated t value lies outside this range. In Example 6.13, the calculated t value of $-.22$ falls within this range, confirming that the difference between means does not qualify as significant.

The confidence interval established in Example 6.15 identifies a range of critical values. Another type of confidence intervals may identify a range of difference scores. However, most beginning statisticians do not refer to the difference-score confidence interval. The distribution of difference scores lacks the symmetry evident in the distribution of critical t values, complicating the process of obtaining their confidence interval.

6.5 EXPLAINING RESULTS OF THE *t* TEST

Having obtained the needed statistical results, the researcher faces the challenge of explaining them to others. In most cases, the audience does not have the knowledge or interest in details of the study such as the manner in which the researcher organized data or the specific value of the standard error. Reports of *t*-test findings, therefore, generally present only values and explanations relevant to the overall understanding of the relationship between means.

The researcher usually begins by providing a brief description of the data, including the sample sizes, means, and standard deviations for each dataset and, in the case of a one-variable *t* test, the population mean. Summaries of results should also include the values of t_{calc}, and, when on the basis of calculations done by the researcher, mention of the α inequality that indicates insignificance or signficance.

Explanations of insignificant results end with the declaration of an accepted null hypothesis.

Example 6.16: Summary of Insignificant Results Accordingly, such a description would follow the independent-variables *t* test presented in Examples 6.10–6.14, which suggested no significant difference between means:

> The five subjects in the freshwater category caught a mean of 3.6 fish, and the five subjects in the saltwater category caught a mean of 4.2 fish. An independent-samples *t* test compared these values. The resulting statistic of $-.22$ corresponds to a significance value larger than .05, resulting in an accepted null hypothesis. The difference between the sample means does not qualify as significant.

Of course, researchers do not need to follow the exact structure of Example 6.16 when presenting their results. They may choose to substitute parenthetical expressions for some or all in-text reference numerical values.

Example 6.17: Summary of Insignificant Results Using Parentheses   The passage below uses parentheses to provide all relevant values, as an alternative to the presenta-·tion of the same information in Example 6.16:

> Results of an independent-samples *t* test ($t = -.22$) indicate no significant difference between the mean number of fish caught by those fishing in freshwater locations ($n = 5$, $\overline{X} = 3.6$) and by those fishing in saltwater locations ($n = 5$, $\overline{X} = 4.2$). Thus, the null hypothesis of equality between means is accepted ($p > .05$).

When rejecting the null hypothesis, however, the researcher must provide additional information. For a complete understanding of the difference that exists, the audience must know which mean exceeds the other.

Example 6.18: Summary of Significant Results   The results of the one-sample *t* test, presented earlier in this chapter, can provide the basis for such a description:

> Rejection of the null hypothesis reflects the results of a one-sample *t* test conducted at the .05 level of significance. The *t* value of -3.55 indicates that the 10 fishermen in the sample ($\overline{X} = 3.9$) have significantly fewer daily catches than do those in the population ($\mu = 8.5$).

6.6   CONCLUSION

The existence of various types of *t* tests, applicable to different data-gathering contexts, allows for widespread use of the analysis. The *t* test, in its single sample, paired-samples, or independent-samples form, can compare any two means. Researchers regularly use *t* tests in their analyses of differences between males and females, Republicans and Democrats, college graduates and non–college graduates, and many other dichotomous groupings or conditions. One should not forget, however, that *t* tests can also compare data from two specified groups of a nondichotomous variable, such as followers of two particular religions or students at two particular schools.

Further, this chapter describes only the primary function of the *t* test, that of indicating whether to accept or reject the null hypothesis of equality between means. We shall see that *t* tests can serve another important purpose as well. Chapter 7, which presents the analysis of variance, includes references to the *t* test as a method of providing information about the origin of difference that produce significant results from this assessment. The *t* test can also serve as a precursor for the chi-square test presented in Chapter 5. One unhappy with insignificant differences, as evidenced by a $t_{calc} < t_{crit}$, may choose to downgrade the analysis to a chi-square statistic by categorizing the dependent-variable data. With a categorical independent variable and dependent variable, a chi-square test could compare the frequencies within each combination of categories to determine whether they differ significantly. Because the chi-square test is not as specific an analysis as the t test is, it sometimes provides significant results when the t test indicated a lack of significance. Such results, however, do not provide as much support for the claim of group effects as significant t test results do.

Despite differences in the reasons for performing t tests, the process of doing so follows the same general procedure used for all tests of significance. Without the use of SPSS, the researcher computes the calculated value using appropriate formulas and then compares this value to the critical value. Calculated values that exceed critical values indicate significant differences between the values compared. When using SPSS, the researcher simply considers the value of p in relation to α. The researcher rejects the null hypothesis, representative of a significant difference between values, only when $p \leq \alpha$. Analogous similarities exist with regard to the processes involved in determining confidence intervals for all statistical tests as well. Thus, the benefits of becoming familiar with the steps involved in conducting the t test and the reasons for them do not remain confined to this data analysis context alone. This knowledge enhances one's understanding of the theoretical framework for and practical applications of inferential statistics in general.

STATISTICAL RESOURCES FOR SPSS

SPSS output for the t test provides you with the same t_{calc} that you would obtain through the calculations presented in Section 6.3 of this chapter. SPSS output provides this value as well as the degrees of freedom and relevant standard deviations. When one uses SPSS, however, the decision about whether to accept or reject the null hypothesis rests on the relationship between p and α rather than the relationship between t_{calc} and t_{crit}.

Requesting this information from SPSS always begins with your selection of the "Compare Means" option under the "Analyze" heading. You can, then, specify the type of t test that you want SPSS to perform. In addition to the basic instructions for the one-sample, paired-samples, and independent-samples t tests that follow, detailed information about using SPSS to conduct the tests appears in this book's companion website.

www.moravian.edu/aqd

One-Sample t Test in SPSS

For a one-sample t test, SPSS provides you with the window shown in Figure 6.3.

The variables that you wish to analyze, in SPSS terminology, become test variables, and the population mean becomes the test value. SPSS compares the mean values for any variable that you move to the "Test Variable(s) box."

Output consists of two tables. One provides descriptive statistics for the test variable(s) that you have identified. The other contains t_{calc} and a significance (p) value. A comparison of p to your chosen α indicates whether the sample mean differs from the population mean. The value of p also indicates the probability making a type I error by claiming that these two means differ when they really do not. You should not reject

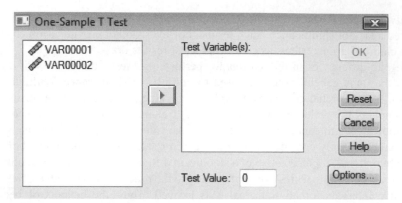

Figure 6.3. SPSS one-sample *t*-test box. The user performs a one-sample *t* test by selecting the appropriate variable from those listed in the box above and moving it to the "Test Variable(s)" box and should then enter the population mean into the "Test Value" box.

the null hypothesis when *p* exceeds α because you selected the value of α to indicate the greatest chance of making a type I error that you are willing to take. A *p* that lies below α, though, indicates a sufficiently small chance of incorrectly rejecting the null hypothesis, and you can characterize the difference as significant.

Because you do not need to compare t_{calc} and t_{crit} if you know the *p* value, SPSS does not provide t_{crit}. The program does, however, provide t_{calc}, and this value should appear in the report of your findings. The appearance of SPSS *t*-test output differs slightly with the different types of *t* test you perform, but all contain these values as well as relevant descriptive statistics.

Output from a one-sample *t* test consists of two tables. Table 6.1 provides descriptive values for your sample, including the sample mean that the *t* tests compares to the population mean. SPSS actually refers to the population mean as the test statistic, and this value appears in Table 6.2. This table also contains the two-tailed significance value (*p*) that you use as a basis for your decision to accept or reject the null hypothesis.

Example 6.19: SPSS Output for One-Variable *t* Test An SPSS analysis of the daily catch data first presented in Example 6.2 produces the output presented in Table 6.2.

From the output in Tables 6.1 and 6.2, you can see that the *t* test compared the sample mean of 3.9 to the population mean of 8.5. The *p* value of .006, found under the "Significance (Two-Tailed)" heading of Table 6.2, indicates that, unless you have chosen to use an α lower than .006, you should reject the null hypothesis. Therefore, you can claim that those in the sample caught fewer fish than those in the general population do.

With the exception of *p*, which you cannot obtain through your own calculations, the values in Example 6.19 match those from Example 6.3. You could, conceivably, use the t_{calc} as a basis of comparison to t_{crit}, obtained from Appendix C. The SPSS out-

TABLE 6.1. SPSS Output for One-Sample *t* Test: One-Sample Text[a]

	N	Mean	Standard Deviation	Standard Error Mean
Fish	10	3.9000	4.09471	1.29486

[a]This table displays the descriptive statistics from the sample.

TABLE 6.2. SPSS Output for One-Sample *t* Test: One-Sample Text[a]

					95% Confidence Interval of the Difference	
	T	Degrees of freedom	Significance (Two-Tailed)	Mean Difference	Lower	Upper
Fish	−3.553	9	.006	−4.60000	−7.5292	−1.6708

Test Value = 8.5

[a]This table contains the values related to the actual comparison between the sample mean and the population mean. The researcher pays particular attention to the significance value (p), which indicates whether to accept or reject the null hypothesis.

put's p value, however, gives you more information than you would get from comparing t values. A comparison between t_{calc} and t_{crit} tells you a bit of information about p. You know that a t_{calc} that exceeds t_{crit} corresponds to a p that lies below α because both of these situations lead to a rejected null hypothesis. Conversely, when t_{calc} is smaller than t_{crit}, p must lie above α. But this logic does not tell you the exact value of p. To obtain this value, which you may find useful in selecting α or for reporting purposes, you must use a statistical program like SPSS.

Paired-Samples *t* Test in SPSS

SPSS can conduct a paired-samples t test only if you have entered an equal number of data points in two columns on the "Data View" screen. The program knows that each row contains data from a single subject or from matched subjects.

As with the one-sample t test, the process of requesting a paired-samples t test from SPSS begins with your selection of the "Compare Means" option from the "Analyze" pulldown menu. When you specify that you would like to conduct a paired-samples t test, a "Paired-Samples T Test" window appears on the screen (Fig. 6.4).

As with the other SPSS procedures described in this chapter, the process of conducting a paired-samples t test receives additional attention on this book's companion website.

www.moravian.edu/aqd

The SPSS output first displays a paired-samples statistics table (Table 6.3), which contains descriptive statistics. This table, appearing at the end of the output, contains

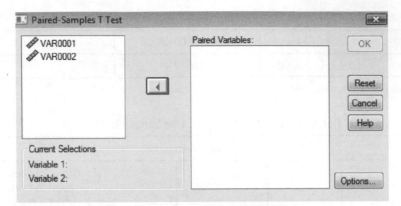

Figure 6.4. SPSS paired-samples *t*-test window. The user performs a paired-samples *t* test by selecting the appropriate category names from those listed in the box above. The names of these categories transfer to the "Paired Variables" box simultaneously.

TABLE 6.3. SPSS Output for Paired-Samples *t* Test: Paired-Samples Statistics[a]

Pair 1	Mean	N	Standard Deviation	Standard Error Mean
Freshwater	3.6000	5	3.50714	1.56844
Saltwater	4.2000	5	5.01996	2.24499

[a]This table displays descriptive statistics from the samples.

the t_{calc} and significance (p) values as well as many of the values that you see while calculating t. The same rule regarding the relationship between the p value and α used with other tests of significance applies to this test as well. A p value smaller than the researcher's chosen α indicates a significant difference and, thus, a rejected null hypothesis.

Along with the statistics table and test table, SPSS output for a dependent-sample t test contains a correlations table. The correlation coefficient indicates the predictability with which one set of values increases as the other increases, designated by a positive value, or with which one set of values decreases as the other increases, designated by a negative value. Chapter 8 provides a full explanation of correlation coefficients as well as a description of the situations in which researchers might find them useful.

Example 6.20: SPSS Output for Paired-Variables *t* Test   An SPSS analysis (see output in Tables 6.4 and 6.5) of the research scenario comparing mean daily catches for subjects who fish in freshwater and in saltwater provides the same descriptive statistics, the degree-of-freedom value and t_{calc} obtained in Example 6.7.

The two-tailed significance value (p) and the correlation coefficient, however, provide new information. In this case, the p value of .878 greatly exceeds the standard α of .05. The decision to accept the null hypothesis on the basis of the p value is the same decision made when comparing t_{calc} and t_{crit} in Example 6.8. Information from the "Paired-Samples Correlations" table corroborates this finding. The significance value

TABLE 6.4. SPSS Output for Paired-Samples *t* Test: Paired-Samples Correlations[a]

Pair 1	N	Correlation	Significance
Freshwater and Saltwater	5	−.846	.071

[a]This table contains correlation values.

TABLE 6.5. SPSS Output for Paired-Samples *t* Test: Paired-Samples Test[a]

Pair 1	Paired Differences					T	Degrees of Freedom	Significance (Two-Tailed)
	Mean	Standard Deviation	Standard Error Mean	95% Confidence Interval of the Difference				
				Upper	Lower			
Freshwater, saltwater	−.60000	8.20366	3.66879	−10.78619	9.58619	−.164	4	.878

[a]This table contains the values related to the actual comparison between the sample means. The researcher pays particular attention to the significance value (*p*), which indicates whether to accept or reject the null hypothesis.

in this table deserves primary attention. Its value of .071, judged using the same standards as used to evaluate a *p* value, suggests that the correlation does not qualify as significant at $\alpha = .05$. Thus, although the number of fish caught may differ predictably according to location, minimal distinctions between scores render this trend negligible.

Independent-Samples *t* Test in SPSS

This book's companion website contains instructions for entering data into the SPSS program screen, which is the most difficult part of conducting an independent-samples *t* test in SPSS. After identifying each subject's category placement and dependent-variable score, you can proceed to the "Analyze" menu to request the independent-samples *t* test.

www.moravian.edu/aqd

The prompt for the independent-samples *t* test appears in the "Compare Means" option, along with the prompts for the other *t* tests described in this chapter. The process of identifying variables involved in the analysis, however, is a bit more complex for the independent-samples test than for either of the others. The "Independent-Samples *t* Test" window contains an area labeled "Test Variable(s)," into which you must move the name of the dependent variable(s) as well as an area labeled "Grouping Variable," into which you must move the name of the independent variable.

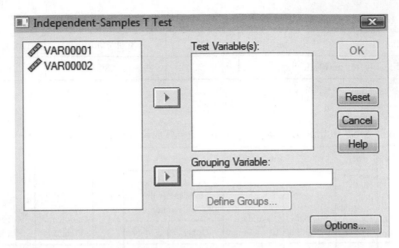

Figure 6.5. SPSS "Independent-Samples T Test" box. The user performs an independent-samples t test by selecting the names of the independent variable, which becomes the grouping variable, and the dependent variable, which becomes the test variable from those listed in the box above. The "Define Groups" button allows the user to specify the two groups of the independent variable that is to be compared.

TABLE 6.6. SPSS Output for Independent-Samples t Test: Group Statistics[a]

	Fishing Location	N	Mean	Standard Deviation	Standard Error Mean
Number of fish caught in one day	Freshwater	5	3.60	3.507	1.568
	Saltwater	5	4.20	5.020	2.245

[a]This table presents descriptive statistics from the samples.

SPSS, however, needs direction regarding the specific groups that you wish to compare. If you have a nondichotomous independent variable, you must indicate which two group means the program should consider. Also, you can create artificial groupings from a continuous independent variable by identifying the value that you would like to serve as the division point. Clicking on the "Define Groups" button (see Fig. 6.5) allows you to provide this sort of information to SPSS.

The table that provides t_{calc} and p for the independent-samples t test contains more values than the comparable tables for the one-sample and the paired-samples t test do. The "Group Statistics" table (Table 6.6) presents descriptive statistics for the two samples. The "Independent-Samples Test" table (Table 6.7)presents the values used to assess significance. In particular, the t_{calc} and relevant significance (p) values appear in a portion of the second table that refers to the t test for equality of means. As always, the p value is smaller than α when group means differ significantly.

TABLE 6.7. SPSS Output for Independent-Samples *t* Test: Independent-samples Test[a]

Variance		Levene's Test for Equality of Variances		*t* Test for Equality of Means						95% Confidence Interval of the Difference	
		F	Significance	T	Degrees of Freedom	Significance (Two-Tailed)	Mean Difference	Standard Error Difference		Upper	Lower
Number of fish caught in one day	Equal variances assumed	2.110	.184	-.219	8	.832	-.600	2.739		-6.915	5.715
	Equal variances not assumed	—	—	-.219	7.153	.833	-.600	2.739		-7.048	5.848

[a]This table contains the values related to the actual comparison between the sample means. In this table, the researcher pays particular attention to the two-tailed significance value (*p*), which indicates whether to accept or reject the null hypothesis. Unless, for some reason, the samples contain data with vastly different ranges, the researcher should assume equal variances and, thus, consider only values in the top row of this table.

SPSS does not provide a correlation table such as the one that appears in output for the paired-samples *t* test because correlation values apply only to situations in which each data point in one category has a counterpoint in the other category.

Example 6.21: SPSS Output for Independent-Variables *t* Test   The output presented in Tables 6.6 and 6.7, produced by an SPSS independent-variables *t*-test analysis using the data first presented in Example 6.11, provides many of values involved in the calculation of *t*, as well as t_{calc} and *p*.

The *p* value of .832, which lies well above any reasonable α value, indicates that no significant difference exists between means of the two samples. This value indicates that the difference between sample means correctly characterizes the population only 16.7% of the time. Thus, the researcher, unwilling to take an 83.2% chance of making a type I error by incorrectly claiming that those who fish in freshwater and those who fish in saltwater have different daily catches, would accept the null hypothesis.

The "Independent-Samples T Test" table actually contains two significance values. The significance value under the "Levene's Test for Equality of Variance" heading does *not* tell you whether to accept or reject your null hypothesis of equality between category means. You should use this value, instead, to determine whether to look at the top or the bottom row on the right side of the table. If the Levene significance value exceeds the α that you have chosen, then the variances of the two categories in the analysis do not differ significantly, and you should refer to the values in the top row on the right of the table. A Levene's significance value lower than α indicates a significant difference between the categories' variances. In this case, you should refer to the values in the bottom row on the right side of the table. Any difference that you see between the values in these two rows results from a slight modification to the calculations needed when you cannot assume equality between variances.

Explaining Results of an SPSS *t*-Test Analysis

If the researcher obtained t_{calc} from SPSS, then his or her explanation should revolve around the relationship between α and *p*. Examples 6.10 and 6.11, which reflect the use of SPSS, contain the same information as Examples 6.16–6.18 do with the exception of identifying *p* rather than t_{crit}.

Example 6.22: Summary of Insignificant *t*-Test Results from SPSS   An independent *t* test produced a *t* value of −.22 and a *p* value of .831. These numbers necessitate the acceptance of the null hypothesis, indicating that mean values of 3.6 and 4.6, referring to the number of fish caught in caught by those fishing in freshwater locations ($n = 5$) and in saltwater locations ($n = 5$), do not differ significantly.

Example 6.23: Summary of Significant *t*-Test Results from SPSS   A one-sample *t* test compared the sample mean of 3.9 to the population mean of 8.5. Results of this test ($t = -3.55$, $p = .006$) indicate that those in the sample ($n = 10$) caught significantly fewer fish than those in the general population do. Consequently, the null hypothesis is rejected.

REVIEW QUESTIONS

Determine whether each of the following null hypotheses should be tested with a single-sample t test, a paired-samples t test, or an independent-samples t test.

6.1. Blue-collar workers earn the same amount of money as white-collar workers do.

6.2. Gasoline prices in a particular state are no different from the mean national price.

6.3. Children's maturity levels do not change from third to fourth grade.

6.4. Men tend to have careers with the same prestige rankings as those of their fathers.

6.5. Fraternal twins finish each other's sentences equally as often as identical twins do.

Real estate professionals generally consider 30 days the mean amount of time in which a home sells. Recent economy changes, however, have prompted a particular home market analyst to claim that it now takes longer to sell a home, and conducts a survey to investigate the issue. Information gathered from nine randomly selected individuals who recently sold homes are presented below.

Home	Days on Market
1	24
2	10
3	76
4	19
5	37
6	42

6.6. State the null hypothesis for the relevant *t* test.

6.7. Find the calculated *t* statistic.

6.8. Determine the number of degrees of freedom to use for this test.

6.9. Find the critical statistic at $\alpha = .01$, $\alpha = .05$, and $\alpha = .10$.

6.10. Is the null hypothesis rejected at $\alpha = .01$? At $\alpha = .05$? at $\alpha = .10$?

6.11. Write a short summary of results for each of the significance values addressed in Question 6.10.

Many of the students who visit the counseling center at Getumsmart University suffer from anxiety. The counselors know that a possible association may exist between doing yoga and having low anxiety levels, and they wonder if they should implement a yoga program for students. To assess the success of such a program, they select six pairs of roommates. One roommate attends yoga session for a month and the other doesn't. At the end of the month, the counselors measure each students' anxiety level using a scale from 1 to100 (1—low anxiety; 100—high anxiety). The results are given as follows:

Yoga	No Yoga
50	62
32	47
51	77
53	46
41	60

6.12. State the null hypothesis for the relevant *t* test.

6.13. Find the calculated *t* statistic.

6.14. Determine the number of degrees of freedom to use for this test.

6.15. Find the critical statistic at $\alpha = .01$, $\alpha = .05$, and $\alpha = .10$.

6.16. Is the null hypothesis rejected at $\alpha = .01$? At $\alpha = .05$? At $\alpha = .10$?

6.17. Write a short summary of results for each of the significance values addressed in Question 6.16.

Travel and tourism analysts wish to determine whether individuals spend longer on vacation in destinations that are warmer or colder than their hometowns are. They ask 16 randomly selected individuals about the destinations (warmer or colder than their hometowns) and lengths of their last vacations. The number of nights spent on vacation by those who traveled to warmer and to colder than those in their hometowns are as follows:

Warmer Climate	Colder Climate
7	4
3	4
10	5
6	7
7	2
6	6
9	
5	
13	
9	

6.18. State the null hypothesis for the relevant *t* test.

6.19. Find the calculated *t* statistic.

6.20. Determine the number of degrees of freedom to use for this test.

6.21. Find the critical statistic at $\alpha = .01$, $\alpha = .05$, and $\alpha = .10$.

6.22. Is the null hypothesis rejected at $\alpha = .01$? At $\alpha = .05$? At $\alpha = .10$?

6.23. Write a short summary of results for each of the significance values addressed in Question 6.22.

7

ANALYSIS OF VARIANCE: COMPARING CONTINUOUS-VARIABLE DATA AMONG NONDICHOTOMOUS GROUPS

7.1 INTRODUCTION

Conceptually, the analysis of variance (ANOVA) is simply an expanded version of a t test. As you recall, the t test compares two means. The ANOVA makes a similar comparison, but can accommodate independent variables with more than two groups.

Example 7.1: ANOVA versus t Test If, for example, the researchers conducting the fishing study, referenced throughout Chapter 6, wish to compare the number of fish caught in three different environments, they could not use a t test. Although the t test suffices when comparing fishing success in freshwater and saltwater locations, it would not do so if the comparison involved three locations. An ANOVA, however, can compare an infinite number of means. The researchers would also need to use an ANOVA if they added additional independent variables. It seems reasonable that the type of bait used may also relate to the number of fish caught. An ANOVA could simultaneously compare the number of fish caught by individuals in each location and using different types of bait.

Analyzing Quantitative Data: An Introduction for Social Researchers, First Edition. Debra Wetcher-Hendricks.
© 2011 John Wiley & Sons, Inc. Published 2011 by John Wiley & Sons, Inc.

The similarities between t tests and ANOVAs usually provoke two questions for novice researchers.

1. You may wonder why you can't just always use an ANOVA, figuring that it should work for two groups in the same way that it works for more than two groups. In truth, it does. However, as you'll see from the formulas and calculations presented later in this chapter, performing an ANOVA involves much more work performing a t test does. (Of course, if you use a statistical software program to perform your tests, it doesn't really make much difference.) Those who, for some reason, use an ANOVA accidentally when a t test would have sufficed, can obtain t by finding the square root of F.

2. Another common question relates to the possibility of performing multiple t tests in place of an ANOVA. It may seem that comparing two groups at a time accomplishes the same thing as an ANOVA does. This strategy works sometimes, but not always. In particular, you can perform multiple t tests when the analysis involves only one independent variable. To compare means for four categories of an independent variable, for instance, you would need to perform six t tests on the basis of the following null hypotheses:

$$H_{0_1}: \mu_1 = \mu_2$$

$$H_{0_2}: \mu_1 = \mu_3$$

$$H_{0_3}: \mu_1 = \mu_4$$

$$H_{0_4}: \mu_3 = \mu_3$$

$$H_{0_5}: \mu_2 = \mu_4$$

$$H_{0_6}: \mu_3 = \mu_4$$

Even though each individual t test is less complicated than the ANOVA, performing so many consecutive t tests becomes rather tedious. The ANOVA examines all pairs of variables simultaneously. If the ANOVA indicates significance, you can further investigate the source of the significance with t tests, as explained in Section 7.4 of this chapter. But, by doing the omnibus ANOVA first, you can determine whether it is necessary to contrast pairs of categories with t tests.

The strategy of using multiple t tests in place of an ANOVA does *not* work when the study involves more than one independent variable. Section 7.3.2 of this chapter explains that significant ANOVA results may reflect interactions between independent variables. Multiple t tests cannot provide a complete analysis of significance because they do not address these interactions between the variables.

For all intents and purposes, then, you should use the ANOVA to test null hypotheses in the forms of

$$H_0: \mu_1 = \mu_2 = \mu_3 \cdots \mu_k$$

for which k represents the number of groups involved in the analysis. This null hypothesis predicts equality between the means of as many datasets as you wish to compare. Determining the source of significant results requires some post hoc testing, which receives attention later in this chapter. Should the ANOVA indicate a lack of significance, however, you can assume that no differences exist between means of individual categories or between means of combined categories.

The ANOVA produces an F statistic. Use of the F symbol honors Ronald Aylmer Fisher (1890–1962), who made great contributions to modern statistics. Interestingly, Fisher's technique of comparing group means doesn't directly involve means at all. Instead, as demonstrated in Section 7.3.1, it uses a ratio of the variation between group means to the variations of scores within the groups. This ratio constitutes the calculated F value. A comparison of the calculated F value to the critical F value indicates whether the ratio has occurred by chance.

7.2   THE F DISTRIBUTION

The decision about whether to accept or reject the null hypothesis for an ANOVA is based on the F distribution. This curve is a density function. It illustrates the probability of obtaining any F value using the calculations presented later in this chapter. The value of F indicates the size of the difference between category means, with large F values resulting from large differences and small F values resulting from small differences.

7.2.1   The F Distribution versus the Normal Distribution

If you performed multiple ANOVA tests and recorded the resulting F value for each test, you could use a histogram to display the frequencies of various F values. The outline of this histogram forms the F distribution.

Section 7.3.1 of this chapter explains that the F value is actually the ratio of two χ^2 values. As a result of its relationship to the χ^2 statistic, the F distribution resembles the χ^2 distribution, presented in Chapter 5. Both distributions are nonparametric, meaning that they do not necessarily follow the path of the normal curve (Fig. 7.1).

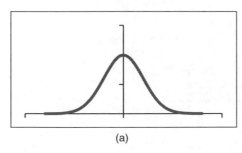
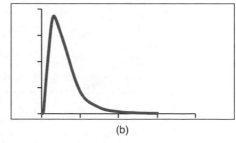

(a)   (b)

Figure 7.1. Normal distribution (a) versus F distribution (b). As evident from the graphs, the F distribution (b) differs from the normal distribution (a). F values appear along the x axis, and frequencies or probabilities appear along the y axis of the x distribution.

Most often, you will be concerned with *cumulative probabilities*, which are identi-fied by the area under the curve. You usually focus on the area under the curve to the right of or to the left of a particular F value on the x axis. The area under the curve to the right of a particular F value, called the *right-tail area*, indicates the probability of that F value occurring by chance. As the F value increases in size, this probability decreases. Your choice of α determines when this probability is small enough to reject the null hypothesis of equality between means. Section 7.2.3 further explains the rela-tionship between α, F, and the right-tail area.

7.2.2 Variations in the *F* Distribution

Changes in the appearance of the F distribution follow a general pattern similar to changes in the appearance of the χ^2 distribution. As sample sizes and, thus, degrees of freedom increase, the F distribution slowly loses its skewness. However, increasing the degrees of freedom is not as straightforward for the ANOVA as for the chi-square test. The ANOVA uses two types of degrees of freedom: one pertaining to the number of categories involved in the analysis and one pertaining to the number of subjects within each category. The F distribution's progression from the strongly skewed curve to the roughly normal curve reflect increases to both of these values (see Fig. 7.2).

The two degree of freedom (df) values, one pertaining to the numbers of subjects (n) in each category and one pertaining to the number of categories, influence the size of the residual. The *residual*, in this case, refers to disparities between scores within a particular category as well as the disparities between category means. Each added category has the potential for expanding the range of means being compared. So, an analysis involving many categories likely has a larger disparity between means than one with few categories does. A similar situation exists with respect to the number scores within each category. With each subject comes the possibility of a score that vastly differs from the others in that category. As the number of categories and the number of subjects within each category increase, residuals tend to increase.

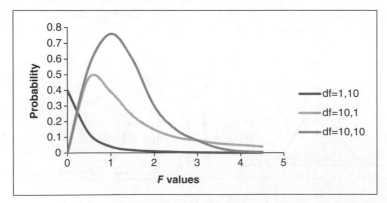

Figure 7.2. *F* distributions. The graph shows probability curves for *F* values with various degrees of freedom. The distribution begins to resemble the normal curve as degrees of freedom increase.

The residual plays a large part in the calculation of F. The numerator of the F ratio addresses the residual between categories, and the denominator of the F ratio addresses the residual within categories. Because of the relationship between the sizes of residuals and degrees of freedom, the value of F relies greatly on degrees of freedom. With small n values and a small number of categories, residuals between groups and within groups tend to differ only slightly. F distributions based on small category sizes and few categories are, therefore, generally tallest near $F = 1$. However, the addition of categories increases opportunities for disparities between mean category scores. These changes raise the value of the F ratio's numerator, which causes the overall F value to increase. As F values become larger, the tallest portion of the distribution slowly moves to the right until the curve resembles the normal distribution.

7.2.3 F Probabilities

Distinguishing between significant and nonsignificant F values requires the identification of a critical value. The critical F value creates right-tail area that contains the highest α proportion of F values. Values that lie in the right-tail area occur so rarely that they have no more than an α probability of resulting from random variation between means. If calculations produce an F value so large that it falls into the right-tail area of the distribution, you can reject your null hypothesis.

In Figure 7.3, the right-tail area, based on the standard of $\alpha = .05$, corresponds to calculated F values greater than or equal to the critical value of approximately 3.5. These values constitute the largest 5% of scores, which are the only ones indicating significant differences between means. With $\alpha = .05$, no more than a 5% chance of a type I error exists if F_{calc} falls into the right-tail area. For this example, an F_{calc} greater than 3.5 lies in the right-tail area and, thus, should lead to a rejected null hypothesis. Given these circumstances, less than 5% chance of incorrectly characterizing differences as significant exists. But an F_{calc} less than 3.5 should result in an accepted null

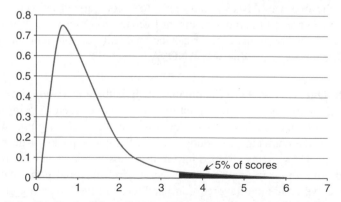

Figure 7.3. F distribution in right-tail area with $\alpha = .05$. The darkened right-tail area of the distribution contains values that lie in the highest 5% of the range of all F scores. The distinction between the highest 5% of scores and the remaining 95% of scores reflects the decision to use an α of .05.

hypothesis. Values less than 3.5 do not lie in the right-tail area, which suggests more than a 5% chance of incorrectly rejecting the null hypothesis.

Of course, α does not necessarily have to be .05. Your choice of α determines the size of the right-tail area in the F distribution. An α value smaller than .05 has a critical value higher than the $\alpha = .05$ critical value. Small α values create strict standards for rejecting the null hypothesis, but minimize the chances of making a type I error. On the other hand, if you have little concern about incorrectly characterizing a difference as significant, you can use an $\alpha > .05$, which increases the size of the right-tail area by lowering the critical value.

7.3 PERFORMING ANOVAs

The complexity of the ANOVA varies with the number of variables involved. Comparisons of means for a single variable's categories, such as the three groups of the location variable described in Example 7.1, require a one-way ANOVA, described in Section 7.3.1. If you wish to compare means of categories formed by combinations of variables, such as the location and bait variables also mentioned in Example 7.1, you would use a two-way ANOVA, described in Section 7.3.2. The ANOVA can expand to accommodate an infinite number of variables. The addition of each variable makes the ANOVA computations and analysis of results increasingly complex. However, as described in the following sections, these progressions follow very predictable and logical patterns.

7.3.1 One-Way ANOVA

The simplest test in the ANOVA family compares means from categories of a single independent variable. Statisticians refer to this test as the one-way ANOVA because subjects are divided into categories according to only one set of criteria. Section 7.1 explains that the one-way ANOVA can apply to a comparison between two means. However, most reserve it for comparing means from three or more categories. Situations involving one nondichotomous categorical independent variable and one continuous dependent variable, *require* a one-way ANOVA.

Example 7.2: One-Way ANOVA Scenario   Such a situation is exemplified by a study that attempts to determine whether a relationship exists between chewing-gum flavor and the amount of time it takes an individual to finish a pack of gum. Suppose that those conducting the chewing-gum study provide five-piece packs of gum to each of 24 randomly selected subjects, divided into four groups. Subjects in one group receive mint-flavored gum, those in another group receive fruit-flavored gum, and those in a third group receive cinnamon flavored gum, and those in the remaining group receive traditionally flavored bubble gum. Each subject must contact the researchers after finishing the five pieces of gum in the pack. The researchers record the number of days needed by each of the 24 subjects in each of the four groups to finish the pack of gum. These hypothetical values, as well as the category sums and means, appear as follows:

Flavor

Mint	Fruit	Cinnamon	Bubblegum
5	10	5	2
3	4	6	1
1	7	3	5
4	6	3	6
3	6	6	3
1	8	7	3
$\Sigma X_M = 17$	$\Sigma X_F = 41$	$\Sigma X_C = 30$	$\Sigma X_B = 20$
$\bar{X}_M = 2.83$	$\bar{X}_F = 6.83$	$\bar{X}_C = 5.00$	$\bar{X}_B = 3.33$

The ANOVA determines whether the four sample means differ enough to characterize the corresponding population means as different. Thus, an appropriate hypothesis for the ANOVA, based on four flavors of gum (mint, fruit, cinnamon, and traditionally flavored bubblegum) would appear as

$$H_0: \mu_M = \mu_F = \mu_C = \mu_B$$

Significant ANOVA results would lead to the rejection of this null hypothesis, and insignificant results would lead to the null hypothesis' acceptance.

This investigation would have obvious value to those involved in the candymaking/ marketing industry. Results of the one-way ANOVA comparison can help these individuals to adjust their production levels for the different flavors of gum as well as to determine the amount of each flavor supplied to retailers.

One-Way ANOVA Formulas. Unlike most of the other inferential statistics presented thus far in this book, the formula used to calculate F does not contain familiar values. F consists of the ratio of the mean-square between-groups value (MS_B) to the mean-square within-group value (MS_W):

$$F = \frac{MS_B}{MS_W} \tag{7.1}$$

MS_B recognizes distinctions between mean scores of the categories involved in the analysis. MS_W refers to the disparity of scores within each category. So, essentially, these values are measures of variation.

www.moravian.edu/aqd

The derivation of Equation (7.1), shown on this chapter's website, demonstrates how MS_B and MS_W provide the measures of variation needed for the ANOVA. Obtaining

MS_B and MS_W, however, requires a series of steps. Computation of these values as well as the F ratio follows the process outlined in Equations (7.2)–(7.10). Equation (7.11) restates Equation (7.1) in the context of the overall procedure. An example, using the chewing-gum data introduced in Example 7.2, accompanies each step in calculating F;

Step 1. Perform preliminary computations. Formulas at later stages in the process require knowledge of three values that you must calculate. It is best to calculate these values first. Then, you can easily substitute them into the relevant formulas without having to stop your momentum later for "side calculations."

 a. The most tedious preliminary computation involves finding the sum of squared values, ΣX^2. To begin, you must square each value in the dataset. Adding the squared values produces ΣX^2. This sum of squared values appears in the SS_T formula [Eq. (7.3)].

 b. The squared sum of values for each category, $(\Sigma X_k)^2$, appears in the SS_B formula [Eq. (7.4)]. This value differs slightly from the sum of squared values for each category. Obtaining each category's $(\Sigma X_k)^2$ requires first adding the data point values for that category and then squaring the sum.

 c. Another squared value, represented as C, appears in the formulas for both SS_T and SS_B. This value consists of the ratio between the squared sum of all values in the entire sample and the number of subjects. The following equation (7.2) provides the formula for C:

$$C = \frac{\left(\sum X\right)^2}{N} \tag{7.2}$$

Adding all values in the dataset and squaring this sum produces the numerator in Equation (7.2). The value of C consists of this squared sum divided by the total sample size.

Example 7.3: One-Way ANOVA Preliminary Calculations With respect to the chewing-gum data, calculations produce C as shown.

Step 1.

 a. Squaring each data point results in the following values. The sum of the squared values within each category constitutes $\sum X_k^2$ for that category.

$(\text{Mint})^2$	$(\text{Fruit})^2$	$(\text{Cinnamon})^2$	$(\text{Bubblegum})^2$
25	100	25	4
9	16	36	1
1	49	9	25
16	36	9	36
9	36	36	9

(Mint)^2	(Fruit)^2	(Cinnamon)^2	(Bubblegum)^2
1	64	49	9
$\Sigma X^2_M = 61$	$\Sigma X^2_F = 301$	$\Sigma X^2_C = 164$	$\Sigma X^2_B = 84$

b. Although obtaining $(\Sigma X)^2$ for each category also involves adding values and squaring, these operations take place in the opposite order as they do to obtain ΣX^2_k. Addition occurs first. Then, the sum for each category is squared:

$$\left(\sum X_M\right)^2 = 17^2 = 289$$

$$\left(\sum X_F\right)^2 = 41^2 = 1681$$

$$\left(\sum X_C\right)^2 = 30^2 = 900$$

$$\left(\sum X_B\right)^2 = 20^2 = 400$$

c. The numerator of the formula for C requires another arrangement of addition and squaring. Squaring takes place only after adding all values in the dataset. Category sums were obtained during the process of computing values in step 2 (above, in this example). It is easiest to simply add these values to obtain the sum of all values in the sample. This value is then squared and divided by N:

$$C = \frac{\left(\sum X\right)^2}{N} = \frac{(17+41+30+20)^2}{24} = \frac{108^2}{24} = 486.00$$

Step 2. Compute sample sums of squares. Three separate sum of squares values exist.

a. The *total sum of squares* (SS$_T$) acknowledges the differences between each individual score and all other scores in the sample:

$$SS_T = \sum X^2 - C \tag{7.3}$$

Simply subtracting the result from step 1c from the result of step 1a produces SS$_T$. The entire formula consists of values obtained during your preliminary calculations from step 1.

b. The *between-groups sum of squares* (SS$_B$) refers to differences between groups. It compares the scores from each category to the scores from the other categories in the sample:

$$SS_B = \frac{\left(\sum X_1\right)^2}{n_1} + \frac{\left(\sum X_2\right)^2}{n_2} + \cdots + \frac{\left(\sum X_k\right)^2}{n_k} + -C \tag{7.4}$$

This formula requires you to first divide the squared sum from each category by the number of subjects in that category and then subtract C from the sum of these quotients to produce the SS_B value. So, this formula utilizes results from steps 1b and 1c.

c. The *within-group sum of squares* (SS_W) contrasts each individual score from the others in its category. Researchers sometimes refer to the within-group sum of squares as the *error sum of squares* because it reflects random differences between individual data points within a category. Assuming that you have already calculated SS_T and SS_B, calculating SS_W requires only simple subtraction.

$$SS_W = SS_T - SS_B \tag{7.5}$$

If you calculated correctly, the sum of SS_B and SS_W should equal SS_T.

Example 7.4: One-way ANOVA Sum-of-Squares Calculations Calculations for the total sum of squares and the between groups sum of squares, respectively denoted in Equations (7.3) and (7.4), utilize the results from the preliminary computations performed in Example 7.3:

Step 2.

a. $SS_T = \Sigma X^2 - C = 610 - 486 = 124$

b.
$$SS_B = \frac{\left(\sum X_1\right)^2}{n_1} + \frac{\left(\sum X_2\right)^2}{n_2} + \cdots + \frac{\left(\sum X_k\right)^2}{n_k} + -C$$

$$= \frac{289}{6} + \frac{1681}{6} + \frac{900}{6} + \frac{400}{6} - 486 = 59$$

c. $SS_W = SS_T - SS_B = 124 - 59 = 65$

Step 3. Compute degrees of freedom. Each of the three sums of squares has a corresponding degree-of-freedom value:

$$df_T = N - 1 \tag{7.6}$$

$$df_B = K - 1 \tag{7.7}$$

$$df_W = N - K \tag{7.8}$$

To verify your calculations, add the values of df_B and df_W. The sum of these two values should equal df_T.

Example 7.5: One-Way ANOVA Degree-of-Freedom Calculations Equations (7.6), (7.7) and (7.8) provide the formulas to compute degrees of freedom that correspond to the three sum of squares values for the chewing-gum study:

$$df_T = N - 1 = 24 - 1 = 23$$

TABLE 7.1. ANOVA Summary Table[a]

Source	SS	df	MS	F
Between groups	SS_B	df_B	MS_B	F
Within group	SS_W	df_W	MS_W	
Total	SS_T	df_T	—	

[a]The table provides a structure for obtaining mean squares and the F statistic. Values for the sum of squares and degrees of freedom appear in rows labeled with the appropriate source of variation. Calculations using these values produce mean squares for each source as well as the F ratio.

$$df_B = K - 1 = 4 - 1 = 3$$
$$df_W = N - K = 24 - 4 = 20$$

Just as the sum of within-group and between-groups sum-of-squares values equal the total sum of squares, the sum of the within-group and between-groups degrees of freedom equals the total degrees of freedom.

Step 4. Create an ANOVA summary table (see Table 7.1). The table should contain a column that lists the sums of squares obtained in step 2 and a column that contains degrees of freedom obtained in step 3. You should also include columns labeled for mean square (MS) values and for the F statistic.

You already know the SS and df values. So, you can immediately insert them into the table. Use Equations (7.9), (7.10) and (7.11) to obtain values for MS_B, MS_W, and F, respectively.

$$MS_B = \frac{SS_B}{df_B} \qquad (7.9)$$

$$MS_W = \frac{SS_W}{df_W} \qquad (7.10)$$

$$F = \frac{MS_B}{MS_W} \qquad (7.11)$$

Example 7.6: One-Way ANOVA Summary Table   The sums of squares and degrees of freedom from Examples 7.4 and 7.5 can be placed in the summary table immediately (Table 7.2). Equations (7.9) and (7.10) provide the means to compute the between groups and within groups mean-square values. The F value consists of the ratio of the mean squares, as shown in Equation (7.11).

Interpreting the One-Way Calculated F Value. A *critical F* (F_{crit}) table provides values to which you must compare the calculated F obtained using Equation (7.11). The table organizes F_{crit} values according to between-groups degrees of freedom (df_B), the within-group degrees of freedom (df_W), and α.

TABLE 7.2. ANOVA Summary Table with Sample Data[a]

Source	SS	df	MS	F
Between	59	3	$MS_B = \dfrac{SS_B}{df_B} = \dfrac{59}{3} = 19.67$	
Within	65	20	$MS_W = \dfrac{SS_W}{df_W} = \dfrac{65}{20} = 3.25$	$F = \dfrac{MS_B}{MS_W} = \dfrac{19.67}{3.25} = 6.05$
Total	124	23		

[a]The SS and df columns contain values determined before creating the table. Formulas in the MS and F columns explain how to obtain these values. Researchers do not compute a total mean-square value as it plays no role in the computation of F.

Appendix D of this book provides one version of a critical F table. Other tables may arrange the critical values differently, but all critical F tables require knowledge of df_B, df_W, and α. Appendix D actually contains separate F tables for $\alpha = .10$, $\alpha = .05$, and $\alpha = .01$, the three most commonly used α values. So, you should begin by locating the correct table according to the α that you have chosen to use. Then, you should look for the appropriate df_B value along the top of the table and for the appropriate df_W value along the left of the table. The critical F appears at the intersection of the df_B (or df numerator) column and the df_W (or df denominator) row.

As with comparisons of the critical and calculated t or χ^2 values. A calculated value less than the critical value indicates no significant difference between population means, which should prompt you to accept the null hypothesis. You can reject the null hypothesis only when the calculated value equals or exceeds the critical value. In this situation, less than an α probability of incorrectly claiming that population means differ, otherwise known as a type I error, exists. Increasing the value of α allows you to improve your chances of rejecting the null hypothesis, but also improves the chances of making a type I error. Decreasing the value of α does just the opposite in that it lowers your chances of rejecting the null hypothesis, but also lowers the chances of making a type I error.

Example 7.7: Critical F Value Comparisons of Example 7.6's calculated F statistic of 6.05 to the critical F values from Appendix D indicate whether the means for the four types of gum differ significantly. For this study, the critical F values lie at the intersection of the column labeled "df = 3" and the row labeled "df = 20." The critical F value of 3.098 appears in this spot on the $\alpha = .05$ table. According to the rule that one rejects the null hypothesis when $F_{calc} > F_{crit}$, the researcher must reject the null hypothesis of equality between the four means. One can state that a significant difference exists with more than 95% certainty.

The rejected hypothesis at $\alpha = .05$ implies that a similar comparison using $\alpha = .10$ would also indicate significance. If a type I error has less than a 5% chance of occurring, then it certainly has greater than a 10% chance of occurring! Rejecting the null hypothesis at $\alpha = .10$ requires a smaller calculated F than needed to do so at $\alpha = .05$. (For the record, $_{.10}F_{3.20} = 2.380$, which verifies this logic.)

One who desires more than a 95% guarantee that a significant difference exists, however, may wish to decrease the α value. Using $\alpha = .01$ allows for only a 1% chance of making a type I error and, consequently, has the largest critical F value. For this particular example, the calculated value of 6.05 still exceeds the critical value of 4.938. But it does not do so as comfortably as in the $\alpha = .10$ or $\alpha = .05$. Still, even under the stringent conditions of $\alpha = .0176$, the researcher can claim that a significant difference exists between the mean amounts of days that it takes individuals to finish a pack of each of the four flavors of chewing gum.

The declaration that a significant difference exists actually raises more questions than it answers. Most evidently, you must determine the source of the significant difference. This issue didn't arise in the t-test situation because the analysis involves only two values, making the reason for the significant difference obvious. Significant differences obtained from an ANOVA can reflect disparities between any two means or any combinations of means involved in the analysis. Thus, when ANOVA results indicate a significant difference between means, post hoc testing must take place. Section 7.4 provides information about post hoc tests used to investigate sources of significant ANOVA results.

7.3.2 Two-or-More-Way ANOVA

Forms of ANOVA more complex than the one-way ANOVA can accommodate many independent variables. Just as the one-way ANOVA compares category means for one variable, a two-way ANOVA compares category means for two variables, a three-way ANOVA compares category means for three variables, and so on, using as many categories as needed. For the sake of a generic reference, the remainder of this chapter refers to ANOVAs that involve more than one independent variable as multiway ANOVAs.

To use multiway ANOVAs, all the independent variables must be categorical and the dependent variable must be continuous. The independent variables, essentially, separate subjects into groups within groups or, more succinctly, into subgroups.

Example 7.8: Data Subgroups   Such subgroups would exist if the researcher who performed the study presented in Example 7.3 expands the investigation to distinguish between sugarless and sugared gum. This investigation would compare the mean number of days it takes to finish packs of gum that fall into each combination of the sugar content and flavor categories. The researcher, therefore, needs to identify packs of gum not only by their flavor (M = mint; F = fruit; C = cinnamon; B = bubblegum), but also according to their sugar content (N = no sugar; S = sugar). So, each flavor grouping would contain subgroupings of sugarless and sugared gum. One could alternatively refer to flavor subgroupings within each sugar content category.

Factorial Designs. Data for a multiway ANOVA often appear in a *factorial design*. The factorial design resembles the crosstabulation, presented in Chapter 2 and discussed further in Chapter 5 of this book. As in the crosstabulation, each cell of the factorial represents a combination of two or more variables' categories. However, the contents of the factorial cells differ from the contents of the crosstabulation cells. Rather than providing the number of subjects that fall into a particular combination of categories, each cell of a factorial provides subject scores, sums of scores, or mean scores for those who fall into a particular category.

The arrangement of the factorial design depends on the number of independent variables present. For an investigation involving two independent variables, the factorial consists of rows and columns. Researchers describe such a factorial by referring to the number of rows (R) and the number of columns (C) as an "R by C factorial," denoted as $R \times C$.

Example 7.9: Factorial Design Assigning chewing-gum flavor to the column position and sugar content to the row position produces the 2×4 factorial shown in Table 7.3. According to this factorial design, half of the subjects in each flavor category received sugarless gum and half received sugared gum.

The multiway ANOVA compares row means, column means, and cell means. To prepare data for analysis, many researchers prefer to rearrange data into nested columns.

The formation shown in Table 7.4 makes it easy to identify the sums, squared sums, and means for scores in each category. All of these values have roles in the multiway ANOVA calculations.

A factorial applied to represent data from more than two independent variables uses layers in addition to rows and columns. Researchers would refer to a factorial for three variables as an $R \times C \times L$ factorial, in which R, C, and L respectively indicate the number of rows, columns, and levels. Such a factorial could take the form of a three-dimensional box or could appear as a double-nested or double-split design.

TABLE 7.3. 2×4 Factorial[a]

Sugar Content	Flavor				
	Mint	Fruit	Cinnamon	Bubblegum	Σ
Sugarless	5	10	5	2	—
	3	4	6	1	52
	1	7	3	5	—
Sugared	4	6	3	6	—
	3	6	6	3	56
	1	8	7	3	—
Σ	17	41	30	20	108

[a]Each cell in the factorial contains the scores of the three subjects in that particular combination of categories. When categories contain many subjects, the factorial cells may indicate the number of subjects (n) and mean for each category rather than listing individual scores.

TABLE 7.4. Two-Way ANOVA Data in Column Format[a]

Statistic	Sugarless Gum Flavor				Sugared Gum Flavor				Total
	Mint	Fruit	Cinnamon	Bubble	Mint	Fruit	Cinnamon	Bubble	
—	5	10	5	2	4	6	3	6	—
—	3	4	6	1	3	6	6	3	—
—	1	7	3	5	1	8	7	3	—
ΣX_{rc}	9	21	14	8	8	20	16	12	108
$\bar{X}_{rc}$	3.00	7.00	4.67	2.67	2.67	6.67	5.33	4.00	—
$\Sigma(X_{rc}^2)$	35	165	70	30	26	136	94	54	580

[a]The data points from Table 7.3 appear in columns, with each column containing the scores from one cell. Subscripts rc, in the notation for descriptive statistics, indicate the corresponding factorial row and column. The sum of scores, sum of squared scores, and mean for each cell from Table 7.3 appears at the end of the appropriate column in the table.

With the inclusion of each additional independent variable, the factorial design gains another layer. The number of layers and, hence, the number of elements included in references to the factorial increase as the number of independent variables increases. A study involving four independent variables, for instance, would produce a $R \times C \times L_1 \times L_2$ factorial.

Main Effects and Interaction Effects. The multiway ANOVA assesses more than just differences between means of the factorial's rows, columns, or layers. These differences are called *main effects*. Simply examining main effects would require nothing more complicated than a one-way ANOVA. However, when two or more independent variables exist, other effects, called *interactions*, exist as well and must receive attention.

An *interaction effect* indicates an inconsistency in the way that one subgroup's means change within the categories of an independent variable. The portion of the multiway ANOVA that addresses the interaction effect does not compare all subgroups' means to each other (the main effect portion of the ANOVA focuses on this aspect) but, rather, compares the pattern of changes in means within each category.

Line graphs can clarify this concept. To begin, consider a simpler situation than the one presented in Example 7.8. Given two independent variables, A and B, each with two categories, the two-way ANOVA compares four dependent-variable means. To put this hypothetical depiction into context, you can imagine that half of the subjects in the sample receive a stimulus and the other half do not, constituting two categories for variable A. Then, variable B identifies subjects by preexisting conditions (such as male and female), creating two subgroups within each of the two categories originally established by variable A (Table 7.5).

Each point on Figure 7.4 represents the mean for one of these groups. The position of these points with respect to the y axis indicates the value of the means. The x axis contains designations for the two conditions of variable A, receiving and not receiving the stimulus. The lines, themselves, represent subjects' variable B groups.

TABLE 7.5. Means for Two Dichotomous Variables[a]

		Variable B	
	Group	Category 1	Category 2
Variable A	Stimulus	$\bar{X}_{S1}$	$\bar{X}_{S2}$
	No stimulus	$\bar{X}_{N1}$	$\bar{X}_{N1}$

[a]Subjects are divided according to some preexisting condition and their contact with the stimulus. Half of those who receive the stimulus (the experimental group) fall into category 1, and half fall into category 2. Half of those who do not receive the stimulus (the control group) fall into category 1, and half fall into category 2.

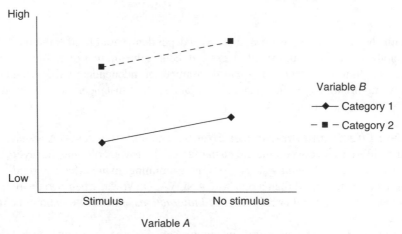

Figure 7.4. No interaction effect. For subjects in both of variable B's categories, the dependent-variable mean for those who did not receive the stimulus exceeds the mean for those who did receive the stimulus. The parallel lines suggest that this difference is consistent among both variable B categories. Thus, no interaction effect exists.

Figure 7.4 indicates no interaction effect. The parallel lines in the graph demonstrate a consistent difference in mean dependent-variable scores among subjects exposed to the stimulus and those not exposed to the stimulus regardless of their variable B categories. In both categories, subjects exposed to the stimulus have lower means than do those not exposed to the stimulus. Not only do "no stimulus" means exceed "stimulus" means in both cases; they do so by the same amount.

With only two categories per variable, as demonstrated in Figure 7.1, determining whether an interaction exists poses little challenge. If, however, one of your variables involves more than two groupings, your graph may contain disjointed lines or may contain more than two lines. You can assume that no interaction exists only if all cor-

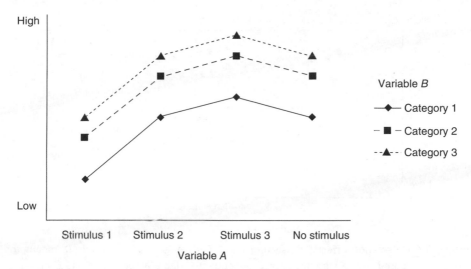

Figure 7.5. No interaction effect expansion. Each portion of the line representing a variable *B* category is parallel to its counterparts. The parallel lines indicate that differences between means are consistent among those in the three variable *B* categories. Thus, no interaction effect exists.

responding means remain relatively equidistant, as shown in Figure 7.5 (based on three categories within one variable and four categories within another).

Figures 7.4 and 7.5 represent situations in which subjects are classified according to only two criteria, variables *A* and *B*. But your study may also involve more than two independent variables. Assessing interaction effects for investigations involving more than two independent variables involves multi-dimensional graphs, but the same principle applies. All corresponding lines must remain parallel to signify the lack of an interaction.

Nonparallel lines, such as those in Figure 7.6, signify an interaction. According to this graph, the relationship between means for those who do and do not receive the stimulus does not remain consistent among categories of variable *B*. Mean dependent-variable scores for all those in category 1 and mean dependent-variable scores for all those in category 2 lie about midway between the "high" and "low" designations. But, among those in category 1, subjects who received the stimulus have low mean scores and subjects who received no stimuli have high mean scores; the opposite is true for those in category 2. This distinction reflects particular combinations of variable *A*'s stimulus condition and variable *B*'s categories, meaning that an interaction between the variables exists.

Even lines that do not blatantly intersect on the graph, itself, can indicate an interaction effect. The lines in Figure 7.7 depict inconsistency in patterns in which means vary across the independent-variables categories. Although the lines do not intersect, you can clearly see that means for subjects each of variable *B*'s categories do not follow similar patterns of change with respect to the stimulus.

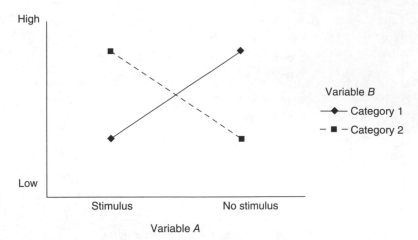

Figure 7.6. Interaction effect (intersecting lines). For category 1 of variable *B*, means for those not exposed to the stimulus exceed dependent-variable means for those exposed to the stimulus. However, the opposite situation characterizes those in category 2 of variable *B*. The intersecting lines indicate a change in the order of means for those in variable *B* categories.

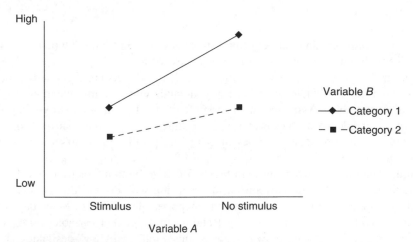

Figure 7.7. Interaction effect (nonintersecting lines). The dependent-variable means for those in category 1 of variable *B* exceed the mean for those in category 2 with respect to both of variable *A*'s conditions. The different slopes of the lines, however, indicate inconsistencies in the sizes of the differences between means for the two categories.

When an interaction exists, results of the omnibus multiway ANOVA indicate significance. A one-way ANOVA would fail to find such significance because it can test only for main effects. It may appear, from an examination of main effects only, that no significant differences exist. As explained earlier, an examination of Figure 7.6 suggests that the overall mean for those in category 1 of variable *B* (the combination of those who did and did not receive the stimulus) likely does not differ significantly from the overall mean of those in category 2. Similarly, the overall mean of those exposed to the stimulus (the combination of those from categories 1 and 2) does not differ significantly from the mean of those subjects exposed to the stimulus. It is only when you compare the means for each of the variable's subgroups that significance becomes evident. The nonparallel lines in Figures 7.6 and 7.7 indicate different dependent-variable scores based not only on category or stimulus condition but also on particular combinations of the two. The interaction of this category and stimulus leads to a difference in scores of the subgroups, which manifests itself as significant multiway ANOVA results.

Two-Way ANOVA Formulas. The procedure for performing a multiway ANOVA follows the same general blueprint as does the procedure for performing a one-way ANOVA. You must first perform preliminary calculations. Using the values obtained by the preliminary calculations and the appropriate formulas, you can obtain sum-of-squares and degree-of-freedom values. Then, you can create an ANOVA summary table in which you compute mean-square values and, ultimately, the F ratio. Finally, comparison of the F ratio that appears in the table to the critical F value indicates whether you should accept or reject the null hypothesis.

Each of these steps, however, is more complicated for the multiway ANOVA than for the one-way ANOVA. To account for main effects of more than one independent variable as well as interaction effects between variables, the multiway ANOVA involves more comparisons, resulting in more sum-of-squares and degree-of-freedom formulas than needed for the one-way situation. The following steps, each accompanied by an example based on the chewing-gum data presented in Example 7.9, outlines the procedures for obtaining the F values for a two-way ANOVA. Expansions to these steps can adjust the procedure to account for studies involving more than two independent variables.

Step 1. Perform preliminary computations. Beginning with calculations of the descriptive statistics needed for the sum-of-squares formulas allows for easy substitution in step 2 of this process.

    a. Sum-of-squares formulas require knowledge of the sum of all values in the dataset, denoted as ΣX or T. If you have arranged your data as shown in Table 7.4, you can find this value at the end of the row labeled ΣX_{rc}.

    b. T^2 represents represents the sum-of-squares values for the entire sample. With data arranged as shown in Table 7.4, obtaining T^2 appears at the end of the row labeled $\Sigma(X_{rc}^2)$.

    c. In addition to the sum-of-squares (SS) values for all cells, you must compute the values for the rows, $(T_{R.}^2)$, and columns $(T_{.C}^2)$. These values differ from T^2 because they require addition of row or column values *before* squaring takes place.

$$T_{R.}^2 = \sum\left(\sum X_{r.}^2\right) \tag{7.16}$$

$$T_{.C}^2 = \sum \left(\sum X_{.c}^2 \right) \tag{7.17}$$

Luckily, the marginal values in the factorial, in Table 7.3, provide the sum of values for each column and row, $\Sigma X_{.C}$ and $\Sigma X_{R.}$, respectively. Squaring these values and adding the results provides the needed quantities.

d. To compute the necessary sum-of-squares values, you must also obtain the squared sums of values for each cell in the crosstabulation, represented as T_{RC}^2. You can use the following formula to do so:

$$T_{RC}^2 = \sum \left(\sum X_{RC}^2 \right) \tag{7.18}$$

The row labeled ΣX_{RC} in Table 7.4 contains sums of values for each cell. Equation (7.18) instructs you to square each of these values and then add. Notice that, in contrast to the procedure used to obtain ΣX^2, calculating T_{RC}^2 requires adding the scores in each cell *before* squaring.

Example 7.10: Two-Way ANOVA Preliminary Computations   Some preliminary computations using the data from Example 7.9, specifically those for ΣX and T^2, have already taken place. Others require some arithmetic.

Step 1.

a. The value of ΣX, sometimes represented as T, represents the sum of all individual scores in the sample, in this case 108. It should appear at the end of the row labeled ΣX_{rc}.

b. The value of T^2 represents the sum-of-squares scores in the entire sample. It should appear at the end of the row labeled $\Sigma(X_{rc}^2)$ in the column format of the two-way ANOVA data. For this example, $T^2 = 580$.

c. Inserting marginal row values from the factorial into Equation (7.16) produces $T_{R.}^2$:

$$T_{R.}^2 = \sum \left(\sum X_{r.}^2 \right) = 52^2 + 56^2 = 5840$$

Inserting marginal column values from the factorial into Equation (7.17) produces $T_{.C}^2$.

$$T_{.C}^2 = \sum \left(\sum X_{.c}^2 \right) = 17^2 + 41^2 + 30^2 + 20^2 = 3270$$

d. The summed squares of all cell totals, as shown below, constitutes T_{RC}^2:

$$T_{RC}^2 = \sum \left(\sum X_{RC}^2 \right) = 9^2 + 21^2 + 14^2 + 8^2 + 8^2 + 20^2 + 16^2 + 12^2 = 1646$$

Step 2. Compute mediating values. The mediating values are patterns of the values obtained in step 1 of this process and appear repeatedly in the sum-of-squares formula, similar to the role that C played in many formulas for the one-way test. Computing the mediating values minimizes the amount of calculations needed after substitution into the sum-of-squares formulas.

a.
$$[T] = \frac{\left(\sum X\right)^2}{N} \tag{7.19}$$

This formula requires you to first add all values in the dataset, producing the value described in step 1a. Then, you must square this sum and divide the squared value by the total number of subjects in the sample:

b.
$$[X] = S(X^2) \tag{7.20}$$

Formally, the equation for $[X]$ requires division of $\Sigma(X^2)$ by 1. However, because dividing by 1 does not change the value of the dividend, step 1b has already produced this value:

c.
$$[R] = \frac{T_{R.}^2}{nC} \tag{7.21}$$

Equation (7.16) produces the value for the numerator of this equation. The denominator consists of the product of the number of subjects in each cell and the number of columns in the factorial:

d.
$$[C] = \frac{T_{.C}^2}{nR} \tag{7.22}$$

Equation (7.17) produces the value for the numerator of this equation. The denominator consists of the product of the number of subjects in each cell and the number of rows in the factorial:

e.
$$[RC] = \frac{T_{RC}^2}{n} \tag{7.23}$$

Equation (7.18) produces the value for the numerator of this equation. The denominator consists of the number of subjects in each cell.

Example 7.11: Two-Way ANOVA Mediating Values Calculations   For the two-variable chewing-gum example, Equations (7.19)–(7.23) require calculations involving the preliminary values obtained in Example 7.10.

Step 2.

a. The value of $[T]$ represents the ratio of $(\Sigma X)^2$ to the total number of subjects in the sample:

$$[T] = \frac{\left(\sum X\right)^2}{N} = \frac{108^2}{24} = 486$$

b. This value has actually already been computed in step 1b. It consists of the sum of all squared values in the sample:

$$[X] = \sum (X^2) = 580$$

c. The formula for $[R]$ requires the division of $T_{R.}^2$ by the total number of subjects in each row of the factorial. Step 1c produces the first of these values. Multiplying the number of subjects in each cell (n) by the number of columns (C) provides the denominator for the equation:

$$[R] = \frac{T_{R.}^2}{nC} = \frac{5840}{(3)(4)} = 486.67$$

d. As the counterpart to $[R]$, $[C]$ results from dividing $T_{.C}^2$, computed in step 1d by the total number of subjects in each column of the factorial. The second of these values consists of the product of the number of subjects in each cell (n) and the number of rows (R) in the factorial:

$$[C] = \frac{T_{.C}^2}{nR} = \frac{3270}{(3)(2)} = 545$$

e. The mediating value representing the interaction effect focuses on within-cell variations. The respective formula uses two known values T_{RC}^2, available from step 1e, and the number of subjects in each cell of the factorial:

$$[RC] = \frac{T_{RC}^2}{n} = \frac{1646}{3} = 548.67$$

Step 3. Compute sums of squares. For a two-way ANOVA, five separate sum-of-squares values exist. Four of these five values represent differences similar to those that exist in the one-way situation. The fifth sum of squares pertains to interaction effects:

a. The *total sum of squares* (SS$_T$) acknowledges the differences between each individual score and all others in the sample. Essentially, it combines elements of all other sums of squares:

$$\text{SS}_T = [X] - [T] \qquad\qquad (7.24)$$

b. The one-way ANOVA, which had to account for differences on the basis of only one variable, compared category means for that one variable using a between-groups sum of squares. But a two-way ANOVA must address main effects among categories of each of the two individual variables. The two-way ANOVA's *row sum of squares* (SS_R) accounts for half of the one-way's between-groups sum of squares. SS_R compares the scores from each row to the scores from the other rows in the sample:

$$SS_R = [R]-[T] \qquad (7.25)$$

c. The *column sum of squares* (SS_C) accompanies the row sum of squares. SS_C compares the mean value for each column to those for the other columns in the factorial. When considered together, the column sum of squares and the row sum of squares describe main effects, specifically contrasting groups of each variable:

$$SS_C = [C]-[T] \qquad (7.26)$$

d. To compare the means for subgroups, otherwise known as *interaction effects*, you must compute the *interaction sum of squares* ($SS_{R \times C}$). This value summarizes the differences between each combination of the two variables' categories, represented by a particular cell, and the other cells in the factorial:

$$SS_{R \times C} = [RC]+[T]-[R]-[C] \qquad (7.27)$$

e. The two-way ANOVA's counterpart to the one-way's *within-group sum of squares*, is sometimes called the *error sum of squares*. It compares each individual score to the other scores within its factorial cell. The notation for the within-group sum of squares ($SS_{S/RC}$), indicates the focus on each particular subject within a row–column combination.

$$SS_{S/RC} = [X]-[RC] \qquad (7.28)$$

SS_T should equal the sum of all other SS values. This phenomenon reflects the fact that the total sum of squares addresses the disparity between the largest collection of scores, namely, the mean for the entire sample, and scores pertaining to individual subjects. The other sum-of-squares values provide summaries of disparities for various assemblages of scores between these two extremes.

Example 7.12: Two-Way ANOVA Sum-of-Squares Calculations   Substituting the appropriate mediating values from Example 7.11 into Equations (7.24)–(7.28) allows for computation of the sums of squares needed for the two-way ANOVA table:

Step 3.

    a. Steps 2a and 2b provide the values needed to compute the total sum of squares. The value of SS_T represents the discrepancy between mean time for those in each cell of the factorial and the overall sample mean, which includes those with each flavor–sugar content combination:

$$SS_T = [X] - [T] = 580 - 486 = 94$$

    b. The formula for the row sum of squares is defined as the difference between $[R]$ and $[T]$. SS_R represents the disparities between the entire sample mean and the row means:

$$SS_R = [R] - [T] = 486.67 - 486 = 0.67$$

For the example at hand, SS_R contrasts number of days it takes to finish packs of gum in each sugar content category from the number of days it takes to finish all packs of all types of gum.

    c. The value that emerges from the formula for the column sum of squares represents disparities between the sample mean and column means:

$$SS_R = [C] - [T] = 545 - 486 = 59$$

For the example at hand, it contrasts the number of days it takes to finish packs of gum in each flavor from the number of days it takes to finish all packs of all types of gum.

    d. The interaction sum of squares is the most complex of the sum of squares values in terms of both its meaning and its formula. This value pertains to contrasts between each cell in the factorial and all of the other cells. As such, the formula makes reference to cell, row, column, and the overall sample means:

$$SS_{R \times C} = [RC] + [T] - [R] - [C] = 548.67 + 486 = 486.67 - 545 = 3$$

    e. The difference between $[X]$, corresponding to individual scores, and $[RC]$, corresponding to cell means, produces a value that describes the variation within cells:

$$SS_{S/RC} = [X] - [RC] = 580 - 548.67 = 31.33$$

The within-group sum of squares exists as the most intricate measure of disparities, comparing the mean number of days needed for those with the exact same types of chewing gum to finish the packs that they receive.

It is good practice to confirm that $SS_R + SS_C + SS_{RC} + SS_{S/RC} = SS_T$. For this example, $0.67 + 59 + 3 + 31.33 = 94$.

Step 4. Compute degrees of freedom. Each of the five sums of squares has a corresponding degree-of-freedom value:

$$df_T = N - 1 \tag{7.29}$$

$$df_R = R - 1 \tag{7.30}$$

$$df_C = C - 1 \tag{7.31}$$

$$df_{R \times C} = (C - 1)(R - 1) \tag{7.32}$$

$$df_{S/RC} = (R)(C)(n - 1) \tag{7.33}$$

Verify your calculations by checking to ensure that the value of df_T equals the sum of all other df values.

Example 7.13: Two-Way ANOVA Degree-of-Freedom Calculation   The following computations, based on cell, row, column, and sample sizes from Figure 7.5, provide degrees of freedom for the chewing-gum study:

$$df_T = N - 1 = 24 - 1 = 23$$

$$df_R = R - 1 = 2 - 1 = 1$$

$$df_C = 4 - 1 = 3$$

$$df_{R \times C} = (C - 1)(R - 1) = (2 - 1)(4 - 1) = 3$$

$$df_{S/RC} = (R)(C)(n - 1) = (2)(4)(3 - 1) = 16$$

The values of df_R, df_C, $df_{R \times C}$, and $df_{S/RC}$ should always sum to df_T, as they do in this example.

Step 5. Create an ANOVA summary table (see Table 7.6). The table should contain a column that lists the sums of squares obtained in step 3 and a column that contains degrees of freedom obtained in step 4. You should also include columns labeled for mean-square values and for the calculated F statistic. The two-way ANOVA produces three F values, one representing the difference between category means of the "row" variable, one representing the difference between category means of the "column" variable, and one representing differences between cell means.

You already know the SS and df values. So, you can immediately insert them into the table. Dividing these values as shown in Equations (7.34)–(7.37) produces MS_R, MS_C, $MS_{R \times C}$, and $MS_{S/RC}$. You need not compute total mean squares.

$$MS_R = \frac{SS_R}{df_R} \tag{7.34}$$

TABLE 7.6. Two-Way ANOVA Summary Table[a]

Source	SS	df	MS	F_{calc}
Row (R)	SS_R	df_R	MS_R	F_R
Column (C)	SS_C	df_C	MS_C	F_C
Interaction ($R \times C$)	$SS_{R \times C}$	$df_{R \times C}$	$MS_{R \times C}$	$F_{R \times C}$
Within-group (S/RC)	$SS_{S/RC}$	$df_{S/RC}$	$MS_{S/RC}$	—
Total	SS_T	df_T	—	—

[a]This table provides a structure for obtaining mean squares and the F statistics for columns, rows, and interaction effects. Values for the sum of squares and degrees of freedom appear in rows labeled with the appropriate source of variation. Calculations with these values produce mean squares for each source as well as the F ratios.

$$MS_C = \frac{SS_C}{df_C} \tag{7.35}$$

$$MS_{R \times C} = \frac{SS_{R \times C}}{df_{R \times C}} \tag{7.36}$$

$$MS_{S/RC} = \frac{SS_{S/RC}}{df_{S/RC}} \tag{7.37}$$

The within groups mean square value serves as the denominator for all F ratios. Computing each F ratio, then, involves dividing MS_R, MS_C, or $MS_{R \times C}$, by $MS_{S/RC}$. Equations 7.38 through 7.40 present the relevant formulas.

$$F_R = \frac{MS_R}{MS_{S/RC}} \tag{7.38}$$

$$F_C = \frac{MS_C}{MS_{S/RC}} \tag{7.39}$$

$$F_{R \times C} = \frac{MS_{R \times C}}{MS_{S/RC}} \tag{7.40}$$

Example 7.14: Two-Way ANOVA Summary Table   The ANOVA table 7.7 contains the sum-of-squares values from Example 7.12 and the values from Example 7.14, as well as mean-square and F values. Calculations for the mean-square and F values, using data from the chewing-gum study, are also given.

Interpreting the Two-Way Calculated **F** *Value.*   Each of the three F values that emerges from the two-way ANOVA requires individual attention. With respect to the degrees of freedom used to calculate each, you must obtain the critical F value and compare this value to the calculated value. The comparison using F_R indicates whether significant difference exists among means for the categories of the variable assigned to

TABLE 7.7. Two-Way ANOVA Summary Table with Sample Data[a]

Source	SS	df	MS	F_{calc}
Row (R)	0.67	1	$\dfrac{\text{SS}_R}{\text{df}_R} = 0.67$	$\dfrac{\text{MS}_R}{\text{df}_{S/RC}} = 0.34$
Column (C)	59	3	$\dfrac{\text{SS}_C}{\text{df}_C} = 19.67$	$\dfrac{\text{MS}_C}{\text{df}_{S/RC}} = 10.36$
Interaction ($R \times C$)	3	3	$\dfrac{\text{SS}_{R \times C}}{\text{df}_{R \times C}} = 1$	$\dfrac{\text{MS}_{R \times C}}{\text{df}_{S/RC}} = 0.51$
Within-group (S/RC)	31.33	16	$\dfrac{\text{SS}_{S/RC}}{\text{df}_{S/RC}} = 1.96$	
Total	94	23		

[a]This table presents F statistics for effects of chewing-gum sugar content, flavor, and the interaction between the two. Information in the MS and F columns explains how to obtain these values. Researchers do not compute a total mean-square value as it has no role in the computations of F.

the row position in the factorial. The comparison using F_C indicates whether significant difference exists among means for the categories of the variable assigned to the column position in the factorial. The comparison using $F_{R \times C}$ indicates whether significant difference exists among means for the cells in the factorial. In all cases, a calculated F value that exceeds the critical F value suggests significance.

The same table used for one-way ANOVAs, located in Appendix D of this book, provides critical values for multiway ANOVAs. The degree-of-freedom values listed along the left side of the table represent the $\text{df}_{S/RC}$, or, as sometimes labeled, the degrees of freedom associated with the denominator of the F ratio. Accordingly, then, the values that appear along the top of the table pertain to the degrees of freedom associated with the numerator of each F ratio, either df_R, df_C, or $\text{df}_{R \times C}$. Each effect, thus, has its own critical F to compare to the corresponding calculated F.

Unless you have some compelling reason to change the value of α, you should use the same α value for all tests within a two-way ANOVA. An accepted null hypothesis for the two-way ANOVA at the chosen α reflects insignificant row, column, and interaction effects. If any of the calculated F ratios exceed the critical values, then you must reject the omnibus hypothesis of equality between sample means.

Example 7.15: Two-Way ANOVA F values pertaining to the factorial design involving chewing-gum sugar content and flavor represent effects for each of these two independent variables as well as the interaction between them.

Comparisons between each calculated F value and the corresponding critical value indicate whether its means differ significantly. The critical F pertaining to the row effect is based on 1 numerator degree of freedom and 16 denominator degrees of freedom. You would find the critical value for this portion of the analysis at the intersection of the column labeled "1" and the row labeled "16" on the appropriate critical F table. Using the standard α of .05, the critical $_{.05}F_{1,16}$ is 4.49. In this particular analysis, the tests for column and interaction effects both have 3 numerator degrees of freedom and 16 denominator degrees of freedom. The critical F value for this portion of the analysis, therefore, appears at the interaction of the column labeled "3" and the row labeled "16" on the critical F table that appears in Appendix D. $_{.05}F_{3,16} = 2.34$.

A critical value that exceeds the calculated value suggests no significant difference. This situation exists with respect to row and interaction effects. The calculations in Example 7.14 produce a calculated F_R of 0.34, which is smaller than the $_{05}F_{1,16}$ of 4.49. Similarly, the calculated $F_{R\times C}$ of 0.51, also shown in Example 7.14, does not exceed the $_{05}F_{3,16}$ of 2.34. Thus, one could conclude that no row or interaction effects exist. A column effect, however, *does* exist. The calculated F_C of 7.15 from Example 7.14 greatly exceeds the $_{05}F_{1,16}$ of 2.34. In summary, any difference between the times needed to finish packs of sugared or sugarless gum or to finish packs of gum in each of the eight combinations of sugar content and flavor are so small that they cannot be considered significant. However, when ignoring sugar content and considering subjects only on the basis of the flavor of gum that they received, group means differ significantly.

The α value may have to be changed to suit the researcher's purposes as long as she or he considers type I error issues. An α of .10 provides a greater chance of rejecting the investigation's null hypotheses than $\alpha = .05$ does. The tradeoff for this leniency is the increased probability of making a type I error. To minimize the chances of making a type I error, you may opt to use an α value of .01, which allows for fewer rejected hypotheses than does $\alpha = .05$. Interestingly, though, the results of the chewing-gum study remain the same at all three of these α levels. For each of these α values, F_R and $F_{R\times C}$ remain below the critical value and F_C lies above the critical value. Because at least one of these tests indicated significance, one must reject the null hypothesis tested by the two-way ANOVA.

Once again, the next step in the analysis depends on the results of the multiway ANOVA. No further testing must take place when all critical F values exceed their respective calculated F values. In this situation, you can move to the process of explaining and reasoning about the insignificance between category means. A rejected null hypothesis, reflecting significant results for some effect, however, demands post hoc testing. The portions of the multiway ANOVA that drive a rejected null hypothesis provide hints regarding a starting point for post hoc testing. Section 7.4.2 contains information about post hoc tests for ANOVAs involving two or more independent variables.

7.4   POST HOC TESTING

Chapter 5 of this book explains post hoc testing in the context of chi-square tests. The same principles apply to post hoc tests following an ANOVA. The tests determine why the original, or omnibus, test identified a significant difference. The omnibus difference may reflect a disparity between two individual categories, one category and the remainder of the sample, or one combination of categories compared to another. Post hoc testing compares independent-variable categories or combinations of independent-variable categories with the hopes of finding at least one source of the significant omnibus results.

7.4.1 One-Way ANOVA Post Hoc Tests

Examining the descriptive statistics for each category may help you determine the starting point for the post hoc tests. Because the one-way ANOVA considers categories of a single independent variable, you may easily notice a blatant disparity between category means. This difference should become the basis of your first post hoc comparison. If this comparison yields significant results, then you have successfully found at least one reason for the rejected omnibus hypothesis. Insignificant results from this comparison require you to perform additional post hoc tests, contrasting various categories or combinations of categories, until you find the source of the omnibus significance. Sometimes, you need to perform many post hoc tests before finding this source.

The actual post hoc tests for an omnibus ANOVA test require t tests because they involve comparisons between two values. The simplest post hoc tests compare means from two individual categories. In this case, you can just substitute the means and standard deviations for these categories into the t-test formulas presented in Chapter 6. When your post hoc tests involve comparisons between combinations of categories, though, you must recalculate means, standard deviations, and sample sizes before using these formulas.

Example 7.16: Post Hoc Tests for One-Way ANOVA Post hoc tests for the rejected null hypothesis that packs of the four different flavors of gum last the same number of days requires this sort of contemplation. One can easily see that the means for fruit-flavored ($\overline{X}_F = 6.83$) and for cinnamon-flavored ($\overline{X}_C = 5.00$) gum lie well above the means for mint-flavored $\overline{X}_M = 2.83$) and bubblegum-flavored ($\overline{X}_B = 3.33$) gum. Comparing the combined mean for the fruit and cinnamon flavors ($\overline{X}_{FC} = 5.92$) to the combined mean for the mint and bubblegum flavors ($\overline{X}_{MB} = 3.72$), therefore, seems a reasonable point at which to begin the post hoc comparisons.

The t test applied compare $\overline{X}_{FC}$ to $\overline{X}_{MB}$ uses Equations (6.5) and (6.6). Each of these combined means and the corresponding sample sizes, which are both 12, fit into these formulas. The formulas also require knowledge of each category's standard deviation. Equation (3.2) produces a standard deviation value of 2.02 for the fruit/cinnamon-flavored category and a standard deviation value of 1.68 for the mint/bubblegum-flavored category. The pooled variance (s_p), a component of the t-test formula, relies on these values. Calculations using Equation (6.7) provide a pooled variance of 1.85. The calculations below, based on Equation (6.5), demonstrate the remainder of the process for obtaining t_{calc}:

$$t_{calc} = \frac{\overline{X}_1 - \overline{X}_2}{s_p \sqrt{(1/n_1) + (1/n_2)}} = \frac{5.92 - 3.72}{1.85\sqrt{\dfrac{1}{12} + \dfrac{1}{12}}} = \frac{2.84}{.76} = 3.74$$

You must also calculate the degrees of freedom using Equation (6.6).

$$df = n_1 + n_2 - 2 = 12 + 12 - 2 = 22$$

The $\alpha = .05$ critical value, using 22 degrees of freedom is 1.72. Because $t_{calc} > t_{crit}$, the difference between the combined mean for fruit/cinnamon-flavored gum and the mean for mint/bubblegum flavor qualifies as significant. This difference explains at least part of the reason for the rejected omnibus hypothesis. Other sources of difference, perhaps between mean scores for individual categories or mean scores for combinations of categories other than the one addressed in this example, may exist as well.

Had this particular investigation indicated that the means compared do not differ significantly, other comparisons must take place. The researcher should continue post hoc tests using different arrangements of means until the post hoc t test provides significant results.

7.4.2 Two-or-More-Way ANOVA Post Hoc Tests

Sources of significant results for an ANOVA involving more than one independent variable may exist among the categories of any variable involved or among interactions between variables. Post hoc testing for a rejected omnibus hypothesis should not include comparisons of effects for which the calculated F value does not exceed the critical value. If, for example, $F_R < F_{crit}$, then you can assume that row means do not differ significantly. Because differences between row means to contribute to the overall significant difference, performing post hoc comparisons of row means will never yield a rejected hypothesis. Instead, you should focus your post hoc tests on the effects deemed significant according to values in the ANOVA summary table.

Example 7.17: Post Hoc Tests for Two-Way ANOVA The two-way ANOVA summary table shown in Example 7.14 suggests that the source of the overall significance lies in differences between columns, which pertain to flavors of chewing gum. This fact should come as no surprise because the flavor categories differed significantly in the one-way ANOVA shown in Examples (7.3)–(7.6).

Just as the difference between fruit-flavored gum and the other flavors of gum helped to explain the rejected omnibus hypothesis for the one-way ANOVA (See example 7.16), it helps to explain the rejected omnibus hypothesis for the two-way ANOVA. This disparity, however, may not be the only reason for the significant omnibus results. Differences between other categories or other combinations of categories may also play a role. Therefore, researchers must use care when describing the sources of significance. They cannot describe a particular difference between categories as *the* reason for a rejected omnibus test, but rather as a contributing factor to the rejection.

On uncovering a source of the significant omnibus difference, you may choose to end your post hoc analyses or to continue searching for additional sources. You should base this choice on your audience and the rationale for your study. If you choose to continue your post hoc analysis, you should try to explain each effect deemed significant by the two-way ANOVA. In the case of the two-way ANOVA using the chewing-gum data, you needed only to examine column means. However, if the ANOVA results had indicated that a row effect, a column effect, and an interaction effect exist, you would have needed to search for a significant difference between row means, between column means, and between cell means.

7.5 CONFIDENCE INTERVALS

Researchers often wish to know the range of F_{calc} values that lead to an accepted null hypothesis. These values are less than F_{crit} and, thus, lie to the left of the right-tail area on the F distribution. An F_{calc} in this range reflects a difference between means that has more than an α probability of occurring by chance. Because the F distribution lies entirely to the right of the y axis, the lowest value in the confidence interval is always 0. F_{crit} forms the upper boundary.

If your calculations produce any of these values at the $\alpha = .05$ level of significance, you can accept the null hypothesis with 95% confidence. Hence, this range is called the 95% *confidence interval*. F_{calc} values that lie within this range lead to an accepted null hypothesis because they lie to the left of the right-tail area on the F distribution. With α-.05, only the 5% of scores that lie in the right-tail area lead to a rejected null hypothesis.

Example 7.18: Confidence Interval   The 95% confidence interval for the one-way ANOVA presented in Examples 7.3–7.6 include the range of values from 0 to 3.098, formally written as CI:$[0 < F < 3.098]$. The fact that the one-way ANOVA's F_{calc} of 6.05 led to a rejected null hypothesis (see Example 7.7) should come as no surprise. It lies well outside of the 95% confidence interval, indicating less than a 5% chance that the differences between means reflect something other than the effects being examined.

The size of the confidence interval can change according to the α value used. A 90% confidence interval contains F values that correspond to differences in means that have as much as a .10 probability of occurring by chance. Consequently, the highest 10% of F scores lie in the right-tail area and the F_{crit} value that serves as the lower boundary of the right-tail area lies farther to the left of the distribution when $\alpha = .10$ than when $\alpha = .05$. Thus, a 90% confidence interval, based on an α value of .10, is smaller than a 95% confidence interval, leading to an increase in the number of rejected null hypotheses. However, by basing your analysis on a significance value of .10, you allow as much as a 10% percent chance of incorrectly rejecting the null hypothesis.

Using an α smaller than .05 has the opposite effect in that it increases the size of the confidence interval. An α of .01, for instance, allows you to reject the null hypothesis only if F_{calc} lies within the highest 1% of scores. So, the right-tail area contains only the highest 1% of F scores. The remaining F_{calc} values, which lie between 0 and F_{crit}, constitute the 99% confidence interval. Should your ANOVA produce any of these values, you can reject the null hypothesis with 99% confidence that the differences between means occurred by chance.

7.6   EXPLAINING RESULTS OF THE ANOVA

Before presenting results of the ANOVA test, you should provide your audience with basic information about your sample and the data that it produced. All reports of data analysis should identify the category sizes for each categorical variable and, when necessary, describe the scale used for each continuous variable. To fully understand ANOVA comparisons, the audience also needs to know the mean dependent-variable score for each independent-variable category or combination of independent-variable categories. It is not uncommon for standard deviations to accompany each of these mean values.

You can provide means and standard deviations either before presenting the ANOVA results or within the context of describing significant and insignificant differences. In the first of these techniques, all categories, including, and their means standard deviations, are provided simultaneously, either within the text or, in the case of multiple independent variables, by providing a factorial diagram.

Example 7.19: Reporting Category Means and Standard Deviations   The results of the one-way ANOVA introduced in Example 7.3 could begin with the following sort of statement, which includes mention of means. You may also report standard deviations if you believe your audience has an interest in them.

> Equal numbers of subjects received mint-flavored, fruit-flavored, cinnamon-flavored, and bubblegum-flavored chewing gum, creating four categories containing six subjects each. Packs of mint-flavored gum were finished in a mean of 2.83 days; packs of fruit-flavored gum, in a mean of 6.83 days; packs of cinnamon-flavored gum, in a mean of 5.00 days; and packs of bubblegum-flavored gum, in a mean of 3.33 days. A one-way ANOVA compared these values to determine whether they differ significantly.

With the method shown in Example 7.19, the audience can see relationships between the values in different categories for themselves before you provide them with the formal ANOVA results. Some researchers, however, do not provide this information before explaining the ANOVA results. Rather, they begin with an explanation of whether significant row, column, and cell effects exist and provide means as they become relevant in the explanation. The remainder of the examples in this section use this method to present means.

Your key task, when presenting results, is to inform the audience whether means differ significantly. You should do so either by stating that you cannot reject the null hypothesis, further explaining that this decision reflects the lack of a significant difference, or that you can reject the null hypothesis, further explaining that this decision reflects the presence of significant differences.

Accepted null hypotheses require less explanation than rejected null hypotheses do. With no significant differences to interpret, you simply need to provide F_{calc}, F_{crit}, α, and the means, following a pattern similar to that shown for the insignificant t-test results. (See Example 6.22.)

For a rejected null hypothesis, the explanation must also identify the source(s) of this significance. The presentation of results for a rejected null hypothesis can begin with the same general format as Example 7.20 does, except for the designation of the difference as significant rather than insignificant. You would simply supplement this summary by noting the post hoc t tests that indicated significance, characterizing differences between the compared categories as contributing factors to the omnibus rejection. Should your post hoc tests involve combined means, as shown in Example 7.16, you must provide these means in the context of your discussion about the comparisons.

Example 7.20: Summary of Significant Results   The results from the Example 7.6's one-way analysis indicate a significant difference between means and, therefore, can serve as an example. The following explanation mentions not only the overall omnibus significance, but also the results of post hoc analyses conducted to find the source of this significance.

A one-way ANOVA ($\alpha = .05$) produced an F_{calc} of 6.05, which, when compared to the test's F_{crit} of 3.098, leads to a rejected null hypothesis. The number of days needed to finish a pack of mint-flavored ($\overline{X} = 6.83$), fruit-flavored ($\overline{X} = 6.83$), cinnamon-flavored ($\overline{X} = 5.00$), or bubblegum-flavored ($\overline{X} = 6.83$) gum differs significantly. The clear disparity between the two higher means and the two lower means formed the basis for post hoc investigations. According to the post hoc comparison ($F_{calc} = 3.74$ and $F_{crit} = 1.72$ at $\alpha = .05$), the mean for the combination of fruit-flavored and cinnamon-flavored gums ($\overline{X} = 5.92$) differs significantly from the mean for the combination of mint-flavored and bubblegum-flavored gums ($\overline{X} = 3.72$). This distinction contributes to the omnibus ANOVA significance.

Example 7.20 uses parentheses to present means, but integrates values of F_{calc} into the main sentence structures. This format is just one of many ways to present results. Your own writing style should determine your method of informing your audience of these values. Chapter 11 of this book provides detailed directions and guidance for describing statistical tests and their results.

7.7 CONCLUSION

You could claim that the ANOVA contains elements of both the t test and the chi-square test. As explained in Section 7.1, both the t test and the ANOVA compare means of groups. Many, in fact, consider the t test a special case of the ANOVA, simplified by inherent lack of interaction effects and obvious source of significant differences. The relationship between the ANOVA and the chi-square test becomes clear in Section 7.3.1, where you see the derivation of the ANOVA formula. This derivation begins with the ratio between χ^2 values. Containing aspects of both the t test and the χ^2 test, the ANOVA is clearly the most complex analysis presented thus far in this book.

The relationship between the ANOVA and the other two tests of significance some-times leads researchers to simplify ANOVA data with the intention of performing a t test or a χ^2 test. You would most likely use this strategy when you had hoped that the ANOVA would suggest a rejected hypothesis, but it doesn't. Often, similar categories from a one-way ANOVA can be combined to form two large categories. A t test, then, could compare the two category means. In other cases, you could categorize the depen-dent variable using an operational definition to create class limits, as explained in Chapter 2. A crosstabulation would present the frequency for each combination of independent- and dependent-variable categories, and a χ^2 test could determine whether these frequencies differ significantly.

You should understand that the t test and χ^2 test, when used on artificially catego-rized data, do not provide as specific analyses as the ANOVA does. For example, the χ^2 test described in the previous paragraph cannot examine the differences between individual data points, as the ANOVA does. Rather, it examines the allocation of sub-jects into the newly created categories. With the chi-square analysis, the difference in scores of those within a particular category does not matter; only the fact that they fit into that category matters. So, in some situations, the chi-square provides significant results when the ANOVA doesn't. You should realize, though, that using a chi-square test in hopes of finding significance when an ANOVA fails to do so is a "demotion." A significant χ^2 does not provide as much support for your original claim of significance as a significant F value would have.

The ANOVA can also serve as a foundation for even more intricate statistical procedures. Chapter 8 mentions the ANOVA in the context of regression analysis. Variations of the basic ANOVA also exist. Chapter 9 explains that you can adjust the ANOVA to accommodate situations comparable to the paired-subjects t test, in which the same subjects are members of all categories. Chapter 9 also describes ways to accommodate more than one dependent variable and to predict subjects' independent-variable group placement on the basis of their dependent-variable scores. Both of these analyses stem from the ANOVA presented in this chapter. These expansions of the ANOVA's functions may make the ANOVA the most widely used statistical test. Thus, knowledge of the ANOVA and the ability to interpret its results are very valuable tools for data analysis.

STATISTICAL RESOURCES FOR SPSS

You already know that, when $F_{calc} < F_{crit}$, you should accept the null hypothesis because $p > \alpha$ and that when $F_{calc} > F_{crit}$, you should reject the null hypothesis because $p < \alpha$. But the main portion of this chapter never mentions the actual value of p. To obtain this value, you must use a statistical software package such as SPSS. Options in SPSS's

"Analyze" pulldown menu allow the user to perform ANOVA's using any number of independent variables.

One-Way ANOVAs in SPSS

The "Compare Means" option from the "Analyze" pulldown menu in SPSS contains an option for the one-way ANOVA. On selection this option, a "One-Way ANOVA" window should appear on the screen (Fig. 7.8).

For the one-way ANOVA, SPSS refers to the independent variable, used to define categories of subjects, as the *factor*. The program asks you to identify this factor, along with the name of the dependent variable. To conduct a basic test, you need only to move the names of the independent and dependent variables to the appropriate boxes and click "OK". However, you may also find some of the buttons on the right side of the window useful, most often to instruct SPSS to include category means in its output. This chapter's companion website contains descriptions of when and how to use these buttons.

www.moravian.edu/aqd

The main output generated by SPSS is an ANOVA summary table. This table contains all of the values in Table 7.2 as well as the p value. A p value that exceeds α suggests that the calculated F does not exceed the critical F, thus prompting the acceptance of the null hypothesis. A p value less than or equal to α, however, leads to a rejected null hypothesis because it suggests that the calculated F exceeds the critical F.

Example 7.21 shows the output corresponding to the one-way ANOVA presented in Examples 7.3–7.6.

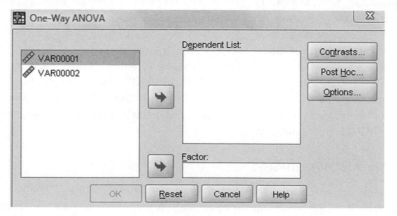

Figure 7.8. SPSS one-way ANOVA window. The user performs a one-way ANOVA by selecting the appropriate category names from those listed in the box above. The name of the independent variable should be moved to the factors area, and the name of the dependent variable should be moved to the dependent list area.

TABLE 7.8. SPSS Output for One-Way ANOVA: Descriptives[a]

					95% Confidence Interval for Mean			
Flavor	N	Mean	Standard Deviation	Standard Error	Lower Bound	Upper Bound	Minimum	Maximum
Mint	6	2.83	1.602	.654	1.15	4.51	1	5
Fruit	6	6.83	2.041	.833	4.69	8.98	4	10
Cinnamon	6	5.00	1.673	.683	3.24	6.76	3	7
Bubblegum	6	3.33	1.862	.760	1.38	5.29	1	6
Total	24	4.50	2.322	.474	3.52	5.48	1	10

Days:

[a]This table lists descriptive statistics from the samples. This table does not appear unless the user selects "descriptive" from the options available in the SPSS "One-Way ANOVA" window.

TABLE 7.9. SPSS Output for One-Way ANOVA: ANOVA[a]

Days:

Variation	Sum of Squares	df	Mean Square	F	Significance
Between groups	59.000	3	19.667	6.051	.004
Within group	65.000	20	3.250	—	—
Total	124.000	23	—	—	—

[a]The values in this summary table indicate whether category means differ significantly. The significance value (p) indicates the exact probability that the difference between these means reflects nothing but chance.

Example 7.21: SPSS Output for One-Way ANOVA   Tables 7.8 and 7.9 contain the output produced by a one-way ANOVA performed in SPSS using the data from Example 7.3. With the exception of the p value, all of the values in the tables are the same as those that appear in the chapter's one-way ANOVA calculations.

Table 7.8's descriptive values simply provide a framework for understanding the values in Table 7.9. The p value of .004 in Table 7.10 indicates that the differences between category means occur by chance 0.4% of the time. This situation meets the criteria for rejecting the null hypothesis at the .10 and .05 levels of significance, but not at the .01 level of significance.

Two-Way ANOVAs in SPSS

Even though the multiway ANOVA compares means, no multiway ANOVA option exists among the "Compare Means" options in SPSS's "Analyze" pulldown menu. The multiway ANOVA function, instead, can be found by clicking on the "Analyze" menu's "General Linear Model" option. The "Univariate" option, implying the presence of only one dependent variable, applies to this situation. If this option is selected, a "Univariate" window should appear on the screen (Fig. 7.9).

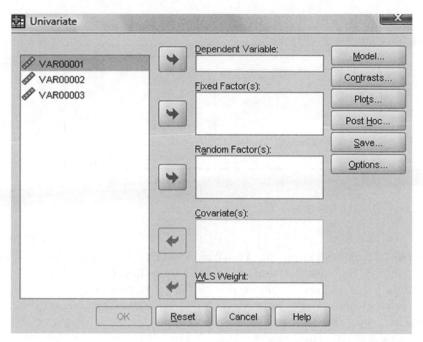

Figure 7.9. SPSS univariate window. The user performs a multiway ANOVA by selecting the appropriate category names from those listed in the box above. The names of the independent variables should be moved to the fixed factor(s) area, and the name of the dependent-variable should be moved to the dependent-variable box.

The independent variables, labeled as factors in the one-way scenario, are called *fixed factors* in the multiway scenario. Moving the independent variables and the dependent variables to the appropriate areas in the "Univariate" screen prepares SPSS to perform the appropriate multiway ANOVA. Once again, detailed descriptions of how to conduct this test, including use of the buttons on the right side of the "Univariate" windows, appear on this book's companion website.

www.moravian.edu/aqd

As in the case of the one-way ANOVA, SPSS produces a summary table for the two-way ANOVA. This table contains the values identified in Table 7.6. If you wish, you can compare the calculated F value to the critical value. However, with knowledge of p value, which appears in the rightmost column of the output, you do not need to do so. A p value that is smaller than α suggests a significant difference between means and, therefore, a rejected null hypothesis.

The SPSS two-way ANOVA output also contains a "Between-Subject Factors" table (Table 7.10). This table provides frequencies for all categories of the independent variables involved in the analysis. Category means do not appear in the output unless you have specifically requested them.

TABLE 7.10. SPSS Output for Two-Way ANOVA: Between-Subjects Factors[a]

Factor		Value Label	N
Flavor	1	Mint	6
	2	Fruit	6
	3	Cinnamon	6
	4	Bubblegum	6
Sugar content	0	Sugarless	12
	1	Sugar	12

[a]The factors listed in this table provide the user with information regarding the categories involved in the analysis.

Example 7.22: SPSS Output for Two-Way ANOVA   For the data from Example 7.7, the three SPSS output tables are presented here as Tables 7.10–7.12.

All the values in Table 7.7 also appear in Table 7.12's summary table. Table 7.12 also contains a significance column, which provides p values for each tested difference. Of the effects being assessed, only the p value pertaining to flavor categories lies below the standard α of .05. These results suggest that means for the flavor categories differ significantly, but means for sugar content categories and for the combination of flavor and sugar content categories do not. Example 7.7's comparison of the F_{calc} and F_{crit} values led to the same conclusion.

Explaining Results of an SPSS ANOVA

Your explanation of SPSS output for an ANOVA should contain p values rather than F_{crit} values, as described in Section 7.5. The p values tell your audience members the exact probability of making a type I error if you reject your null hypothesis. Then, they can compare this value to your chosen α or to another α value that they prefer to use.

Example 7.23: Summary of Insignificant ANOVA Results from SPSS   Adjusting the description of omnibus signficance given in Example 7.20 to include the SPSS output from Example 7.21 might produce an explanation similar to the following:

The ANOVA F value of 6.05 ($p = .004$) leads to a rejected null hypothesis at $\alpha = .05$. The number of days needed to finish a pack of mint-flavored ($\overline{X} = 6.83$), fruit-flavored ($\overline{X} = 6.83$), cinnamon-flavored ($\overline{X} = 5.00$), or bubblegum-flavored ($\overline{X} = 6.83$) gum differs significantly.

Presentation of results from at least one post hoc test that helps to explain this significant difference would complete the explanation.

TABLE 7.11. SPSS Output for Two-Way ANOVA: Descriptive Statistics[a]

Dependent variable: days				
Flavor	Sugar Content	Mean	Standard Deviation	N
Mint	Sugarless	3.00	2.000	3
	Sugar	2.67	1.528	3
	Total	2.83	1.602	6
Fruit	Sugarless	7.00	3.000	3
	Sugar	6.67	1.155	3
	Total	6.83	2.041	6
Cinnamon	Sugarless	4.67	1.528	3
	Sugar	5.33	2.082	3
	Total	5.00	1.673	6
Bubblegum	Sugarless	2.67	2.082	3
	Sugar	4.00	1.732	3
	Total	3.33	1.862	6
Total	Sugarless	4.33	2.605	12
	Sugar	4.67	2.103	12
	Total	4.50	2.322	24

[a]The descriptive statistics provided in this table deserve the most attention. This table displays the mean values compared by the two-way ANOVA. This table does not appear unless the user selects "descriptive" from the options available in SPSS's "Univariate" window.

TABLE 7.12. SPSS Output for Two-Way ANOVA: Tests of Between-Subjects Effects[a]

Dependent variable: days					
Source	Type III Sum of Squares	df	Mean Square	F	Significance
Corrected model	62.667[b]	7	8.952	2.335	.076
Intercept	486.000	1	486.000	126.783	.000
Flavor	59.000	3	19.667	5.130	.011
Sugar content	0.667	1	0.667	0.174	0.682
Flavor * Sugar content	3.000	3	1.000	0.261	0.853
Error	61.333	16	3.833	—	—
Total	610.000	24	—	—	—
Corrected total	124.000	23	—	—	—

[a]The p values presented in this table deserve the most attention. Researchers use these p values in the "significance" column of this table as a basis for determining whether to accept or reject the null hypotheses of equality between category means (between-group effects) and between means for each combination of categories (interaction effects).
[b]$r^2 = .505$ (adjusted $r^2 = .289$).

REVIEW QUESTIONS

7.1. Suppose that a researcher performs an ANOVA to compare groups of a dichotomous variable and later realizes that a t test would have sufficed. If the ANOVA
produced an F of 3.61, what would the t statistic for the t test have been?

*Consider the following scenario for Questions 7.2–7.13. Swim team members are timed
for a 25-yard swim of their best stroke. The times for those who swam freestyle, backstroke, breaststroke, and butterfly, in seconds, are as follows:*

Freestyle	Backstroke	Breaststroke	Butterfly
20.2	21.4	19.2	20.1
17.8	19.9	18.8	18.6
19.9	21.4	21.8	22.8
20.5		18.9	20.7
18.8		21.0	19.3
18.7			

7.2. State the null hypothesis for the relevant ANOVA test that compares mean times.

7.3. Compute the mean time for each stroke category.

7.4. Compute the sum-of-squares values $(\sum X_k^2)$ for each category.

7.5. Compute the squared sum of values $((\sum X_k)^2)$ for each category.

7.6. Compute C.

7.7. Compute the following sum-of-squares values:

(A) total sum of squares (SS_T)

(B) between-groups sum of squares (SS_B)

(C) within-group sum of squares (SS_B).

7.8. Determine the following degree-of-freedom values:

(A) total degrees of freedom (df_T)

(B) between-groups degrees of freedom (df_B)

(C) within-group degrees of freedom (df_W)

7.9. Create an ANOVA summary table that contains all sum-of-squares and degree-
of-freedom values. Calculate between-groups mean-square (MS_B) and within-
groups mean-square (MS_T) values. Add these values to the ANOVA summary
table.

7.10. Find the calculated F statistic.

7.11. Find the critical F value at $\alpha = .01$, $\alpha = .05$, and $\alpha = .10$.

7.12. Is the null hypothesis rejected at $\alpha = .01$? At $\alpha = .05$? At $\alpha = .10$?

7.13. Write a short summary of the results for each of the significance values addressed
in Question 7.11.

*Consider the following scenario for questions 7.14–7.19. An environmentalist wishes
to determine whether people recycle equal amounts of metal, glass, and plastic. The*

environmentalist gathers data by recording the percentages of 90 randomly selected bins, 30 labeled for each product, that are filled. The mean percentage for bins labeled for metal is 66.5%, the mean percentage for bins labeled for glass is 48.2%, and the mean percentage for bins labeled for plastic is 70.7%.

7.14. State the null hypothesis for the relevant one-way ANOVA.

7.15. Find the calculated F value. Assume $\Sigma X^2 = 352,405.20$.

7.16. Find the critical F value at $\alpha = .01$, $\alpha = .05$, and $\alpha = .10$.

7.17. Is the null hypothesis rejected at $\alpha = .01$? At $\alpha = .05$? At $\alpha = .10$?

7.18. Write a short summary of the results for each of the significance values addressed in Question 7.17.

7.19. Perform post hoc tests to determine at least one source of significance for each rejected null hypothesis from Question 7.17.

7.20. Family therapists wonder whether a relationship exists between the times of the day that parents work and the amount of time that they spend with their children. They ask 12 parents, 4 of whom work first shift (7:00 A.M.–3:00 P.M.), 4 of whom work second shift (3:00 P.M.–11:00 P.M.), and 4 of whom work third shift (11:00 P.M.–7:00 A.M.) to keep track of the number of hours they spend with their families during a particular week. The results are as follows:

First Shift	Second Shift	Third Shift
25	10	25
45	30	30
30	20	25
40	20	40

(A) Perform a one-way ANOVA using $\alpha = .05$ to address the null hypothesis that the mean number of hours for those in each category do not differ significantly.

(B) Determine whether post hoc testing is necessary. If so, determine at least one source of the significant difference.

For questions 7.21–7.35, consider a variation of the scenario described in Question 7.20 for which subjects' jobs are categorized as blue-collar or white-collar. A factorial categorizes subjects according to both the shift they work and the type of job that they have as follows. Each cell contains the number of hours that subjects fitting into each combination of categories spent with their families.

Type	Shift		
	First	Second	Third
Blue-collar	25	10	20
	45	30	40
White-collar	30	20	25
	40	20	35

7.21. State the null hypothesis for the relevant ANOVA test that compares mean times for those in the six categories.

7.22. Compute the mean time for each of the six categories.

7.23. Compute the sum of all values (ΣX or T)

7.24. Compute the sum-of-squares values (T^2).

7.25. (A) Compute the sum-of-squares values for rows ($T_{R.}^2$).

(B) Compute the sum-of-squares values for columns (T_C^2).

7.26. Compute the square sums of values for the cells (T_{RC}^2).

7.27. Compute the following mediating values:

(A) $[T]$

(B) $[X]$

(C) $[R]$

(D) $[C]$

(E) $[RC]$

7.28. Compute the following sum-of-squares values:

(A) total sum of squares (SS_T)

(B) row sum of squares (SS_R)

(C) column sum of squares (SS_C)

(D) interaction sum of squares ($SS_{R \times C}$)

(E) within-group sum of squares (SS_B)

7.29. Determine the following degree-of-freedom values:

(A) total degrees of freedom (df_T)

(B) row degrees of freedom (df_R)

(C) column degrees of freedom (df_C)

(D) interaction degrees of freedom ($df_{R \times C}$)

(E) within-group degrees of freedom (dr_B)

7.30. Create an ANOVA summary table that contains all sum-of-squares and degree-of-freedom values. Calculate mean-square values. Add these values to the ANOVA summary table.

7.31. Find the calculated F statistics.

7.32. Find the critical F values at $\alpha = .01$, $\alpha = .05$, and $\alpha = .10$.

7.33. Is the omnibus null hypothesis rejected at $\alpha = .01$? At $\alpha = .05$? At $\alpha = .10$?

7.34. Write a short summary of the results for each of the significance values addressed in Questions 7.32 and 7.33.

7.35. Draw a line graph of mean values for each job-type category. On the basis of this graph, explain why no interaction effect exists.

Consider the following scenario for Questions 7.36–7.41. Dr. Stopsneze, an allergist, wonders whether differences exist between out-of-pocket expenses (costs not paid by insurance) for her patients with various allergy sources and levels of exposure to that source. She creates the following factorial to summarize the mean out-of-pocket expenses for a total of 45 patients, five in each combination of source and exposure categories, during the most recent calendar year:

Exposure to Primary Allergen	Source			
	Hayfever	Mold/Mildew	Animals	
Limited	$\bar{X} = 85$	$\bar{X} = 81$	$\bar{X} = 101$	$\bar{X} = 87$
	$s = 3.00$	$s = 4.37$	$s = 7.08$	$s = 3.76$
Moderate	$\bar{X} = 86$	$\bar{X} = 80$	$\bar{X} = 99$	$\bar{X} = 83$
	$s = 2.69$	$s = 8.87$	$s = 6.37$	$s = 6.61$
Frequent	$\bar{X} = 90$	$\bar{X} = 88$	$\bar{X} = 106$	$\bar{X} = 102$
	$s = 3.95$	$s = 2.76$	$s = 4.76$	$s = 6.46$
	$\bar{X} = 89$	$\bar{X} = 88.33$	$\bar{X} = 94.67$	
	$s = 10.12$	$s = 10.17$	$s = 90.9$	

7.36. Find the calculated F values. (Use $\Sigma X^2 = 374{,}322.50$.)

7.37. Find the critical F values at $\alpha = .01$, $\alpha = .05$, and $\alpha = .10$.

7.38. Is the omnibus null hypothesis rejected at $\alpha = .01$? At $\alpha = .05$? At $\alpha = .10$?

7.39. Perform post hoc tests to determine at least one source of significance for each rejected null hypothesis from Question 7.39.

7.40. (A) Find the range of standardized values within which a researcher could be 95% confident that the calculated F value would fall given nine degrees of freedom.

(B) Find the range of standardized values within which a researcher could be 99% confident that the calculated F value would fall given nine degrees of freedom.

(C) Why is the 99% confidence interval larger than the 95% confidence interval is?

8

CORRELATION AND REGRESSION: COMPARING CHANGES AMONG CONTINUOUS-VARIABLE SCORES

8.1 INTRODUCTION

Statisticians disagree about whether regression–correlation analysis falls into the category of descriptive statistics or inferential statistics. It has characteristics of both. Regression and correlation values can describe the relationship between subjects' scores on continuous variables. However, you can also use them to make predictions about one's dependent-value score on the basis of one's independent value score(s), making it somewhat like inferential statistics, which allow for speculation based on sample data.

Null hypotheses for these regression and correlation analyses propose that no relationship exists between independent-variable scores and dependent-variable scores, as the null hypotheses for chi-square tests, *t* tests, and ANOVAs do. Unlike the inferential tests, however, discussed in Chapters 5–7, you do not compare a calculated value to a critical value to determine whether to reject the null hypothesis for a correlation–regression analysis. The statistics, formulas, and illustrations, themselves, tell you

Analyzing Quantitative Data: An Introduction for Social Researchers, First Edition. Debra Wetcher-Hendricks.
© 2011 John Wiley & Sons, Inc. Published 2011 by John Wiley & Sons, Inc.

whether an independent variable can predict independent-variable scores.[1] The basic analyses use a *linear* model, referring to a line that describes the trend between independent- and dependent-variable values as well as how closely follows this line.

The regression analysis and the correlation analysis each uses its own formula, and each produces statistics that look very different. Together, though, they provide a full picture of the linear relationship between continuous-variable scores. The between-correlation coefficients and regression equations become clear when considering the scatterplot arrangement of data points for two variables. (Please see Chapter 3 for basic information about scatterplots.)

Example 8.1: Scatterplot   An examination of the relationship between the number of students in a class and the number of hedgers (um . . , er . . . , uh . . . , etc.) that the teacher uses during a 60-minute class period lends itself to a basic regression and correlation analysis involving two variables. In this case, the number of students in the class is the independent variable, and the number of hedgers used per hour by the teacher is the dependent variable.

One might reason that classes with few students have relatively relaxed atmospheres and, thus, teachers of these classes speak somewhat informally. But as the amount of students in the class increases, the teacher begins to adopt a more formal demeanor and tends to take care to speak correctly, which includes avoiding the use of hedgers. The opposite, however, could also be true. Some teachers may become nervous as class size grows, and an increase in the use of hedgers may reflect tentative speech or minor anxiety that sometimes results from nervousness. A scatterplot helps to determine which, if either, of these possibilities more correctly represents the relationship between the variables. For this graph, using hypothetical data from bogus 40 teachers, values along the x axis correspond to the number of students in a class, and values along the y axis correspond to the number of hedgers used by the teacher during a 60-minute class period.

Figure 8.1 shows a general tendency for y values to increase as x values increase. On the basis of this graph, you could safely state that the second of the earlier conjectures has more support than the first one does. The strength of the tendency for the number of hedgers used to increase as the number of students increases is evident from the degree to which the points follow a linear path. In this case, although the points generally move in an upward direction, there are many exceptions to this trend. So, the predictability of one variable from another is far from guaranteed.

A regression equation provides a mathematical representation of the line that best describes the arrangement of points on a scatterplot such as Figure 8.1. The correlation

---

[1] Any references to critical and calculated F values or to probabilities result from an ANOVA, not from a correlation–regression analysis. This ANOVA, like other ANOVAs, determines whether dependent-variable scores differ in relation to independent-variable categories. However, this analysis could compare as many as n groups because, with the independent variable's continuous nature, each subject may constitute his or her own group.

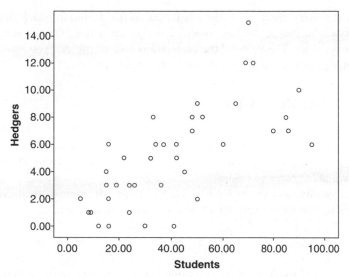

Figure 8.1. Scatterplot. Each point on the scatterplot represents the number of students in a particular class and the number of hedgers used per hour by the class' teacher. The arrangement of points provides information about the linear relationship between these two variables.

coefficient describes how closely points lie along this line. The sign (+ or −) of the regression equation's slope and of the correlation coefficient indicate the overall direction of the trend between the independent variable and the dependent variable. Later sections of this chapter further explain the links between the regression equation and the correlation coefficient and also expand on the context of Example 8.1 to include more than two variables and to acknowledge the possibility of nonlinear relationships between variables.

8.2   BIVARIATE RELATIONSHIPS

Most often, references to regression and correlation analysis focus on two variables, making them *bivariate*. Analyses of bivariate relationships produce a bivariate regression equation and a *pairwise* correlation coefficient. The term "pairwise" simply reflects the fact that the analysis regards each independent variable score and its corresponding dependent-variable score as partners of a pair. The analysis compares changes between these pairs for each subject in the sample.

Regression and correlation analyses focus on the direction and consistency of these changes to assess the possibility of predicting dependent-variable scores from independent-variable scores. Both of these statistics indicate, through the use of a positive or negative sign, the slope of the line that best fits the scatterplot points. The regression equation, in and of itself, allows you to make the necessary predictions. But the success in making these predictions is based on the degree to which they are scattered about on the graph. As the points converge on a line, the equation becomes increasingly accurate. The value of the correlation coefficient tells you how accurately the regression equation can predict dependent-variable scores.

8.2.1   Bivariate Regression

You already know that scatterplots visually present data from two continuous variables. Regression analysis provides a mathematical equation that characterizes the arrangement of points representing subjects' independent-variable scores (x values) and dependent-variable scores (y values).

Basic regression analysis is based on the evidence of a linear trend. So, it uses a linear equation. You have likely seen linear equations in the form of

$$y = mx + b \qquad\qquad (8.1)$$

before in algebra class. The regression equation follows the same format. However, some of the notation differs. In this context, the equation appears as

$$y = a + bx \qquad\qquad (8.2)$$

The commutative property of addition allows for rearrangement of the components after the equality sign. In Equation (8.2), a represents the y intercept on the graph and b represents the slope of the line. To review these concepts, consider the following example.

Example 8.2: y Intercept and Slope   Figure 8.2 presents a line with a y intercept of 4 and a slope of $-.75$.

The y intercept of 4 indicates that the line crosses the vertical axis at 4 and the slope of $-.75$ indicates that, the value of y decreases by .75 units for each unit increase in x.

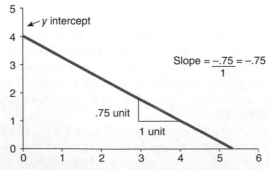

Figure 8.2. Line. The line in the graph can be represented by the equation $y = 4 + (-.75x)$ or, more simply, $y = 4 -.75x$. Added remarks on the graph explain the y-intercept and slope values.

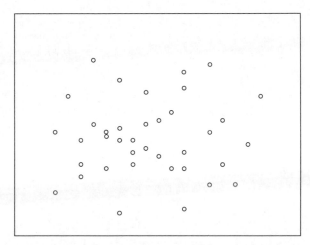

<u>Figure 8.3.</u> The arrangement of points on the scatterplot does not blatantly indicate a trend between the independent and dependent variables. One cannot easily determine whether the regression line should have a positive or negative slope.

The $y = a + bx$ line follows the general direction of points on a scatterplot. The sign of the slope (b) tells you whether the variables have a direct or inverse relationship. A negative slope exists when values for one variable increase as values for the other variable decrease. A positive slope exists when values for one variable increase while values for the other variable also increase. However, when points are very scattered, such as in Figure 8.3, there may not be a positively sloped or a negatively sloped line that seems to coincide at all with the arrangement of points.

You would likely have difficulty determining the relationship between x and y in Figure 8.3. Dependent-variable scores do not increase or decrease consistently with respect to increases in independent-variable scores. Thus, the regression line that describes this scatterplot will not provide accurate predictions of dependent-variable scores from independent-variable scores.

Sometimes, even when points suggest a very evident regression line, you may have difficulty characterizing the relationship between variables. Specifically, this situation occurs when the points seem to collect around a vertical or horizontal line.

The horizontal line that best represents the arrangement of points in Figure 8.4 will not help you very much when trying to predict dependent variable scores from independent variable scores. By definition, horizontal lines have an equation of y equal to some constant ($y = C$). Without the presence of x in the equation, it is clear that y values (representing the dependent variables) have no relationship to x values (representing the independent variable). All x values have the same y value. Thus, you cannot use independent-variable scores to predict dependent-variable scores. A similar condition would exist if the points on the scatterplot were to converge around a vertical line. This situation would produce an equation of $x = C$, which suggests that all y values have the same x value. However, for scatterplots in which points have a distinct upward or

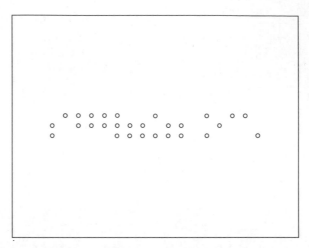

Figure 8.4. The arrangement of points in the scatterplot clusters around a line. However, this line is horizontal and thus does not represent a consistent change between independent- and dependent-variable scores. A horizontal regression line predicts the same dependent-variable score (*y*) for all independent-variable scores (*x*).

downward sloping pattern, the regression equation can represent the trend between the independent and dependent variables well.

Example 8.3: Regression Line   Figure 8.1 provides an example of a relatively evident upward-sloping pattern. Even without the presence of a regression line, the arrangement of points suggests a direct relationship between the number of students in a class and the number of hedgers used by the teacher of that class. However, the addition of the line provides specific information about that relationship.

The equation of the line in Figure 8.5 is $y = 1.02 + .10x$, indicating that it has a y intercept of 1.02 and a slope of +.10. The positive slope, although obvious from the scatterplot, confirms that increases in independent-variable scores tend to correspond to increases in dependent-variable scores. In this case, the y intercept provides little practical information as no class sizes of 0 exist. But, in other situations, it may prove useful in that it indicates the dependent-variable score when the independent-variable score equals 0.

You can use the equation of regression line to predict the dependent-variable score given any independent-variable score. Because, according to the equation, the values of x and y vary with respect to one another, each value substituted into the equation for the x component produces a different y value. The resulting y value that results indicates the estimated dependent-variable value that corresponds to the independent-variable value that replaced x.

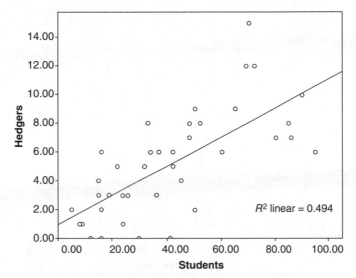

Figure 8.5. Regression line. The regression line helps to characterize the dispersion of points from Figure 8.1. According to the position of the line, researchers can use the number of students in the class to predict the number of hedgers used per hour by the teacher of that class.

Example 8.4: Prediction of Dependent-Variable Scores (Bivariate) Using Equation (8.2), then, one could estimate the number of hedgers used by one who teaches a class with 25 students. None of the teachers who provided data had classes containing exactly 25 students. So, a researcher has no way to characterize this situation other than estimating. Replacing the x in the equation with a 25 produces

$$y = 1.02 + .10(25).$$

With arithmetic simplification, the equation becomes $y = 3.52$. This number is an estimate of the number of hedgers used per hour by a teacher who has a class of 25 students. The ordered pair of (25, 3.52) lies on the regression line. Obviously, a teacher can't really use a fractional number of hedgers. The formula provides only a best guess for the y value based on the overall goal of minimizing differences between predicted and actual values.

The accuracy with which you can make predictions of dependent-variable scores from independent-variable scores reflects the degree to which the scatterplot points follow the regression line. The exact placement of this line is determined through an iterative method involving the sum of squares of residuals. For any line on the scatterplot, the vertical distance between each point and the line, the residual, is measured. Figure 8.6 shows the residual distances for some points on the scatterplot for the hedger

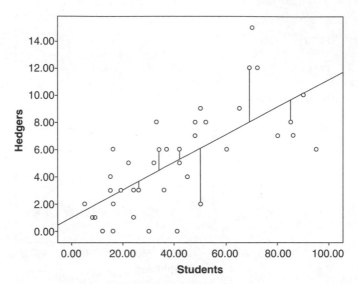

Figure 8.6. Residuals. The vertical lines that connect points to the regression line represent the residuals associated with those points. Points below the line have negative residuals and above the line, positive residuals. Squaring the residuals and then adding them provides a representation of the line's ability to characterize the points on the scatterplot.

data. It would be impossible to show all of the residual distances without making the graph look cluttered. But the lines on the graph demonstrate the concept.

This residual is squared, and the sums of the squared residuals for all points represents an overall measure of the line's representativeness of the scatterplot. As the line's representativeness increases, the sum of the squared residuals decreases. So, the line that produces the smallest sum of squared residuals qualifies as the regression line. In fact, some formally refer to this line as the *least-squares regression line* to acknowledge the way in which it is selected.

8.2.2 Pairwise Correlation

Correlation values indicate how well one variable predicts the other. Scatterplots and regression analysis are closely related to correlation values. With knowledge of a correlation coefficient, you can determine the degree to which points on the scatterplot follow the path of the regression line and, thus, the extent to which the regression equation fits the data.

The Pairwise Correlation Coefficient. The most commonly used correlation coefficient was introduced by Karl Pearson[2] in 1896, based on earlier work by Sir Francis Galton.[3] A key step in obtaining this coefficient requires you to add products

[2] Karl Pearson also deserves credit for developing the chi-square test and for coining the term "standard deviation."

of values associated with each of the two variables involved in the analysis. Hence, it is formally called the *Pearson product moment correlation coefficient.* Statisticians symbolize the correlation coefficient with an *r* or, when related to the variables *x* and *y*, as r_{xy}.

Statisticians define r_{xy} as the covariance of *x* and *y* (C_{xy}) divided by the product of the *x* and *y* standard deviations:

$$r_{xy} = \frac{\sum C_{xy}}{\sigma_x \sigma_y}. \tag{8.3}$$

Unless you have already computed covariances, however, this formula does not allow for easy computation of r_{xy}. You may find the following equation

$$r_{xy} = \frac{N\Sigma(xy) - (\Sigma x)(\Sigma y)}{\sqrt{N\Sigma x^2 - (\Sigma x)^2}\sqrt{N\Sigma y^2 - (\Sigma y)^2}} \tag{8.4}$$

more useful than Equation (8.3) because it requires knowledge only of sums and sums of products. Chapter 8's companion website shows the equivalence between the two formulas.

www.moravian.edu/aqd

Equation (8.4) is actually one of many formulas besides Equation (8.3) that is commonly used to compute the correlation coefficient. Other formulas use standardized (*z*) scores or means. If you have these values, then you may prefer one of these versions of Equation (8.4). However, most often, you will have only values for *x* and *y*, making Equation (8.4). most useful. For this reason, Example 8.5 uses Equation (8.4) rather than another version of the formula in its demonstration of calculating a pairwise correlation coefficient.

Example 8.5: Pairwise Correlation Coefficient   Consider a relatively simple version the hedgers study, involving only five subjects.

	X (Class Size)	Y (Hedgers/Class)
	9	9
	19	4
	71	14
	35	10
	54	17
Σ	188	54

[3]Pearson, while obtaining his doctoral degree, was a student of Galton's. The work of both Galton (1889, 1890) and Pearson (1894, 1896, 1900) focused on genetics, specifically, eugenics. Development of the correlation coefficient discussed occurred within this context.

Although this sample size would probably not meet the qualifications for a generalizable study, it provides a good first example of the computations needed to obtain r. Before actually using Equation (8.4), some preliminary calculations must take place. Because the equation includes the sums of the products of each x and y as well as sums of x^2 and y^2, it is useful to calculate these values first:

	X^2	Y^2	XY
	81	81	81
	361	16	76
	5041	196	994
	1225	100	350
	2916	289	916
Σ	9624	682	2419

The sums at the bottom of these columns and the columns for each of the raw scores, along with the n of 5, fit into Equation (8.3):

$$r = \frac{5(2419) - (188)(54)}{\sqrt{5(9624) - (188)^2} \sqrt{5(682) - (54)^2}}$$

Simplification as shown eventually produces a correlation coefficient of +.77.

$$r = \frac{12,095 - 10,152}{\sqrt{48,120 - 35,344} \sqrt{3410 - 2916}}$$

$$= \frac{1943}{(113.03)(22.23)} = +.77$$

The numerical value of r indicates the strength of the linear relationship between variables. It always ranges from -1.00 to $+1.00$. The sign of the coefficient indicates whether the variables have a direct or inverse relationship.

This information closely resembles the description of a dataset provided by a scatterplot. In fact, the the correlation coefficient helps to determine the slope (b) of the regression equation because

$$b = r\left(\frac{\sigma_y}{\sigma_x}\right). \tag{8.5}$$

The sign of the correlation coefficient, therefore, is always the same as the sign of the regression equation's slope. If a perfect positive correlation, indicated by $r = +1.00$, exists, increases in the values associated with one variable correspond to perfectly predictable increases in the values associated with the other variable. All of the points on a scatterplot would fall exactly on a positively sloped line. In the case of a perfect negative correlation, indicated by $r = -1.00$, the values associated with one variable

TABLE 8.1. Correlation Ranges[a]

$|r|$ Values	Strength
$0 \leq |r| < .149$	Very weak
$.150 \leq |r| < .299$	Weak
$.300 \leq |r| < .699$	Moderate
$.700 \leq |r| < .849$	Strong
$.850 \leq |r| < 1.00$	Very strong

[a]Verbal descriptions of linear relationships between variables correspond to particular correlation coefficient ranges. These descriptions provide general suggestions for the characterization of correlation coefficients. The ranges may change to reflect contextual issues or researcher intentions for a particular investigation.

correspond to perfectly predictable decreases in the values associated with the other variable. This situation would produce a scatterplot in which all points would fall exactly on a negatively sloped line.

Perfect correlations rarely exist. But the closer r lies to $+1.00$ or -1.00, the stronger the linear relationship between the two variables is. Correlation coefficients that lie near 0, whether positive or negative, indicate large residuals and suggest little, if any, linear relationship between the variables. Opinions about the boundaries within which a correlation coefficient must fall for it to receive various verbal descriptions vary. However, you can use the rubric in Table 8.1 as a rough guide to describe the strength of a linear relationship based on the value of the correlation.

Example 8.6: Describing the Linear Relationship According to the standards provided in Table 8.1, Example 8.5's correlation coefficient of $+.77$ suggests a strong linear relationship. The coefficient's positive sign indicates that increases in the independent variable coincide with increases in the dependent variable. Considering these two aspects together, one could predict rather comfortably that teachers of large classes use more hedgers during class than teachers of small classes do.

Unless $r = +1.00$ or $r = -1.00$, you cannot predict, with total certainty, one variable from another. You know that, as the absolute value of the correlation coefficient rises, predictability increases. But the correlation coefficient itself does not tell you the exact proportion of changes in one variable's values that can be explained by changes in the other variable's values. A manipulation of the correlation coefficient, called the *coefficient of determination*, however, does provide this information.

The Coefficient of Determination. On its surface, the correlation coefficient may seem to be an arbitrarily defined representation of the linear relationship between variables. Rest assured, though, that the value produced by Equation (8.4) has a very important meaning. The squared correlation coefficient, called the *coefficient of determination* and denoted as R, indicates the proportion of variance in one variable's scores that can be explained by variance in the other variable's scores:

$$R = r^2 \qquad (8.6)$$

To fully understand this concept, you should realize that individual independent- and dependent-variable scores vary for many reasons. Differences in dependent-variable scores may correspond to differences in independent-variable scores (and vice versa), but may also reflect other factors, such as an intervening variable (described in Section 8.3.3), or random variation. The coefficient of determination tells you the extent to which you can associate changes in dependent-variable scores with changes in independent-variable scores. Many researchers prefer to consider the value of the coefficient of determination in percentage form, stating that variations in the independent-variable scores account for a particular percentage of variations in the dependent-variable scores. The remainder of the variation in the dependent score reflects unknown factors.

Example 8.7: Coefficient of Determination   The coefficient of determination for Example 8.5's data is .59, obtained by squaring the correlation coefficient of .77. This R value suggests that differences in class size can explain 59% of differences in the number of hedgers used by professors. The remaining 41% of the variation in the number of hedgers used occurs for other reasons.

8.2.3   Curvilinear Relationships

You have read that regression–correlation analysis provides information about linear trends between data points. However, the importance of the term *linear* in that description has received little attention thus far. It is essential, though, that you recognize the limitations associated with the linear context of regression–correlation analysis.

The lack of a strong linear relationship, as evidenced by a correlation coefficient near 0, does not necessarily indicate the lack of an overall relationship. A linear relationship is only one of many relationships that a variable can have. Examining various scatterplot formations may help to clarify this idea. Figures 8.7 and 8.8 show points in curvilinear, rather than linear, arrangements.

Arrangement of points like those in Figures 8.7 and 8.8 occur rather frequently. In fact, curvilinear patterns more complicated than those shown, such as quartic curves (with three bends) or even circles and ellipses, can exist. Clearly, such arrangements suggest relationships between x and y values. However, because the x and y coordinates do align themselves in a linear fashion, regression–correlation analysis may overlook these relationships.

Example 8.8: Curvilinear Relationship   An analysis of police presence and crime in various cities might produce a graph similar to Figure 8.7. The x variable could represent the number of police per hundred citizens on the police forces for the cities in the sample, and the y variable could represent the crime rate for each city.

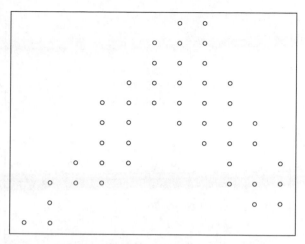

<u>Figure 8.7.</u> Quadratic relationship. As values increase along the X axis, Y values increase and then decrease. A least-squares regression line describing the left portion of the graph would have a positive slope; a least-squares regression line describing the right portion of the graph would have a negative slope. No single least-squares regression line could produce consistently small residuals. Thus, a low correlation coefficient would result.

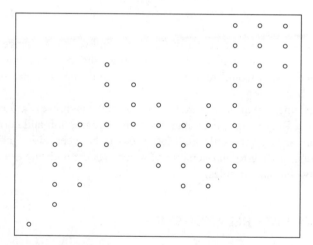

<u>Figure 8.8.</u> Cubic relationship. The trend in Y values changes twice as X values increase. A positively sloped least-squares regression line could describe the leftmost and rightmost portions of the graph; the center of the graph suggests a negatively sloped least-squares regression line. No single least-squares regression line could produce consistently small residuals. Thus, a low correlation coefficient would result.

The arrangement of points in Figure 8.9 could occur for various reasons. Perhaps, administrators of cities with low "criminal subcultures" see no need for large police forces. These cities correspond to the points that lie in the low x–y range on Figure 8.9. But many scatterplot points also lie in the high x–low y range. Cities with large police forces that can effectively control crime may account for these points. The rising and

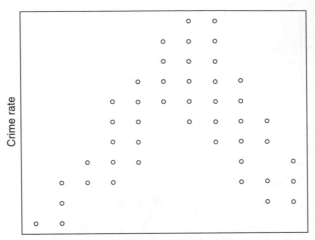

Figure 8.9. Police force size and crime rate. Figure 8.7, placed into the context of the relationship between the size of cities' police forces and cities' crime rates, suggests that the highest crime rates, exist in cities with police forces in the middle of the range. Cities with very small or very large police forces have comparatively low crime rates.

then falling *y* values toward the center of the graph represent the change from the first of these situations to the second. The high crime rates that occur in cities with moderately sized police forces would reflect both an active criminal subculture and inadequately sized police forces.

A clear curvilinear relationship exists. Linear analysis, however, does not address curvilinear trends. Relying on linear analysis such as regression and correlation might lead one to believe that very little association exists between cities' crime rates and police force sizes, leading to an oversight of a very strong and important trend in the relationship between the variables.

8.3   MULTIVARIATE RELATIONSHIPS

Studies are not always so simple that they entail only two variables. You may find that, to fully explain a relationship, you need to acknowledge the influence of additional variables. Because these situations involve more than two variables, they require *multivariate analyses*.

Unlike the bivariate context, which involves only one standard technique of regression–correlation analysis, different forms of multivariate analysis exist for different circumstances. Your intentions determine the appropriate multivariate technique to use. The remainder of this section presents the multiple regression–multiple correlation analysis as well as the partial correlation and part correlation analyses. You can use the multiple regression–correlation analysis for situations in which you wish to examine the combined effects of two or more dependent variables. Partial and part correlations address situations in which at least one other variable interferes with the relationship between a single independent variable and a single dependent variable.

8.3.1 Multiple Regression

Multiple-regression analysis can provide a scatterplot and equation for situations in which two or more independent variables work collectively to predict scores on the dependent variable. Not surprisingly, the scatterplot for a regression analysis involving more than two variables has more than two dimensions. Each independent variable corresponds to an axis on the scatterplot. With many variables, the scatterplot becomes very difficult to illustrate on a two-dimensional surface. However, a sample analysis involving three variables can help you understand the general idea. This analysis uses data points measured along x, y, and z axes.

Example 8.9: Three-Variable Scatterplot A slight modification to the hedgers study described earlier in this chapter might rest on the idea that the number of students in a class in conjunction with the number of questions asked per hour by students creates a dynamic in the classroom that relates to teachers' use of hedgers. A subsequent investigation would attempt to determine whether the combination of the number of students (X) and the number of student questions per hour (Z) can predict the number of hedgers used per hour by the teacher (Y).

We can characterize both the number of students enrolled in the course and the number of questions asked per hour by these students as independent variables. These two variables, together, create a certain atmosphere in the classroom that may predict teachers' use of hedgers. In particular, one might wonder whether the combination of the number of students (X) and the number of questions that they ask (Z) used by the professor can predict the number of hedgers used per hour by teachers (Y).

The addition of the questions variable makes a three-dimensional scatterplot necessary. This illustration can appear as an open box, as shown in Figure 8.10.

The X and Y axes have the same positions as they do in the two-dimensional graph. The Z variable adds a dimension of depth, although it is somewhat difficult to perceive in a two-dimensional illustration. Each point on the graph appears suspended within the box at the intersection of the number of students, hedgers, and question that it represents.

Points on a three-dimensional scatterpolot suggest a least-squares regression plane, as opposed to the least-squares regression line on a two-dimensional scatterplot. The smallest sum-of-squares residuals determines the placement of the regression plane, which shows the predicted horizontal–vertical–depth arrangement of points. Such an illustration, however, is very difficult to see on a two-dimensional page in a book.

Still, you can obtain the equation for this plane. The multivariate regression equation expands to accommodate each new variable. With Y representing the dependent variable and X and Z representing independent variables, the regression equation appears as

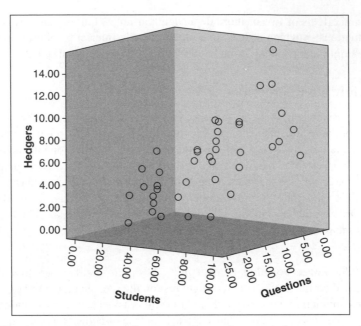

Figure 8.10. Three-variable scatterplot. Each point on the scatterplot represents the number of students enrolled in a particular class, the number of questions asked per hour by students in that class, and the number of hedgers used per hour by the teacher of that class. The arrangement of points provides information about the linear relationship between these three variables.

$$y = a + b_1 x + b_2 z \tag{8.7}$$

To perform a regression analysis using more than two independent variables, you would simply add the extra variables and their respective slopes to the right side of Equation (8.7).

Example 8.10: Three-Variable Regression Equation The equation $y = .228 + .091x + .087z$ describes the regression plane for the scatterplot shown in Figure 8.10. Because a two-dimensional page does not easily show a three-dimensional image, it is more difficult to see the associations between the graph and the equation than in the bivariate situation. But similar relationships exist.

The y intercept is .228. The values that precede x and z in the equation represent slopes. Each of these values refers to the change in y values as its corresponding variable increases. The positive slopes suggest that y increases as both x and z increase. For each unit increase in the number of students (X), the number of hedgers used (Y) increases .091 units. For each unit increase in the number of questions asked (Z), the number of questions asked increases by .087 units.

As in the bivariate situation, you can use the regression equation to predict a y score given particular x and z scores. You need only to substitute the x and y values into the regression equation and perform the appropriate arithmetic.

Example 8.11: Prediction of Dependent-Variable Scores (Multivariate) For example, a researcher may wish to predict the number of hedgers used by the teacher of a class with an enrollment of 75 (not one of the class sizes used to create Fig. 8.13 in the Statistical Resources for SPSS section, which follows the main text of the chapter). Suppose that this course has an enrollment of 75 and that, during an observation, the researcher counts 8 questions asked by students during an hour-long class.

Substituting these numbers into the regression equation presented in Example 8.10 produces

$$y = .228 + .091(75) + .087(8)$$

So, $y = 7.75$, meaning that one could predict 7.75 hedgers per hour from the teacher of this class. One cannot assume that the teacher uses 7.75 hedger questions, but can only recognize that this y value lies on the regression line, which minimizes residuals between predicted and actual scores.

8.3.2 Multiple Correlation

Multiple-correlation values describe the effectiveness of the regression equation, just as bivariate correlation values do. The multiple-correlation coefficient, however, indicates the strength of the linear relationship between a combination of at least two independent variables and a single dependent variable.

The Multiple-Correlation Coefficient. A multiple-correlation coefficient involving two independent variables is denoted as R_{YXZ}. The subscript maintains the role of X as an independent variable and Y as a dependent variable, but adds Z as a second independent variable. If you wish to address more than two independent variables, the notation expands accordingly: R_{YWXZ} signifies three independent variables, R_{YVWXZ} signifies four independent variables, and so on. In all of these cases, Y corresponds to the dependent variable.

Before beginning computations for R_{YXZ}, you should obtain values for all pairwise correlation coefficients. Equation (8.8) shows the arrangement of pairwise coefficients that produces the multiple-correlation coefficient for a situation involving two dependent variables. The formula emerges from a blend of the variances and covariances of the independent variables and the dependent variable:

$$R_{Y.XZ}\sqrt{\frac{r_{XY}^2 + r_{YZ}^2 - 2r_{XY}r_{XZ}r_{YZ}}{1 - r_{XZ}^2}} \tag{8.8}$$

If you wish to address the relationship between more than two independent variables and the dependent variable, you can incorporate the additional variables into Equation

(8.8). This process, however, becomes very cumbersome as the formula becomes increasingly complicated with the addition of each variable. Matrices can help you organize all of the relevant pairwise coefficients and computations.

Example 8.12: Multiple-Correlation Coefficient   For the sake of an uncomplicated example, consider a situation in which a researcher wishes to use a combination of two independent variables to predict scores on the dependent variable. The following dataset simply expands on that presented in Example 8.5 by defining Z as the number of questions asked per hour by students, based on the reasoning that this issue may help to predict the number of hedgers used by teachers. Once again, the dataset is rather small, but appropriate to show the basic procedure for calculating $R_{y.xz}$:

X (Class Size)	Y (Hedgers/Hour)	Z (Questions/Hour)
9	9	3
19	4	6
71	14	10
35	10	6
54	17	11

For this analysis, $r_{XY} = .77$, $r_{XZ} = .91$, and $r_{YZ} = .76$. These values fit into Equation (8.8):

$$R_{y.xz} = \sqrt{\frac{.77^2 + .76^2 - 2(.77)(.91)(.76)}{1 - .91^2}}$$

$$= \sqrt{\frac{.105}{.172}} = +.78$$

Table 8.1 characterizes a correlation coefficient of .78 as strong. The number of students in a class and the number of student questions per hour, when considered together, predict the number of hedgers used per hour by the class' teacher rather well. In other words, the regression equation provides accurate estimates of y.

You should remember, however, that the correlation coefficient addresses only linear relationships. Had the data in Example 8.12 produced a low multiple correlation coefficient, you could not assume that the variables have absolutely no relationship. The possibility for a curvilinear relationship still exists.

The Coefficient of Multiple Determination.   The coefficient of determination plays the same role for the multivariate context as it did in the bivariate context. Squaring the multiple-correlation coefficient (or, more simply, ending the calculations for the multiple-correlation coefficient before taking the square root) produces a value that represents the percentage of variation in dependent-variable scores explained by changes in the scores for the independent variables. The remainder of changes in dependent-variable scores reflects aspects not included in the analysis.

Example 8.13: Coefficient of Multiple Determination   Obtaining the coefficient of determination for the data from Example 8.12 simply involves squaring the correlation coefficient of +.78. The resulting value, .61, suggests that 61% of differences in the number of hedgers used per hour by a teacher can be explained by differences in the combination of class size and the number of questions asked per hour by students. Factors other than these two independent variables can explain the remaining 39% of changes in dependent-variable scores.

8.3.3   Partial and Part Correlations

Researchers do always address situations involving more than two variables with a multiple regression–correlation analysis. Sometimes, they wish to examine the relationship between a single independent variable and a single dependent variable, free of the influences that other intervening variables may have. *Intervening variables*, sometimes called *confounding variables*, are factors that impact scores on the dependent variable or on both the independent and dependent variables, complicating the direct relationship between the two. When intervening variables exist, a pairwise correlation coefficient can misrepresent the linear relationships between the independent and dependent variables.

Example 8.14: Intervening Variable   A researcher may realize, for instance, that the course topic may influence both the number of students in a particular class and the number of hedgers used by teachers of that class. The researcher may reason that math and natural science courses tend to have lower enrollments than courses in other subjects, such as those in the social sciences and humanities. Further, the researcher might contend that math and natural science topics tend to have their bases in confirmed facts, leading to little hesitation in the speech patterns of the teacher. But humanities and social sciences courses often challenge or question proposed ideas, resulting in frequent use of hedgers by teachers who consider and carefully phrase their words during class. Because the degree to which course material contains factual information may affect values for both the independent and dependent variables, pairwise correlation values may be misleading. Figure 8.11 illustrates the role of the intervening variable in this relationship.

According to this diagram, the number of students in the class and the number of hedgers used per hour by the teacher both change in conjunction with the amount of factual information in course material. These links can explain the relationship between the independent- and dependent-variable scores. Although the strong positive correlation (see Example 8.5) may seem to imply that the number of students in a class directly affects the number of hedgers used by the teacher of that class, the relationship may not be so simple. The simultaneous increases in independent- and dependent-variable scores may result from the fact that changes in both of these variables' scores reflect changes in the intervening variable's scores.

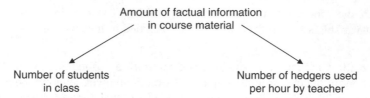

<u>Figure 8.11.</u> Intervening variable causal diagram. Each arrow in the diagram signifies the direction of causality. The intervening variable of amount of factual information in course material influences both the number of students in the class and the number of hedgers used per hour by the teacher of that class.

An intervening variable can raise or lower a correlation coefficient. In some cases, the intervening variable provides an indirect connection between the independent and dependent variables that further supports a preexisting relationship between the two. This situation leads to a correlation coefficient that overestimates the pure relationship between the independent and dependent variables. In contrast, the intervening variable may change independent- and dependent-variable scores so that they do not change as consistently with respect to each other as they would on their own. An artificially low correlation would, therefore, result.

Of course, not every correlation analysis involves intervening variables, and the pairwise correlation coefficient often suffices. However, if you suspect that an intervening variable plays a role in a linear relationship, you may find partial and part correlations useful. Using the partial–part correlation analysis allows you to, in effect, pretend that intervening variables do not exist. The formulas for partial and part correlation coefficients provide estimates of the correlation between the independent and the dependent variable while controlling for intervening variables.

Partial Correlation. A *partial correlation* analysis holds steady the influence of intervening variables on both the independent and dependent variables. The formula for the partial correlation ensures that intervening-variable variances do not affect the relationship between X and Y. The basis behind this formula is that subtracting the correlation coefficient for each intervening variable and X and the correlation coefficient for each intervening variable and Y from r_{XY} leaves you with a representation of the pure relationship between X and Y. Deriving the partial correlation coefficient formula involves dividing this difference by the product of standard deviations related to the intervening variables. (Note that this procedure follows the same general pattern as that used to derive the pairwise coefficient, described in Section 8.22.) This procedure, along with substitutions based on statistical equivalences and algebraic simplification, produces the following formula for the partial correlation coefficient that removes the effects of a single intervening variable, W:

$$r_{XY.W} = \frac{r_{XY} - r_{WX}r_{WY}}{\sqrt{1 - r_{WX}^2}\,\sqrt{1 - r_{WY}^2}} \tag{8.9}$$

The notation $r_{XY.W}$ indicates that the coefficient describes the linear relationship between X and Y independent of W.

Example 8.15: Partial Correlation Coefficient Equation (8.9) can be applied to the situation described in Example 8.14. The partial correlation, in this case, indicates the strength of the linear relationship between the number of students in a class (X) and the number of hedgers used per hour by the teacher (Y) while ignoring any effect that the amount of factual information in course material (W) has on either of the other two variables.

The following dataset includes hypothetical values for W, measured by the percentage of course material based on confirmed fact, along with the sample values already used for X and Y earlier in this chapter:

W (Factual Information)	X (Class Size)	Y (Hedgers/Hour)
91	9	9
68	19	4
56	71	14
50	35	10
44	54	17

From Equation (8.5), one can determine that $r_{WX} = -.75$, $r_{WY} = -.58$, and $r_{XY} = +.77$. Calculation of the partial correlation coefficient begins with the insertion of these values into Equation (8.9):

$$r_{XY.W} = \frac{.77 - (-.75)(-.58)}{\sqrt{1 - (-.75)^2}\sqrt{1 - (-.58)^2}}$$

$$= \frac{.77 - .435}{\sqrt{.438}\sqrt{.664}} = \frac{.335}{.540} = +.62$$

The partial correlation coefficient of +.62, compared to the pairwise correlation coefficient of +.77, suggests that the intervening variable enhances the trend between independent- and dependent-variable scores. In other words, the influence of the amount of factual information in course material makes the linear relationship between the number of students in a class and the number of hedgers used per hour by the teacher seem a bit stronger than it really is.

Example 8.15 addresses a relatively simple scenario in that it involves only three variables. A similar procedure, however, can remove the effects of any number of intervening variables. To adjust Equation (8.9) so that you can remove the effects of more than one intervening variable, you simply need to include correlation values involving those intervening variables in the numerator and the denominator. Equation

(8.10) presents a generic version of the formula, in which n represents the number of intervening variables:

$$r_{XY.W \cdots n} = \frac{r_{XY} - r_{WX}r_{WY} \cdots r_{nX}r_{nY}}{\sqrt{1-r_{WX}^2}\sqrt{1-r_{WY}^2} \cdots \sqrt{1-r_{nX}^2}\sqrt{1-r_{nY}^2}} \qquad (8.10)$$

Part Correlation. When removing the effects of intervening variables, you usually need to address their influences on both the independent and dependent variables as the partial correlation coefficient does. Occasionally, however, you may find that the intervening-variable effects change scores for only the independent variable. In this situation, the pairwise correlation coefficient (r_{XY}) would be based on altered x values, but unaffected by y values. Thus, obtaining the "pure" value involves removing the effect of the intervening variables on the independent variable. The *part correlation* accomplishes this task. Notation for the part correlation involving a single intervening variable uses W to represent this variable and $r_{Y(X.W)}$ for the correlation coefficient. The parentheses in the coefficient notation group the independent and intervening variables to indicate that the procedure controls for W only with respect to its influence on X.

The formula for a partial correlation coefficient looks very similar to the formula for a partial correlation coefficient. In fact, the two equations have identical numerators. Without the need to remove the influence that W has on Y, though, the denominator of the part correlation coefficient formula does not contain the r_{WY} term:

$$r_{Y(X.W)} = \frac{r_{XY} - r_{WX}r_{WY}}{\sqrt{1-r_{WX}^2}} \qquad (8.11)$$

Because it is a shortened version of the partial correlation, some refer to the part correlation as the *semipartial correlation*.

Example 8.16: Part Correlation Coefficient One would find the part correlation coefficient useful if one believed that the amount of factual information presented in a course (W) affects the number of students enrolled in that course (X), but has no direct impact on number of hedgers used by a teacher (Y). The steps below produce a value that describes the linear relationship between X and Y, independent of any association between W and X:

$$r_{Y(X.W)} = \frac{.77-(-.75)(-.58)}{\sqrt{1-(-.75)^2}}$$

$$= \frac{.77-.435}{\sqrt{.438}} = \frac{.335}{.661} = +.51$$

This part correlation coefficient, like the partial correlation coefficient obtained in Example 8.15, is smaller than the pairwise correlation coefficient of .77. Apparently, the impact that the intervening has on the independent variable alters the trend in independent-variable scores so that r_{XY} implies a stronger linear relationship with dependent-variable scores than really exists. Controlling for the relationship between the amount of factual information in course material and the number of students in a course, therefore, reduced the correlation coefficient value.

Equation (8.12) provides a generic version of the part correlation coefficient equation comparable to the generic version of the partial correlation coefficient equation shown in Equation (8.10). Once again, n represents the number of intervening variables involved in the analysis. By including relevant terms in the numerator and denominator, you can calculate a part correlation coefficient that removes the effects of any number of intervening variables upon the independent variable:

$$r_{Y(X.W\cdots n)} = \frac{r_{XY} - r_{WX}r_{WY}\cdots r_{nX}r_{nY}}{\sqrt{1 - r_{(WX}^2} \cdots \sqrt{1 - r_{(n-1)X}^2}\sqrt{1 - r_{nX}^2}} \tag{8.12}$$

8.4 THE PHI COEFFICIENT

Section 8.1 of this chapter explains that regression and correlation analysis pertains to situations involving only continuous variables. However, a value similar to the correlation coefficient, called the *phi coefficient*(Φ), can assess relationships between two dichotomous categorical variables. The relationships described by the Φ coefficient are not linear, as they are for correlations. Linear relationships can exist only when patterns of increasing and decreasing values among the variables can exist. As you know from Chapter 2, categorical variables produce nominal data, which have no numerical value. Still, trends in the frequencies among combinations of the categorical variables' groups may exist and this aspect is what the Φ coefficient addresses.

You can interpret Φ values similarly to the way you interpret correlation coefficients. Values near 0 indicate very weak relationships, and values near -1.00 or $+1.00$ indicate very strong relationships. A 2×2 crosstabulation can help to clarify the phi coefficients' meaning (see Table 8.2). Figure 8.17 uses A, B, C, and D to represent cell frequencies.

TABLE 8.2. Phi Coefficient Crosstabulation[a]

		Dependent Variable (Y)		
		Y_1	Y_2	Σ
Independent Variable (X)	X_1	A	B	$A + B$
	X_2	C	D	$C + D$
	Σ	$A + C$	$B + D$	$A + B + C + D$

[a]In this table, X_1 and X_2 represent the two independent-variable categories; Y_1 and Y_2 represent the two dependent-variable categories. The letter in each cell represents the frequency for the relevant combination of independent- and dependent-variable categories. Marginal values consist of sums across rows, columns, or for all cells in the table.

An association among variables exists if frequencies along one diagonal greatly exceed frequencies along the other diagonal. So, if the values of A and D are much higher than the values of B and C are, then Φ signifies a relationship between the independent variables. The same occurs if the values of B and C are much higher than the values of A and D are. In the first of these cases, a positive Φ results and in the second of these cases, a negative Φ results. The sign, however, is just an outcome of the way in which you enter data into the crosstabulation.

To contrast the frequencies along each diagonal in the crosstabulation, the numerator of the Φ formula requires you to find the difference between products of A and D and of B and C. The fact that the (AD) term appears first in the formula explains the distinction between positive and negative Φ values. The denominator of the formula simply consists of the square root of all marginal values:

$$\Phi = \frac{AB - CD}{\sqrt{(A+B)(C+D)(A+C)(B+D)}} \tag{8.13}$$

Example 8.17: Phi Coefficient   The continuous data used for examples earlier in this chapter are not appropriate for a phi analysis. However, had a researcher categorized these data, he or she could make use of Φ. Rather than describing class enrollment with a number, for example, a researcher might describe classes as having fewer than 30 students or at least 30 students. Similarly, the researcher might create one category for teachers who use fewer than five hedgers per hour and another for teachers who use at least five hedgers per hour. On the basis of these standards, the crosstabulation in Table 8.3 summarizes frequencies for data used to create Figure 8.1.

This particular crosstabulation happens to blatantly show a positive association among variables with higher values for A and D than for B and C. The phi coefficient, however, provides numerical proof of the relationship:

$$\Phi = \frac{(13)(21) - (2)(4)}{\sqrt{(15)(25)(17)(23)}}$$

$$= \frac{273 - 8}{\sqrt{146,625}} = \frac{265}{382.92} = +.69$$

TABLE 8.3. Students × Hedgers Crosstabulation[a]

		Number of Hedgers per Hour		
		<5	≥5	Σ
Number of Students	<30	13	2	15
	≥30	4	21	25
	Σ	17	23	40

[a]Rows of the crosstabulation distinguish between classes with fewer than 30 students and with at least 30 students. Columns of the crosstabulation distinguish between classes in which the teacher uses fewer than five hedgers per hour and in which the teacher uses at least five hedgers per hour. Each cell contains the frequency of classes that fall into a particular combination of variable categories.

The positive value of Φ indicates that large values exist along the AD diagonal as opposed to the BC diagonal. A negative value would have resulted if larger values existed along the BC diagonal than along the AD diagonal. With an absolute value of .69, one could characterize the relationship between the independent and dependent variables as moderate, bordering on strong. These two aspects, when considered together, suggest that teachers of small classes tend to use few hedgers and teachers of large classes tend to use many hedgers. Had a more equal dispersion of frequencies than that shown in Figure 8.18 existed, a trend in frequencies would not have been so evident. Therefore, Φ would have fallen closer to 0.

8.5 EXPLAINING RESULTS OF CORRELATION–REGRESSION ANALYSIS

8.5.1 Regression and Correlation

The most important thing to remember when explaining results of the analyses described in this chapter is not to overstate a relationship. Most overstatements result from neglecting to consider the linear nature of regression and correlation analyses. In explanations of regression and correlation values, you should use "linear," or describe the way in which the dependent-variable scores change in response to changes in scores of the independent variable(s). With a low correlation coefficient, you should avoid claims that no relationship exists because such statements overlook the possibility of curvilinear relationships.

Also, you should avoid using causal terms when describing relationships. The fact that two variables have a linear relationship does not necessarily mean that changes in the independent variable cause changes in the dependent variable. Intervening variables or causal time order issues[4] may explain the relationship.

Beyond these general cautions, you can choose to report the statistics that you believe best suit your purposes. Some situations call for you to include a scatterplot, a regression equation, and a correlation coefficient. For other situations, usually when your audience has little knowledge of statistics and responds best to visual representations, a scatterplot, alone, suffices. You may wish to display the least-squares regression line on this scatterplot and provide the equation for this line, explaining how it can predict dependent-variable scores.

---

[4]Issues of causal time order arise when a researcher cannot determine whether the changes in independent-variable scores cause changes in dependent-variable scores or vice versa. For example, if a positive correlation exists between individuals' love of animals (measured according to some numeric scale) and the number of pets that they've had during their lifetimes, it may be difficult to determine whether having a lot of pets causes people to love animals or whether loving animals caused people to have a lot of pets.

Example 8.18: Presentation of Regression Analysis   Findings from the bivariate regression analyses provided in Section 8.2.1 may, therefore, be summarized as follows:

The arrangement of points indicates a clear tendency for the number of hedgers used per hour by a class' teacher to increase as the number of students in the class increases. See the scatterplot in Figure 8.12.

The equation of the regression line that describes this arrangement of points, $y = 1.02 + .10x$, verifies this fact. The positive coefficient for an x regression line has a positive slope, indicating a direct linear relationship between the independent and dependent variables. Further, with knowledge of a class' size, one can predict the number of hedgers used per hour by the teacher of that class, represented by y. Replacing the x for the class size and performing the necessary arithmetic produces this value.

Results of the multivariate regression analysis presented in Section 8.3.1 could be presented in a similar manner.

Researchers, however, tend to present correlation coefficients alone more often than they present scatterplots and regression equations alone. The level of your audience's knowledge determines the extent to which you must explain the meaning of the correlation coefficient. If necessary, you should characterize the value according to Table 8.1. If you believe that your audience would understand the concepts of percent-

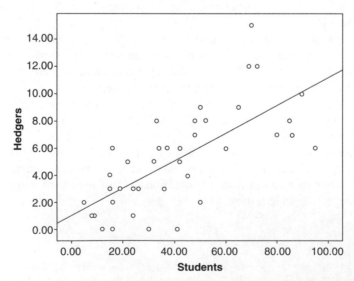

Figure 8.12. Scatterplot for presentation of regression analysis. Points in the scatterplot follow the general pattern of the positively sloped regression line. This arrangement indicates that the number of hedgers used by teachers increases in conjunction with class enrollment.

ages better than the concept of correlations, then you may find it useful to provide and explain the coefficient of determination.

Example 8.19: Presentation of Correlation Coefficient   The correlation coefficient and a coefficient of determination from the examples in Section 8.2.2 can a serve as a basis for this sort of description.

> Calculations produced a correlation coefficient (r) of +.77. According to this value, the number of students in a particular class serves as a strong predictor of the number of hedgers used per hour by the teacher of that class. The correlation coefficient's positive value suggests that increases in the number of students in a class correspond to increases in the number of hedgers used by teachers.

> The value of r^2 signifies of the proportion of variance in scores on one variable that can be explained by variance in scores on the other variable. In this case, $r^2 = .59$, meaning that 59% of differences in the number of hedgers used by teachers relates to differences in the number of students in the class. Other, as yet unknown, factors explain the remaining 41% of variation in teachers' use of hedgers.

Descriptions similar to this one, but obviously expanded, can address the multiple-correlation coefficient, the partial correlation coefficient, and the part correlation coefficient.

Although Examples 8.18 and 8.19 provide relevant statistics within the main content of the explanation, you may vary the presentation of this information. The use of parentheses, references to appendixes that contain diagrams, and many other techniques are perfectly acceptable. Chapter 11 includes detailed suggestions for effectively presenting findings from regression and correlation analyses.

8.5.2   Relationships between Dichotomous Variables

Most likely, you would not use a phi coefficient in very basic analysis. So, the need to present and report it arises much less frequently than the need to discuss correlation coefficient and regression equations does. Those interested in the phi coefficient generally have some background in statistical analysis and, thus, you can likely assume that they understand what a phi coefficient is.

For situations in which you must explain the role of the phi coefficient, however, you may find it helpful to begin with by presenting the 2×2 crosstabulation. The phi coefficient's role within a two-dichotomous-variable context should then become clear. Then, you can present the value and explain that it describes the distribution of subjects among diagonals of the crosstabulation's cells.

Example 8.20: Presentation of Phi Coefficient   Explaining the trend of frequencies in Figure 8.10, for example, involves only a short paragraph.

> Clearly, the upper left and lower right cells of this crosstabulation contain higher frequencies than do the other two cells. Accordingly, $\Phi = +.69$. This value indicates a moderate—bordering on strong—trend of low use of hedgers in small classes and high use of hedgers in large classes.

Again, you should use Example 8.20 only as a basis for your own presentation of results. Your research goals, familiarity with your audience, writing style, and many other factors may determine the way in which you choose to present and explain the phi coefficient.

8.6 CONCLUSION

With the exception of the mean, regression, and correlation values may receive more mention in the everyday world than results of any other statistical analysis do. Computing the correlation coefficient and obtaining a regression equation requires a reasonable amount of familiarity with statistical procedure. However, a general understanding of the correlation coefficient, itself, as well as the regression equation and the scatterplot, requires little knowledge of statistics. This quality makes them appealing and understandable to the public. Those with little statistical knowledge likely do not know the role of a chi-square test, a t test, or an ANOVA and would have difficulty comprehending the concept of "significant difference." Therefore, public sources, such as news agencies, tend to simply describe trends in relationship by presenting correlation coefficients and graphs.

Unfortunately, however, many use the term "correlation" in too general a sense. Having read this chapter, you realize that regression and correlation analyses apply to situations involving continuous variables and that they describe only linear relationships. However, inexperienced statisticians often make such statements as "There is a correlation between gender and violence." You should trust your instinct that such a correlation cannot exist, given the independent variable's categorical nature, but also understand that such reports refer to "correlation" in the popular sense, not the statistical sense.

Still, these analyses hold a very as important a role within the context of genuine statistical analysis. As explained early in the chapter, you could not examine the relationships between scores on two or more continuous variables without considering regression and correlation. An understanding of the topics in this chapter will help you better understand the inferential statistics presented in previous chapters. For example, you can now appreciate why some might use an ANOVA, along with regression–correlation analysis, to assess the relationship between two continuous variables. Such an analysis would involve considering each individual independent-variable score as a category in and of itself, potentially creating as many independent-variable categories as subjects. Comparing the dependent-variable scores (or, when necessary, the mean dependent-variable scores) for each independent variable score, essentially constitutes an ANOVA. Many perform this analysis in conjunction with regression–correlation analysis. The regression and correlation values describe trends in the way that dependent-variable scores change in relation to changes in independent-variable scores, and the ANOVA F value indicates whether these changes are significant.

Further, many of the principles described in this chapter contribute to advanced procedures, some of which receive attention in Chapter 9. These procedures can address the covariance, which plays a role in determining the correlation coefficient, as described in Section 8.2. Chapter 9 demonstrates how considering a trend in variables' scores within the context of other statistical tests allows you to address a wide variety of research contexts.

STATISTICAL RESOURCES FOR SPSS

For regression and correlation analyses as well as for a phi analysis, SPSS output produces the very same values that you can obtain yourself by using the formulas shown throughout this chapter. The regression and correlation functions in SPSS can provide scatterplots, regression equations, correlation coefficients, and coefficients of determination.

Examples of this output appear in Figure 8.13 and Tables 8.4–8.8. This chapter's companion website contains additional examples and explanations for these analyses.

Bivariate Regression and Correlation in SPSS

The screens used to obtain scatterplots, regression equations, and correlation coefficients in SPSS each, in some way, ask you to identify your analysis as bivariate or multivariate. Bivariate analyses produce a simple scatterplot, coefficient for a bivariate regression, and pairwise correlation coefficients.

Scatterplots. A number of methods exist for producing scatterplots in SPSS. One of the simplest methods uses the "Legacy Dialogues" option, located under the "Graphs" heading on the toolbar. The "Legacy Dialogues" pulldown menu lists the names of many graphs, including one entitled "Scatter/Dot." With this selection, a box allowing you to specify the particular type of scatterplot that you need, appears.

A simple scatterplot serves the purpose of a bivariate linear regression. With your identification of the independent and dependent variables, SPSS produces the

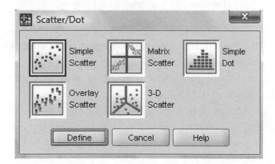

Figure 8.13. SPSS "Linear Regression" window. The SPSS "Scatter/Dot" window allows the user to choose from five types of graphs. The simple scatter refers to a bivariate scatterplot. The resulting graph situates independent-variable scores along the *x* axis and dependent-variable scores along the *y* axis.

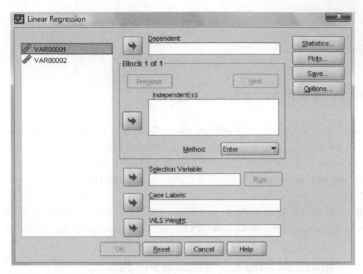

<u>Figure 8.14.</u> SPSS "Linear Regression" window. The user obtains regression and correlation values by moving the independent- and dependent-variable names to appropriate areas in the window. For a bivariate analysis, each box should contain the name of only one variable.

appropriate scatterplot. The scatterplots in this chapter are examples of SPSS's scatterplot output. (Although the vertical lines used to illustrate residuals have been added to Fig. 8.6.)

Once this output appears on the screen, you may adjust the appearance of the graph by making changes such as including the regression line and modifying x- and y-axis scales.

Regression Equation Coefficients. To perform regression and correlation analyses in SPSS, you must use the "Analyze" pull-down menu. If you choose the "Regression" and then the "Linear" options, a "Linear Regression" window appears (Fig. 8.14).

Output contains the values of r, r^2, a, and b.

Example 8.21: SPSS Output for Bivariate Regression Analysis Output for the analyses using the scenario described in Section 8.2.1 includes the correlation coefficient, coefficient of determination, shown in Table 8.4, and information about the regression equation, shown in Table 8.5.

According to the "Model Summary" (Table 8.4), the x and y variables have a correlation of .70 (rounded to two decimal places). Although you could square this value yourself to obtain the coefficient of determination, the model summary provides this value as well. Values for the regression equation appear in the B column of Table 8.5. The y intercept is the first value in the column, and the slope is the second value in the column. Placing these values into their appropriate places produces the equation shown in Table 8.4. (Tables 8.4 and 8.5 are two of the four tables included in the SPSS regression output for the data from examples in Section 8.2.1.)

TABLE 8.4. SPSS Bivariate Regression Output. Model Summary[a]

Model	r	r^2	Adjusted r^2	Standard Error of the Estimate
1	.703[b]	.494	.481	2.59045

[a]Values of the correlation coefficient and coefficient of determination appear as r and r^2, respectively, in this table.
[b]Predictors: (constant), students.

TABLE 8.5. SPSS Bivariate Regression Output: Coefficients[a]

	Unstandardized Coefficients		Standardized Coefficient		
Model	B	Standard Error	β	t	Significance
1 (Constant)	1.017	.799	—	1.272	.211
Students	0.101	.017	.703	6.096	.000

[a]Dependent variable: hedgers. This table provides the y intercept and slope for the regression equation under the column labeled B.

Correlation Coefficients. If you wish only to obtain the pairwise correlation coefficient or would like to obtain correlation coefficients for many combinations of variable, you may wish to use the "correlation" function. The prompt for this analysis is also in the "Analyze" pulldown menu. You should choose "bivariate correlation coefficient" from the options provided. A window entitled "Bivariate Correlations" appears (Fig. 8.15).

SPSS calculates r for all pairs of variables placed into the "variables" area of the window shown in Figure 8.15. The output for this process consists of a correlation matrix.

Example 8.22: SPSS Bivariate Correlation Matrix Output   Table 8.6 is a correlation matrix containing the pairwise correlation coefficient obtained through calculations shown in Table 8.5.

TABLE 8.6. SPSS Bivariate Correlation Output: Correlations[a]

		Students	Hedgers
Students	Pearson correlation	1.000	.703[b]
	Significance (two-tailed)		.000
	N	40	40
Hedgers	Pearson correlation	.703[b]	1.000
	Significance (two-tailed)	.000	
	N	40	40

[a]The correlation matrix summarizes data used in Section 8.2. The correlation coefficient describing the linear relationship between the number of students in a class and the number of hedgers used per hour by the teacher of that class lies at the intersection of the appropriate row and column.
[b]Correlation is significant at the 0.01 level (two-tailed).

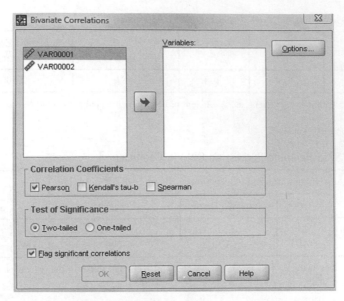

Figure 8.15. SPSS "Bivariate Correlations" window. The names of variables for which a correlation is desired should be moved to the "Variables" area of the window. If this area contains the names of more than two variables, SPSS will provide the correlation coefficient for each pair of variables listed.

All correlation matrices are symmetric along the diagonal from the upper left to the bottom right corner. Values of +1.00 appear at the intersections of rows and columns that pertain to the same variable because all variables correlate perfectly with themselves. The correlations of interest, though, lie at the intersection of the rows and columns representing different variables. Although Example 8.6 includes data for only two variables, correlation matrices can address many correlations at once, providing an *r* value for each pair of variables.

Multivariate Regression and Correlation in SPSS

The "Analyze" and "Graphs" menus contain the commands used to obtain multivariate regression and multiple correlation information. Just as in the bivariate situation, the multivariate scatterplot and the multivariate regression equation output contain the multiple-correlation coefficient. You can find details on using these functions for the multivariate situation as well as for interpreting the output on this chapter's companion website. Obtaining partial and part correlation coefficients, however, requires a different procedure.

www.moravian.edu/aqd

Scatterplots. The "3-D Scatter" option in the "Scatter/Dot" window (see Fig. 8.13) allows you to create a scatterplot that shows the arrangement of points for scores on three variables. This process actually produced Figure 8.10.

Regression Equation Coefficients. To perform a multiple, rather than a bivariate, regression analysis, you need only move more than one variable name to the "Independent Variable" areas of the "Linear Regression" window. Output includes the multiple-correlation coefficient, the coefficient of multiple determination, and values for the regression equation.

From SPSS regression output, you can obtain the multiple correlation coefficient and multiple coefficient of determination from the table labeled "Model Summary" (Table 8.4) and coefficients for the regression equation from the table labeled "Coefficients" (Table 8.5).

Correlation Coefficients. SPSS does not provide multiple-correlation matrixes. You should obtain a multiple-correlation coefficient from the regression equation output. You can, however, instruct SPSS to produce matrices of partial and part correlation coefficients.

Although you must still select the "Correlation" option from those listed under the "Analyze" heading, you must then deliberately instruct SPSS to calculate a partial correlation coefficient. After selecting "partial" from the "Correlation" menu, a "Partial Correlations" window appears.

The "Variables" label in the "Partial Correlations" window (Fig. 8.16) refers to the independent and dependent variables. You can begin by moving the names of these variables to that area of the window. The names of intervening variables should be moved to the area of the window labeled "Controlling for." By doing so, you indicate to SPSS that you wish to hold this variable's scores constant while assessing the linear relationship between the independent and dependent variables. The resulting output consists of a correlation matrix for partial correlation coefficients.

Example 8.23: SPSS Partial Correlation Matrix Output   The name of the intervening variable from Example 8.15, factualinfo, appears under the title of "Control Variables" in the SPSS partial correlation matrix.

Therefore, you know that the values in the correlation matrix result from removing the influence of the intervening variable(s) listed on the left side of the output.

TABLE 8.7. SPSS Partial Correlation Output: Correlations[a]

Control Variables			Students	Hedgers
factualinfo	Students	Correlation	1.000	.628
		Significance (two-tailed)	—	.372
		Degrees of freedom	0	2
	Hedgers	Correlation	.628	1.000
		Significance (two-tailed)	.372	—
		Degrees of freedom	2	0

[a]SPSS lists the control variables(s) along the left side of the partial correlation matrix. Otherwise, the partial correlation matrix has the same appearance as the pairwise correlation matrix does.

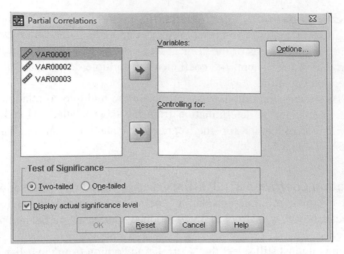

Figure 8.16. SPSS "Partial Correlations" window. This window contains an area for the names of the independent and dependent variables as well as an area for the name of the variable or variables that the researcher wishes to remove from the relationship. Placing the name of each variable in the appropriate area of the window produces a partial correlation coefficient.

The matrix for a partial correlation closely resembles the pairwise correlation matrix as well. However, SPSS includes the name of the intervening variable(s), called the *control variable* in SPSS terminology, in the partial correlation matrix.

On request, SPSS can also include partial correlation coefficients in its regression output. This output also contains part correlation coefficients. In fact, SPSS does not produce part correlation matrices, as it does for partial correlation coefficients. Requesting the part correlation within the "Linear Regression" window is the only way to obtain part correlation coefficients from SPSS.

Clicking on the "Statistics" button in the "Linear Regression" window brings a "Linear Regression: Statistics" window to the screen (Fig. 8.17).

A list on the right side of the window contains an option for part and partial correlations. If you select this option, the values appear in the regression output's coefficients table. Additional information about this output, as well as the process of obtaining multiple and part correlation information from SPSS, appears in this chapter's companion website.

www.moravian.edu/aqd

Phi Coefficient Output

Because a phi analysis addresses two categorical values and, thus, does not assess a linear relationship, SPSS's regression and correlation commands do not apply. The command to provide Φ is found within the SPSS "Crosstabs" window. In addition to

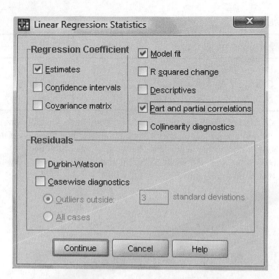

<u>Figure 8.17.</u> "Linear Regression: Statistics" window for part and partial correlations. The user can request part and partial correlations in SPSS's linear regression output by clicking on the box next to the "Part and partial correlations" listing on the right side of the window. The output contains coefficients for the linear relationship between the dependent variable and each independent variable, holding constant the effects of all other independent variables as appropriate for the part or partial analysis.

the following basic explanations of the process for obtaining and interpreting Φ, this chapter's companion website provides detailed steps.

www.moravian.edu/aqd

Chapter 2 contains information on requesting a crosstabulation from SPSS, and Chapter 5 expands on this information by explaining how to obtain a chi-square value by using the "Crosstabs" window's "Statistics" function. Just below the "Chi-square" option in the "Crosstabs: Statistics" window is an area labeled "nominal." The prompt for a phi coefficient, labeled "Phi and Cramer's V," lies within this area (see Fig. 8.18).

When you select this option, SPSS includes the phi value in its crosstabulation output. You are already familiar with SPSS's crosstabulation output from Chapter 2. If you request a phi coefficient within the context of the crosstabulation analysis, the crosstabulation output includes a table entitled, "Symmetric Measures," which identifies Φ.

Example 8.24: SPSS Phi Coefficient Output The "Symmetric Measures" table (Table 8.8) contains the phi coefficient found through calculations in Example 8.18.

TABLE 8.8. SPSS Symmetric Measures Table[a]

Nominal by Nominal	Value	Significance
Phi	.692	~.000
Cramer's V	.692	~.000
N of valid cases	40	—

[a]The Φ value of .692 indicates a moderate trend in the distribution of subjects into categories. Cramer's V value (although not discussed in this book) refers to the dependence between scores of the two variables in the analysis. As the identical scores indicate, it is very closely related to the phi value.

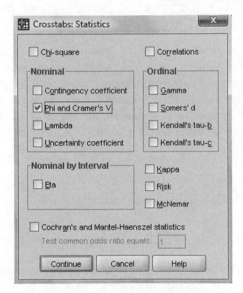

Figure 8.18. "Crosstabs: Statistics" window for phi coefficient. The user instructs SPSS to include Φ in its crosstabulation output by selecting the "Phi and Cramer's V" option in the "Crosstabs: Statitistics" window. The resulting value describes the trend in category frequency for variables in the crosstabulation.

Even though Φ analyses basically apply to dichotomous variables, SPSS can also provide Φ coefficients for crosstabulations based on variables with more than two categories. The value of Φ in this case, however, can reflect much more complicated trends than those that determine the value of Φ in the standard two-dichotmous-variable situation.

REVIEW QUESTIONS

For Questions 8.1–8.5, determine whether the analysis, described by its independent variable and dependent variable (i.v. and d.v.), would most likely produce a regression line with a positive slope, a negative slope, or neither.

8.1.   i.v.: the amount of time per week a child practices piano

  d.v.: the number of mistakes the child makes during her or his piano recital performance

8.2.   i.v.: the number of floors in an office building

  d.v.: the percentage of workers in the building who use the stairs to get to their offices

8.3.   i.v.: the cost of a child's Halloween costume

  d.v.: the amount of candy the child receives while trick-or-treating

8.4.   i.v.: the number of pages in a novel

  d.v.: the amount of time it takes to read the novel

8.5.   i.v.: the size of a dog

  d.v.: the number of times per day that the dog is walked

Use the following scatterplot for Questions 8.6–8.9. The points represent data from a hypothetical market test of peanut butter's "stickiness" and refers to the number of seconds needed for subjects to say the alphabet with different amounts of peanut butter in their mouths.

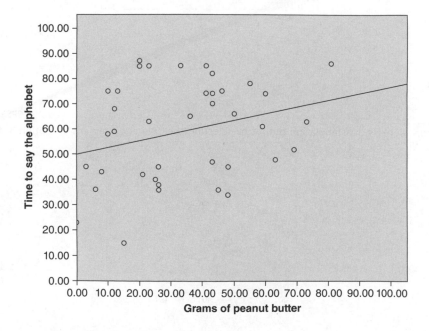

8.6. About what is the regression line's slope?

8.7. What is the regression line's y intercept?

8.8. What is the equation of the regression line?

8.9. How long does the regression equation predict to it will take one who eats 100 grams of peanut butter to recite the alphabet?

8.10. Explain the relationship between the value of the correlation coefficient (*r*) and the effectiveness of the regression equation in making predictions.

For Questions 8.11–8.14, use the scatterplots to determine the associated correlation coefficient's sign (positive, negative, or neither) and estimate the strength of the correlation (using the descriptions in Table 8.1).

8.11.

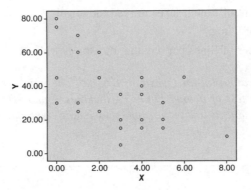

8.12.

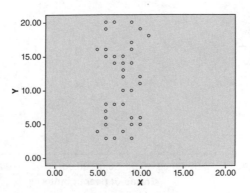

8.13.

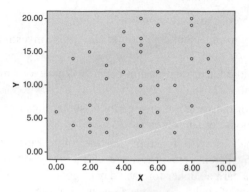

8.14.

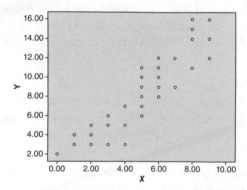

8.15. Calculate the pairwise correlation coefficient given the following X and Y values. On the basis of this value, describe the relationship between X and Y:

X	Y
22	2
45	3
16	6
30	7
26	7
18	8

8.16. Find the coefficient of determination for the data in Question 8.15. What does this value indicate?

Use the following scenario to answer Questions 8.17–8.20. Suppose that a researcher measures the ounces of sunscreen that 200 individuals use before and during a day at the beach and the severity of the subjects' sunburns (0 = none; 10 = severe) at the end of the day. For these two variables, r = −.65.

8.17. What is the sign of the regression line's slope?

8.18. Describe the arrangement of points for this investigations' data on a scatterplot.

8.19. How strong is the linear relationship between ounces of sunscreen used and the severity of sunburn?

8.20. What percent of the variation in severity of sunburn can be explained by variations in the amount of sunscreen used?

8.21. Behavioral analysts wish to study the use of reward charts, often used in schools and by parents, to encourage children's good behavior. With these charts, children earn a sticker for each day of good behavior and, after obtaining a certain amount of stickers, receive a reward. For their analysis, the researchers find 100 children for whom reward charts are used. Data for each child include the number of stickers needed for a reward and the number of stickers that the child earns each week. These two variables have a very weak linear relationship ($r = +.14$). Why is it incorrect for the analysts to assume that no relationship exists between the variables? What type(s) of relationship should they investigate further? Why?

Determine whether a multiple, partial, or part correlation is most appropriate for the scenarios described in Questions 8.22–8.25. Identify the independent variable(s) (i.v.), dependent variable (d.v.), and, if applicable, the intervening variable (I.v.) for each.

8.22. an investigation to determine whether the numerical grade that one receives in a typing class, irrespective of one's typing speed, can predict the number of typographical errors per page that one makes

8.23. an investigation into the number of calories consumed for dinner as predicted by a combination of the calories consumed for breakfast and for lunch

8.24. an investigation in which the researchers wish to determine whether the size of the print on a page, independent of subjects' levels of vision (from a vision test), can predict the amount of time needed to complete a brain-teaser puzzle

8.25. an investigation into the relationship between temperature and plants' rate of growth independent of the influence that humidity level may have on both of these factors

8.26. Suppose that a potential candidate for political office wishes to determine the extent to which the amount of money spent on past campaigns (X) corresponds to the percentages of popular votes that candidates receive (Y). During the investigation, however, the potential candidate realizes that the number of weeks spent on the campaign trail (Z) may also play a role in the relationship. The condidate gathers the following data for each of these three variables from eight past political candidates:

X	Y	Z
($ million)	(% popular vote)	(weeks)
8.2	38	34
5.2	62	28
11.1	30	19
6.5	61	39
4.6	47	42
9.7	43	36
10.6	53	26
6.9	72	38

(A) Find r_{XY}, r_{XZ}, and r_{YZ}.

(B) Calculate the multiple-correlation coefficient, R_{YXZ}.

(C) Explain the meaning of the results from (B) in terms of the linear relationship between money spent during campaigns, weeks spent campaigning, and percentage of popular vote.

8.27. Find the coefficient of multiple determination for the data presented in Question 8.26. What does this value indicate?

For questions 8.28 and 8.29, consider the following scenario. Suppose that a researcher believes that the relationship between the age at which individuals marry (X) and the number of children they have (Y) is confounded by the individuals' age at the time of data collection (W). (Middle-age and elderly individuals may have married early and had many children because, years ago, it was more common to do so than it is today.) So, the correlation between age at the time of marriage and number of children may reflect a "hidden" effect of subjects' current ages. To begin the analysis, the researcher calculates pairwise correlation coefficients for each pair of variables: $r_{WX} = +.68$; $r_{WY} = +.16$; $r_{XY} = -.32$.

8.28. (A) Calculate the partial correlation coefficient, (r_{XYW}), to assess the relationship between age at the time of marriage and number of children, independent of any relationship that either of these variables may have with age at the time of data collection.

(B) Explain the meaning of the results from (A).

8.29. (A) Calculate the part correlation coefficient, [$r_{Y(X.W)}$] to assess the relationship between age at the time of marriage and number of children, independent of any relationship age at the time of marrage may have with age at the time of data collection.

(B) Explain the meaning of the results from (A).

8.30. Frequencies in the following crosstabulation represent the number of adults and of children/teenagers (determined by asking subjects their ages) who visit three randomly selected fast-food restaurants and three randomly selected full-service restaurants during the course of a particular day. Find the value of Φ and meaning of this value in terms of the data.

| | Restaurant Type | | |
Age Group	Fast Food	Full Service	Σ
Adult	312	520	832
Child/teen	192	91	283
Σ	504	611	1115

ADVANCED
STATISTICAL ANALYSES

9.1 INTRODUCTION

The tests presented in Chapters 5–8 focus on easily distinguishable situations and predictions. All of these analyses make straightforward comparisons between groups of subjects or between individual scores. Chapter 5's chi-square test, the t test presented in Chapter 6, and the ANOVA presented in Chapter 7 all use subjects' category placements as predictors. Chapter 8 explains that regression and correlations analysis can predict continuous dependent-variable scores from one or more continuous independent-variable scores.

These tests should serve you well for most general research contexts. Combinations and modifications of them, however, greatly expand your analysis options. The advanced techniques presented in this chapter allow you to account for situations that extend beyond the basic inferential statistical tests. You may wish, for example, to compare dependent-variable scores of the same subjects in different conditions. Other analyses may require you to determine whether a single independent variable can predict scores on multiple dependent variables or to determine whether subjects' scores on a continuous variable's scale can predict their group placement on a categorical variable. Although the tests described in Chapters 5–8 may come close to accommodating these

Analyzing Quantitative Data: An Introduction for Social Researchers, First Edition. Debra Wetcher-Hendricks.
© 2011 John Wiley & Sons, Inc. Published 2011 by John Wiley & Sons, Inc.

sorts of situations, they do not address the intricacies that advanced statistical analyses do.

9.2 REPEATED-MEASURES ANALYSIS OF VARIANCE

Chapter 6, which describes t tests, distinguishes between independent and paired samples. You know, therefore, that you must use a paired-samples t test if each member of one sample has a counterpart in the other group. When the groups do not have such a relationship, you use an independent-samples t test.

You can characterize groups for an ANOVA in the same way. Members of one group may or may not have counterparts in the other groups. Chapter 7's description of the ANOVA is limited only to *between-subjects designs*, the ANOVA's counterpart to the independent-samples t test. This form of the ANOVA is most commonly used and you can consider the independent-samples ANOVA, based on a between-subjects design, the default. In other words, unless otherwise specified, particular members of one group do not correspond to particular members of other groups.

But when member of one group does have counterparts in the other groups, a *within-subject design* exists. You must acknowledge the relationships between subjects by performing a *repeated-measures ANOVA*, named as such because the same subjects repeatedly provide data. The repeated-measures ANOVA is comparable to a paired-samples t test. They differ only in that the paired-samples t test compares mean scores for two independent-variable conditions and the repeated-measures ANOVA compares mean scores for more than two independent-variable conditions.

9.2.1 Capabilities of Repeated-Measures ANOVA

A repeated-measures ANOVA acknowledges the preexisting relationship between subjects. The groups involved in the analysis may contain different subjects with logical one-to-one connections, such as the eldest, middle, or youngest sibling in a family, or may contain the same subjects in different conditions.

Example 9.1: Repeated-Measures ANOVA Scenario The latter of these arrangements might work well for a study comparing the difficulties of crossword puzzles that appear in newspapers, magazines, and crossword puzzle books. The researcher could provide three crossword puzzles, one from each of these sources, to subjects and measure the amount of time needed to complete each puzzle. Assuming that completion time is an accurate measure of difficulty, the puzzle with the longest mean completion time qualifies as the most difficult, and the puzzle with the shortest mean completion time qualifies as the easiest.

Having the same subjects complete all three puzzles ensures that the groups completing the three puzzles have equivalent crossword-puzzle-solving abilities. With different subjects in each group, the possibility of a selection bias exists. One group may have better crossword-puzzle-solvers than the other groups have. Short completion times for this group may reflect competence, not puzzle difficulty. If the same subjects compose each group (making each subject her or his own counterpart), there is no chance that differences in completion time relate to differences in the groups' competencies rather than the puzzles, themselves.

Using the same subjects to provide data under different conditions alters the structure of the ANOVA presented in Chapter 7. You read about the assumption of equal variances in Section 7.3.1. For the repeated-measures ANOVA, this assumption expands to include covariances. Covariances, closely related to correlations, describe the strength and the relationship between values for two continuous variables. Scores from subjects in independent groups, such as those used for Chatper 7's ANOVAs, should have little or no covariance. But the connections between subjects in a within-subject design creates covariances. Thus, variations between groups may occur in conjunction with one another. The repeated-measures ANOVA's within-group sum-of-squares value allows for this possibility. As a result, the repeated-measures ANOVA uses a different formula for calculating sum-of-squares values than the independent ANOVA does.

9.2.2 Performing a Repeated-Measures ANOVA

Most of the steps for performing a repeated-measures ANOVA follows those for performing the ANOVAs described in Chapter 7. The two use the same formulas to compute ANOVA table values for between-groups and total effects. You must, however, redefine the within-group values for the repeated-measures ANOVA.

For the ANOVAs in Chapter 7, $SS_W = SS_T - SS_B$. The total sum-of-squares value compares each subject to all other subjects in the sample. The between-groups sum-of-squares value compares the mean of each category to the means of the other categories. The amount of total variation that the between-groups variation cannot explain is indicated by the between-groups sum-of-squares value. This value represents variations between each subject and the others in its group. With independent groups, you must consider these variations for all subjects in all groups. Each additional category has the potential for expanding the within-subject variability. But when subjects in one group have counterparts in the other groups or, especially when all groups consist of the same subjects, the situation changes. For this within-subject design, you need only to measure each subject against the others in one of the groups. The covariance addresses any linear trends in the patterns of differences from group to group. Example 9.2 shows exactly why a within-group design has less within-group variability than a comparable between-groups design does.

Example 9.2: Within-Subjects Variability Comparing the arrangement of subjects' scores for a between-groups design and a within-group design can demonstrate the differences amounts of within-group variability. Suppose that three independent categories each contain five subjects, creating a between-subjects design (Table 9.1).

Because each category contains different subjects, measuring variability within groups requires comparisons between x_1, x_2, x_3, and x_4; between x_5, x_6, x_7, and x_8; and between x_9, x_{10}, x_{11}, and x_{12}.

The notation of data points, however, changes if the three categories contain the same five subjects. The subscripts in Table 9.2 identify only four subjects, but distinguish each subjects' three scores by the condition from which it emerges.

Each row in Table 9.2 corresponds to a single subject who provided data in all three conditions. Because all groups contain the same subjects, the difference between subjects in one condition should be the same in the other two conditions. So, this design, in theory, has only one-third the amount of within-group variability as the between-groups design, shown in Table 9.1 has.

This reduced amount of variation leads to a lower SS_W value for the within-subject design than for the between-subjects design.

With lowered within-subject values, $SS_T > SS_T + SS_W$. To make an equality, the right side of this expression must contain an additional factor that accounts for the within-group variability lost when all groups contain the same subjects. This new measure, called the *subjects sum of squares* (SS_s), describes the variability for each subject in all conditions and is associated with the covariances explained earlier. For the within-group design shown Example 9.2, SS_s pertains to the variability of each individual subjects' three scores.

TABLE 9.1. Data Organization For Between-Subjects Design[a]

Condition A	Condition B	Condition C
x_1	x_6	x_{11}
x_2	x_7	x_{12}
x_3	x_8	x_{13}
x_4	x_9	x_{14}
x_5	x_{10}	x_{15}

[a]The sample contains a total of 15 subjects, divided into three independent-variable categories. Each x represents a particular subject's dependent-variable score. An ANOVA compares the mean scores for each of the three categories.

TABLE 9.2. Data Organization for Within-Subject Design[a]

Condition A	Condition B	Condition C
x_{1A}	x_{1B}	x_{1C}
x_{2A}	x_{2B}	x_{2C}
x_{3A}	x_{3B}	x_{3C}
x_{4A}	x_{4B}	x_{4C}
x_{5A}	x_{5B}	x_{5C}

[a]The sample contains a total of five subjects, each of whom provide dependent-variable data in three conditions. A repeated-measures ANOVA compares the mean scores for each of the three conditions.

Adding SS_S, SS_W, and SS_B should produce SS_T for a repeated-measures ANOVA. Equation (9.1) produces the SS_S value:

$$SS_S = \sum (\bar{X}_S - \bar{X}_T)^2 \tag{9.1}$$

In this equation, $\bar{X}_S$ represents the mean of a particular subject's scores or matched subjects scores in all categories (e.g., x_{1A}, x_{1B}, x_{1C}). The new sum-of-squares measure has an associated degree-of-freedom measure:

$$df_S = n - 1 \tag{9.2}$$

Remembering that, in general, degree-of-freedom values refer to the number of options available (see Chapter 7) helps to explain this formula. It simply refers to the number of possible arrangements of scores within a group.

The order of subjects must remain constant for all groups because of the one-to-one correspondence between subjects in a within-subject design. This restriction does not exist for a between-subject design. The within-subject design, therefore, has fewer degrees of freedom than the between-subjects design does. The df_S value accounts for the difference between the df_W values in the two designs.

The repetitive arrangement of groups in a within-subject design means that you can multiply the number of options for subjects in one group $(n - 1)$ by the number of options for groups $(K - 1)$ to acquire the within-group degree-of-freedom value:

$$df_W = (n - 1)(K - 1) \tag{9.3}$$

Another way that calculations for the repeated-measures ANOVA differs from calculations for the ANOVAs in Chapter 7 relates to df_T. This value still pertains to the number of options available for scores in the entire dataset, but the formulas in Chapter 7 state that $df_T = N - 1$ because, in that context, each person in the sample provides a single data point. So, the number of subjects N is also the number of scores in the dataset. N, however, does not correctly represent the number of scores for a within-group design. To acknowledge that all categories may contain the same subjects, you must define the total number of scores as $(n)(K)$, rather than N. So, for a repeated-measures ANOVA, we obtain

$$df_T = (n)(K) - 1 \tag{9.4}$$

For a repeated-measures ANOVA, like all ANOVAs, the total degree-of-freedom value equals the sum of all other degree-of-freedom values. So, following the pattern established for sum-of-squares values in a repeated-measures ANOVA, $df_T = df_B + df_S + df_W$.

Example 9.3: Repeated-Measures ANOVA Degrees of Freedom The following calculations, based on the tables from Example 9.2, demonstrate this relationship:

$$df_B = K - 1 = 3 - 1 = 2$$

$$df_S = n - 1 = 5 - 1 = 4$$

$$df_W = (n - 1)(K - 1) = (5 - 1)(3 - 1) = (4)(2) = 8$$

$$df_T = (n)(K) - 1 = (5)(3) - 1 = 15 - 1 = 14$$

$$df_T = df_B + df_S + df_W$$

$$14 = 2 + 4 + 8$$

Having calculated all necessary sum-of-squares and degree-of-freedom values, you can organize them into an ANOVA table similar to the ones presented in Chapter 7. The repeated-measures ANOVA table includes a fourth row to show subject effects. But SS_S and df_S do not have any direct roles in the computation of F. In fact, once you create a one-way repeated-measures ANOVA table, you calculate F for the repeated-measures ANOVA the same way as you do for Chapter 7's one-way ANOVA. Dividing each SS by its corresponding df produces a mean-square (MS) value. The ratio of MS_B to MS_W produces F. Table 9.3 shows all of these relationships.

You interpret the value of the F ratio by comparing it to a critical F. F_{crit} values appear in a "Critical F Values" table such as the one in Appendix D of this book. A significant difference between means exists when $F_{calc} > F_{crit}$, indicating that you should reject the null hypothesis of equality between means. A $F_{calc} < F_{crit}$, though, leads to an accepted null hypothesis. In this case, means do not differ enough at your chosen α for you to claim that these differences reflect something other than random variation.

9.3 MULTIPLE ANALYSIS OF VARIANCE

The ANOVAs presented in Chapter 7 can, in theory, accommodate in infinite number of independent categorical variables. Expanding a one-way ANOVA to a two-way ANOVA allows you to consider the combination of two categorical variables in predicting the dependent variable, using a three-way ANOVA allows you to consider the combination of three categorical variables in predicting the dependent variable, and

TABLE 9.3. Repeated-Subjects ANOVA Summary Table[a]

Source	SS	df	MS	F
Between	SS_B	df_B	$MS_B = SS_B/df_B$	$F = MS_B/MS_W$
Within	SS_W	df_W	$MS_W = SS_W/df_W$	—
Subjects	SS_S	df_S	$MS_S = SS_S/df_S$	—
Total	SS_T	df_T	—	—

[a]The table provides a structure for obtaining mean squares and the F statistic. Values for the sum of squares and degrees of freedom appear in rows labeled with the appropriate source of variation. The mean-square value for each source of variation is the ratio of each sum-of-squares value and the degrees of freedom for that source. Between-groups and within-group values determine the F ratio.

using an n-way ANOVA allows you to consider that the combination of n categorical variables in predicting the dependent variable.

Although the ANOVA acknowledges the fact that you may need many independent variables to successfully predict a dependent-variable score, it does not address the possibility that independent-variable categories may predict values on more than one continuous dependent variable.

Example 9.4: Multiple Dependent Variables   Suppose that a researcher wishes to assess audience memory of a particular story presented in three different ways. If some read the story, some view a film that presents the story, and some watch a Broadway musical version of the story, then these three genres define three independent-variable categories. Subjects' recall of various element of the story, such as setting, characters, and plot, could serve as dependent variables for the study. By asking subjects relevant questions, a researcher could obtain continuous scores for each of these dependent variables. This design resembles an ANOVA in that the researcher wishes to determine whether those in different independent-variable categories have significantly different dependent-variable scores. However, rather than just one dependent variable, three exist.

To analyze a situation such as the one presented in Example 9.4, you need to simultaneously recognize the relationship between all of the dependent variables and the independent variable. A *multiple analysis of variance* (MANOVA) essentially considers a combination of continuous-variable scores as the overall dependent variable. It then determines whether the independent-variable categories have significantly different combined dependent-variable scores. MANOVAs can take one-way or multiway forms depending on the number of independent variables involved.

9.3.1   Capabilities of MANOVA

The logic in combining dependent variables for a MANOVA lies in the interrelationship between dependent variables. For situations in which the dependent variables measure unrelated entities, a MANOVA is unnecessary. You can perform individual ANOVAs to address the relationship between independent-variable categories and subjects' scores on each of the independent variables. With moderately or strongly correlated dependent variables ($r \geq .60$ or so), however, this technique may lead to a misrepresentation of effects, overlooking differences that are not evident when considering each dependent variable separately. The MANOVA avoids this problem by considering a combination of dependent-variable scores, sometimes called the *canonical variate*. It determines whether significant differences exist in mean canonical variate scores for the various independent-variable categories.

Example 9.5: Canonical Variate of Dependent Variables   The situation described in Example 9.4 requires a MANOVA because subjects recall a story's setting, characters, and plot as most likely having some relationship with one other. This relationship could reflect some aspect of the story, itself; the subjects' overall memory capabilities; or any number of other issues.

This common thread, whatever it may be, creates correlations between the dependent variables. To give any overlapping constructs that produce these correlations the appropriate amount of attention, the MANOVA focuses on the canonical variate.

You may wonder what advantage the MANOV has over multiple ANOVAs. In a sense, the MANOVA addresses the possibility of a "whole greater than the sum of its parts" situation. Like the ANOVA, it investigates the difference between independent-variable groups for each of the dependent variables. But the ANOVA cannot examine differences between canonical variates that combine scores on many dependent-variable factors. A MANOVA's canonical variate, on the other hand, can encompass an infinite number of dependent variables.

You should resist the urge, however, to design a study with an abundance of dependent variables. Each dependent variable added to the analysis complicates it because of the possibility of interaction effects. Particular combinations of dependent variables for a MANOVA can interact with one another similarly to the way that independent variables can interact in a multiway ANOVA. Results of the omnibus test become overwhelming and difficult to interpret when many interaction effects exist. Further, error components, usually attributed to random variation in scores, accumulate as you add main and interaction effect to the analysis. So, with may variables, you may run the risk of distorting omnibus test results.

9.3.2 Performing a MANOVA

The MANOVA blends elements of the ANOVA procedures presented in Chapter 7 and the regression analyses presented in Chapter 8. The canonical variate that serves as the combined dependent-variable construct reflects the linear association between these variables. An equation can show the combination of dependent variables that allows for the clearest distinctions between independent-variable categories. In this situation, the canonical variate (C) is a function of weighted dependent-variable z scores[1]. Equation (9.1) uses b to represent weights, just as it does in traditional regression equations, and p to represent the number of dependent variables that compose the canonical variate:

$$C = b_1 z_1 + b_1 z_1 + \cdots + b_p z_p \tag{9.5}$$

The canonical variate values suggested by Equation (9.5) form a matrix, with a vector corresponding to each variable. Therefore, the calculations needed to obtain the necessary statistics involve linear algebra.

Beyond the need to use higher-order algebra to establish dependent measure vectors, the significance test for a MANOVA follows a familiar pattern. As with the ANOVA, calculations produce an F value, consisting of the ratio between mean-square values, that you can compare to the critical value. The mean-square values that consti-

---

[1] The lack of an intercept of the equation results from the use of standardized (z) scores. An equation using raw scores, rather than standardized scores, would have an intercept.

tute the MANOVA's F value consist of the ratio of the sum-of-squares value to the degrees of freedom, just as they do for the ANOVA. The MANOVA's version of the sum of squares, called the *sum of squares and cross-products* (SSCP), acknowledges differences within and between groups and for the total sample.

This increased responsibility is evident when computing SSCP values. Rather than multiplying individual values as you do when calculating SS values (see Section 7.3.1), you need to multiply matrices to calculate SSCP values. Multiplying matrices involves the linear algebra operations mentioned earlier. Specifically, you must use determinants to obtain cross-products of the matrices. Statisticians often create a ratio of these determinants called the *lambda* (Λ) statistic. In fact, many report this statistic, introduced by Wilks in 1932, more often than they report F values for MANOVAs.

The formula for Λ uses to the same within and total designations used in the ANOVA. However, in Equation (9.2), each of these designations refers to a determinant, rather than an SS, df, or MS value. Mathematically, the within and total determinants are respectively represented as $|W|$ and $|T|$:

$$\Lambda = \frac{|W|}{|T|} \tag{9.6}$$

This ratio describes the proportion of variance in mean canonical variate values that independent-variable categories cannot explain. A small Λ value indicates significant differences between groups' mean canonical variates.

Although the Λ statistic receives a lot of attention in literature explaining the results of MANOVAs, you cannot use it to test the null hypothesis as you can with an F value. For a significance test, you must continue the process, changing Λ into SSCP values with a transformation developed by Rao (1951). The SSCP values play the same role in the MANOVA as SS values do in the ANOVA. Moreover, the MANOVA's consists of the ratio between the between and the within groups mean-square values, just as the ANOVA's F does. Equations (9.3)–(9.5) show these relationships:

$$MS_B = \frac{SSCP_B}{df_B} \tag{9.7}$$

$$MS_W = \frac{SSCP_W}{df_W} \tag{9.8}$$

$$F = \frac{MS_B}{MS_W} \tag{9.9}$$

You can organize the values produced by these formulas into a MANOVA table. A one-way MANOVA, which compares mean canonical variate values for categories of one independent variable, produces only one F value (see Table 9.4).

A multiway MANOVA, one using at least two independent variables, produces an F ratio for each independent variable as well as for each interaction between independent variables. So, the MANOVA summary table for a two-way MANOVA (Table 9.5), contains three F values.

TABLE 9.4. One-Way MANOVA Summary Table[a]

Source	SSCP	df	MS	F
Between	$SSCP_B$	df_B	MS_B	F
Within	$SSCP_W$	df_W	MS_W	
Total	$SSCP_T$	df_T		

[a]This table provides a structure for obtaining mean squares and the F statistic. Values for the sum of squares and cross products and for degrees of freedom appear in rows labeled with the appropriate source of variation. Calculations using these values produce mean squares for each source as well as the F ratio.

TABLE 9.5. Two-Way MANOVA Summary Table[a]

Source	SSCP	df	MS	F_{calc}
Row (R)	$SSCP_R$	df_R	MS_R	F_R
Column (C)	$SSCP_C$	df_C	MS_C	F_C
Interaction ($R \times C$)	$SSCP_{R \times C}$	$df_{R \times C}$	$MS_{R \times C}$	$F_{R \times C}$
Within-group (S/RC)	$SSCP_{S/RC}$	$df_{S/RC}$	$MS_{S/RC}$	
Total	$SSCP_T$	df_T		

[a]This table provides a structure for obtaining mean squares and the F statistics for a two-way design, including columns, rows, and interaction effects. Values for the sum of squares and cross-products and for degrees of freedom appear in rows labeled with the appropriate source of variation. Calculations with these values produce mean squares for each source as well as the F ratios.

You interpret the F ratios for a MANOVA the same way that you interpret them for an ANOVA. A critical F table, such as the one in Appendix D, provides values to compare to F_{calc}. If $F_{calc} < F_{crit}$, you must accept the null hypothesis and consider the mean of canonical variates for each independent group equal. Otherwise, you can claim that a significant difference between mean canonical variate values exists. This result requires further investigation to determine the source of this significance. Post hoc tests, similar to the ones described in Chapter 7 can compare mean canonical variates for particular groups or for particular combinations of groups. Differences that produce significant results when assessed with post hoc tests contribute to the rejection of the omnibus hypothesis.

For a situation involving a dichotomous independent variable, you can modify the MANOVA calculations to produce a Hotteling's T^2 (1931). Actually, T^2 can also be described as a generalization of the t-test described in Chapter 6. Just as a t test compares the mean scores on a single dependent variable for two groups of a dependent variable, Hotteling's T^2 compares mean canonical variate scores for two groups when multiple dependent variables exist.

9.4 ANALYSIS OF COVARIANCE

The ANOVAs described in Chapter 7 assume that no predictors of dependent-variable scores other than independent-variable categories exist. In some cases, however, other factors, called *covariates*, may have strong relationships with subjects' independent variable categories. These relationships may make it difficult to determine whether the independent variable, the covariate, or a combination of the two predicts dependent-variable scores.

Example 9.6: Covariates A comparison of relaxation techniques could use an ANCOVA. Cardiologists may wish to know whether a particular relaxation technique reduces heart rate more than others do. To investigate this possibility, they might send one group of subjects to yoga sessions, one group to meditation sessions, and one group to biofeedback therapy sessions. The cardiologists would measure subjects' heart rates before and after one of these sessions and note the change in heart rate.

Given just this information, a comparison of changes in heart rates could be attributed only to differences in the subjects' relaxation technique category. But other factors, such as the length of the relaxation session, may also deserve attention. The yoga, meditation, and biofeedback therapy sessions might last for different amounts of time. If those experiencing the relaxation technique with a longer session than the others experience the largest drop in heart rate, then the cardiologists may not know whether the technique, itself, or the length of the session, or a combination of the two predicts the change in heart rate. So, cardiologists who wish to focus on only the relaxation technique, would consider it the independent variable, change in heart rate as the dependent variable, and initial heart health as a covariate.

An *analysis of covariance* (ANCOVA) recognizes the potential impact of covariates, along with independent-variable categories, as it determines whether significant differences in dependent-variable scores exist. Calculations for an ANCOVA essentially remove the effects of covariates, allowing you to understand the relationship between the independent-variable categories, themselves, and the continuous dependent-variable scores. This idea should remind you of the partial and partial correlations, which remove the effects of a confounding variable on the relationship between two continuous variables. In fact, correlation and regression do play a part in the ANCOVA.

The *multiple analysis of covariance* (MANCOVA) is the MANOVA version of the ANCOVA in that it adjusts for covariates when assessing the significant differences between mean canonical variates. To maintain simplicity in the remaining portion of this chapter, however, tests involving covariates are identified as ANCOVAs with the understanding that this reference also implies the use of MANCOVAs when necessary.

9.4.1 Capabilities of ANCOVA

Example 9.6 describes a situation in which the covariate creates error variance. You could assume that, at the onset of the study, all three groups were equivalent. But, in addition to the independent variable of relaxation technique, the covariate of session length may have given those in one group an advantage over those in another. Because the researchers consider the variation resulting from the covariate extraneous influence on dependent-variable scores, they use an ANCOVA to separate it from the independent variable.

Researchers can also have another rationale for using the ANCOVA. They do not limit their definition of a covariate to a factor *imposed* on the independent variable, arguing that some covariates exist even before a study begins. Such a situation would occur if pre-existing factors distinguish between groups in the same way that the independent variable does.

Example 9.7: Existing Group Differences If, for example, cardiologists tend to recommend different relaxation techniques for patients with different levels of heart health, preexisting differences would exist between the three categories of subjects described in Example 9.6. In this situation, changes in heart rate may reflect more than just differences in relaxation technique.

At the very least, the cardiologists must acknowledge the possibility that the relaxation techniques, in general, may not have as great a benefit for those with very poor heart health than for those with only minor heart problems (or, for the sake of argument, vice versa). Therefore, those with poorer heart health than others, if assigned to the same independent-variable group, may not experience as large a change in heart rate as would the more healthy individuals in the other groups. The cardiologists would be unable to determine whether this difference reflects subject's preexisting conditions, relaxation techniques, or a combination of the two. To investigate the relationship between relaxation technique and change in heart rate, independent of subjects' preexisting conditions, the cardiologists would consider preexisting conditions as a covariate.

The extraneous inequality among groups results from a known sampling bias, not error variance, as with the situation described in Example 9.6. You should know that, as a result, some researchers oppose the use of an ANOVA to remove preexisting disparities between groups. They maintain that this test addresses error variance, and prefer to use other corrections to account for the sampling bias.

The ANCOVAs, for whatever reason you may choose to use them, rely on a number of assumptions about the data. Some of these assumptions stem from the ANOVA characteristics, and some stem from the regression components of the test. Section 7.3.1 first presents the assumption of homogenous variances in the context of deriving one-way ANOVA formulas. This assumption also holds true for the ANCOVA tests. The variances of dependent-variable scores for each independent-variable category must be nearly equal. A similar assumption, homogeneity of regression, requires nearly equal linear relationships between the covariate and the dependent-variable scores for each independent-variable group.

9.4.2 Performing an ANCOVA

With the main goal of an ANCOVA being the comparison of means, you begin the tests by calculating the means for each group. You must, however, calculate means for both the dependent-variable and canonical variate values and for the covariate values. Formulas like the ones presented in Chapter 7 allow you to compute sums of squares for both dependent variables (D) and covariates (C). This process, for a one-way ANCOVA, should produce SS_{B_D}, SS_{W_D}, SS_T, SS_{B_C}, SS_{W_C}, and SS_{T_C}. A multiway test requires you to calculate interaction sums-of-square values as well.

The values described thus far reflect the ANOVA portion of the ANCOVA. They pertain to differences in dependent-variable and covariate means for each independent-variable group. But you have not yet examined the relationship between the covariate and the dependent variable. With its focus on the association between continuous variables, this portion of the analysis requires regression techniques. These techniques produce values, analogous to the sums of squares, called the *sums of codeviates* (SC). This term, however, is just another way to refer to the covariance, which plays a role in correlation analysis. (See Chapter 8.)

To compute covariates or, in this context, SC values, you can then use the following equation:

$$SC_T = \sum (D_i C_i) - \frac{\sum D_i \sum C_i}{N} \tag{9.10}$$

The within-group sums of codeviates (SC_W) addresses the linear relationship between covariate and dependent-variable scores in each independent-variable category. Each category has its own SC_W value. So, for the situation presented in Example 9.7, you would need to calculate a within-groups sum of codeviates for the yoga group, for the meditation group, and for the biofeedback group. The following equation produces each category's sum of co-deviates value, labeled (SC_{W_g}, to stress that each SC value pertains to a particular independent-variable group.

$$SC_{W_g} = \sum (D_{ig} C_{ig}) \frac{\sum D_{ig} \sum C_{ig}}{n_g} \tag{9.11}$$

This formula also has similarities to the correlation coefficient formula shown in Chapter 8. Unlike the total sum-of-codeviates calculations, though, you limit your calculations for the within-group sums of codeviates to one group at a time. The notations of D and C in Equation (9.7) refer to dependent-variable or canonical variate values and to covariate values within each individual group. Adding all SC_{W_g} value provides you with the overall SC_W.

$$SC_W = \sum SC_{W_g} \tag{9.12}$$

Coefficients of determination (see Chapter 8) based on SC values are used to adjust the SS values so that they reflect the covariate. Subtracting a coefficient of determination from its respective SS value produces an adjusted sum of squares for total effects and for within-group effects. Then, to obtain an adjusted between-groups sum of squares, you must simply subtract:

$$SS_{B_{adj}} = SS_{T_{adj}} - SW_{B_{adj}} \tag{9.13}$$

TABLE 9.6. ANCOVA Summary Table[a]

Source	SS_{adj}	df	MS	F
Between	$SS_{B_{adj}}$	df_B	MS_B	F
Within	$SS_{W_{adj}}$	df_W	MS_W	
Total	$SS_{T_{adj}}$	df_T		

[a]This table provides a structure for obtaining mean squares and the F statistic. Values for the adjusted sum of squares and degrees of freedom appear in rows labeled with the appropriate source of variation. Calculations using these values produce mean squares for each source as well as the F ratio.

The SS_{adj} values approximate the sums of squares that would have existed independent of any covariate influence.

The remainder of the process for the one-way ANCOVA follows the same pattern as the one-way ANOVA process does. You divide SS_{adj} values by degrees of freedom to obtain mean-square values (MS). The ratio of MS_B to MS_W constitutes F (see Table 9.6).

For a multiway ANCOVA, just as for a multiway ANOVA, you must calculate an MS value for each interaction effect as well and, consequently, obtain multiple F values.

Determining the meaning of each calculated F value requires a comparison to the critical F value in a critical F table such as the one in Appendix D. An $F_{calc} > F_{crit}$ indicates a significant difference between group means, meaning that you should reject the null hypothesis at the chosen α level. You should accept the null hypothesis of equality when $F_{calc} < F_{crit}$.

9.5 DISCRIMINANT ANALYSIS

To perform the tests described in Chapters 5–7 and in Sections 9.2 and 9.3, you must have categorical independent variables. The tests determine how well one's independent-variable category predicts one's placement on a dependent-variable measure. They do not allow you to use scores on continuous variables as predictors. Certain investigations, however, may have continuous independent variables and categorical dependent variables.

Example 9.8: Continuous Independent Variable and Categorical Dependent Variable Executives at a fence company would encounter this type of situation when trying to use acreage of a residential property to predict the type of fence that their clients choose.

The company's executives could, first, consider the acerage of each client's property. Then, they could classify each fence installed by the company according to its style, identifying it as chain link, wrought iron, wood, or vinyl. (Although a fencing company likely offers other styles of fences, using only four categories keeps this example relatively simple.)

The question of whether the choice of fence has a relationship to the size of the property that it encloses forms the basis of a hypothesis with a continuous independent variable and a categorical dependent variable. Of the many relationships that could exist between these variables, the executives might propose the hypothesis that the popularity of fencing materials change from chain link to vinyl to wrought iron to wood as the size of the property enclosed by the fence increases. Because the existence of the property preceded the existence of the fence, one must consider property size, which is measured continuously, as the independent variable and the type of fence, which is measured categorically, as the dependent variable. None of the tests presented in Chapters 5–8, however, can address this situation.

Sometimes, however, you can restate this sort of hypothesis to make the categorical factor the independent variable and the continuous factor the dependent variable. Doing so makes it possible for you to use a *t* test or an ANOVA.

Example 9.9: Restatement of Hypothesis   The hypothesis from Example 9.8, for instance, may be restructured this way. To make the hypothesis appropriate for a one-way ANOVA, the company executives could restate the hypothesis to suggest that, by knowing what type of fence surrounds a particular property, one can deduce the size of that property. Admittedly, this hypothesis would be somewhat complex as it would need to predict a three-tiered order; properties enclosed by wood fences have higher mean areas than those enclosed by wrought iron fences, properties enclosed by wrought-iron fences have higher mean areas than do those enclosed by vinyl fences, and proper-ties enclosed by vinyl fences have higher mean areas than do those enclosed by chain-link fences. But, because this hypothesis defines categorical measure of fencing material as the independent variable and continuous measure of property size as the dependent variable, a one-way ANOVA is appropriate.

Changes like the one explained in Example 9.9 allow you to analyze data using commonly known statistics. Many researchers, therefore, use this technique to simplify an analysis or to make it understandable to others. However, the results of the altered analysis do not really address the true research question. When possible, it is best to use a discriminant analysis when you have a continuous independent variable and a categorical dependent variable.

9.5.1 Capabilities of Discriminant Analysis

Issues of causal time order (see Chapter 10) can render the type of switch described in Example 9.9 inappropriate or lead to misinterpretation of the results. Discriminant analysis avoids these problems. Rather than determining whether one's category can predict one's score on a continuous measure, *discriminant analysis* determines whether one's continuous-variable score implies one's category.

Discriminant analysis resembles regression–correlation analysis in that both use continuous independent variables. But you can likely note the relationship between discriminant analysis and an ANOVA most easily. In its simplest form, then, discriminant analysis amounts to a one-way ANOVA (or, if only two groups are involved, a t test) in reverse. Rather than the ANOVA categorical independent variables and a continuous dependent variable, discriminant analysis has continuous independent variables and a categorical dependent variable. The name "discriminant analysis" reflects the procedure's attempt to use subjects' scores on the continuous independent variable to discriminate between dependent-variable categories. For this reason, many refer to the continuous independent variable as the *predictor variable* and to the categorical dependent variable as the *grouping variable*.

The research hypothesis for a discriminant analyisis specifies the way in which predictor variable values suggest grouping variable values. Characterizing the relationships between predictor and grouping variable scores as significant uses the same principles as other inferential statistical tests use. Through your choice of α, you can determine how strong of an association between the continuous and categorical values must exist for you to consider it significant. Significant test results tell you when different mean predictor variable scores correspond to different groups. When such distinctions exist, you can determine, with no less than $1 - \alpha$ confidence, a subject's group membership on the basis of that person's predictor variable score.

Most researchers use a discriminant analysis in hopes of classifying subjects according to their scores on a continuous variable. In addition, though, results from a discriminant analysis can help you determine the most effective way to define categories. To understand this role, you must recognize that a categorical variable's ability to predict a continuous variable's score, as addressed by an ANOVA, does not imply the inverse relationship. In other words, although results of an ANOVA might characterize subjects' category membership as a good predictor of that person's dependent-variable score, the dependent-variable score, in and of itself, may not explain subjects' category memberships. The dependent continuous-variable scores may be one of many factors that distinguish between the independent-variable categories.

Example 9.10: Predictability   The property size–fencing investigation introduced in the previous example can help to clarify this idea. Although the type of fence that encloses a property might be a good indicator of the property's size, one cannot assume that all properties of that size have the same kind of fencing. Other factors, possibly land use or the location of the property, may help to predict the type of fencing that surrounds it. Further, even if fencing style, a categorical variable, can predict scores on multiple continuous measures, such as property size, land use, or location, each of these continuous variables may not be a good indicator of fencing style. One must use a discriminant analysis to determine whether any of these continuous variables can predict fencing style.

When presented with many possible continuous predictors, you can use a discriminant analysis to identify the one that best classifies subjects into grouping variable categories. This designation is based on *discriminant loadings*. The discriminant loading for a particular predictor variable characterizes the relationship between changes in scores and distinctions between grouping variable categories. A direct relationship exists between the size of a variable's discriminant loading and degree to which it helps to predict a subject's category. So, the predictor variable that most effectively identifies subjects' category placements has the highest discriminant loading.

Discriminant analysis does not always search for the best single predictor. You can also use it to assess situations in which two or more predictor variables cooperate to determine categories. A *multiple discriminant analysis* uses subject's scores on a combination of continuous factors to identify that person's category membership. This investigation relates to the MANOVA in the same way that the basic discriminant analysis relates to the one-way ANOVA. They address the same variables, but in reverse order.

9.5.2   Performing a Discriminant Analysis

The elements of regression analysis and ANOVA involved in a descriminant analysis become very evident when considering the procedures for and results of the test. The use of a continuous variable to predict scores on another variable requires regressionlike techniques. Additionally, you can use a significance test, like the one used in an ANOVA, to assess the association between continuous-variable ranges and categorical variable groupings. The remainder of this section describes the way in which these two components cooperate to fully depict the relationship between variables.

Although a regression analysis predicts scores on a continuous variable and a discriminant analysis predicts categorical variable scores, they both rely on continuous predictors. Accordingly, they both use linear equations. The discriminant analysis' prediction, called the *discriminant function*, describes the relationship between predictor variable and grouping variable values and grouping variable categories. Like a regression equation, it identifies coefficients for its predictor. The discriminant function's coefficients are discriminant loadings (see Section 3.5.1), each indicating the importance of its corresponding variable in the equation. Equation (9.14) provides a discriminant function that can expand to incorporate as many predictor variables as needed:

$$G = b_1 z_1 + b_1 z_1 + \cdots + b_n z_n \tag{9.14}$$

This equation suggests that a discriminant loading (b) weights each predictor variable's standardized score(z) and that a combination of weighted standardized scores predicts the grouping variable value (G).

Versions of the F test can assess the discriminant function's ability to identify significant distinctions between groups. There is not, however, a single significance test that applies to all discriminant analyses. Your rationale for performing the discriminant analysis dictates the particular test that you should use. The Wilks' lambda (Λ), first

---

[2] If predictor variable scores are not standardized, the equation refers to x, not z, and also contains an intercept (c). Thus, the equation would appear as

$$G = c + b_1 x_1 + b_1 x_1 + \cdots + b_n x_n.$$

described in Section 9.3.2, reflects the possibility of multiple dependent variables. making it a popular statistic to use. Other statistics, such as the Mahalonobis D^2 and Rao's V, can indicate whether the presence of a particular predictor variable amplifies or suppresses the distinctions between categories.

As with the inferential statistical tests described in Chapters 5–8, significant results do not necessarily support your research hypothesis. The tests, themselves, only determine whether values differ; they do not tell you *how* values differ. So, when you find a discriminant function that produces significant results, your analysis must continue to determine whether categories differ in the way that you expected.

9.6 CONCLUSION

The tests presented in this chapter receive significantly less attention than do the chi-square test, the t test, the ANOVA, and regression analysis, which each received its own chapter in this book. The limited attention that the tests described in this chapter receives should emphasize that you should use them only when those described in Chapters 5–8 cannot sufficiently account for the complexities of your data or research context.

The basic information about advanced statistical analyses in this chapter greatly expands your options for inferential tests. Although not presented as such when first introduced, some of the analyses presented in Chapters 5–8 are actually simplified versions of the advanced analyses described in this chapter. In particular, the paired-samples t test is just a repeated-measures ANOVA using a dichotomous independent variable, and the part and partial correlations preview the ANCOVA.

Although the repeated-measures ANOVA, the MANOVA, the ANCOVA, and discriminant analysis all have comparisons between groups as their underlying themes, each accounts for an additional aspect that the tests in Chapters 5–8 cannot address. You may even encounter a research situation involving more than one of these additional aspects. In these cases, you can use combinations of the advanced statistical tests, such as a repeated-measures MANOVA or, as mentioned in Section 9.5, a multiple discriminant analysis. The capabilities of these tests, and combinations of them, make it possible for you to analyze an infinite number of relationships between variables.

STATISTICAL RESOURCES FOR SPSS

SPSS commands and output for the advanced statistical analyses described in this chapter can seem extremely complicated. Not all of the prompts that appear on the SPSS screens or the values that appear in the output, however, pertain to the specific tests addressed in this chapter. The following sections focus on the test results that allow you to assess significant differences in the repeated-measures ANOVA, the MANOVA, and the ANCOVA, as well as to produce the discriminant function.

Repeated-Measures ANOVA

The "General Linear Model" option in SPSS's "Analyze" pulldown menu contains the repeated-measures ANOVA prompt. You should use this prompt for all repeated-measures ANOVAs, regardless of whether they are one-way or multiway designs. A "Repeated Measures Define Factor(s)" window (Fig. 9.1) appears when you select the "Repeated Measures" prompt. In this window, you must prepare SPSS for your comparisons by inputting a name for the factor that distinguishes between groups (time, conditions, etc.) and the number of datasets to compare.

A second window, entitled "Repeated Measures" (Fig. 9.2), allows you to specify the names of the individual variables whose means you wish to compare.

The F ratios and p values that appear in the output indicate whether the means differ significantly. As with all other inferential statistics, you reject the null hypothesis of equality between means when $p < \alpha$.

Of all the tables that appear in SPSS's repeated-measures ANOVA output, the "Tests of Within-Subject Effects" normally provides the most useful information. This table contains the calculated F value and the p value. For the type of repeated-measures ANOVA described in this chapter, you should focus on the row labeled "Sphericity Assumed."

Example 9.11: SPSS Output for One-Way Repeated-Measures ANOVA   Table 9.7 shows the "Tests of Within-Subject Effects" output produced by the hypothetical analysis of crossward puzzles described in Example 9.1.

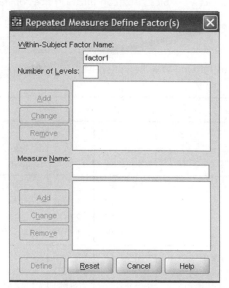

<u>Figure 9.1.</u> SPSS "Repeated Measures Define Factor(s)" window. The user enters general information about the within-group design into this window so that SPSS knows what data to request. The "Within-Subject Factor Name" refers to a term describing the condition that distinguishes between groups. The "Number of Levels" refers to the number of groups involved in the comparison.

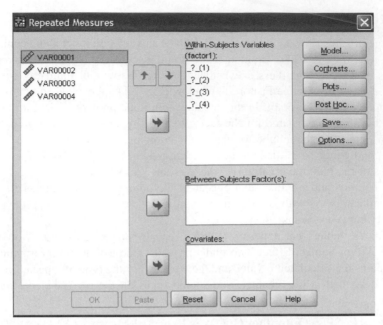

Figure 9.2. SPSS "Repeated Measures" window. SPSS requests information in this window according to the number of levels entered into the "Repeated Measures Define Factors" window. The "Within-Subject Variables" box contains a space for each variable involved in the analysis.

TABLE 9.7. SPSS Output for One-Way Repeated-Measrues ANOVA: Tests of Within-Subject Effects[a]

Measure: MEASURE_1						
Source		Type III Sum of Squares	df	Mean Square	F	Significance
Publication	Sphericity assumed	324.640	2	162.320	2.488	.088
	Greenhouse–Geisser	324.640	1.958	165.840	2.488	.090
	Huynh–Feldt	324.640	2.000	162.320	2.488	.088
	Lower–bound	324.640	1.000	324.640	2.488	.121
Error (publication)	Sphericity assumed	6394.027	98	65.245	—	—
	Greenhouse–Geisser	6394.027	95.920	66.660	—	—
	Huynh–Feldt	6394.027	98.000	65.245	—	—
	Lower–bound	6394.027	49.000	130.490	—	—

[a]Values in the top row of this table refer to the size of the difference between category means. In this case, the relationship between the p value of .088 and the chosen α value indicates whether the researcher should accept the null hypothesis that it takes subjects the same amount of time to complete all three crossword puzzles.

As with all other inferential statistics, means differ significantly when $p < \alpha$. With a p value of .088, the decision about whether to accept or reject the null hypothesis depends highly on the researcher's choice of α for this investigation. The standard α value of .05 would lead one to accept the null hypothesis. But one who chooses to use an α value of .10 could reject the null hypothesis, claiming that the amount of time needed to complete crossword puzzles from newspapers, magazines, and crossword puzzle books differ significantly.

The information in Table 9.7 tells you only whether significant differences exist, not the direction of the differences between means. If the p value from this table is smaller than your chosen α, you must continue your analysis to determine the cause of this significance. You can begin by considering the means for each category. Your judgment about which mean or means seem to differ the most from the others can provide you with a starting point for post hoc analyses. Post hoc analyses for a repeated-measured ANOVA should take the form of paired-samples t tests.

On request, SPSS can provide you with descriptive statistics, such as means, and paired-sample t test results for all pairs of categories involved in your analysis. Instructions for obtaining and interpreting these tables appear in this chapter's companion website.

MANOVA

You can access the SPSS "Multivariate" window (Fig. 9.3) by selecting "Multivariate" from the "General Linear Model" options given in the "Analyze" pulldown menu. This window is designed to accept information for a MANOVA. It contains boxes labeled "Dependent Variables," for all of the components of the canonical variate and "Fixed Factor(s)," for the independent variable or variables.

The SPSS "Multivariate Test" output table contains the values that you need to determine whether to accept or reject the null hypothesis for a MANOVA. In particular, these values appear in the section of the table that refers to the independent variable(s). The method that you have used to obtain the F value determines the row that pertains to your analysis. The "Wilks' lambda" row provides the values that pertain to Section 9.3.2's explanation of how to obtain F via Λ.

Example 9.12: SPSS Output for One-Way MANOVA   For the one-way MANOVA first presented in Example 9.4, the decision regarding whether to accept or reject the null hypothesis depends on the values associated with genre. These values appear in the lower portion of the "Multivariate Tests" table (Table 9.8).

Results of this test unquestionably indicate that subjects' recall of story elements differ significantly for those who read the story, saw it presented as a film, and saw it presented as a Broadway musical. Using Wilks' lambda to obtain the F value of 6.743 and, in turn, the p value of .000, should result in an accepted null hypothesis. Not surprisingly, all of the other tests produce the same result.

Post hoc tests should follow a MANOVA that yields significant results, as the analysis in Example 9.12 does. Your first step, as always, involves determining which

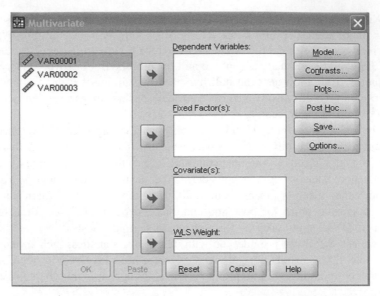

Figure 9.3. SPSS "Multivariate" window. At least two of the variables listed in the box on the left side of the screen must be identified as dependent variables for the MANOVA. For a one-way MANOVA, the "Fixed Factor(s)" box should contain only one variable name. Moving more than one variable name to this box instructs SPSS to perform a multiway MANOVA.

TABLE 9.8. SPSS Output for One-Way MANOVA: Multivariate Tests[ac]

Effect	Value	F	Hypothesis df	Error df	Significance
Intercept					
Pillai's trace	0.954	2039.605	3.000	295.000	.000
Wilks' lambda	0.046	2039.605	3.000	295.000	.000
Hotelling's trace	20.742	2039.605	3.000	295.000	.000
Roy's largest root	20.742	2039.605	3.000	295.000	.000
Genre					
Pillai's trace	.124	6.536	6.000	592.000	.000
Wilks' lambda	.876	6.743	6.000	590.000	.000
Hotelling's trace	.142	6.949	6.000	588.000	.000
Roy's largest root	.142	13.972	3.000	296.000	.000

[a]This table contains inferential statistics based on various tests of significance. For this analysis, values related to the genre indicate significance. The results associated with Wilks' lambda, the F value of 6.743, and the p value of .000, are most relevant for the procedure described in Section 9.3.2.

groups likely account for the significant difference. Comparisons between these groups serve as the starting point for your analysis. With the MANOVA, however, you have more options for post hoc comparisons than you do with the ANOVA. In addition to comparing canonical variate means, you can compare means for various combinations of the dependent variables that constitute the canonical variate. This chapter's companion website explains the many possible sources of significance for a MANOVA and how to examine them with post-hoc tests.

www.moravian.edu/aqd

ANCOVA and MANCOVA

The SPSS "Univariate" window (Fig. 9.4), used for a multiway ANOVA (see Chapter 7), contains a box labeled "Covariate(s)." By placing a variable name in this box, you instruct SPSS to perform an ANCOVA rather than an ANOVA.

A "Covariate(s)" also appears the "Multivariate" window shown as Figure 9.3. This option allows you to identify covariates, changing a MANOVA to a MANCOVA. You can find specific information about how to correctly identify the independent variable, dependent variable, and covariates, for both the ANCOVA and the MANCOVA in this chapter's companion website.

www.moravian.edu/aqd

SPSS performs the calculations needed to remove the influence of any variables identified as covariates in its "Univariate" or "Multivariate" window. Table 9.9 contains the values that indicate whether significant differences exist.

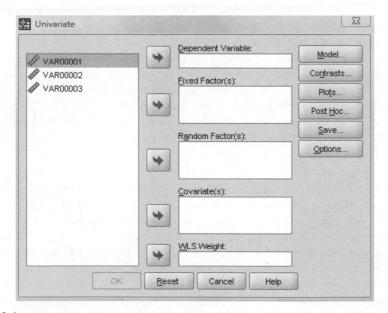

Figure 9.4. SPSS "Univariate" window. The user performs a discriminant analysis by selecting the appropriate variable names from those listed in the box above. The name of the continuous variable(s) should be moved to the "independents" area, and the name of the categorical dependent variable should be moved to the "Grouping Variable" area.

TABLE 9.9. SPSS Output for One-Way ANCOVA: Tests of Between-Subjects Effects[a]

Dependent variable: change					
Source	Type III Sum of Squares	df	Mean Square	F	Significance
Corrected model	34.834[b]	3	11.611	1.640	.183
Intercept	449.240	1	449.240	63.467	.000
Health	1.825	1	1.825	.258	.612
Technique	31.524	2	15.762	2.227	.112
Error	1033.440	146	7.078	—	—
Total	5367.000	150	—	—	—
Corrected total	1068.273	149	—	—	—

[a]Although SPSS output for the ANCOVA contains more information than do the outcomes of "Tests of Between-Subjects Effects," the researcher should focus on this table to determine whether significant differences exist. Values pertaining to the omnibus ANCOVA appear in the top row of this table. These values indicate whether those in the three relaxation technique categories experienced significantly different drops in heart rate.
[b]$r^2 = .033$ (adjusted $r^2 = .013$).

Example 9.13: SPSS Output for One-Way ANCOVA An analysis of the relaxation techniques described in Example 9.6 would require a one-way ANCOVA because it involves only one independent variable. Table 9.9 provides the results, using imaginary data, for such an analysis.

The name of the covariate, in this case, health, appears along with the name of the independent variable in Table 9.9. The "Corrected model" row, however, provides the information needed to accept or reject the null hypothesis regardless of any influence that a subject's health may have on his or her independent-variable category. The corrected model's p value of .183 exceeds most reasonable α levels, suggesting that those who participate in yoga sessions, meditation sessions, and biofeedback therapy do not experience significantly different changes in heart rate.

The sum of squares shown in the "Corrected model" row of Table 9.9 results from having removed any effects that the covariate, subject health, has on group placement. SPSS uses this value, not the standard sum of squares discussed in Chapter 7, to compute mean-square values and, ultimately, the F ratio.

Because of its inclusion of multiple dependent variables, the MANCOVA produces more output than the ANCOVA does. Still, the Table 9.9 provides the information necessary to accept or reject the null hypothesis. To help you understand the results of the information in this table, you can request descriptive information for data on each category used in an ANCOVA or MANCOVA.

ANCOVA output contains only one other table, which tells you the number of subjects in each independent-variable group. If you have conducted a MANCOVA, this table lists the names and sizes of each category for each variable. For additional information about ANCOVA and MANCOVA output, please see this chapter's companion website.

www.moravian.edu/aqd

Discriminant Analysis

In SPSS's "Discriminant Analysis" window (Fig. 9.5), you identify both the continuous independent variable(s) that you wish to use as predictors of subjects' category placements and the grouping variable. When you move the name of the grouping variable to the appropriate box, SPSS asks you to input the range of nominal values used to designate groups. You can obtain this window by selecting "Classify" from SPSS's "Analyze" pulldown menu and then specifying that you would like a discriminant analysis.

The way in which you interpret SPSS discriminant analysis output depends on your motive for conducting the test. If you would simply like a straightforward answer about the significance of differences, you should begin by examining the p value. The Wilks' lambda table (Table 9.10) provides this value in its column entitled "Significance," based on the process of calculating F described in Section 9.5. To understand the strength of the linear relationship between variables, however, you must consider the discriminant function. For analyses with a single predictor, this equation contains an intercept value and a coefficient for the predictor value. As the strength of the linear relationship between the predictor variable and the grouping variable increases, the size

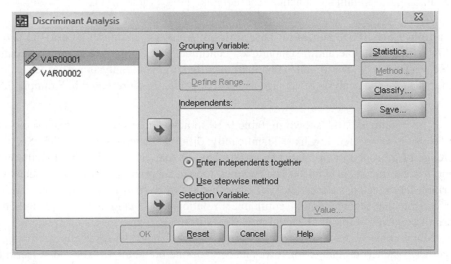

Figure 9.5. SPSS "Discriminant Analysis" window. The user performs a discriminant analysis by selecting the appropriate variable names from those listed in the box on the left side of the window. The name of the continuous variable(s) should be moved to the "Independents" area, and the name of the categorical dependent variable should be moved to the "Grouping Variable" area.

TABLE 9.10. SPSS Output for Discriminant Analysis: Wilks' Lambda[a]

Test of Function(s)	Wilks' Lambda	Chi-Square	df	Significance
1	.927	11.049	3	.011

[a]This table contains the *p* value that indicates whether the predictor variable values differ significantly for each grouping variable category.

TABLE 9.11. Standardized Canonical Discriminant Function Coefficients[a]

	Function
	1
Acreage	1

[a]Coefficients for the discriminating function appear as standardized canonical discriminant function coefficients in this table. Because this analysis involves only one predictor variable, the table contains only one coefficient. Further, it attributes all predictability to that variable.

of the predictor variable's coefficient increases. Coefficients appear in the "Standardized Canonical Discrimininant Function Coefficients" table (Table 9.11).

Example 9.14: SPSS Output for Discriminant Analysis   Tables 9.10 and 9.11 show a Wilks' lambda table and a standardized canonical discriminant function coefficient table, respectively. These tables result from a discriminant analysis performed using mock data for the analysis of acreage and fencing style, first presented in Example 9.8.

The *p* value of .011 shown in Table 9.10 indicates that properties enclosed with different styles of fencing have significantly different acreages at $\alpha = .05$. So, the acreage of a property can predict the type of fence that encloses it. The discriminant function coefficient in Table 9.11 describes the linear relationship between the two variables. Acreage has a coefficient of 1 because the analysis involves only one predictor variable that accounts for the entire linear relationship. Had more than one predictor variables existed, Table 9.11 would provide a different coefficient for each one.

Many consider the results of the significance test and the discriminant function together. When your analysis involves more than one predictor variable, the discriminant function can help you determine the role that each one plays in helping to predict category placements. This information becomes especially useful if results of the significance test indicate that the combination of multiple predictor variables adequately predicts subject's categories ($p < \alpha$). Considering the size of each predictor variable's coefficient may allow you to "streamline" the discriminant function so that it includes only the variables that truly help to predict grouping variable values. This chapter's companion website briefly describes this process as well as providing detailed instructions for conducting a discriminant analysis in SPSS.

www.moravian.edu/aqd

REVIEW QUESTIONS

Determine whether a repeated-measures ANOVA, a MANOVA, an ANCOVA, or discriminant analysis should be used to test each of the following null hypotheses. Explain your reasoning.

9.1. Regardless of the length of a person's hair, females, with blonde, brunette, red, and gray hair spend equal amounts of time per year in beauty salons.

9.2. Considering athletic ability as a combination of strength and speed, members of all college athletic teams have equal athletic ability.

9.3. The use of cars, a van, or a bus to transport students for a class field trip is not related to the number of students in the class.

9.4. Equal numbers of rooms have lights on and off at all levels of the sunlight's intensity.

9.5. No difference exists in peoples' reaction times when tested in the morning, in the afternoon, or in the evening.

9.6. Restaurants that have no dress code, that have a lenient dress code, and that have a strict dress code receive equally high customer ratings, based on food quality, service, and overall atmosphere.

Consider a within-subject design based on observations of four types of perennial flowers over 3 years. The number of days that each type of flower is in full bloom each year, produces the following data:

Year 1	Year 2	Year 3
18	18	16
16	18	15
20	19	16
14	14	13

9.7. Find SS_S.

9.8. Find df_S.

9.9. Find df_W.

9.10. Find df_T.

9.11. Find df_B.

9.12. Find F_{crit} at $\alpha = .05$ for the repeated-measures ANOVA comparing subject performance in the four conditions.

9.13. Suppose that the repeated-measures ANOVA leads to a rejected null hypothesis.

(A) What post hoc comparison should be done first? Why?

(B) What type of t test would be used for post hoc tests?

9.14. What is the advantage to comparing canonical variate means using a MANOVA rather than addressing each means of each dependent variable using multiple ANOVAs?

9.15. Explain the difference between an SS value and an SSCP value.

9.16. (A) Complete the following one-way MANOVA summary table.

Source	SSCP	df	MS	F
Between	112.58	3		
Within	49.36	91		
Total				

(B) Find F_{crit} for this analysis.

(C) Should you reject the null hypothesis for this investigation? Why or why not?

9.17. (A) Complete the following two-way MANOVA summary table.

Source	SSCP	df	MS	F_{calc}
Row (R)	74.89	2		
Column (C)	61.21	2		
Interaction ($R \times C$)	122.25			
Within group (S/RC)		24		
Total	298.39	32		

(B) Find relevant F_{crit} values at $\alpha = .05$ for this analysis.

(C) Should you accept the null hypothesis for this investigation? Why or why not?

9.18. Explain what variations each of the following address:

(A) SS_{B_D}

(B) SS_{W_D}

(C) SS_{T_D}

(D) SS_{B_C}

(E) SS_{W_C}

(F) SS_{T_C}

Consider an ANCOVA that compares the number of months it takes to complete the doctoral program in a particular discipline at two different universities. With different criteria for admitting students, those in each program have different amounts of previous experience (including formal education) in the field.

9.19. (A) What is the independent variable for this study?

(B) What is the dependent variable for this study?

(C) What is the covariate for this study?

For Questions 9.20–9.24, use the following data, based on the scenario described for Question 9.19:

University	Years of Experience	Months in Program
A	40	16
A	33	15
A	42	7
A	43	10
A	30	5
B	42	12
B	33	8
B	40	18
B	29	5
B	39	15

9.20. Find SC_T.

9.21. (A) Find SC_{W_A} and SC_{W_B}.

(B) Find SC_W.

9.22. *Consider the following discriminant analysis scenario. Nutritionists wonder whether a relationship exists between the number of calories consumed during the main course of a meal and the types of desserts people order at restaurants. They obtain information about the number of calories randomly selected restaurant visitors consume from their main courses as well as whether they order no dessert, a dessert to be eaten with a spoon (e.g., ice cream) or a dessert to be eaten with a fork (e.g., cake).*

(A) What is the predictor (independent) variable for the analysis?

(B) What is the grouping (dependent) variable for this analysis?

9.23. Given the following multiple discriminant function

$$G = .32x_1 + .49x_2 + .10x_3 + .13x_4$$

(A) Which predictor variable has the strongest relationship with the grouping variable? How do you know?

(B) Removing which predictor variable would have the least effect on the predictability of the grouping variable? How do you know?

PART III

APPLYING DATA

10

DRAWING CONCLUSIONS

10.1 INTRODUCTION

Social scientists distinguish between the results of a study and the conclusions of a study. The results consist of relevant descriptive and inferential statistics as well as a statement about whether you have accepted or rejected the null hypothesis. Other than referring to variable names, this information contains very little context. It merely explains the deductive process of determining whether a relationship exists between variables.

By combining the results of the study with your contextual understanding of the study's topic, you can draw conclusions. Conclusions of social research describe the ways in which the results of a study can explain conditions or behaviors. They often go so far as to suggest approaches to managing negative conditions or, when possible, behaviors and promoting positive ones.

Example 10.1: Results versus Conclusions   The results of an analysis to determine whether a significant difference exists between the maximum loudness (measured in decibels) of an elementary school classes with and without class pets would focus on the calculated and the critical t values. A t_{calc} that exceeds t_{crit} indicates that the people take significantly different levels of loudness for both types of classes In this case, one

Analyzing Quantitative Data: An Introduction for Social Researchers, First Edition. Debra Wetcher-Hendricks.
© 2011 John Wiley & Sons, Inc. Published 2011 by John Wiley & Sons, Inc.

would reject the null hypothesis (H_0: $\overline{X}_{pet} = \overline{X}_{no\,pet}$), identifying the louder and the quieter of the two types of classes. The null hypothesis would be accepted, suggesting that no difference in loudness exists, if $t_{calc} < t_{crit}$. In addition to addressing the null hypothesis, results could include relevant descriptive statistics, most likely means and standard deviations for a t test such as this one.

The next logical step in describing the outcome of this study would involve recommendations based on the presence or absence of a significant difference. At this point, the researcher moves from results to conclusions. For this study, conclusions might begin with the researcher's description of the relationship between having a class pet and the loudness of the students in the class. If loudness differs in exactly the way that the research hypothesis predicts, the researcher can tout his or her inductive logic. Otherwise, the researcher can rationalize about what accounts for the unexpected results. Conditions such as the choice of schools or limited observations may be offered as explanations.

In their conclusions, researchers may also critique their study and describe plans for follow-up studies. After reflecting on how they conducted their studies, they often believe it important to point out the studies' limitations and imperfections. These issues can range from sampling issues to or unanticipated events during the course of data collection that may have affected the outcome of the study. Researchers can use shortcomings of their studies as bases for new studies. Sometimes, they simply explain plans to replicate, or repeat, their studies using different or broader samples or subjects than they originally did. Other reasons for suggesting the need for further studies can include the researcher's desire to change the attributes or measurements to increase their reliability and accuracy.

10.2 ACCEPTING AND REJECTING HYPOTHESES

The entire goal of inferential statistical analysis revolves around determining whether your research hypothesis correctly predicts the relationship between variables. These tests, however, do not produce outcome that you can immediately apply to the research hypothesis. Rather, they tell you whether you can accept or reject the null hypothesis. You must, then, take the extra step of considering what these results imply about your research hypothesis. There is no simple rule about how to proceed with this step because the relationship between the null and research hypotheses can vary.

10.2.1 The Null Hypothesis–Research Hypothesis Relationship

Reiterating the information about research and null hypotheses in Section 4.3.2, the research hypothesis makes a prediction based on your true expectation for results, and the null hypothesis predicts equality. The two can, on occasion, make the same prediction. Your research goal may involve refuting a common belief or assumption about a distinction between particular situations, groups, or people. In this case, the research hypothesis, which asserts your belief about the relationship between the independent and dependent variables, would propose equality between all individuals or groups, just as the null hypothesis does.

Example 10.2: Identical Research and Null Hypotheses The information that a researcher gathers during a review of the literature for the topic described in Example 10.1 might lead her or him to believe that no relationship exists between having a class pet and the class' maximum loudness. When measured in terms of maximum decibel level, then the mean for classes with pets should equal the mean for classes without pets, making the research hypothesis $H: \bar{X}_{pet} = \bar{X}_{no\,pet}$. This research hypothesis looks identical to the null hypothesis presented in Example 10.1 because the both predict equal dependent-variable scores for the independent-variable groups.

Most often, however, the two are not identical because you intend to demonstrate that individuals differ on the basis of some independent-variable characteristic.

Example 10.3: Different Research and Null Hypotheses A researcher who believes that, unlike the situation presented in Example 10.2, one can predict the loudness of a class on the basis of whether the class has a pet, would propose a research hypothesis that differs from the null hypothesis. In the research hypothesis, the researcher would indicate which of the two independent-variable groups might have the higher maximum decibel level. A researcher who wishes to suggest an association between having pets and having a quiet classroom would state the research hypothesis as $H: \bar{X}_{pet} < \bar{X}_{no\,pet}$. This hypothesis suggests that one can predict the loudness of a class according to whether it has a pet.

This research hypothesis differs from the null hypothesis, which still states $H_0: \bar{X}_{pet} = \bar{X}_{no\,pet}$. Although the researcher believes that, when measuring maximum loudness for classes with and without class pets, one could expect a smaller mean for the former than for the latter, the researcher cannot test this contention directly. She or he must first determine whether a difference in maximum loudness for the two types of classes exists at all. So, as with the scenario from Example 10.2, the researcher begins by testing the null hypothesis.

The results of statistical analyses will tell you whether to accept or reject the null hypothesis of equality. The way in which you interpret these results depends on the relationship between your research and null hypothesis. You cannot take the same steps after accepting null hypothesis in situations involving identical null and research hypotheses and in situations in which they differ. Likewise, the meaning of a rejected null hypothesis in terms of the research hypothesis depends on whether the two are identical or different.

10.2.2 Matching Null and Research Hypotheses

A research hypothesis that suggests no relationship between the independent and dependent variables allows for relatively straightforward analysis. Because this hypothesis states exactly the same thing as the null hypothesis does, you can accept it when you accept the null hypothesis and reject it when you reject the null hypothesis.

Even though the research and null hypotheses are basically identical, statistical tests technically revolve on the null hypothesis. The relationship between the calculated and the critical values indicate whether you should accept or reject the null hypothesis. Subsequent steps involve considering the implications of this acceptance or rejection in terms of the research hypothesis. With identical research and null hypotheses, however, these subsequent steps reduce to the single step of restating the null hypothesis' findings in terms of the research hypothesis.

Example 10.4: Accepting or Rejecting Identical Research and Null Hypotheses   The researcher conducting an analysis of the class' loudness described in Example 10.2 would know whether to accept or reject the research hypothesis almost instantly after comparing t_{calc} and t_{crit}. This comparison, in and of itself, indicates whether one should accept or reject the null hypothesis. In this example, however, the research hypothesis predicts equality between the mean loudness levels for the two categories of classes, just as the null hypothesis does. So, whatever decision the researcher makes about the null hypothesis also applies to the research hypothesis.

10.2.3   Different Null and Research Hypotheses

When a research hypothesis does not predict equality, you must know more than merely whether a difference exists, which suffices for the situations described in Section 10.2.2. But evaluating a research hypothesis that predicts inequality requires you to determine whether it correctly identified the individuals or situations that have higher dependent-variable scores than others. Not only do dependent-variable scores have to differ; they have to differ in the way predicted for you to accept the research hypothesis. Your decision about whether to accept or reject the null hypothesis, therefore, may involve multiple steps. The flowchart in Figure 10.1 provides a visual representation of the thought process needed to consider all possible results.

You've certainly noticed that the side of the flowchart that relates to different research hypotheses has more paths than the side that relates to identical research hypotheses has. As explained in Section 10.2.2, acceptance or rejection of a research hypothesis that, like the null hypothesis, predicts equality, requires only one path. But the multiple judgments needed to accept a research hypothesis that does not predict quality create additional paths. By following these paths, you can assure yourself that you are accepting the research hypothesis only when it correctly predicts the relationship between the independent and dependent variables.

Example 10.5: Accepting or Rejecting Different Null and Research Hypotheses   To make a decision regarding the research hypothesis from Example 10.5, which proposes that classes with pets have lower mean loudness levels than those without pets do, one would focus on the right side of Figure 10.1.

The shorter of the paths of the right side suggests that an accepted null hypothesis leads immediately to a rejected research hypothesis. The lack of any significant difference in mean loudness level, as the accepted null hypothesis indicates, means that no inequality, including the one proposed by the research hypothesis, can exist.

The longer of the paths would have been relevant if results of inferential statistics indicated a significant difference in loudness levels of classes with and without pets. In this case, the research hypothesis might correctly describe the relationship between having a class pet and loudness in the classroom. Suppose, for example, that classes with pets have a mean loudness level (in decibels) of 98.3 and classes without pets have a mean loudness level of 100.4. The researcher, in this case, could accept the null hypothesis because the significant difference exists in the predicted direction, with classes that do not have pets being louder than classes that do have pets.

If, however, the loudness factor of 98.3 referred to classes with pets and the loudness factor of 100.4 referred to classes without pets, the researcher could not accept the research hypothesis. This decision reflects that fact that the values are opposite those predicted by the research hypothesis predicts.

Although determining whether to accept or reject the research hypothesis in Example 10.5 requires multiple steps, the process can become further complicated when the study involves a nondichotomous independent variable. Research hypotheses that describe relationships between more than two variables contain at least two inequalities. Inferential statistical tests produce a calculated value that exceeds the

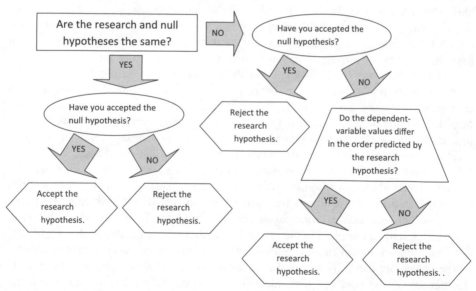

Figure 10.1. Hypothesis decision flowchart. The flowchart illustrates the different approaches needed to accept or reject a research hypothesis given different conditions. Identical research and null hypotheses permit a nearly immediate decision, as shown on the left side of the flowchart. The complexities on the right side pertain to the issues that one must consider before accepting or rejecting a null research hypothesis that differs from the null hypothesis.

critical value if *any* of these inequalities is significant. Before fully accepting the research hypothesis, though, you must make sure that all inequalities have significance and exist in the predicted direction. Otherwise, you can claim only that the data support portions of your research hypothesis.

Example 10.6: Accepting or Rejecting Research Hypothesis with Nondichotomous Categorical Variable   A researcher who wishes to distinguish between types of pets in his or her analysis of the class' loudness levels would have more than two categories of classes and, therefore, need to consider these aspects. The researcher may believe that a glass tank creates the perception of a barrier between students and the pet. Thus, the researcher may reason that behavior of students with a pet in a tank lies somewhere on the continuum between the extreme behaviors of those without a class pet and those with a pet that lives in a cage. The resulting hypothesis, $H: \bar{X}_{\text{caged pet}} > \bar{X}_{\text{tanked pet}} \bar{X} >_{\text{no pet}}$, contains two inequalities. One suggests that classes with caged pets have lower loudness levels than classes with tanked pets have. The other suggests that classes with tanked pets have lower loudness levels than those without pets have. The inequalities imply an order of quietest to loudest classes.

The ANOVA that would test for significant differences between the three means does not need $\bar{X}_{\text{caged pet}} > \bar{X}_{\text{tanked pet}}$ and $\bar{X}_{\text{tanked pet}} \bar{X} >_{\text{no pet}}$ to produce a F_{crit} that exceeds F_{calc}. Even $\bar{X}_{\text{caged pet}} < \bar{X}_{\text{tanked pet}} < \bar{X}_{\text{no pet}}$ could produce significant results. Also, only one of these portions of the overall inequality stated in the research hypothesis needs to be true for the ANOVA to suggest significance. Quite possibly, $\bar{X}_{\text{caged pet}} > \bar{X}_{\text{tanked pet}}$, but $\bar{X}_{\text{tanked pet}} \bar{X} <_{\text{no pet}}$ or vice versa. Although, in this situation, the classes' loudness levels does follow a part of the order predicted in the research hypothesis, the entire research hypothesis is not correct. The researcher, therefore, could not fully accept it.

Even if the mean loudness levels for the classes arrange themselves in the order predicted by the research hypothesis, the researcher must analyze the difference between each pair of category means. An F_{crit} that exceeds F_{calc} suggests only that two category means differ significantly. So, it may be that no significant difference exists between loudness levels of classes with tanked pets and classes with caged pets if the loudness level of classes with no pets is significantly greater than that for classes with tanked pets. A similar situation may exist with respect to a insignificant difference between loudness levels of classes with tanked pets and no pets. Further, each of the inequalities blatantly stated in the hypothesis may prove insignificant if significance exists in the difference between classes with caged pets and no pets. To be confident that each inequality stated and implied in the research hypothesis is associated with a significant difference, the researcher should perform post hoc comparisons, as described in Chapter 7. The researcher can fully accept the research hypothesis if all comparisons indicate significance. If the post hoc tests identify only some differences as significant, the researcher may be able to claim that variations in loudness level with respect to the presence of a class pet exists, but not to the extent predicted.

10.3   DRAWING CONCLUSIONS FROM RESULTS

The designation of a research hypothesis as accepted or rejected may end the analytical portion of the study. But you must still address the contextual basis of the study. Having obtained statistical results, you can return to the foundation of your investigation to characterize, clarify, or provide suggestions about human behavior. These conclusions allow your audience to utilize the information that your study has uncovered.

The way in which you describe the implications of your results depends on your audience and your motive for performing your study in the first place. You should have provided a contextual basis for your study in your literature review. This portion of your research report precedes the introduction of your hypothesis. It contains background information, usually from findings of previous studies, that justifies your study and research hypothesis. Using the analogy of a trip, the literature review provides your audience with a travel brochure, helped to determine the expectations of your audience. Then, the trip, itself—in this case, the voyage through the data collection and analysis process—occurs. After data collection, you present your conclusions as evidence of what you experienced during the process of research, in much the same way that you would show photographs after a trip as evidence of what you experienced on your travels. The conclusions bring your research report full circle by telling the audience whether the data gathered fulfilled the expectations that you instilled in them through your literature review.

The conclusion is the last impression that your audience members have of your research project and, therefore, this section of the report should stress your study's value to them. Most audience members want to know how they could use the results of your study to understand or react to situations that they regularly encounter. They look to your interpretations of the results to provide them with this information. This interpretation should have many elements, including the summary of your findings, reflection on your own study, and speculation about the future of research on the topic of your study. The following sections describe the manners in which you must think about your study's results to acknowledge each of these issues. Each section also provides suggestions for incorporating your thoughts about them into the conclusion.

10.3.1 Summarizing

Knowing why your audience is interested in your study in the first place should help you to focus your conclusions. Every audience and, possibly, every audience member, may value your research for a different reason. Your study's results may help those in your audience to make informed decisions; they may help the audience gain insight into possible foundations of others' decisions and behaviors; they may help your audience members prepare for unfamiliar situations by providing some sort of general picture of the people or circumstances that they may encounter. Each of these applications, as well as the many more that could exist, demands a different approach to contextualizing your results into conclusions.

Example 10.7: Context For example, the study regarding the relationship between having a class pet and class loudness would likely have the most appeal to teachers, educational administrators, and faculty in education departments of colleges and universities. Teachers expect the study's results to aid them in making a decision about whether to allow pets in the classroom or, in the case of the faculty member, whether to encourage future teachers to do so. Academic administrators who must make a decision about whether to create or maintain a "No animals in school" rule may benefit from knowing whether the benefits, in this case a quiet classroom, justifies the potential problems associated with having pets in the classroom.

Audience members could also use the results of the study as a basis for expectations about various classes. The conclusions can help substitute teachers, for example, characterize classes on the basis of whether they have class pets. If a relationship between the variables does exist, substitute teachers, who encounter new and unpredictable situations every day, may scan new classrooms in the morning to help them determine what sorts of behavior to expect from students in the class.

Others involved in the educational process likely have their own reasons for wanting to know whether this relationship exists. School psychologists, curriculum developers, and even students' parents may be interested in different aspects of the connection between having a class pet and students' levels of loudness. Researchers should tailor their presentations of results to satisfy the audiences' particular curiosities.

Stated simply, your conclusions should satisfy your audience's curiosity in the topic. To fully do so, you must recognize not only exactly what your audience members want to know but also their reason for wanting to know this information. For audience members who plan to use the information from your study passively, such as the substitute teacher in Example 10.7, your conclusion should simply interpret the data and summarize any significant trends or differences that exist. However, those, such as the administrators from Example 10.7, who wish to use the newly found information as grounds for policies or interactions, might benefit from your recommendations about how to act on the results of the study.

Because the way in which you summarize your study in the conclusion may have a great impact on audience members' future behavior, it is essential that they have a clear understanding of your study's impact. It doesn't hurt to remind the audience of your study's value. You likely already did so in your literature review. However, at that point, in your audience members' minds, your research existed only in the abstract. Now, having seen or heard concrete results, you audience can truly appreciate the importance of your analysis.

Your audience members, however, really want the valuable information that you promised your findings would provide. Providing this information, for the most part, requires you to expand the technical descriptions of your findings to applicable elements, often in the form of characterizations or recommendations. Audience members may not know what to make of a claim that a significant difference does or does not exist at $\alpha = .05$. But they can understand your suggestions about whether they should regard some situations differently from others. A full explanation of your study's real-world relevance leaves your audience members with an appreciation of how they can benefit from the knowledge that your study's findings provide.

With that said, determining exactly what to include in your conclusions can prove quite challenging, especially for complex research projects with varied audiences. Most summary portions of the "Conclusion" section, however, have similar basic components. You can use the following guidelines as a basis for organizing the summary:

- Remind the audience of the problem that you identified in your literature review and the hypothesis or hypotheses that your investigation tested.
- Remind the audience of the study's most important findings. (For studies that have more than one research hypothesis and, thus, more than one finding, you may wish to list the findings in order of importance.)
- Interpret the meaning of each accepted or rejected research hypotheses with respect to the problem that you identified in your literature review.
- Explain how the audience could use the information uncovered by the research.
- Describe any controversies or new information that have arisen from the study's findings.
- Make predictions, based on past differences and trends, about future differences and trends.

To a great extent, your own perceptions about what is important determine the information that you present and how you present it in your conclusions. Still, you can lose credibility if your conclusions do not logically follow from the information presented earlier in your research report. Additional guidelines can help you avoid a conclusion that confuses your audience or trivializes your findings.

- Do not begin the conclusion with finalizing words, such as "In conclusion," and "Finally."
- Do not use second person.
- Do not introduce new material.
- Do not make overly subjective or emotional statements.
- Do not embellish your study's findings (often done through exaggerated or misleading statements).

10.3.2 Reflecting

Excited about their findings and eager to convince others of their study's value, a researcher generally proclaims her or his study a success in the conclusion of the research report. There is, of course, nothing wrong with pointing out the ways in which your study has broadened awareness about the research topic. A good researcher, however, also uses a critical eye to assess her or his study. In retrospect, you can almost always identify aspects of your study that you consider imperfect. These issues often reflect unavoidable or unpredictable circumstances. Nevertheless, if they have impacted the outcome of your study, then you have the responsibility to make your audience aware of them. A balance of self-praise and self-criticism helps convince your audience that your results and conclusions provide a genuine account of the research topic.

Sampling issues often head the list of aspects that researchers wish they could change about their studies. Because of circumstances such as time and monetary constraints, you may not have acquired the sample size or diversity that you wanted. Factors such as unavailability of subjects and unequal subject groups may have also limited the amount or type of data you could obtain. In your conclusion you should describe your optimal sample and explain why you could not obtain it. Most audience members understand the practical limitations of sampling and realize that you made your best attempt at acquiring a representative sample. They tend to be somewhat forgiving of mild sampling inadequacies, making this issue a good one to mention first.

Other matters that deserve mention in your conclusion vary from study to study. As a general rule, you should address anything that may have impacted the results or applicability of your study. Your goal is not to belittle your study, but rather to avoid misleading your audience. You should, therefore, frankly identify, explain the reasons for, and describe your attempts to rectify the following sorts of situations:

* Budget or time constraints limited the scope of your study.
* You experienced unforseen difficulties in obtaining data from subjects (due to lack of cooperation, faulty tools, etc.).
* You were unable to obtain the exact information desired from subjects (due to ethical considerations, threats to internal validity,[1] etc.).
* Experimental errors occurred.

Although it may seem odd to point out concerns about your own study, doing so actually assures audience members of your capability as a researcher and an expert in your field of research. Members of your audience with knowledge about your research topic or familiar with research methods may have identified some of these shortcomings before reading or hearing the conclusion of your report. Failure to acknowledge them may give the impression that you consider your study flawless. Rather than ignoring your study's imperfections, you should present them as a learning tool, explaining why they occurred and why you could not anticipate or prevent them in your study as well as whether any ways to minimize them in future studies exist.

10.3.3   Speculating

Research on your topic does not end with your study. You probably designed your study on the basis of ideas that you got from others' research, and you should expect the same to happen when your audience reads or hears your research report. In fact, many researchers use a portion of their conclusions to suggest ways in which their studies can serve as starting points for future studies on the same or similar topics.

A common type of follow-up study attempts to replicate a previous study while avoiding the flaws that the researcher identified in her or his conclusions. This type of replication study is often relatively simple because it requires little, if any, prestudy planning. You can usually refer to the original study's literature review to justify the importance of the topic and can use the original study's research and null hypotheses.

[1] Please see Campbell and Stanley (1966) for a detailed discussion of threats to internal validity.

Thus, most of your work on the new project can focus on data collection and analysis.

The results of your study may have also provided you with ideas for follow-up investigations that provide further insight into your topic or related topics. Findings that surprise you, for example, may spur you to search for additional variables to explain the relationships uncovered in your study.

Example 10.8: Investigating Surprising Results One conducting the study described in Example 10.3, based on the research hypothesis that classes with class pets have lower loudness scores than those without class pets do, might be surprised by an accepted null hypothesis. Although his or her background research suggests that $\bar{X}_{\text{pet}} < \bar{X}_{\text{no pet}}$, the researcher would have to acknowledge equal loudness levels between the two types of classes.

With much faith in their predictions, based on information from sources used for the literature review, researchers may choose to further investigate the relationship. Additional review of scholarly material and further speculation may lead researchers to a new hypothesis that they believe specifies the relationship between having class pets and classroom loudness better than the original hypothesis did. The researcher, for instance, may realize that differences in classes' loudness levels may be apparent only in relation to certain types of class pets. Therefore, the researcher may suggest a follow-up study that compares the mean decibel levels in classrooms with no class pets, with class pets kept in cages, and with class pets kept in tanks.

Another approach to expanding your study could seek to broaden your findings. This type of follow-up study can determine whether a relationship that exists among the segment of the population that you tested also exists in other segments of the population.

Example 10.9: Extending the Study Findings that support the research hypothesis presented in Example 10.3, suggesting lower levels of loudness in elementary-school classrooms with pets than in those without pets, could lead to questions about whether similar relationships exist in other conditions. The researcher may, therefore, suggest replicating her or his study in settings such as secondary-school classrooms, college dormitories, or workplaces.

An infinite number of other variations and extensions of your study may exist. Identifying some of the possibilities for future research, founded on the results of your study, ends your research report in an inspiring way.

10.4 CAUTIONS

An accepted research hypothesis can easily entice you into assuming that a direct association exists between the independent and dependent variables. The relationship, however, may not be so simple. Just because your research has uncovered the predicted

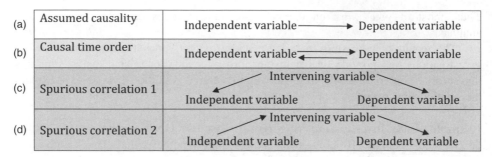

Figure 10.2. Causal diagrams. When changes in the independent variable directly cause changes in the dependent variable, the "assumed causality" diagram (a) suffices. The other three diagrams (b)–(d) illustrate the alternative explanations that can explain statistically significant relationships or linear trends between variables. Complex relationships may even combine elements of the causal time order and spurious correlation diagrams.

difference or correlation doesn't mean that you can make assertions about why the trend exists. Sweeping statements about the reasons for relationships between variables or about individuals within your subject groups can misrepresent the results of your study. Before making suggestions to your audience about how the results of your study apply to "real world" contexts, you should consider four pitfalls that can lead to faulty conclusions.

10.4.1   Alternate Explanations of Causation

Chapter 1 presents the independent variable as the "predictor" and the dependent variable as the "predictee." Chapter 1 also explains that those who think of these variables as the "cause" and "effect", respectively, often overlook the alternative explanations for the causal relationship. It may very well be that a direct causal diagram leading from the independent variable to the dependent variable accurately describes the relationship. But you must also consider the possibilities of causal time order issues or spurious correlations. Either of these alternate explanations may account for a relationship in which dependent-variable scores change predictably with respect to changes in independent-variable scores.

The causal diagrams in Chapter 1 illustrate the potential flows of causality between independent variables, dependent variables, and intervening variables to help you understand the roles that each of these types of variables can play. A short review of these arrangements, however, stresses their importance in relation to drawing conclusions.

Figure 10.2(a) refers to the most commonly assumed relationship, in which an independent variable directly impacts a dependent variable. However, issues of causal time order, represented in Figure 10.2(b), can designate the dependent variable as the cause and the independent variable as the effect. A spurious correlation, involving at least one intervening variable, as shown in Figures 10.2(b)–(d), could also challenge the claim that independent-variable scores determine dependent-variable scores.

Spurious correlation 1 occurs when changes in scores for an intervening variable explain changes in both independent- and dependent-variable scores. Spurious correlation 2 occurs when changes in the independent variable's scores cause changes in an intervening variable's scores and changes in that intervening variable's scores cause changes in the dependent variable's scores.

Example 10.10: Alternative Causal Explanations A rejected null hypothesis for the sample study concerning classroom pets and class' loudness levels could imply any of the possibilities shown in Figure 10.2.

The causal diagram in Figure 10.3(a) correctly depicts the relationship between variables only if having a class pet, in and of itself, really does account for differences in class' loudness levels. Of course, this direct relationship may exist. However, in a non-laboratory setting like a classroom, a researcher seldom can control the data-gathering process enough to eliminate alternative explanations.

Most likely, this study used existing subject groups. Classes that had class pets prior to the beginning of the study provided data, and classes without pets provided data. The researcher, however, has no "history" of these classes. In particular, the researcher does not know the reason for having or not having a pet in each classroom. It could be that initially quiet rooms get class pets and initially loud rooms do not because teachers believe that pets will become scared or agitated in loud rooms. The researcher's comparison of classes in this case would indicate that those with pets have significantly higher loudness levels than those without pets do. But the difference in loudness levels does not exist because of the class pet condition. Rather, the class pet condition exists because of differences in loudness levels. The researcher has no way of knowing whether causality moves in this direction, from the dependent variable to the independent variable, or in the assumed direction, from the independent variable to the dependent variable. The researcher should, therefore, use the causal time order diagram [Fig. 10.3(b)] to illustrate the indefinite direction of causality.

Figures 10.3(c) and 10.3(d), labeled as spurious correlations, accommodate an intervening variable that connects the independent and the dependent variables. Figure 10.3(a) overlooks this possibility. But the spurious correlation diagrams suggest that the link between the independent and dependent variable relies on a "hidden" variable.

For spurious correlation 1, overall student behavior, the intervening variable could influence a teacher's decision about whether to have a pet in the classroom and could serve as a factor that determines the classroom's loudness. Teachers may be hesitant to bring pets into unruly classrooms, possibly believing that the students don't deserve the privilege of having a pet. This situation explains the causal path from "student overall behavior" to "having a class pet." The causal path from "student overall behavior" to "loudness level" may exist because noise level among the student's rises in response to their classmates' rowdy behavior or because the teacher must yell a lot to keep the students under control. The arrangement of these causal paths indicates that no direct relationship exists between having a class pet and loudness level. The intervening variable of overall behavior influences both the independent and the dependent variables.

The diagram for spurious correlation 2 also places the intervening variable between the independent and dependent variables, but gives it a different role than it had in spurious correlation 1. The spurious correlation 2 arrangement suggests that, on getting a class pet, rules in the classroom may change. A teacher may increase the penalties for excessive loudness in the classroom, to keep the pet from becoming scared or agitated. Thus it is not the pet, itself, but the penalties for bad behavior, that cause the reduced loudness in rooms with class pets. Even with a class pet, students may be loud if the teacher hadn't imposed these penalties.

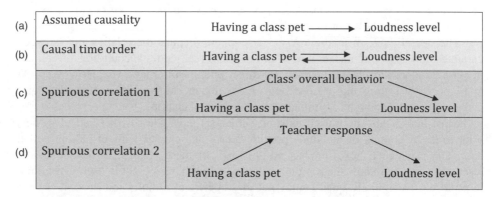

<u>Figure 10.3.</u> Class pet causal diagrams. Any of these four diagrams can illustrate the causal paths that explain a statistically significant relationship between having a class pet and the class' loudness levels.

The causal time order diagram or either of the spurious correlation diagrams in Figure 10.3 could describe the true association between having a class pet and a classroom's level of loudness. Researchers can dismiss the possibility of a causal time order issue only if they have the foresight to pretest and posttest the same class. Likewise, researchers can dismiss the possibility of a causal time order issue only if they can account for every possible intervening variable in their analyses. Otherwise, their conclusions cannot contain terms or phrases suggesting that getting a class pet will decrease noise levels in the classroom.

For relatively simple analyses, you must merely remain mindful of the fact that alternative explanations prevent you from declaring that changes in the independent-variable cause changes in the dependent variable. Some analyses, however, may benefit from your determination of exactly which alternative explanation most likely describes the relationship. In these situations, you must consider not only causal time order issues and spurious correlations but also the combination of the two. Many arrangements of the causal paths shown in Figure 10.2 can exist.

Example 10.11: Combined Alternative Explanations   For example, rather than behavior influencing high levels of loudness, as the spurious correlation 1 diagram in Figure 10.3 depicts, levels of loudness might influence behavior. The dynamic of a quiet classroom may make students feel as though they must refrain from inappropriate behavior. However, without this dynamic, students feel little or no need to restrain themselves. Further, in their efforts to control student behavior, teachers may reward quiet classes with pets, making classroom management techniques an intervening variable. The direction of causality, therefore, flows from level of loudness to classroom management techniques to having a class pet.

The causal diagram in Figure 10.4 looks different from any of those presented in Figure 10.3. It contains the same intervening variable as Figure 10.3's spurious correlation 2 diagram does, but the causal paths point in different directions in the two diagrams. With respect to the direction of causality, the diagram in Figure 10.4 resembles Figure 10.3's causal time order diagram. In both, the independent variable appears as the result, rather than the cause, of the relationship. Without including both the spurious correlation element and the causal time order element, one could not accurately describe this relationship between having a class pet and the class' loudness levels.

Example 10.11 gives only one possibility of how a combination of causal time order and spurious correlations might describe the relationship between variables, and a relatively uncomplicated one at that. The inclusion of additional intervening variables and bi-directional paths between variables can produce some very intricate causal diagrams.

10.4.2   High Alpha Values

A second issue that you should revisit after collecting data pertains to your chosen alpha value. The value of α dictates the possibility of falsely rejecting the null hypothesis, thereby making a type I error. As α increases, the possibility of making a type I error also increases. With a low possibility of making a type I error, you can claim that a significant difference exists with much more certainty than you can when a high possibility of making a type I error exists.

When you selected α , based on the information in Chapter 4, you were likely thinking mostly about whether the standard value of .05 would lead you to reject your null hypothesis. Determining whether to accept or reject the null hypothesis involves comparing the critical value suggested by α to the calculated value, obtained through your computations. If the calculated value is larger than the critical value, you should reject the null hypothesis. However, as Chapter 4 explains, you have some control over the situation because you can alter the value of α.

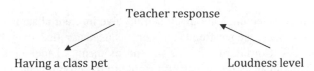

Figure 10.4. Class pet combined alternative explanation causal diagram. Paths indicate that the loudness level of a classroom affects the teachers' classroom management, which, in turn, affects whether the students have a class pet. This relationship involves both causal time order issues and a spurious correlation.

Increasing α causes critical values to decrease. So, one strategy for ensuring a rejected null hypothesis is to increase α to a point at which it suggests a critical value that is smaller than the calculated value. If you increase the standard value of α slightly, to values such as .075 or .10, you may lower the critical value just enough so that you can reject your null hypothesis. Larger increases, however, can create too great a chance of making a type I error. Some actually frown on raising α above .05 at all, as they are unwilling to accept even a 7.5% chance or a 10% of incorrectly claiming that values differ significantly. Still others prefer to use α values lower than the standard of .05 to minimize the chance of making a type I error as much as possible.

As the researcher, you realize that your results cannot provide definite verification of a significant difference. However, your audience may not. You must, therefore, take care to explain significant results in terms of the possibility of a significant difference existing rather than making a concrete declaration of unquestionable significance.

10.4.3   The Ecological Fallacy

Humans, constantly trying to make sense of the world, must rely on certain "mental shortcuts." These shortcuts, often called *heuristics* by social scientists, help us make decisions about unknown individuals or situations. In many cases, heuristics work well. For instance, one who avoids a public swimming pool on a really hot day, thinking that it would be too crowded for the visit to be enjoyable, has used heuristics to make the connection between the weather and people's activities. But careless use of heuristics can lead to incorrect characterizations, such as stereotypes, or biases. Social researchers must take care not to encourage the use of these shortcuts, or to use the shortcuts themselves, to make assertions about individual subjects. Improper use of heuristics can lead to an ecological fallacy.

An *ecological fallacy* occurs when a researcher concludes that each individual in a subject group has the general characteristics of that subject group. A moment of thought about this logic should make its unsoundness clear. In a way, you can think of the ecological fallacy as overgeneralization in reverse. Overgeneralization involves classifying all individuals within a subject group in a certain way on the basis of information about a particular person in that group. This practice can lead to inaccurate depictions of the group. With the ecological fallacy, using general information about a subject group to portray a particular person in that group leads to inaccurate depictions of that person.

A basic form of the ecological fallacy can involve inferential statistics. *Inferential statistics* compare values, such as frequencies or means, that reflect overall group qualities or performances. Considering means for the moment, all members of the group have their own individual scores, which contribute to the group mean, but likely differ from it. Any group member's individual score may lie well below or well above the group mean. You cannot, therefore, make any conjectures about a particular subject's score on the basis of the mean of that person's subject group.

Example 10.12: The Ecological Fallacy with Descriptive Statistics The study that addresses the relationship between having a class pet and classroom loudness provides a perfect opportunity for the ecological fallacy to occur. The t test used for the analysis compares mean loudness levels. Results of this statistical analysis describe the classes' means in relation to one another, but say nothing about particular individuals within those classes. Some students in a class have individual loudness levels lower than the class' mean loudness level, and others have loudness levels higher than the class' mean loudness level.

The t-test results might support the null hypothesis of equality in loudness level of classes with and without pets. However, these results indicate nothing about individual students. The equal means do not imply that a particular student in a class with a pet is exactly as loud as a particular student in a class without a pet. The t-test results do not suggest anything about where, within the range of loudness scores, any particular person falls. They suggest only that the high and low loudness scores for the two types of classes "balance out" in the same way.

You must use the same logic if t-test results indicate a significant difference between loudness levels of classes with and without pets. This result provides no information about individual students' loudness levels. A chosen student from the louder of the two classes may have a loudness level that lies well below that student's class' mean loudness score. Similarly, a chosen student from the quieter of the two classes may have a loudness level that lies well above the class' mean loudness score. In this case, the student from the quieter class may, as an individual, be quieter than the individual student from the quieter class is.

Another version of the ecological fallacy can occur when units of analysis are not people. Data points for comparisons of social institutions do not necessarily refer to individuals within that institution, but may refer to characteristics of the institutions, themselves. The information gathered in these situations provides only a very general picture of the people within it. Therefore, you cannot make any definite comments about the similarities or differences between these people.

Example 10.13: The Ecological Fallacy with Nonhuman Units of Analysis This sort of ecological fallacy occurs most often in correlational analyses. So, it would likely not cause concern for researchers performing the study related to class pets and class loudness levels, presented throughout this chapter. (As explained in Example 10.12, analysis for that study would focus on t tests, not correlations.)

However, a study investigating whether a correlation exists between alcohol consumption in college and college dropout rates might promote this sort of ecological fallacy. For this analysis, colleges serve as the units of analysis. Each independent-variable data point, related to rate of alcohol consumption, and each dependent-variable data point, related to dropout rate, describes a particular college.

If a positive correlation exists between these two variables, the researcher can make only the very general claim that the possibility of dropping out of college increases with the amount of alcohol consumed by students of the college. The researcher cannot conclude that the drinkers and the dropouts are the same people. Perhaps the roommates of heavy drinkers, not the heavy drinkers themselves, become fed up with the circumstances that they must endure and choose to leave the college. In this case, characterizing a college dropout as a drinker would misrepresent that person.

10.4.4   Reductionism

Individuals also try to make sense of their world by drawing on their own backgrounds and knowledge. This strategy may prove useful if you need to anticipate upcoming events or behaviors or, sometimes, to give advice. However, using your experiences as the sole bases for interpreting results of social research often leads you to overlook other important aspects of the relationship between variables. Researchers refer to this situation as *reductionism* because it involves reducing a somewhat complex explanation to an oversimplified version that gives full credit to only one line of reasoning . To avoid reductionism, you cannot allow you own backgrounds or the motives of those sponsoring the research to determine the way that you construe the results.

To provide a whole understanding of the reason for a particular relationship, you need to identify and explain each and every part that constitutes that whole. Focusing on only one aspect does not provide a complete picture. Your audience members may consider this aspect solely responsible for a social relationship, remaining unaware of other social conditions or behaviors that also deserve their attention.

Example 10.14: Reductionism   To avoid such a problem with the class pet study, researchers would need to explore a variety of perspectives about pets in the classroom. Academic professionals such as teachers of principals, who deal with the practicalities of classroom management on a daily basis, might focus on a way that the class pet can serve as a reward to encourage proper behavior in the classroom. Psychologists might show interest in the calming effects that animals can have on humans. Parents of the children in the class may perceive the pet as a "homelike" element of school that encourages behavior that the children would have in their homes. The students, themselves, may have an entirely different view, perhaps enjoying the caretaking responsibilities associated with having a pet and demonstrating what they believe to be appropriate "caretaking" behavior.

Each of these groups, as well as many others not mentioned here, has a unique perspective on the possible relationship between the presence of a pet in the classroom and the loudness of the students in the class. Because researchers cannot offer a causal explanation for the presence or the lack of a relationship between variables, they cannot proclaim any one of these interpretations more or less sound than another. The researchers must also recognize the possibility that no single explanation accounts for different loudness levels in classes with and without pets, assuming that such a difference exists. Possibly, the rationales offered by each of constituencies have little value by themselves. However, when considered together, they may offer a sound explanation of the relationship between having a class pet and the class' loudness. So, the interplay between the elements of discipline, psychology, parenting, and childhood perceptions may create a whole that is greater than the sum of its parts.

10.5 CONCLUSION

Although not explicitly stated, this chapter contains two main themes. One theme deals with critical interpretation. The transition from results to conclusions relies on your willingness and ability to consider the social ramifications of your findings so that you can provide your audience with an accurate understanding of what your results suggest about the world. You must, therefore, clearly describe the causal paths between variables rather than allow your audience to assume that changes in the independent variable cause changes in the dependent variable. Also, by choosing your value responsibly, you avoid overly eager reactions to your results by subjects who do know about type I errors. The second theme, objectivity, actually sets the foundation for the entire research process in that social research (or any research, for that matter) should strive to provide an unbiased description of the relationships between variables. A lack of objectivity can lead to the ecological fallacy or reductionism.

Critical interpretation and objectivity helps to ensure that valid results do not become invalid conclusions. If you remember, critical interpretation and objectivity played roles in the early stages of your research as well. Your research hypothesis, for example, emerged from your critical evaluation of previous studies, leading to your identification of a void that your study could fill. In your attempts to provide an objective analysis of your research topic, you chose the indicators for your variable, your sample, and your method of data collection to maximize value neutrality. You should have the same awareness of these issues when you interpret the results of your analyses.

The challenge of providing your audience with a complete and correct understanding of the relationship between your variables is, in many ways, greater than the challenges associated with statistical analyses. The statistical analyses described in Chapters 5–8 can intimidate new researchers or those uncomfortable with mathematical processes. However, these analyses have very specific uses and structures. If necessary, you could follow a list of instructions for how to choose and perform a statistical analysis without knowing how or why the analysis provides the information you need. You cannot follow such a script when determining how to apply your results to the "real world." For this task, you must rely on your insight into the research context as well as your ability to recognize and avoid the pitfalls that could lead you to misrepresent your results. Once you have passed this hurdle, having correctly identified the social implications of your study's results, you can focus your attention on the way in which to present your conclusions to your audience. In your conclusions, you can return to the aesthetic principles that you used to effectively entice your audience in the introduction and literature review portions of your research report. Chapter 11 suggests strategies for leaving your audience with an accurate and complete answer to your research question.

REVIEW QUESTIONS

Base your answers to Questions 10.1–10.3 on the research hypothesis that no difference exists in the numbers of males with mustaches, with beards, with both mustaches and beards, and with neither mustaches nor beards.

10.1. State the null hypothesis.

10.2. What does failure to reject the null hypothesis indicate about the research hypothesis? Why?

10.3. What does a rejected null hypothesis indicate about the research hypothesis? Why?

Answer Questions 10.4–10.6 on the basis of the research hypothesis that more males have only beards than have only mustaches, have both mustaches and beards, or have neither mustaches nor beards.

10.4. State the null hypothesis.

10.5. What does failure to reject the null hypothesis indicate about the research hypothesis? Why?

10.6. What does a rejected null hypothesis indicate about the research hypothesis? Why?

Consider the following scenario for Questions 10.7–10.9. A researcher hypothesizes that people spend more time reading the local sections than the national or sports sections of their newspapers. To test this hypothesis, the researcher observes 150 subjects as they read their newspapers and records the number of minutes spent reading each section. Subjects take a mean of 14.75 minutes to read the local section, a mean of 12.81 minutes to read the national section, and a mean of 14.97 minutes to read the sports section.

10.7. If a repeated-measures ANOVA produces an F_{calc} that is smaller than F_{crit}, can you conclude that the research hypothesis is correct? Why or why not?

10.8. If a repeated-measures ANOVA produces an F_{calc} that exceeds F_{crit}, can you conclude that the research hypothesis is correct? Why or why not?

10.9. Suppose it took subjects a mean of 13.97, rather than 14.97 minutes, to read the sports section. Can you accept the research hypothesis given the F values described in Question 10.8? Why or why not?

For Questions 10.10–10.14, determine whether an ecological fallacy, reductionism, both, or neither has occurred and why.

10.10. A content analysis of movies indicates that action movies contain more cursewords than comedy movies do. A newspaper article summarizing the study tells readers, therefore, that the newly released comedy movie contains fewer cursewords than the newly released action movie does.

10.11. Results of a study indicate a negative correlation between the number of gang members and the number of arrests in cities across the nation. The research report explains that racial profiling can explain the high arrest rate of gang members because most gangs consist of racial minorities.

10.12. According to a survey, the general public does not consider males who wear a single earring as odd today as they did years ago. Researchers present these data as an example of changing public attitudes toward male appearance.

10.13. A study of supermarket purchases indicates that individuals purchase fewer fresh fruits and vegetables than they did 10 years ago. The researcher concludes that inflation has led shoppers to buy frozen or canned fruits and vegetables, which are cheaper than the fresh items.

10.14. A review of records provided by 100 ski resorts nationwide shows a positive correlation between the number of children's ski tickets purchased and the number of injuries on the slopes per year. Researchers, therefore, suggest that the ski slopes implement mandatory safety-training programs for children.

11

WRITING RESEARCH REPORTS

11.1 INTRODUCTION

Do not think that your audience has the emotional attachment to your study that you have. You, not they, have devoted the time and energy to determining appropriate hypotheses, gathering data, analyzing data, and drawing conclusions. The research report that audience members read or hear provides the only contact that they have with your study and, therefore, drive their impression of it. Thus, you must effectively communicate your rationales for performing your study, choosing the analyses you used, and drawing your conclusions.

From your original conceptualization of the study and until you drew your conclusions, you followed a very regimented path. Conventions for data gathering and analysis dictated the way in which you proceeded. Writing your research report, however, introduces an element of aesthetics that had no part in these steps of the research process.

The aesthetic element shows itself mostly in your writing style. In any context, not just research, the way in which someone depicts a situation determines an audience's perception of it. Those in the fine arts have based their careers on this fact! As a researcher, you do not have quite as much aesthetic freedom as artists, who are held to few boundaries, might have. But, to some extent, you can control your audiences' views

Analyzing Quantitative Data: An Introduction for Social Researchers, First Edition. Debra Wetcher-Hendricks.
© 2011 John Wiley & Sons, Inc. Published 2011 by John Wiley & Sons, Inc.

about your topic and the information that your study has uncovered by the way in which you describe your study and its results. Section 11.2 presents information about choosing a tone, including language and demeanor, for your research report that suits your audience members and effectively communicates the information that you want your audience to glean from your study.

Each of the remaining sections of the chapter provide suggestions for packaging the vast amount of explanation that you could provide into manageable and understandable segments for your audience. Researchers usually separate their reports into sections that correspond to the steps in the research process. Thus, most research reports contain at least four sections. Reports generally begin with a "Presentation of Hypothesis," which essentially consists of a literature review that provides background information to justify the study. The "Methods" section describes the research process, including aspects such as sampling, measurement, and analysis of data. The "results" section presents information about the outcomes of these analyses. Interpretations of and suggestions based on the results appear in the "Conclusions". (Please see Chapter 10 for information about drawing legitimate conclusions.) These sections, collectively, provide your audience with the full story of your study.

11.2   TONE

You already know what you need to say in your research report, but you have probably not given much attention to how you should say it. Your report's tone, described by literature experts as the attitude with which you convey your message, greatly affects the way in which your audience perceives your work.

You may best understand the importance of a message's tone by considering its effects outside of the realm outside of writing.

Example 11.1: Effects of Tone   People associate medical malpractice suits with misdiagnoses or mistreatments of patients' conditions. In his book *Blink*, however, Malcolm Gladwell points out that these suits often stem from patients' dissatisfaction with the way physicians addresses them (Gladwell 2005). Regardless of the medical situation, patients file malpractice charges against physicians whose tones lack sensitivity more often than they file charges against physicians who use tones that convey respect, empathy, and concern. The way the physician delivers her or his message, not the message itself, has the most impact on patients' perceptions of their physicians' competence.

Example 11.1 indicates that, when interacting with their audiences (patients), physicians must concern themselves with not only the most effective way to communicate with patients but also the most appropriate way. As a researcher, you must do so as well.

Finding the most effective and appropriate way to describe your study to an audience begins with your consideration of the audience, itself. The most important issue for you to recognize is your audience members' purposes for reading or listening to your research report. The reasons for your audience's interest in your study should help you determine the angle from which you should present your study and its findings. Once you have decided the best approach to take, you can focus on your presentation style, ranging from the words you choose to use to the illustrations that you include in your report.

Some audiences, such as administrators who have hired you to research a topic or situation, may wish to use the results of your study as a basis for decisionmaking. Another type of audience can consist of those with expertise in the field of your research. They probably hope to use the results of your study to validate their beliefs or to provide new opportunities to expand their knowledge in the field. Even those with little knowledge about your research topic may find your report beneficial in helping them to broaden their understanding of their own areas of interest or, in some cases, in providing them with a basic understanding of a new topic.

These audiences are far from the only ones who might choose to read or listen to your research report. Thus, part of your prewriting exercises should include an inquiry into how the audience perceives you and what they wish to gain from reading or listening to your research report. With this knowledge, you can match your writing to the audience's perception of you as a teacher, a factfinder, an advocate, a storyteller, or in some other role.

11.2.1 Language

The role that the audience expects you to take should determine the language, including aspects such as word choice, sentence composition, and punctuation, used to convey your ideas. Literary analysts have explained how these elements help to create a "voice" for the presentation. Conversational speech, which may use slang and other casual phrases, creates to an informal or, even, lighthearted voice. For a research report, however, an informal voice may trivialize your work and findings. To impress the value of your study on your audience, you should use a somewhat formal voice. Suggestions for maintaining a formal voice emphasize writing principles that you learned during your early years of schooling:

- Use active voice as much as possible. Passive voice, marked by forms of "to be," such as "is," "was," and "have been" (although not every use of these words constitutes passive voice) followed by a past-participle verb, places the object at the end of the sentence. Using passive voice does not necessarily violate any rules of grammar. However, it sometimes creates more complicated-than-necessary sentence structures, which can lead to misinterpretations by your audience members, who expect to read or hear the subject, of the sentence first. Active verbs follow the subject, and, therefore, you should choose them when you can.
- Avoid using second person. Addressing audience members directly, using "you" or "your," implies an expectation about the subjects' knowledge base or abilities. This sort of familiar speech can appeal to audiences of personal or instructional texts (like this book), but have no place in formal writing.

- Use first person sparingly and judiciously. References to yourself can create a subjective tone. To maintain the objectivity that researchers should have, you should refer to yourself only when describing what you have done as part of the research process and, even then, only when necessary. "I" or "we" should never be used for justifications.
- Be gender-neutral when possible. Today's gender equality has made gender-specific speech unacceptable in formal presentations. Pronouns should also be gender-neutral, either by using plural terms such as "they" or by using and alternating male and female counterparts, such as "he or she" and "she" and "he" in different hypothetical examples.
- Do not use slang. This relaxed speech creates a casual tone for your presentation and, thus, your audience may take a lackadaisical approach to considering your study's arguments and benefits. Also, because slang terms and their meanings vary by subculture, your points may not be clear to all audiences.
- Do not use colloquial expressions. Although similar to slang, colloquial expressions have widely recognized meanings. Like slang terms, though, colloquial expressions have a conversational quality that compromises the formal tone of the presentation.
- Do not use trite expressions. Once, these sayings may have made dramatic and emphatic points. But, through overuse, they have lost their meanings and do not have the intended effect on audiences. You can usually find a way to express your ideas more directly than a trite expression can.
- Do not use contractions. Combining words, as contractions do, basically amounts to a shortcut. Audiences may consider one who uses contractions in a formal presentation, especially a written one, lazy.

Example 11.2: Formal Voice   Examples of inappropriate and appropriate words and phrases can help to clarify these principles (see Table 11.1).

Writing with a formal mindset can also have some disadvantages. Overzealous use of formal language can make your report too lofty to appeal to your audience. So, while following the guidelines for maintaining a formal voice, you should be careful that you don't threaten the readability (which, from this point forward, also implies listenability for spoken presentations) of your report. Reports with the highest readability use simple language. Uncommon and unnecessarily complex speech can make readers stop reading or listening so that they can decipher what you are trying to say.

Stated plainly, the language that you use should not detract from the importance of the information contained in your report. The following guidelines can help you provide an easily understandable presentation. You may find that you need to adjust these guidelines for particular audiences. However, you should have a compelling reason (e.g., orders from a superior) to entirely disregard any of them.

- Avoid jargon. Terms and phrases that are considered jargon have relevance within a particular field, but have little meaning outside of that context. Those

TABLE 11.1. Principles for Using Formal Voice[a]

Principle	Instead of saying . . .	Say . . .
Use active voice as much as possible.	"Data were provided by randomly selected individuals across the country."	"Randomly-selected individuals from across the country provided data."
Do not use second person.	"When visiting, you should present your host or hostess with a gift."	"A visitor should present the host or hostess with a gift."
Use first person sparingly and judiciously.	"We asked each host or hostess to send us a list of the gifts that they received and to rate their satisfaction with each one."	Hosts and hostesses received instructions to submit a list of gifts they received along with their satisfaction ratings for each one"
		or (if some first person is acceptable)
		"We requested that each host or hostess submit a list of gifts they received along with their satisfaction ratings for each one."
Be gender-neutral when possible.	"Each host submitted his list and ratings at the end of the month."	"Hosts and hostesses submitted their lists and ratings at the end of the month"
		or
		"Each host submitted his or her list and ratings at the end of the month."
Do not use slang.	"A really cool pattern emerged among the satisfaction levels associated with different types of gifts."	"An interesting pattern emerged among the satisfaction levels associated with different types of gifts."
Do not use colloquial expressions.	"Giving a gifts says thanks to the host or hostess."	"Giving a gift shows appreciation to the host or hostess."
Do not use trite expressions.	"Visitors should stick to the basics when choosing gifts for their hosts."	"Visitors should choose traditional gifts for their hosts."
Do not use contractions.	"The rejected null hypothesis indicates that hosts and hostesses aren't equally satisfied with all gifts."	"The rejected null hypothesis indicates that hosts and hostesses are not equally satisfied with all gifts"
		or
		"The rejected null hypothesis indicates that hosts and hostesses like some gifts more than others."

[a]To maintain a formal voice, words and phrases that appear in the column on the right should replace those that appear in the center column of the table.

TABLE 11.2. Principles for Enhancing Readability[a]

Guidelines	Instead of saying . . .	Say . . .
Avoid jargon.	"Networking"	"Forming business relationships"
Use simple terms.	"Residential Dwelling"	"Home"
Be concise.	"At some time in the future"	"Later"
Use the audience's native language.	"Crème de la crème"	"Best"

[a]For maximum readability, words and phrases that appear in the column on the right should replace those that appear in the center column of the table.

unfamiliar with the details of your study's topic may not understand discipline-related jargon.

- Use simple terms. Avoid artificial expressions. Complicated ways to say simple things can make your explanations ambiguous or, even, incomprehensible to your audience.
- Be concise. Avoid longer-than-necessary phrases. Using unnecessary words to describe a simple thing or idea detracts from the ideas you wish to emphasize.
- Use the audiences' native language. If you use foreign words and phrases, you take the chance that your audience members will not necessarily recognize these terms. Also, because every language has its own structure, phrases from one language may not fit neatly into another language, making your sentences awkward. With the English language having evolved from combinations of other languages, you should use your judgment about what terms and phrases would be unfamiliar to your audience.

Example 11.3: Readability   Table 11.2 provides examples of phrases that reduce readability and their reader-friendly counterparts.

Like all rules, those listed in Tables 11.1 and 11.2 have exceptions. Direct quotes, for instance, are not subject to these principles. You should never change an individual's words to suit presentation style. Other valid reasons for disregarding suggestions provided in the tables also exist. You should, though, strongly consider your justification any time you choose to violate a standard of formality or readability.

11.2.2   Presentation of Facts

For nonfiction works, such as a research report, writing style accounts for only part of the tone. Your presentation of facts associated with the study, ranging from the background information used to justify your research to outcomes of your statistical tests, also affects the tone of your report. You must carefully choose not only the way in which you present these facts but also the facts that you choose to report. Audiences with little familiarity about your study's topic may need you to start from the beginning, providing as much background information about the topic as possible. Those who view you as a resource for providing them evidence to support their existing opinions, however, may be insulted by your inclusion of such facts. Similarly, the detail with which you explain the data-gathering and testing procedures used for your study should vary according to the familiarity that your audience members have with these techniques. Providing meticulous explanations of these processes might appeal to those who view you as a teacher, but might annoy an audience that regard you as a fact-finder or advocate.

You should remember, though, that all of your audience members have turned to you because they trust your skills of research and your manner of communicating the facts that they want to know. Chapters 1–9 focus on the first of these issues. But your audience can easily lose sight of even the most interesting and applicable facts uncovered by your study if you fail to present them effectively. To do so, you should exude a degree of confidence in both your findings and your audience's ability to critically evaluate them.

These instructions may seem contradictory. In one sense, you don't want to seem timid when presenting your facts. But you must also avoid making assumptions about your audiences' capabilities to draw their own inferences. The key to satisfying both of these requirements lies in the terms that you use to introduce your facts or, more correctly, the terms that you *do not* use when introducing your facts. Terms and phrases in the left column of Table 11.3, called *hedgers*, indicate uncertainty. The presumptive terms and phrases on the right subtly impart your opinion about what your audience should find evident. You can find the right balance between tentativeness and audacity by avoiding both hedgers and presumptives. Table 11.3 presents a partial list of these terms.

You do not necessarily need to avoid these terms every single time you'd like to use them. The degree to which they affect the tone of your presentation depends on the context in which you use them. These terms do affect tone as much when used to

TABLE 11.3. Hedgers and Presumptives[a]

Hedgers	Presumptives
It seems as though/it seems that	Absolutely
Possibly	Certainly
Pretty/pretty much	Definitely
Probably	Obviously
Relatively	Of course
Seemingly	Surely
Some	Without question
Somewhat	Undoubtedly
Sort of	
To some extent	

[a]Terms and phrases listed in the "Hedgers" column tend to make the presenter seem unconfident or her or his statements. A tone of overconfidence, however, can be created with the terms listed in the "presumptives" column.

describe your research processes or statistical analyses as when used to convey background information or findings of your study.

Example 11.4: Placement of Presumptives   A statement such as "Obviously, people enjoy some gifts more than they enjoy others" may suggest to the audience that they should have known this fact. Audience members may consider this sort of statement condescending.

Using the term "obviously" to describe the rationale for statistical tests, however, does not give the same impression. Explaining the need for a *t* test by stating "The mean satisfaction level associated with the different types of gifts obviously differ, but a one-way ANOVA can determine whether they differ significantly" can actually have the opposite effect. It assures audience members that they have correctly observed a difference between values presented earlier in the report.

Example 11.4 demonstrates the way in which the use of a presumptive can change the tone of a sentence. But the same holds true for hedgers. You should, therefore, use hedgers and presumptives cautiously and sparingly.

11.3   SECTIONS OF THE RESEARCH REPORT

The tone of your report can reflect more than just language. The research report's organization and the depth of details that it provides also help establish the tone. With the exception of giving the audience members a preview of your results, stating your major findings to entice them to read or listen, a chronological explanation of your research activities usually works best.

Some audiences, specifically those familiar with the scientific method, may be satisfied with basic statements of your hypothesis, methods, results, and conclusions. For other audiences, you may need to provide detailed accounts of these four components. Regardless of the depth in which you must describe your research activities, however, these four sections should form the basis of your report.

11.3.1   Presentation of Hypothesis

Before learning about your data collection and analysis, your audience needs to know how your study fills a void or expands on past research on the topic. Research reports, therefore, begin with a literature review, which guides audience members to your research hypothesis.

The depth of your literature review should reflect your audience's degree of preexisting knowledge about your research topic. A literature review's most important job is to explain how your research can provide knowledge that helps to expand understanding of your research topic. You must, therefore, provide a logical flow of information, citing studies performed by others and describing the relationships between them, so that, on reaching your research hypothesis, the audience has an "Oh, that makes perfect sense" reaction.

Your literature review should try to take your audience down the same path that you followed in devising your hypothesis. Common rationales for hypotheses include filling a gap in knowledge, building on past research, connecting findings of previous studies, and contradicting past findings. The following sections provide suggestions for arranging information, including examples, to guide your audience in each of these contexts.

Filling a Gap in Knowledge. Because every study has a unique focus, it often takes results from multiple studies to piece together a full understanding of a social phenomenon. Different studies address different aspects of a general topic and, when considered together, provide a well-rounded analysis of that topic. However, if you believe that these studies have not acknowledged an element that you consider important, you can use this element as a basis for your own investigation.

Example 11.5: Identification of a Gap in Knowledge Researchers interested in appropriate gifts to give a host or hostess, for instance, wish to pursue the research topic implied in Example 11.4, which addresses the satisfaction levels associated with different types of gifts. Those investigating the best type of gift to give a host or hostess may realize that past analyses on the topic has focused primarily on wine and candy, but failed to include flowers. A subsequent investigation, thus, could add flowers to the list of gifts assessed. This investigation provides an important contribution to the overall knowledge needed to determine what type of gift a host or hostess would appreciate most.

The researchers may refer to findings of previous studies or documented information regarding issues such as people's expectations for gifts and gift(s) deemed appropriate for various occasions. On the basis of this information, the researcher should predict the relationship between each type of gift and the host's or hostess' satisfaction level with it in comparison to the other gifts. The research hypothesis, then, formally states a predicted order of satisfaction levels, perhaps, $H: \bar{X}_C > \bar{X}_W > \bar{X}_F$, to suggest that hosts and hostesses prefer receiving candy to receiving wine and prefer receiving wine to receiving flowers.

To understand your rationale for a study like the one described in Example 11.5, your audience needs to know why the original lack of knowledge prevents a full understanding of the research topic. The majority of your literature review should present and describe previously performed studies and their findings as well as other documented information relevant to the general topic. It is important for you to point out connections between these facts, using references to each other and appropriate transitions. These explanations should make your audience aware of the extent of overall understanding about the general issue. Most importantly, though, they make your audience aware of the information still needed to provide a full understanding. Then, your audience members can appreciate how the investigation proposed by your research hypothesis, presented at the end of the literature review, attempts to fill one of these gaps.

Building on Past Research. Even if you have found no gaps in knowledge, you can expand on findings about topics of interest. For as many questions as social research answers, more questions develop. You can, therefore, use findings of others' research as starting points for new studies.

As explained in Chapter 10, a portion of your conclusions should focus on speculation about how others might build on your findings. There is no reason why you can't simply take the role of the "other," with your study building on others' findings. Hypotheses for this sort of investigation focus on the possibilities of relationships brought to the audiences' (or your) attention by the findings of past studies. Follow-up studies often provide interested audiences with further insight into the research topic by focusing on a particular condition in more detail than past studies did or by addressing a new question that these studies raised.

Example 11.6: Identifying a Foundation for Building on Past Research   The same background information that prompted the study described in Example 11.5 could also prompt a study that focuses on details of use of the gifts presented to hosts and hostesses. Suppose that results of others' studies indicate equal levels of satisfaction with wine and candy gifts. This finding might raise the question of whether satisfaction level relates to the intended use of the gift, specifically whether the visitor brings the gift to be consumed during his or her visit or for the host to save until later.

A hypothesis based on this research question could suggest that hostesses and hosts have higher satisfaction levels with gifts intended for immediately used than with gifts intended for use at some other time. The literature review that prompts this sort of hypothesis might include information about concepts such as the types of occasions that demand immediately usable gifts according to etiquette experts or the concept of immediate gratification, which describes the tendency for individuals to choose short-term over long-term pleasure.

With the intention of building on past research, as described in Example 11.6, you must provide your audience members with a complete summary of known information on your topic. Without being told what information has already been discovered, they cannot appreciate the way in which your study furthers understanding.

As with all literature reviews, one that suggests further investigation into other studies' findings should consist mostly of your explanations about past research. The way in which you present this information, however, differs from the critical argument that you would give in a "knowledge gap" literature review. A "building" literature review should describe how one study has built on findings of another to progressively increase knowledge about the research topic. With these descriptions and your commentary on them, you can establish a gradual unfolding of information, allowing your audience to accept your study and its research hypothesis as the next step in this process.

Contradicting Past Findings. A more critical approach to a literature review than filling a gap in knowledge and building on past research requires you to identify weaknesses of others' studies. These weaknesses may pertain to design flaws that the original researcher overlooked or could not control, which would lead you to perform a study that does not have these problems. They may also reflect the fact that, over time or as a result of specific events in society, results of old, well-done studies have become obsolete, making a replication, or repeat, of the study in present social conditions necessary. Either way, the expectation that your study will provide different results than past research has serves as the justification for your research.

Example 11.7: Identifying a Foundation for Contradicting Past Findings Suppose, for instance, that somebody has already performed a study based on the originally described research scenario of comparing the satisfaction levels of hosts and hostesses who receive gifts of wine and candy. Another researcher who questions the original researcher's methods may decide to adjust the study to correct for the flaw. Maybe the new researcher believes that the original researcher used a biased sample and wishes to conduct the study using a broader selection of subject. Perhaps the original researcher gathered data using a survey and the new researcher believes that observation would provide the most valid data. Perhaps the new researcher does not think that the original researcher measured the dependent variable of satisfaction level appropriately. Any of these reasons, as well as many others, could compel the new researcher to perform her or his own study on the topic.

In a literature review suggesting the need to correct or improve on a past study (or studies), you must explain why you believe that findings of the past study or studies do not adequately portray the research topic. To show courtesy to fellow researchers, you should take a respectful approach to presenting these contentions.

Even though your reason for citing a particular study in your literature review is to call attention to its shortcomings, you should begin by focusing on the value of the study. In addition to highlighting some of the evidence regarding the topic's importance, you can discuss the potential uses for information uncovered by the original investigation. The key to justifying your own study lies in revealing to the audience members that past research did not meet its goal of providing this useful information because of invalid or unreliable results. If other researchers made errors in designing their studies or in collecting data, you should identify and explain these errors. You can explain how you plan to modify past studies so that your results provide usable information. If the results of past research have simply become outdated, you should explain why.

The main portion of your literature review should consist of presentation, criticism, and descriptions of your proposed modification to a past study or studies. Unlike many other types of literature reviews, one that introduces a study performed to contradict past findings does not need to lead the audience, step by step, to a new and unique hypothesis. In fact, your research hypothesis for this type of study may actually mimic, word for word, the research hypothesis for the study that you criticize. This type of literature review should end with a promise to correctly investigate the hypothesis so that your audience has more valid and reliable information on the topic than other studies provided.

Connecting Past Findings. Arguably the most common type of literature review points out connections between findings of previously conducted studies. Many scholars refer to social science as *interdisciplinary*, meaning that it encompasses many interrelated topics. Findings of a study based in one discipline, when considered along with findings of a study based in another discipline, can often help social scientists identify new issues worthy of investigation. If you identify such an issue, you can develop a study to investigate a relationship between variables never before considered together.

Example 11.8: Identifying Findings to Connect   A researcher might, for example, try to link findings of the study described in Example 11.6, to findings of economic research on the topic of reciprocity. Suppose that results of economic and psychological studies demonstrate an association between the extent to which one's expectations of the relationship with another person are met and the amount of effort one devotes to the relationship. This information, considered along with findings that support the hypothesis regarding and hostesses' levels of satisfaction with gifts, presented in Example 11.6, can create the foundation for a new study.

One section of the literature review should explain how levels of satisfaction can vary with the type of gift received, based on the findings of the Example 11.6 study. Another section of the literature review should present information about the association between satisfied expectations of a relationship and high amounts of effort devoted to that relationship. The researcher's only remaining task in the literature review involves providing speculation about the way in which these findings suggest a new hypothesis.

The researcher can lead the audience to this hypothesis by using "if–then" reasoning. If higher levels of satisfaction accompany immediately usable gifts than gifts intended for later use, and if the amount of effort devoted to a relationship increases as the satisfaction with that relationship increases, then hosts and hostesses devote more effort to a relationship with a visitor if that visitor has given an immediately usable gift than if the visitor had given a gift intended for later use.

The "then" portion of the last sentence in Example 11.8 serves as the new study's hypothesis. In most cases, you can follow this transitive model to design a literature review for a study that attempts to connect past findings. *Transitive arguments*, which state that, if $a = b$ and $b = c$, then $a = c$, provide a clear structure for your contention because they identify overlapping pieces of knowledge.

You can arrange your transitive argument in three sections, as the description in Example 11.8 does. The first section provides background information and details that past research has provided about your study's independent variable. The second section provides background information and details that past research has provided about your study's dependent variable. In the third section, you explain the connection between the findings of studies related to the independent variable and the dependent variable. This structure makes your audience fully aware of how you have pulled together pieces of others' studies to formulate your own hypothesis.

11.3.2 Description of Methods

From your report's literature review, your audience members should know what results you expect to obtain. In the "Methods" section of your research report, you describe the steps that you took to obtain and evaluate data to test your hypothesis. The way in which you organize these descriptions depends on the tone of your report. Generally, though, you should separate your "Methods" section into subsections, each addressing a particular aspect of the methods that you used. Each section should have a heading that describes its contents.

You can use the subheadings that you believe allow you to most clearly and concisely describe your method. One common way to divide the "Methods" section of a research report into subsections uses headings similar to the following:

- *Subjects*—this subsections contains detailed information about the sampling method that you have used, as well as a rationale for your choice.
- *Measures*—this subsection identifies your approach to data gathering, specifically mentioning the instruments that you used and, when possible, providing copies of them as well as rationales for your choices.
- *Procedure*—this subsection contains descriptions of the steps you took to obtain data using the previously-described design.

Some researchers may divide the "Methods" sections of their report differently or into subsections smaller than these three. Regardless of how you choose to title and organize the information in your "Methods" section, however, it must always contain information about your sampling techniques, your approach to gathering data, and the steps taken to obtain data from your subjects. The following sections of this chapter, therefore, describe the content of these three subsections. You can rearrange or redistribute the information for each as you see fit for your own report.

Subjects. Section 4.3.1, entitled, "The Importance of Good Sampling," points out that a good study has external validity, meaning that you can generalize data. *Generalizablity* allows you to correctly characterize your study's population on the basis of information that you have gathered from the sample. The most important factor in obtaining generalizable results is using a *representative* sample, one that has the same proportional makeup as the population does. In your research report, you must prove to your audience that you have obtained a representative sample by (1) identifying the study's population and (2) describing the sampling method.

POPULATION. For audiences unfamiliar with the concept of subject selection, you may want to begin this portion of your "Methods" section by explaining the difference between a population and a sample. You can describe the sample as a miniature population, with a makeup that should mirror the makeup of the population. This explanation makes it clear that data from your sample should be similar to the data that you would have gathered from the population.

All research reports should identify the study's population as well as the particular issues of time, money, and access that prevented you from obtaining data from the population. Informing your audience members of these limitations helps you convince them of your need to select a sample of subjects.

Example 11.9: Population For the study concerning host and hostess gifts, the population consists of every single person in the world who every received a gift from a guest. After identifying this population to her or his audience, the researcher must explain the impossibility of obtaining population data. A researcher might cite obstacles such as the need to travel throughout the world and find ways to communicate with individuals who speak languages other than her or his own as reasons for gathering data from a sample rather than from the population.

SAMPLING METHODS. The fact that you must use data from a sample rather than from a population raises the question of exactly how you selected your sample. Your audience members want to know that you have chosen a representative sample. Thus, you must provide them with a detailed explanation of the sampling methods that you used.

If you used a sampling frame other than the entire population, your explanations must begin with a description of the sampling frame. A *sampling frame* consists of individuals who can potentially be selected as subjects for the study. If your sampling frame does not differ from the population, meaning that any individual in the population could serve as a subject, you do not need to discuss this issue. However, if you needed to limit the possible subjects to a particular region (e.g., United States residents) or accessibility method (e.g., those with phone numbers listed in the public phone directory), your sampling frame deserves attention. You should identify the subset of the population that constitutes your sampling frame and assure your audience members that the sampling frame won't lead to an unrepresentative sample.

Example 11.10: Sampling Frame Selecting subjects from the population identified in Example 11.10 may prove too time-consuming and costly for a researcher. Researchers who do not have the money or the time to gather information from subjects in distant countries or remote areas should describe these limitations to their audiences.

Researchers who wish to speak to each subject in person may define their sampling frames according to geographic location. They may find it possible to travel only a certain distance from their homes or offices. Thus, the sampling frame would consist of all individuals living within a designated radius. In another context, a researcher who wishes to distribute surveys over the Internet may not have the problem of geographic location, and may consider anyone, worldwide, who has an email account as a part of the sampling frame.

Although both of these potential sampling frames greatly simplify the process of gathering data, they may produce biased samples. With this sampling frame, the researcher automatically eliminates the chance of obtaining subjects who have ideas and values that differ from those in the immediate area. Using electronic mail to contact subjects worldwide solves this problem, but creates a different problem. The subjects obtained through email may not represent the overall population because, especially in underdeveloped countries, more upper-income than lower-income individuals have email accounts. If the sampling frame underrepresents the lower-income class, then the sample chosen from it underrepresents the lower-income class as well.

The research report should mention such shortcomings, but not dwell on them. Geographic, technologic or other limitations almost always prevent researchers from defining sampling frame that perfectly represents the entire population. The audience should know that, even with these limitations, the sampling frame still consists of subjects who can provide a general understanding of people's satisfaction levels with different types of gifts.

Most of your explanation about sampling methods should focus on the way in which you selected particular individuals from the population or sampling frame to serve as subjects. In addition to the name of the particular type of sampling method you used, you should provide details about how you used this sampling method. The report should always contain the number of subjects who provided data and relevant demographic distributions of subjects. Other details vary according to the type of sampling method used. Table 11.4 contains suggestions about relevant information for common sampling methods.

You should try to convince your audience that the method you chose produced the most representative sample possible. If you have not knowingly limited your sample so that it provides ungeneralizable data, you can simply say so. However, it is not uncommon for practicality or ethical considerations (voluntary participation, the harm standard, etc.) to have limited the representativeness of a sample. For these situations, you should (1) identify these limitations, (2) explain why you could not avoid them, and (3) describe how they affect the representativeness of your sample.

Example 11.11: Sampling Method Suppose that the researcher conducting the study regarding satisfaction with gifts decides to conduct interviews by telephone. Wanting to avoid long-distance telephone charges, the researcher may use a sampling frame of all individuals who have phone numbers listed in the local phone directory. After explaining these choices, the researcher should describe the procedure used to select particular names of individuals to call.

Many methods of selecting particular subjects from the phone directory exist. The researcher might describe how she or he used a simple random method based on computer-generated lists of random values to identify phone directory pages and listings on those pages. One who used systematic sampling rather than simple random sampling would need to inform the audience of the value of n. With an n of 50, for example, the audience would know that the sample consisted of every 50th person listed in the book. Explanations of other sampling methods that the researcher may have used should follow the suggestions provided in Table 11.4.

Measures. The "Measures" portion of your "Methods" section describes the tools that you used to obtain data from your subjects. You can begin by telling your audience whether you used an observation, a survey, an experiment, existing sources

TABLE 11.4. Sampling Method Details[a]

Sampling Method	Details to Include in Report
Convenience	Where, when, and how subjects were obtained
Snowball	Where, when, and how initial subjects were obtained
	Relationships between initial subjects and those who they recruited as second-round subjects
	Relationships between second-round subjects and those who they recruited as third-round subjects, etc.
Quota	Factors (e.g., race, gender) used to balance the sample
	Where, when, and how subjects were obtained
Purposive	Reason why specifically chosen subjects were needed
	Where, when, and how subjects were obtained
Selecting informants	Relationships between informants and subjects
	Reasons why subjects, themselves, could not provide data
	Where, when, and how subjects were obtained
Simple random	Random technique used
Systematic	Value used as n to choose every (nth) individual of the sampling frame as a subject
Stratified	Factors (e.g., race, gender) used to balance the sample
	Random technique used within each stratum
Probability proportionate to size	Factors (e.g., race, gender) used to balance the sample
	Each stratum's proportion of the sample
	Random technique used within each stratum
Cluster	Composition of clusters (e.g., those residing on particular city blocks, those attending particular schools)
	Random technique used to select clusters

[a]The column on the left lists commonly used sampling methods. The first five methods listed use nonrandom techniques, and the second five methods listed use random techniques to select subjects. Points in the column on the right should appear in the research report to describe details of how each sampling method was used.

of data, or a combination of these techniques. Further explanation can address the way in which you implemented the technique(s) and your interactions with subjects.

Because each of the four data-gathering techniques have different design elements, no general structure for the "Measures" portion exists. Table 11.5 presents issues relevant to descriptions of the four main techniques. In your report's "Measures" section, you should address those associated with the data-gathering technique(s) you used.

In addition to the information that Table 11.4 identifies as relevant to your chosen data-gathering technique, your audience may also wish to know your rationale for choosing the technique that you used. This explanation should focus on internal validity, the ability of the instrument to measure the construct that you wish to measure. You can also mention the detail of the information provided by your chosen technique, issues of practicality, and any other points that support your decision.

Procedure. Having provided your audience with an understanding of the framework for your study's methods by describing your subjects and measures, you can focus

TABLE 11.5. Data-Gathering Technique Issues[a]

Data-Gathering Technique	Details to Include in Report
Observation	People, conditions, and behaviors observed
	Place and time of observation(s)
	Participant or nonparticipant (whether the researcher participated in the activities that he or she observed)
	Covert or open (whether the subjects knew that they were being observed)
Survey	Open-ended or closed-ended questions
	Typologies (measuring categories), indices (measuring value), or scales (measuring degrees)
	Incentives to subjects for participation
	Interview or questionnaire
	For questionnaires only: *Attach a copy of the questionnaire*
	Self-administered or monitored (whether subjects complete the questionnaire in the presence of the researcher)
	For interviews only: *Attach a copy of the script*
	Probing and follow-up questions
Experiment	Stimulus
	Blinded or not blinded
	Experimental design
	Use of pretests and posttests
	Use of experimental and control groups
	Random group assignment or matching
Existing sources	Sources used

[a]The column on the left lists data-gathering techniques. The column on the left identifies components of each technique that deserves attention in the research report.

on the actual experience of data gathering and analysis. When describing the procedures that you used, you unveil the steps that you took from the time you first contacted subjects to your decisions about appropriate statistical tests. The "Procedures" section provides your audience with a chronological "play-by-play" narrative of your research activities.

The amount of existing knowledge that your audience has, of both research methods and of your study's topic, determines steps that you include and the detail with which you describe them in the "Procedures" section. When making decisions about how much information to give your audience, consider how much information your audience members need to know for a full understanding of your study. You do not, for example, need to explain "false starts," situations in which you began collecting data, but had to abandon your efforts in favor of a more feasible sample or measure than your original one. The following list contains points that you may wish to include in your "Procedure" section.

- A description of Internal Review Board issues, including how your subjects provided informed consent

- An explanation or copy of instructions given to subjects
- Presentation of coding frames and coding sheets
- Identification of instruments (e.g., videorecorder) used to record data
- A schedule of time spent gathering data in particular settings or from particular subjects
- Description of the use of follow-up and probing questions
- Response rate
- A description of challenges encountered when attempting to access existing data
- A description of any debriefing activities
- Presentation of interrater reliability standards if more than one individual interpreted data
- The number of subject groups used for categorical analyses and qualifications for each group analyses
- An explanation of statistical tests (what the tests do)
- Justification of statistical tests (why they are the best tests to use)

You may certainly add to this list if you consider other aspects of your research activities important for your audience to know. As a rule, the "Procedures" section of your report should provide your audience members with the information that they would need to replicate your study.

11.3.3   Presentation of Results

Sometimes, researchers begin presenting their results, specifically descriptive statistics, within the "Methods" sections of their reports. Including basic information about your sample, such as sample size and descriptive information about its demographics, may help with the flow of information and reduce the amount of values that you have to present in your report's "Results" section. If, however, you have not yet provided this information to your audience, it should appear early in the "Results" section.

The "Results" section's main function, however, is to tell the audience whether the data support your hypotheses. You should clearly state your decision regarding null hypothesis and provide all descriptive statistics needed to substantiate your decision. Then, you can explain how your decision about the null hypothesis influenced your decision regarding the research hypothesis (see Fig. 10.1), addressing post hoc analyses if necessary.

Table 11.6 lists additional information, specific to the tests presented in Chapters 5–8, that should appear in your results.

Chapters 5–8 contain sections that provide suggestions for ways to arrange relevant information about results of the tests they address. The way in which you choose to present this information depends on the number of variables you have measured, the natures of these variables, and the number and types of tests you have conducted. When you have conducted a single test with few variables, verbal descriptions of your results may suffice.

TABLE 11.6. Reportable Results[a]

Statistical Test	Details to Include in Report
Chi-square	Number of subjects in each category Category frequencies and marginal frequencies Your chosen α value Critical and calculated χ^2 values (if you have performed computations) p value (if you have used SPSS) Critical and calculated χ^2 values or p values for any post hoc analyses
t test	Number of subjects in each category Category means and, if appropriate, standard deviations Your chosen α value Critical and calculated t values (if you have performed computations) p value (if you have used SPSS)
ANOVA	Number of subjects in each category Category means and, if appropriate, standard deviations Your chosen α value Critical and calculated F values (if you have performed computations) p value (if you have used SPSS) Critical and calculated F values or p values for any post hoc analyses
Regression/correlation	Correlation coefficient Coefficient of determination Regression equation Scatterplot

[a]The column on the left lists commonly used inferential statistical tests. The column on the right identifies values or other information that should be reported when discussing results of these statistical tests. Descriptions of results for advanced statistical analyses, such as those described in Chapter 9, may include data associated with more than one of the tests listed in this table.

Example 11.12: Verbal Description of Results Example 11.5 suggests that past research concerning gift giving may have compared the satisfaction levels of hosts and hostesses who receive wine and who receive candy. The results of this analysis, which requires a t test, lend themselves well to verbal description.

Assuming that each subject received a satisfaction score, perhaps ranging from 0 to 10, with 0 indicating extreme dissatisfaction and 10 indicating extreme satisfaction, the researcher should summarize the scores for those who received wine and for individuals who received candy. The "Results" section should report the means and, when needed, the standard deviation of each category's scores. Descriptions of the outcome of the t test must contain the critical and calculated t values (or, if you used SPSS, the p value) for the test. Comments about these values, then, tell the audience whether the means differ significantly by identifying the null hypothesis as rejected or not rejected.

A sample explanation of results, using bogus means and standard deviations, may state:

The mean satisfaction of 6.6 ($s = 1.1$) for hosts and hostesses who receive gifts of wine and the mean satisfaction score of 7.1 ($s = 2.3$) for those who receive gifts of candy do not differ significantly. A t test comparing these means produced a calculated value of 1.35. This t_{calc} does not exceed the critical t value of 1.80 at $\alpha = .05$. So, the null hypothesis cannot be rejected.

You can use similar processes to describe the results of chi-square tests and ANOVAs. Your presentation of results from a regression or correlation analysis, though, differs a bit because these tests, in and of themselves, do not address significant differences. For this situation, you can describe the linear relationship as positive or negative and characterize it by using terms such as "weak," "moderate," or "strong." The regression equation can also help to depict the arrangement of data points.

Data analyses do not, however, always remain as simple as the scenario described in Example 11.12. You may find that tables or graphs present data most effectively in the situations.

- If you have performed the same sort of tests multiple times with different variables, you might want to consider the suggestions offered in Example 11.13.

Example 11.13: Table of Multiple t Test Results   After adding the possibility of receiving a gift of flowers, as Example 11.5 describes, the researcher may wish to determine whether satisfaction levels of those who receive flowers differs significantly from satisfaction levels of those who receive either wine or candy. A researcher whose interest lies in promoting flowers as a gift does not need to perform an ANOVA but instead might perform two separate t tests, each comparing the mean for those who received flowers to the mean for those who received one of the other types of gifts. After providing descriptive statistics for those in the flower category (suppose a mean of 5.5 and a standard deviation of 1.5 for this example), Table 11.7, or a similar arrangement can present the results of these analyses.

To declare each of the two null hypotheses as supported or rejected, one may add an additional column to Table 11.7 identifying the null hypothesis as "accepted" or "rejected." One may, instead, follow the table with a short paragraph explaining that the mean satisfaction score for those receiving flowers differs significantly from the mean satisfaction score of those receiving candy ($t_{calc} > t_{crit}$), but not from the mean satisfaction score of those receiving wine ($t_{calc} < t_{crit}$). For the significant difference, the "Results" section should remind the audience about the direction of this difference, specifically stating that the mean for those who receive candy exceeds the mean for those who receive flowers.

- If you have performed multiple post hoc analyses, you might want to consider the suggestions presented in Example 11.14.

TABLE 11.7. Results of Multiple t-Tests[a]

Comparison Factor to $\bar{X}_{\text{flowers}} = 5.5$	$\bar{X}$	$.05t_{\text{calc}}$	$.05t_{\text{crit}}$
Wine	6.6	1.17	1.78
Candy	7.1	2.01	1.77

[a]The upper left cell in the table informs the audience that the mean of 5.5, describing the satisfaction level of those in the flower category, serves as a constant comparison factor for the t tests. Each of the bottom two rows contains information about a separate t test comparison. The leftmost cell in each of these rows identifies the second factor in the t test that it addresses. The other cells in the table provide the means being compared to $\bar{X}_{\text{flowers}}$ in each t test and the values used to make a decision regarding the differences. The table can also include a column listing standard deviations if appropriate.

TABLE 11.8. Results of Pos Hoc Analyses[a]

Post Hoc Hypothesis	$.05t_{\text{calc}}$	$.05t_{\text{crit}}$
H_o: $\bar{X}_{\text{wine}} = \bar{X}_{\text{candy}}$	1.35	1.80
H_o: $\bar{X}_{\text{wine}} = \bar{X}_{\text{flowers}}$	1.17	1.78
H_o: $\bar{X}_{\text{candy}} = \bar{X}_{\text{flowers}}$	2.01	1.77
H_o: $\bar{X}_{\text{wine}} = \bar{X}_{\text{candy and flowers}}$	1.50	1.70
H_o: $\bar{X}_{\text{candy}} = \bar{X}_{\text{wine and flowers}}$	1.21	1.70
H_o: $\bar{X}_{\text{flowers}} = \bar{X}_{\text{wine and candy}}$	1.98	1.70

[a]The left column of the table identifies the tests that the researcher performs to determine which differences in means help to explain significant omnibus ANOVA results. By comparing the critical and calculated t values, the audience can ascertain whether each null hypothesis was supported or rejected.

Example 11.14: Table of Post Hoc Analyses Results A researcher interested in differences between all combinations of the independent-variable categories mentioned in Example 11.12 would begin his or her analysis with an ANOVA. A rejected null hypothesis for this ANOVA indicates that at least two of the means involved in the analysis differ significantly. As many as six post hoc analyses, attempting to determine the source of this significance, may follow.

Rather than tediously describing each post hoc analysis and its results, a researcher may choose to list the tests and their results as shown in Table 11.8.

For audiences unfamiliar with the concept of post hoc testing or the practice of comparing calculated and critical values, the researcher may add an additional column to the table identifying each null hypothesis as "accepted" or "rejected." A short description preceding or following the table can highlight the differences deemed significant as those that contribute to the rejected omnibus hypothesis.

• If you believe that a scatterplot most clearly describes continuous data, you might want to consider the following suggestion.

For visual learners in your audience, actually seeing the arrangement of points on a scatterplot may make more sense than a correlation coefficient and regression equation do. You may also find it useful to show your audience members a scatterplot when variables have a curvilinear relationship. A scatterplot showing a curvilinear relationship makes it very clear to your audience that, despite a low correlation coefficient, your variables have a definite relationship.

11.3.4 Presentation of Conclusions

This book devotes an entire chapter, Chapter 10, to guiding you through the process of drawing conclusions and warning you about common mistakes made when doing so. With as much care as you took to be sure that you did not misinterpret your results, leading to faulty conclusions, you want to make sure that the "Conclusions" section of your report clearly informs audience members of the extent and limits of your study's applicability.

Using the structure of summarizing, reflecting, and speculating, as described in Chapter 10, should help you to present your conclusions in a way that your audience can easily understand. In your summary, you should explain the findings of your study in a real-world context, rather than in reference to the hypotheses that you discussed in the "Results" section of your report. Your reflections about how these findings might impact characterizations or behaviors in the real-world context should follow. Finally, you can speculate about subsequent research based on your findings and how these follow-up studies may expand knowledge of the topic.

11.4 CONCLUSION

Ironically, writing the research report can challenge researchers more than the data-gathering and analysis process does. It is sometimes impossible to predict the knowledge base of audience members and, thus, to know how much detail about your research procedure they need. Therefore, the activity of writing a research report often involves much drafting and revising.

As a starting point, however, you can use the structure provided in Section 11.3. The distinct sections in which you present your hypothesis, methods, results, and conclusions lead your audience members chronologically through your research process. You have many choices about the ways that you explain these steps, ranging from the wording you use to the illustrations that you provide.

You should make these decisions with the objective of providing the fullest and most understandable explanation of your study and its findings. Your audience members have no contact with your research other than the report that you provide to them. Without your careful and detailed explanations and, in some cases, justifications, they cannot appreciate you efforts. As some have said, "It's all in the presentation."

REVIEW QUESTIONS

Rewrite each of the following sentences so that it uses formal voice:

11.1. For hayfever sufferers, springtime can be a pain in the neck.

11.2. If you use email regularly, your telephone rings less often than it does if you do not use email regularly.

11.3. Employees are more laid back when they have flexible schedules than when they have strict work hours.

11.4. After all is said and done, people end up paying just as much in veterinarian bills for their cats as for their dogs.

11.5. There's a positive correlation between a student's numerical grade in a class and how he rates the professor of that class on the course evaluation.

11.6. The kids were asked by the researcher to list their favorite and least favorite foods.

Rewrite each of the following sentences to increase readability:

11.7. Local newspaper reporters scoop national newspaper reporters more often than national reporters scoop local reporters.

11.8. To avoid subjects responding to interview questions ad infinitum, there will be a time limit for all surveys.

11.9. Students were not allowed to use handheld computational devices while participating in the testing session.

Rewrite the following sentences so that they do not contain hedgers or presumptives:

11.10. The results of the investigation are pretty clear.

11.11. A new study could certainly investigate a linear relationship between the number of spelling mistakes and the number of grammar mistakes made when writing.

11.12. Without question, cousins share somewhat fewer secrets with each other than siblings do.

Suppose that imaginary studies have revealed the information presented in questions 11.13–11.16. For each question, put the statements in order to create a line of reasoning for a new study:

11.13. (A) A subsequent investigation could test the research hypothesis that those who consume drinks containing electrolytes before exercising have fewer headaches and lower levels of fatigue after exercise than do those who do not consume drinks containing electrolytes before exercising.

    (B) Biochemical research performed by Rattan and Lewis (1998) suggests that, unlike water, drinks with electrolytes can replace sodium and potassium that the body loses through sweat.

    (C) Some symptom of low sodium and potassium levels in the body are headache and fatigue (Easton 1999).

11.14. (A) This study investigates the hypothesis that those who do not listen to the radio at all have fewer traffic violations than do those who listen to music on the radio and those who listen to music on the radio have fewer traffic violations than do those who listen to talk radio while driving.

(B) Thirteen percent of drivers say that they do not listen to the radio while driving (Lowe, 2008).

(C) A comparison of driving habits (Jamison 2004), found fewer traffic violations among those who listen to talk radio while driving than among those who listen to music on the radio while driving.

(D) Research on those who commit traffic violations has not considered drivers who do not listen to the radio at all.

(E) If drivers do not listen to the car radio, they can devote all of their attention to driving.

11.15. (A) Ingram et al. (2005) claim that their results apply to all spelling bee contestants even though they gathered data only during the final round of the competition.

(B) An adapted version of the original study increases the generalizablity of results by expanding the sample to include all spelling bee competitors, not just those who qualified for the final round.

(C) Results of a 2005 study performed by Ingram, Witt, and Clegelman support the research hypothesis that the spelling bee contestants incorrectly spell a higher percentage of words beginning with consonants than words beginning with vowels.

11.16. (A) According to Opp (1992), very high or very low tones are not pleasing to the human ear.

(B) Further investigation into which singers receive the most attention in choral concerts raises the question of whether this philosophy also applies to soloists.

(C) Arrangers of choral music, knowing that audiences prefer to hear voices in the middle of the vocal range, try to avoid having the soprano section singing alone in a musical piece (Cayet and Kline, 2000).

(D) This question suggests the hypothesis that fewer sopranos than altos, tenors, baritones, or bases sing solos during choir concerts.

For questions 11.17 and 11.18, write a short summary of the information presented.

11.17. H: There is a negative correlation between the age difference, in years, of checkers opponents and the length, in minutes, of their checkers game.

H_0: There is no correlation between the age difference, in years, of checkers opponents and the length, in minutes, of their checkers game.

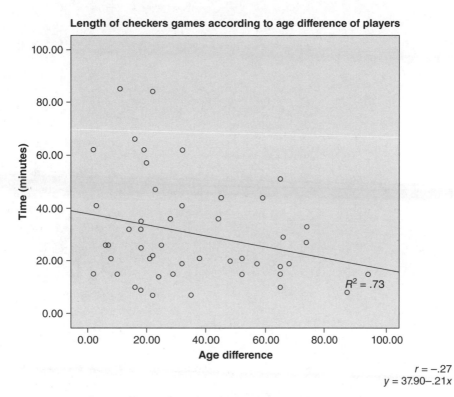

Length of checkers games according to age difference of players

$r = -.27$
$y = 37.90 - .21x$

11.18. H: A lower percentage of people who wear wristwatches than people who don't wear wristwatches arrive late for appointments.

H_0: An equal percentage of people who do and who do not wear wristwatches arrive late for appointments.

		Was subject late for the appointment?		
		No	Yes	Σ
Was subject wearing	No	121	73	194
a wristwatch?	Yes	195	61	256
	Σ	316	134	450

$$\chi^2_{calc} = 10.05$$
$$_{.05}\chi^2_1 = 3.84$$

APPENDIXES

APPENDIXES

APPENDIX A: Z-SCORE TABLE

Find the probability that a score lies between 0 and a particular z score by locating the value at the intersection of row indicating the z score's ones and tens digit and the column indicating the z score's hundredths digit.

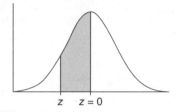

	0.00	0.01	0.02	0.03	0.04	0.05	0.06	0.07	0.08	0.09
0.0	0.0000	0.0040	0.0080	0.0120	0.0160	0.0199	0.0239	0.0279	0.0319	0.0359
0.1	0.0398	0.0438	0.0478	0.0517	0.0557	0.0596	0.0636	0.0675	0.0714	0.0753
0.2	0.0793	0.0832	0.0871	0.0910	0.0948	0.0987	0.1026	0.1064	0.1103	0.1141
0.3	0.1179	0.1217	0.1255	0.1293	0.1331	0.1368	0.1406	0.1443	0.1480	0.1517
0.4	0.1554	0.1591	0.1628	0.1664	0.1700	0.1736	0.1772	0.1808	0.1844	0.1879
0.5	0.1915	0.1950	0.1985	0.2019	0.2054	0.2088	0.2123	0.2157	0.2190	0.2224
0.6	0.2257	0.2291	0.2324	0.2357	0.2389	0.2422	0.2454	0.2486	0.2517	0.2549
0.7	0.2580	0.2611	0.2642	0.2673	0.2704	0.2734	0.2764	0.2794	0.2823	0.2852
0.8	0.2881	0.2910	0.2939	0.2967	0.2995	0.3023	0.3051	0.3078	0.3106	0.3133
0.9	0.3159	0.3186	0.3212	0.3238	0.3264	0.3289	0.3315	0.3340	0.3365	0.3389
1.0	0.3413	0.3438	0.3461	0.3485	0.3508	0.3531	0.3554	0.3577	0.3599	0.3621
1.1	0.3643	0.3665	0.3686	0.3708	0.3729	0.3749	0.3770	0.3790	0.3810	0.3830
1.2	0.3849	0.3869	0.3888	0.3907	0.3925	0.3944	0.3962	0.3980	0.3997	0.4015
1.3	0.4032	0.4049	0.4066	0.4082	0.4099	0.4115	0.4131	0.4147	0.4162	0.4177
1.4	0.4192	0.4207	0.4222	0.4236	0.4251	0.4265	0.4279	0.4292	0.4306	0.4319
1.5	0.4332	0.4345	0.4357	0.4370	0.4382	0.4394	0.4406	0.4418	0.4429	0.4441
1.6	0.4452	0.4463	0.4474	0.4484	0.4495	0.4505	0.4515	0.4525	0.4535	0.4545

Analyzing Quantitative Data: An Introduction for Social Researchers, First Edition. Debra Wetcher-Hendricks.
© 2011 John Wiley & Sons, Inc. Published 2011 by John Wiley & Sons, Inc.

	0.00	0.01	0.02	0.03	0.04	0.05	0.06	0.07	0.08	0.09
1.7	0.4554	0.4564	0.4573	0.4582	0.4591	0.4599	0.4608	0.4616	0.4625	0.4633
1.8	0.4641	0.4649	0.4656	0.4664	0.4671	0.4678	0.4686	0.4693	0.4699	0.4706
1.9	0.4713	0.4719	0.4726	0.4732	0.4738	0.4744	0.4750	0.4756	0.4761	0.4767
2.0	0.4772	0.4778	0.4783	0.4788	0.4793	0.4798	0.4803	0.4808	0.4812	0.4817
2.1	0.4821	0.4826	0.4830	0.4834	0.4838	0.4842	0.4846	0.4850	0.4854	0.4857
2.2	0.4861	0.4864	0.4868	0.4871	0.4875	0.4878	0.4881	0.4884	0.4887	0.4890
2.3	0.4893	0.4896	0.4898	0.4901	0.4904	0.4906	0.4909	0.4911	0.4913	0.4916
2.4	0.4918	0.4920	0.4922	0.4925	0.4927	0.4929	0.4931	0.4932	0.4934	0.4936
2.5	0.4938	0.4940	0.4941	0.4943	0.4945	0.4946	0.4948	0.4949	0.4951	0.4952
2.6	0.4953	0.4955	0.4956	0.4957	0.4959	0.4960	0.4961	0.4962	0.4963	0.4964
2.7	0.4965	0.4966	0.4967	0.4968	0.4969	0.4970	0.4971	0.4972	0.4973	0.4974
2.8	0.4974	0.4975	0.4976	0.4977	0.4977	0.4978	0.4979	0.4979	0.4980	0.4981
2.9	0.4981	0.4982	0.4982	0.4983	0.4984	0.4984	0.4985	0.4985	0.4986	0.4986
3.0	0.4987	0.4987	0.4987	0.4988	0.4988	0.4989	0.4989	0.4989	0.4990	0.4990

Source: TABLES in www.statsoft.com/textbook.

APPENDIX B: TABLE FOR CRITICAL χ^2 VALUES

Find a critical χ^2 value by reading across the row with the appropriate degrees of freedom and down the column for the selected maximum probability (otherwise known as α). Reject the null hypothesis if the calculated value exceeds the critical value.

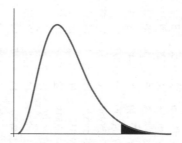

Analyzing Quantitative Data: An Introduction for Social Researchers, First Edition. Debra Wetcher-Hendricks.
© 2011 John Wiley & Sons, Inc. Published 2011 by John Wiley & Sons, Inc.

Critical Values of Chi-Square Distribution

df/p	.995	.990	.975	.950	.900	.750	.500	.250	.100	.050	.025	.010	.005
1	0.00004	0.00016	0.00098	0.00393	0.01579	0.10153	0.45494	1.32330	2.70554	3.84146	5.02389	6.63490	7.87944
2	0.01003	0.02010	0.05064	0.10259	0.21072	0.57536	1.38629	2.77259	4.60517	5.99146	7.37776	9.21034	10.59663
3	0.07172	0.11483	0.21580	0.35185	0.58437	1.21253	2.36597	4.10834	6.25139	7.81473	9.34840	11.34487	12.83816
4	0.20699	0.29711	0.48442	0.71072	1.06362	1.92256	3.35669	5.38527	7.77944	9.48773	11.14329	13.27670	14.86026
5	0.41174	0.55430	0.83121	1.14548	1.61031	2.67460	4.35146	6.62568	9.23636	11.07050	12.83250	15.08627	16.74960
6	0.67573	0.87209	1.23734	1.63538	2.20413	3.45460	5.34812	7.84080	10.64464	12.59159	14.44938	16.81189	18.54758
7	0.98926	1.23904	1.68987	2.16735	2.83311	4.25485	6.34581	9.03715	12.01704	14.06714	16.01276	18.47531	20.27774
8	1.34441	1.64650	2.17973	2.73264	3.48954	5.07064	7.34412	10.21885	13.36157	15.50731	17.53455	20.09024	21.95495
9	1.73493	2.08790	2.70039	3.32511	4.16816	5.89883	8.34283	11.38875	14.68366	16.91898	19.02277	21.66599	23.58935
10	2.15586	2.55821	3.24697	3.94030	4.86518	6.73720	9.34182	12.54886	15.98718	18.30704	20.48318	23.20925	25.18818
11	2.60322	3.05348	3.81575	4.57481	5.57778	7.58414	10.34100	13.70069	17.27501	19.67514	21.92005	24.72497	26.75685
12	3.07382	3.57057	4.40379	5.22603	6.30380	8.43842	11.34032	14.84540	18.54935	21.02607	23.33666	26.21697	28.29952
13	3.56503	4.10692	5.00875	5.89186	7.04150	9.29907	12.33976	15.98391	19.81193	22.36203	24.73560	27.68825	29.81947
14	4.07467	4.66043	5.62873	6.57063	7.78953	10.16531	13.33927	17.11693	21.06414	23.68479	26.11895	29.14124	31.31935
15	4.60092	5.22935	6.26214	7.26094	8.54676	11.03654	14.33886	18.24509	22.30713	24.99579	27.48839	30.57791	32.80132
16	5.14221	5.81221	6.90766	7.96165	9.31224	11.91222	15.33850	19.36886	23.54183	26.29623	28.84535	31.99993	34.26719
17	5.69722	6.40776	7.56419	8.67176	10.08519	12.79193	16.33818	20.48868	24.76904	27.58711	30.19101	33.40866	35.71847
18	6.26480	7.01491	8.23075	9.39046	10.86494	13.67529	17.33790	21.60489	25.98942	28.86930	31.52638	34.80531	37.15645
19	6.84397	7.63273	8.90652	10.11701	11.65091	14.56200	18.33765	22.71781	27.20357	30.14353	32.85233	36.19087	38.58226
20	7.43384	8.26040	9.59078	10.85081	12.44261	15.45177	19.33743	23.82769	28.41198	31.41043	34.16961	37.56623	39.99685
21	8.03365	8.89720	10.28290	11.59131	13.23960	16.34438	20.33723	24.93478	29.61509	32.67057	35.47888	38.93217	41.40106
22	8.64272	9.54249	10.98232	12.33801	14.04149	17.23962	21.33704	26.03927	30.81328	33.92444	36.78071	40.28936	42.79565
23	9.26042	10.19572	11.68855	13.09051	14.84796	18.13730	22.33688	27.14134	32.00690	35.17246	38.07563	41.63840	44.18128
24	9.88623	10.85636	12.40115	13.84843	15.65868	19.03725	23.33673	28.24115	33.19624	36.41503	39.36408	42.97982	45.55851
25	10.51965	11.52398	13.11972	14.61141	16.47341	19.93934	24.33659	29.33885	34.38159	37.65248	40.64647	44.31410	46.92789
26	11.16024	12.19815	13.84390	15.37916	17.29188	20.84343	25.33646	30.43457	35.56317	38.88514	41.92317	45.64168	48.28988
27	11.80759	12.87850	14.57338	16.15140	18.11390	21.74940	26.33634	31.52841	36.74122	40.11327	43.19451	46.96294	49.64492
28	12.46134	13.56471	15.30786	16.92788	18.93924	22.65716	27.33623	32.62049	37.91592	41.33714	44.46079	48.27824	50.99338
29	13.12115	14.25645	16.04707	17.70837	19.76774	23.56659	28.33613	33.71091	39.08747	42.55697	45.72229	49.58788	52.33562
30	13.78672	14.95346	16.79077	18.49266	20.59923	24.47761	29.33603	34.79974	40.25602	43.77297	46.97924	50.89218	53.67196

Source: TABLES in www.statsoft.com/textbook.

APPENDIX C: TABLE FOR CRITICAL *t* VALUES

Find a critical t value by reading across the row with the appropriate degrees of freedom and down the column for the selected maximum probability (otherwise known as α). Reject the null hypothesis if the calculated value exceeds the critical value.

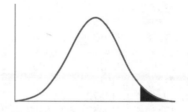

Analyzing Quantitative Data: An Introduction for Social Researchers, First Edition. Debra Wetcher-Hendricks.
© 2011 John Wiley & Sons, Inc. Published 2011 by John Wiley & Sons, Inc.

Critical Values of t Distribution

df/p	.40	.25	.10	.05	.025	.01	.005	.0005
1	0.324920	1.000000	3.077684	6.313752	12.70620	31.82052	63.65674	636.6192
2	0.288675	0.816497	1.885618	2.919986	4.30265	6.96456	9.92484	31.5991
3	0.276671	0.764892	1.637744	2.353363	3.18245	4.54070	5.84091	12.9240
4	0.270722	0.740697	1.533206	2.131847	2.77645	3.74695	4.60409	8.6103
5	0.267181	0.726687	1.475884	2.015048	2.57058	3.36493	4.03214	6.8688
6	0.264835	0.717558	1.439756	1.943180	2.44691	3.14267	3.70743	5.9588
7	0.263167	0.711142	1.414924	1.894579	2.36462	2.99795	3.49948	5.4079
8	0.261921	0.706387	1.396815	1.859548	2.30600	2.89646	3.35539	5.0413
9	0.260955	0.702722	1.383029	1.833113	2.26216	2.82144	3.24984	4.7809
10	0.260185	0.699812	1.372184	1.812461	2.22814	2.76377	3.16927	4.5869
11	0.259556	0.697445	1.363430	1.795885	2.20099	2.71808	3.10581	4.4370
12	0.259033	0.695483	1.356217	1.782288	2.17881	2.68100	3.05454	4.3178
13	0.258591	0.693829	1.350171	1.770933	2.16037	2.65031	3.01228	4.2208
14	0.258213	0.692417	1.345030	1.761310	2.14479	2.62449	2.97684	4.1405
15	0.257885	0.691197	1.340606	1.753050	2.13145	2.60248	2.94671	4.0728
16	0.257599	0.690132	1.336757	1.745884	2.11991	2.58349	2.92078	4.0150
17	0.257347	0.689195	1.333379	1.739607	2.10982	2.56693	2.89823	3.9651
18	0.257123	0.688364	1.330391	1.734064	2.10092	2.55238	2.87844	3.9216
19	0.256923	0.687621	1.327728	1.729133	2.09302	2.53948	2.86093	3.8834
20	0.256743	0.686954	1.325341	1.724718	2.08596	2.52798	2.84534	3.8495
21	0.256580	0.686352	1.323188	1.720743	2.07961	2.51765	2.83136	3.8193
22	0.256432	0.685805	1.321237	1.717144	2.07387	2.50832	2.81876	3.7921
23	0.256297	0.685306	1.319460	1.713872	2.06866	2.49987	2.80734	3.7676
24	0.256173	0.684850	1.317836	1.710882	2.06390	2.49216	2.79694	3.7454
25	0.256060	0.684430	1.316345	1.708141	2.05954	2.48511	2.78744	3.7251
26	0.255955	0.684043	1.314972	1.705618	2.05553	2.47863	2.77871	3.7066
27	0.255858	0.683685	1.313703	1.703288	2.05183	2.47266	2.77068	3.6896
28	0.255768	0.683353	1.312527	1.701131	2.04841	2.46714	2.76326	3.6739
29	0.255684	0.683044	1.311434	1.699127	2.04523	2.46202	2.75639	3.6594
30	0.255605	0.682756	1.310415	1.697261	2.04227	2.45726	2.75000	3.6460
INF	0.253347	0.674490	1.281552	1.644854	1.95996	2.32635	2.57583	3.2905

Source: TABLES in www.statsoft.com/textbook.

APPENDIX D: TABLE FOR CRITICAL *F* VALUES

To find a critical F value, begin by locating the table that corresponds to the selected maximum probability (otherwise known as α). Then, read across the row of the appropriate degrees of freedom for the numerator of the F ratio (df_1) and down the column of the appropriate degrees of freedom for the denominator of the F ratio (df_2). Reject the null hypothesis if the calculated value exceeds the critical value.

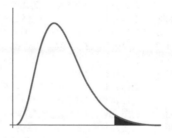

Analyzing Quantitative Data: An Introduction for Social Researchers, First Edition. Debra Wetcher-Hendricks.
© 2011 John Wiley & Sons, Inc. Published 2011 by John Wiley & Sons, Inc.

Critical Values of the F Distribution

$df_1 \rightarrow df_2 \downarrow$	1	2	3	4	5	6	7	8	9
$\alpha = .10$									
1	39.86346	49.50000	53.59324	55.83296	57.24008	58.20442	58.90595	59.43898	59.85759
2	8.52632	9.00000	9.16179	9.24342	9.29263	9.32553	9.34908	9.36677	9.38054
3	5.53832	5.46238	5.39077	5.34264	5.30916	5.28473	5.26619	5.25167	5.24000
4	4.54477	4.32456	4.19086	4.10725	4.05058	4.00975	3.97897	3.95494	3.93567
5	4.06042	3.77972	3.61948	3.52020	3.45298	3.40451	3.36790	3.33928	3.31628
6	3.77595	3.46330	3.28876	3.18076	3.10751	3.05455	3.01446	2.98304	2.95774
7	3.58943	3.25744	3.07407	2.96053	2.88334	2.82739	2.78493	2.75158	2.72468
8	3.45792	3.11312	2.92380	2.80643	2.72645	2.66833	2.62413	2.58935	2.56124
9	3.36030	3.00645	2.81286	2.69268	2.61061	2.55086	2.50531	2.46941	2.44034
10	3.28502	2.92447	2.72767	2.60534	2.52164	2.46058	2.41397	2.37715	2.34731
11	3.22520	2.85951	2.66023	2.53619	2.45118	2.38907	2.34157	2.30400	2.27350
12	3.17655	2.80680	2.60552	2.48010	2.39402	2.33102	2.28278	2.24457	2.21352
13	3.13621	2.76317	2.56027	2.43371	2.34672	2.28298	2.23410	2.19535	2.16382
14	3.10221	2.72647	2.52222	2.39469	2.30694	2.24256	2.19313	2.15390	2.12195
15	3.07319	2.69517	2.48979	2.36143	2.27302	2.20808	2.15818	2.11853	2.08621
16	3.04811	2.66817	2.46181	2.33274	2.24376	2.17833	2.12800	2.08798	2.05533
17	3.02623	2.64464	2.43743	2.30775	2.21825	2.15239	2.10169	2.06134	2.02839
18	3.00698	2.62395	2.41601	2.28577	2.19583	2.12958	2.07854	2.03789	2.00467
19	2.98990	2.60561	2.39702	2.26630	2.17596	2.10936	2.05802	2.01710	1.98364
20	2.97465	2.58925	2.38009	2.24893	2.15823	2.09132	2.03970	1.99853	1.96485
21	2.96096	2.57457	2.36489	2.23334	2.14231	2.07512	2.02325	1.98186	1.94797
22	2.94858	2.56131	2.35117	2.21927	2.12794	2.06050	2.00840	1.96680	1.93273
23	2.93736	2.54929	2.33873	2.20651	2.11491	2.04723	1.99492	1.95312	1.91888
24	2.92712	2.53833	2.32739	2.19488	2.10303	2.03513	1.98263	1.94066	1.90625
25	2.91774	2.52831	2.31702	2.18424	2.09216	2.02406	1.97138	1.92925	1.89469
26	2.90913	2.51910	2.30749	2.17447	2.08218	2.01389	1.96104	1.91876	1.88407
27	2.90119	2.51061	2.29871	2.16546	2.07298	2.00452	1.95151	1.90909	1.87427
28	2.89385	2.50276	2.29060	2.15714	2.06447	1.99585	1.94270	1.90014	1.86520
29	2.88703	2.49548	2.28307	2.14941	2.05658	1.98781	1.93452	1.89184	1.85679
30	2.88069	2.48872	2.27607	2.14223	2.04925	1.98033	1.92692	1.88412	1.84896
40	2.83535	2.44037	2.22609	2.09095	1.99682	1.92688	1.87252	1.82886	1.79290
60	2.79107	2.39325	2.17741	2.04099	1.94571	1.87472	1.81939	1.77483	1.73802
120	2.74781	2.34734	2.12999	1.99230	1.89587	1.82381	1.76748	1.72196	1.68425
INF	2.70554	2.30259	2.08380	1.94486	1.84727	1.77411	1.71672	1.67020	1.63152
$\alpha = .05$									
1	161.4476	199.5000	215.7073	224.5832	230.1619	233.9860	236.7684	238.8827	240.5433
2	18.5128	19.0000	19.1643	19.2468	19.2964	19.3295	19.3532	19.3710	19.3848
3	10.1280	9.5521	9.2766	9.1172	9.0135	8.9406	8.8867	8.8452	8.8123
4	7.7086	6.9443	6.5914	6.3882	6.2561	6.1631	6.0942	6.0410	5.9988
5	6.6079	5.7861	5.4095	5.1922	5.0503	4.9503	4.8759	4.8183	4.7725
6	5.9874	5.1433	4.7571	4.5337	4.3874	4.2839	4.2067	4.1468	4.0990
7	5.5914	4.7374	4.3468	4.1203	3.9715	3.8660	3.7870	3.7257	3.6767
8	5.3177	4.4590	4.0662	3.8379	3.6875	3.5806	3.5005	3.4381	3.3881
9	5.1174	4.2565	3.8625	3.6331	3.4817	3.3738	3.2927	3.2296	3.1789
10	4.9646	4.1028	3.7083	3.4780	3.3258	3.2172	3.1355	3.0717	3.0204
11	4.8443	3.9823	3.5874	3.3567	3.2039	3.0946	3.0123	2.9480	2.8962
12	4.7472	3.8853	3.4903	3.2592	3.1059	2.9961	2.9134	2.8486	2.7964

10	12	15	20	24	30	40	60	120	INF
60.19498	60.70521	61.22034	61.74029	62.00205	62.26497	62.52905	62.79428	63.06064	63.32812
9.39157	9.40813	9.42471	9.44131	9.44962	9.45793	9.46624	9.47456	9.48289	9.49122
5.23041	5.21562	5.20031	5.18448	5.17636	5.16811	5.15972	5.15119	5.14251	5.13370
3.91988	3.89553	3.87036	3.84434	3.83099	3.81742	3.80361	3.78957	3.77527	3.76073
3.29740	3.26824	3.23801	3.20665	3.19052	3.17408	3.15732	3.14023	3.12279	3.10500
2.93693	2.90472	2.87122	2.83634	2.81834	2.79996	2.78117	2.76195	2.74229	2.72216
2.70251	2.66811	2.63223	2.59473	2.57533	2.55546	2.53510	2.51422	2.49279	2.47079
2.53804	2.50196	2.46422	2.42464	2.40410	2.38302	2.36136	2.33910	2.31618	2.29257
2.41632	2.37888	2.33962	2.29832	2.27683	2.25472	2.23196	2.20849	2.18427	2.15923
2.32260	2.28405	2.24351	2.20074	2.17843	2.15543	2.13169	2.10716	2.08176	2.05542
2.24823	2.20873	2.16709	2.12305	2.10001	2.07621	2.05161	2.02612	1.99965	1.97211
2.18776	2.14744	2.10485	2.05968	2.03599	2.01149	1.98610	1.95973	1.93228	1.90361
2.13763	2.09659	2.05316	2.00698	1.98272	1.95757	1.93147	1.90429	1.87591	1.84620
2.09540	2.05371	2.00953	1.96245	1.93766	1.91193	1.88516	1.85723	1.82800	1.79728
2.05932	2.01707	1.97222	1.92431	1.89904	1.87277	1.84539	1.81676	1.78672	1.75505
2.02815	1.98539	1.93992	1.89127	1.86556	1.83879	1.81084	1.78156	1.75075	1.71817
2.00094	1.95772	1.91169	1.86236	1.83624	1.80901	1.78053	1.75063	1.71909	1.68564
1.97698	1.93334	1.88681	1.83685	1.81035	1.78269	1.75371	1.72322	1.69099	1.65671
1.95573	1.91170	1.86471	1.81416	1.78731	1.75924	1.72979	1.69876	1.66587	1.63077
1.93674	1.89236	1.84494	1.79384	1.76667	1.73822	1.70833	1.67678	1.64326	1.60738
1.91967	1.87497	1.82715	1.77555	1.74807	1.71927	1.68896	1.65691	1.62278	1.58615
1.90425	1.85925	1.81106	1.75899	1.73122	1.70208	1.67138	1.63885	1.60415	1.56678
1.89025	1.84497	1.79643	1.74392	1.71588	1.68643	1.65535	1.62237	1.58711	1.54903
1.87748	1.83194	1.78308	1.73015	1.70185	1.67210	1.64067	1.60726	1.57146	1.53270
1.86578	1.82000	1.77083	1.71752	1.68898	1.65895	1.62718	1.59335	1.55703	1.51760
1.85503	1.80902	1.75957	1.70589	1.67712	1.64682	1.61472	1.58050	1.54368	1.50360
1.84511	1.79889	1.74917	1.69514	1.66616	1.63560	1.60320	1.56859	1.53129	1.49057
1.83593	1.78951	1.73954	1.68519	1.65600	1.62519	1.59250	1.55753	1.51976	1.47841
1.82741	1.78081	1.73060	1.67593	1.64655	1.61551	1.58253	1.54721	1.50899	1.46704
1.81949	1.77270	1.72227	1.66731	1.63774	1.60648	1.57323	1.53757	1.49891	1.45636
1.76269	1.71456	1.66241	1.60515	1.57411	1.54108	1.50562	1.46716	1.42476	1.37691
1.70701	1.65743	1.60337	1.54349	1.51072	1.47554	1.43734	1.39520	1.34757	1.29146
1.65238	1.60120	1.54500	1.48207	1.44723	1.40938	1.36760	1.32034	1.26457	1.19256
1.59872	1.54578	1.48714	1.42060	1.38318	1.34187	1.29513	1.23995	1.16860	1.00000
241.8817	243.9060	245.9499	248.0131	249.0518	250.0951	251.1432	252.1957	253.2529	254.3144
19.3959	19.4125	19.4291	19.4458	19.4541	19.4624	19.4707	19.4791	19.4874	19.4957
8.7855	8.7446	8.7029	8.6602	8.6385	8.6166	8.5944	8.5720	8.5494	8.5264
5.9644	5.9117	5.8578	5.8025	5.7744	5.7459	5.7170	5.6877	5.6581	5.6281
4.7351	4.6777	4.6188	4.5581	4.5272	4.4957	4.4638	4.4314	4.3985	4.3650
4.0600	3.9999	3.9381	3.8742	3.8415	3.8082	3.7743	3.7398	3.7047	3.6689
3.6365	3.5747	3.5107	3.4445	3.4105	3.3758	3.3404	3.3043	3.2674	3.2298
3.3472	3.2839	3.2184	3.1503	3.1152	3.0794	3.0428	3.0053	2.9669	2.9276
3.1373	3.0729	3.0061	2.9365	2.9005	2.8637	2.8259	2.7872	2.7475	2.7067
2.9782	2.9130	2.8450	2.7740	2.7372	2.6996	2.6609	2.6211	2.5801	2.5379
2.8536	2.7876	2.7186	2.6464	2.6090	2.5705	2.5309	2.4901	2.4480	2.4045
2.7534	2.6866	2.6169	2.5436	2.5055	2.4663	2.4259	2.3842	2.3410	2.2962

df$_1$→df$_2$↓	1	2	3	4	5	6	7	8	9
13	4.6672	3.8056	3.4105	3.1791	3.0254	2.9153	2.8321	2.7669	2.7144
14	4.6001	3.7389	3.3439	3.1122	2.9582	2.8477	2.7642	2.6987	2.6458
15	4.5431	3.6823	3.2874	3.0556	2.9013	2.7905	2.7066	2.6408	2.5876
16	4.4940	3.6337	3.2389	3.0069	2.8524	2.7413	2.6572	2.5911	2.5377
17	4.4513	3.5915	3.1968	2.9647	2.8100	2.6987	2.6143	2.5480	2.4943
18	4.4139	3.5546	3.1599	2.9277	2.7729	2.6613	2.5767	2.5102	2.4563
19	4.3807	3.5219	3.1274	2.8951	2.7401	2.6283	2.5435	2.4768	2.4227
20	4.3512	3.4928	3.0984	2.8661	2.7109	2.5990	2.5140	2.4471	2.3928
21	4.3248	3.4668	3.0725	2.8401	2.6848	2.5727	2.4876	2.4205	2.3660
22	4.3009	3.4434	3.0491	2.8167	2.6613	2.5491	2.4638	2.3965	2.3419
23	4.2793	3.4221	3.0280	2.7955	2.6400	2.5277	2.4422	2.3748	2.3201
24	4.2597	3.4028	3.0088	2.7763	2.6207	2.5082	2.4226	2.3551	2.3002
25	4.2417	3.3852	2.9912	2.7587	2.6030	2.4904	2.4047	2.3371	2.2821
26	4.2252	3.3690	2.9752	2.7426	2.5868	2.4741	2.3883	2.3205	2.2655
27	4.2100	3.3541	2.9604	2.7278	2.5719	2.4591	2.3732	2.3053	2.2501
28	4.1960	3.3404	2.9467	2.7141	2.5581	2.4453	2.3593	2.2913	2.2360
29	4.1830	3.3277	2.9340	2.7014	2.5454	2.4324	2.3463	2.2783	2.2229
30	4.1709	3.3158	2.9223	2.6896	2.5336	2.4205	2.3343	2.2662	2.2107
40	4.0847	3.2317	2.8387	2.6060	2.4495	2.3359	2.2490	2.1802	2.1240
60	4.0012	3.1504	2.7581	2.5252	2.3683	2.2541	2.1665	2.0970	2.0401
120	3.9201	3.0718	2.6802	2.4472	2.2899	2.1750	2.0868	2.0164	1.9588
INF	3.8415	2.9957	2.6049	2.3719	2.2141	2.0986	2.0096	1.9384	1.8799

$\alpha = .025$

	1	2	3	4	5	6	7	8	9
1	647.7890	799.5000	864.1630	899.5833	921.8479	937.1111	948.2169	956.6562	963.2846
2	38.5063	39.0000	39.1655	39.2484	39.2982	39.3315	39.3552	39.3730	39.3869
3	17.4434	16.0441	15.4392	15.1010	14.8848	14.7347	14.6244	14.5399	14.4731
4	12.2179	10.6491	9.9792	9.6045	9.3645	9.1973	9.0741	8.9796	8.9047
5	10.0070	8.4336	7.7636	7.3879	7.1464	6.9777	6.8531	6.7572	6.6811
6	8.8131	7.2599	6.5988	6.2272	5.9876	5.8198	5.6955	5.5996	5.5234
7	8.0727	6.5415	5.8898	5.5226	5.2852	5.1186	4.9949	4.8993	4.8232
8	7.5709	6.0595	5.4160	5.0526	4.8173	4.6517	4.5286	4.4333	4.3572
9	7.2093	5.7147	5.0781	4.7181	4.4844	4.3197	4.1970	4.1020	4.0260
10	6.9367	5.4564	4.8256	4.4683	4.2361	4.0721	3.9498	3.8549	3.7790
11	6.7241	5.2559	4.6300	4.2751	4.0440	3.8807	3.7586	3.6638	3.5879
12	6.5538	5.0959	4.4742	4.1212	3.8911	3.7283	3.6065	3.5118	3.4358
13	6.4143	4.9653	4.3472	3.9959	3.7667	3.6043	3.4827	3.3880	3.3120
14	6.2979	4.8567	4.2417	3.8919	3.6634	3.5014	3.3799	3.2853	3.2093
15	6.1995	4.7650	4.1528	3.8043	3.5764	3.4147	3.2934	3.1987	3.1227
16	6.1151	4.6867	4.0768	3.7294	3.5021	3.3406	3.2194	3.1248	3.0488
17	6.0420	4.6189	4.0112	3.6648	3.4379	3.2767	3.1556	3.0610	2.9849
18	5.9781	4.5597	3.9539	3.6083	3.3820	3.2209	3.0999	3.0053	2.9291
19	5.9216	4.5075	3.9034	3.5587	3.3327	3.1718	3.0509	2.9563	2.8801
20	5.8715	4.4613	3.8587	3.5147	3.2891	3.1283	3.0074	2.9128	2.8365
21	5.8266	4.4199	3.8188	3.4754	3.2501	3.0895	2.9686	2.8740	2.7977
22	5.7863	4.3828	3.7829	3.4401	3.2151	3.0546	2.9338	2.8392	2.7628
23	5.7498	4.3492	3.7505	3.4083	3.1835	3.0232	2.9023	2.8077	2.7313
24	5.7166	4.3187	3.7211	3.3794	3.1548	2.9946	2.8738	2.7791	2.7027
25	5.6864	4.2909	3.6943	3.3530	3.1287	2.9685	2.8478	2.7531	2.6766
26	5.6586	4.2655	3.6697	3.3289	3.1048	2.9447	2.8240	2.7293	2.6528
27	5.6331	4.2421	3.6472	3.3067	3.0828	2.9228	2.8021	2.7074	2.6309

10	12	15	20	24	30	40	60	120	INF
2.6710	2.6037	2.5331	2.4589	2.4202	2.3803	2.3392	2.2966	2.2524	2.2064
2.6022	2.5342	2.4630	2.3879	2.3487	2.3082	2.2664	2.2229	2.1778	2.1307
2.5437	2.4753	2.4034	2.3275	2.2878	2.2468	2.2043	2.1601	2.1141	2.0658
2.4935	2.4247	2.3522	2.2756	2.2354	2.1938	2.1507	2.1058	2.0589	2.0096
2.4499	2.3807	2.3077	2.2304	2.1898	2.1477	2.1040	2.0584	2.0107	1.9604
2.4117	2.3421	2.2686	2.1906	2.1497	2.1071	2.0629	2.0166	1.9681	1.9168
2.3779	2.3080	2.2341	2.1555	2.1141	2.0712	2.0264	1.9795	1.9302	1.8780
2.3479	2.2776	2.2033	2.1242	2.0825	2.0391	1.9938	1.9464	1.8963	1.8432
2.3210	2.2504	2.1757	2.0960	2.0540	2.0102	1.9645	1.9165	1.8657	1.8117
2.2967	2.2258	2.1508	2.0707	2.0283	1.9842	1.9380	1.8894	1.8380	1.7831
2.2747	2.2036	2.1282	2.0476	2.0050	1.9605	1.9139	1.8648	1.8128	1.7570
2.2547	2.1834	2.1077	2.0267	1.9838	1.9390	1.8920	1.8424	1.7896	1.7330
2.2365	2.1649	2.0889	2.0075	1.9643	1.9192	1.8718	1.8217	1.7684	1.7110
2.2197	2.1479	2.0716	1.9898	1.9464	1.9010	1.8533	1.8027	1.7488	1.6906
2.2043	2.1323	2.0558	1.9736	1.9299	1.8842	1.8361	1.7851	1.7306	1.6717
2.1900	2.1179	2.0411	1.9586	1.9147	1.8687	1.8203	1.7689	1.7138	1.6541
2.1768	2.1045	2.0275	1.9446	1.9005	1.8543	1.8055	1.7537	1.6981	1.6376
2.1646	2.0921	2.0148	1.9317	1.8874	1.8409	1.7918	1.7396	1.6835	1.6223
2.0772	2.0035	1.9245	1.8389	1.7929	1.7444	1.6928	1.6373	1.5766	1.5089
1.9926	1.9174	1.8364	1.7480	1.7001	1.6491	1.5943	1.5343	1.4673	1.3893
1.9105	1.8337	1.7505	1.6587	1.6084	1.5543	1.4952	1.4290	1.3519	1.2539
1.8307	1.7522	1.6664	1.5705	1.5173	1.4591	1.3940	1.3180	1.2214	1.0000
968.6274	976.7079	984.8668	993.1028	997.2492	1001.414	1005.598	1009.800	1014.020	1018.258
39.3980	39.4146	39.4313	39.4479	39.4562	39.465	39.473	39.481	39.490	39.498
14.4189	14.3366	14.2527	14.1674	14.1241	14.081	14.037	13.992	13.947	13.902
8.8439	8.7512	8.6565	8.5599	8.5109	8.461	8.411	8.360	8.309	8.257
6.6192	6.5245	6.4277	6.3286	6.2780	6.227	6.175	6.123	6.069	6.015
5.4613	5.3662	5.2687	5.1684	5.1172	5.065	5.012	4.959	4.904	4.849
4.7611	4.6658	4.5678	4.4667	4.4150	4.362	4.309	4.254	4.199	4.142
4.2951	4.1997	4.1012	3.9995	3.9472	3.894	3.840	3.784	3.728	3.670
3.9639	3.8682	3.7694	3.6669	3.6142	3.560	3.505	3.449	3.392	3.333
3.7168	3.6209	3.5217	3.4185	3.3654	3.311	3.255	3.198	3.140	3.080
3.5257	3.4296	3.3299	3.2261	3.1725	3.118	3.061	3.004	2.944	2.883
3.3736	3.2773	3.1772	3.0728	3.0187	2.963	2.906	2.848	2.787	2.725
3.2497	3.1532	3.0527	2.9477	2.8932	2.837	2.780	2.720	2.659	2.595
3.1469	3.0502	2.9493	2.8437	2.7888	2.732	2.674	2.614	2.552	2.487
3.0602	2.9633	2.8621	2.7559	2.7006	2.644	2.585	2.524	2.461	2.395
2.9862	2.8890	2.7875	2.6808	2.6252	2.568	2.509	2.447	2.383	2.316
2.9222	2.8249	2.7230	2.6158	2.5598	2.502	2.442	2.380	2.315	2.247
2.8664	2.7689	2.6667	2.5590	2.5027	2.445	2.384	2.321	2.256	2.187
2.8172	2.7196	2.6171	2.5089	2.4523	2.394	2.333	2.270	2.203	2.133
2.7737	2.6758	2.5731	2.4645	2.4076	2.349	2.287	2.223	2.156	2.085
2.7348	2.6368	2.5338	2.4247	2.3675	2.308	2.246	2.182	2.114	2.042
2.6998	2.6017	2.4984	2.3890	2.3315	2.272	2.210	2.145	2.076	2.003
2.6682	2.5699	2.4665	2.3567	2.2989	2.239	2.176	2.111	2.041	1.968
2.6396	2.5411	2.4374	2.3273	2.2693	2.209	2.146	2.080	2.010	1.935
2.6135	2.5149	2.4110	2.3005	2.2422	2.182	2.118	2.052	1.981	1.906
2.5896	2.4908	2.3867	2.2759	2.2174	2.157	2.093	2.026	1.954	1.878
2.5676	2.4688	2.3644	2.2533	2.1946	2.133	2.069	2.002	1.930	1.853

df₁→df₂↓	1	2	3	4	5	6	7	8	9
28	5.6096	4.2205	3.6264	3.2863	3.0626	2.9027	2.7820	2.6872	2.6106
29	5.5878	4.2006	3.6072	3.2674	3.0438	2.8840	2.7633	2.6686	2.5919
30	5.5675	4.1821	3.5894	3.2499	3.0265	2.8667	2.7460	2.6513	2.5746
40	5.4239	4.0510	3.4633	3.1261	2.9037	2.7444	2.6238	2.5289	2.4519
60	5.2856	3.9253	3.3425	3.0077	2.7863	2.6274	2.5068	2.4117	2.3344
120	5.1523	3.8046	3.2269	2.8943	2.6740	2.5154	2.3948	2.2994	2.2217
INF	5.0239	3.6889	3.1161	2.7858	2.5665	2.4082	2.2875	2.1918	2.1136

$\alpha = .01$

	1	2	3	4	5	6	7	8	9
1	4052.181	4999.500	5403.352	5624.583	5763.650	5858.986	5928.356	5981.070	6022.473
2	98.503	99.000	99.166	99.249	99.299	99.333	99.356	99.374	99.388
3	34.116	30.817	29.457	28.710	28.237	27.911	27.672	27.489	27.345
4	21.198	18.000	16.694	15.977	15.522	15.207	14.976	14.799	14.659
5	16.258	13.274	12.060	11.392	10.967	10.672	10.456	10.289	10.158
6	13.745	10.925	9.780	9.148	8.746	8.466	8.260	8.102	7.976
7	12.246	9.547	8.451	7.847	7.460	7.191	6.993	6.840	6.719
8	11.259	8.649	7.591	7.006	6.632	6.371	6.178	6.029	5.911
9	10.561	8.022	6.992	6.422	6.057	5.802	5.613	5.467	5.351
10	10.044	7.559	6.552	5.994	5.636	5.386	5.200	5.057	4.942
11	9.646	7.206	6.217	5.668	5.316	5.069	4.886	4.744	4.632
12	9.330	6.927	5.953	5.412	5.064	4.821	4.640	4.499	4.388
13	9.074	6.701	5.739	5.205	4.862	4.620	4.441	4.302	4.191
14	8.862	6.515	5.564	5.035	4.695	4.456	4.278	4.140	4.030
15	8.683	6.359	5.417	4.893	4.556	4.318	4.142	4.004	3.895
16	8.531	6.226	5.292	4.773	4.437	4.202	4.026	3.890	3.780
17	8.400	6.112	5.185	4.669	4.336	4.102	3.927	3.791	3.682
18	8.285	6.013	5.092	4.579	4.248	4.015	3.841	3.705	3.597
19	8.185	5.926	5.010	4.500	4.171	3.939	3.765	3.631	3.523
20	8.096	5.849	4.938	4.431	4.103	3.871	3.699	3.564	3.457
21	8.017	5.780	4.874	4.369	4.042	3.812	3.640	3.506	3.398
22	7.945	5.719	4.817	4.313	3.988	3.758	3.587	3.453	3.346
23	7.881	5.664	4.765	4.264	3.939	3.710	3.539	3.406	3.299
24	7.823	5.614	4.718	4.218	3.895	3.667	3.496	3.363	3.256
25	7.770	5.568	4.675	4.177	3.855	3.627	3.457	3.324	3.217
26	7.721	5.526	4.637	4.140	3.818	3.591	3.421	3.288	3.182
27	7.677	5.488	4.601	4.106	3.785	3.558	3.388	3.256	3.149
28	7.636	5.453	4.568	4.074	3.754	3.528	3.358	3.226	3.120
29	7.598	5.420	4.538	4.045	3.725	3.499	3.330	3.198	3.092
30	7.562	5.390	4.510	4.018	3.699	3.473	3.304	3.173	3.067
40	7.314	5.179	4.313	3.828	3.514	3.291	3.124	2.993	2.888
60	7.077	4.977	4.126	3.649	3.339	3.119	2.953	2.823	2.718
120	6.851	4.787	3.949	3.480	3.174	2.956	2.792	2.663	2.559
INF	6.635	4.605	3.782	3.319	3.017	2.802	2.639	2.511	2.407

Source: TABLES in www.statsoft.com/textbook.

10	12	15	20	24	30	40	60	120	INF
2.5473	2.4484	2.3438	2.2324	2.1735	2.112	2.048	1.980	1.907	1.829
2.5286	2.4295	2.3248	2.2131	2.1540	2.092	2.028	1.959	1.886	1.807
2.5112	2.4120	2.3072	2.1952	2.1359	2.074	2.009	1.940	1.866	1.787
2.3882	2.2882	2.1819	2.0677	2.0069	1.943	1.875	1.803	1.724	1.637
2.2702	2.1692	2.0613	1.9445	1.8817	1.815	1.744	1.667	1.581	1.482
2.1570	2.0548	1.9450	1.8249	1.7597	1.690	1.614	1.530	1.433	1.310
2.0483	1.9447	1.8326	1.7085	1.6402	1.566	1.484	1.388	1.268	1.000
6055.847	6106.321	6157.285	6208.730	6234.631	6260.649	6286.782	6313.030	6339.391	6365.864
99.399	99.416	99.433	99.449	99.458	99.466	99.474	99.482	99.491	99.499
27.229	27.052	26.872	26.690	26.598	26.505	26.411	26.316	26.221	26.125
14.546	14.374	14.198	14.020	13.929	13.838	13.745	13.652	13.558	13.463
10.051	9.888	9.722	9.553	9.466	9.379	9.291	9.202	9.112	9.020
7.874	7.718	7.559	7.396	7.313	7.229	7.143	7.057	6.969	6.880
6.620	6.469	6.314	6.155	6.074	5.992	5.908	5.824	5.737	5.650
5.814	5.667	5.515	5.359	5.279	5.198	5.116	5.032	4.946	4.859
5.257	5.111	4.962	4.808	4.729	4.649	4.567	4.483	4.398	4.311
4.849	4.706	4.558	4.405	4.327	4.247	4.165	4.082	3.996	3.909
4.539	4.397	4.251	4.099	4.021	3.941	3.860	3.776	3.690	3.602
4.296	4.155	4.010	3.858	3.780	3.701	3.619	3.535	3.449	3.361
4.100	3.960	3.815	3.665	3.587	3.507	3.425	3.341	3.255	3.165
3.939	3.800	3.656	3.505	3.427	3.348	3.266	3.181	3.094	3.004
3.805	3.666	3.522	3.372	3.294	3.214	3.132	3.047	2.959	2.868
3.691	3.553	3.409	3.259	3.181	3.101	3.018	2.933	2.845	2.753
3.593	3.455	3.312	3.162	3.084	3.003	2.920	2.835	2.746	2.653
3.508	3.371	3.227	3.077	2.999	2.919	2.835	2.749	2.660	2.566
3.434	3.297	3.153	3.003	2.925	2.844	2.761	2.674	2.584	2.489
3.368	3.231	3.088	2.938	2.859	2.778	2.695	2.608	2.517	2.421
3.310	3.173	3.030	2.880	2.801	2.720	2.636	2.548	2.457	2.360
3.258	3.121	2.978	2.827	2.749	2.667	2.583	2.495	2.403	2.305
3.211	3.074	2.931	2.781	2.702	2.620	2.535	2.447	2.354	2.256
3.168	3.032	2.889	2.738	2.659	2.577	2.492	2.403	2.310	2.211
3.129	2.993	2.850	2.699	2.620	2.538	2.453	2.364	2.270	2.169
3.094	2.958	2.815	2.664	2.585	2.503	2.417	2.327	2.233	2.131
3.062	2.926	2.783	2.632	2.552	2.470	2.384	2.294	2.198	2.097
3.032	2.896	2.753	2.602	2.522	2.440	2.354	2.263	2.167	2.064
3.005	2.868	2.726	2.574	2.495	2.412	2.325	2.234	2.138	2.034
2.979	2.843	2.700	2.549	2.469	2.386	2.299	2.208	2.111	2.006
2.801	2.665	2.522	2.369	2.288	2.203	2.114	2.019	1.917	1.805
2.632	2.496	2.352	2.198	2.115	2.028	1.936	1.836	1.726	1.601
2.472	2.336	2.192	2.035	1.950	1.860	1.763	1.656	1.533	1.381
2.321	2.185	2.039	1.878	1.791	1.696	1.592	1.473	1.325	1.000

REFERENCES

CHAPTER 1

Stevens, S. S. (1946), On the theory of scales of measurement, *Science* **103**:677–680.

CHAPTER 4

DeMoivre, A. (1733), *The Doctrine of Chances: Or a Method of Calculating the Probabilities of Events in Play*, 2nd ed., H. Woodfall, London.

CHAPTER 5

Bayes, T. (1763), An Essay Towards Solving a Problem in the Doctrine of Chances, *Philosophical Transactions of the Royal Society of London*, **53**:370.

CHAPTER 6

Student (Gosset, W. S.) (1908), On the probable error of a mean, *Biometrika* **6**:1–25.

CHAPTER 7

Fisher, R. A. (1925), *Statistical Methods for Research Workers*, Oliver & Boyd, Edinburgh.

Analyzing Quantitative Data: An Introduction for Social Researchers, First Edition. Debra Wetcher-Hendricks.
© 2011 John Wiley & Sons, Inc. Published 2011 by John Wiley & Sons, Inc.

CHAPTER 8

Galton, F. (1889), Correlations and their measurement, chiefly from anthropometric data, *Nature* **39**:238.

Galton, F. (1890), Kinship and correlation, *North Am. Rev.* **150**:419–431.

Pearson, K. (1894), On the dissection of asymmetrical frequency curves, *Phil. Trans. Roy. Soc. Lond. A* **185**:719–810.

Pearson, K. (1896), Mathematical contributions to the theory of evolution. III. Regression, heredity and panmixia, *Phil. Trans. Roy. Soc. A* **187**:253–318.

Pearson, K. (1900), On the criterion that a given system of deviations from the probable in the case of correlated system of variables is such that it can be reasonably supposed to have arisen from random sampling, *Phil. Mag.* **50**:157–175.

CHAPTER 9

Hotelling, H. (1931), The generalization of Student's ratio, *Ann. Math. Statist.* **2**(3):360–378.

Rao, C. R. (1951), An asymptotic expansion of the distribution of Wilks' lambda criterion, *Bull. Intnatl. Statist. Inst.* **23**(Part II):177–180.

Wilks, W. S. (1932), Certain generalizations in the analysis of variance, *Biometrika* **24**:471–494.

CHAPTER 10

Campbell, D. T. and Stanley, J. C. (1966), *Experimental and Quasi-Experimental Designs for Research*, Rand McNally, Chicago.

ANSWERS TO
REVIEW QUESTIONS

1.1. A. colleges
  B. people
  C. people
  D. sets of twins

1.2. A. i.v. = number of acres; d.v. = number of students enrolled
  B. i.v. = coffee consumption; d.v. = blood pressure level
  C. i.v. = sex; d.v. = time spent playing videogames
  D. i.v. = type of twins; d.v. = number of times one's sentence is finished by the other

1.3. *Many correct answers exist. Examples follow.*
  A. i.v. attribute = number appearing on deed under label of "acerage" on deed or tax records
  d.v. attribute = number appearing under label of "enrollment" in latest college catalog
  B. i.v. attribute = subjects' response to question "How many cups of coffee do you drink in a typical day?"
  d.v. attribute = blood pressure reading recorded on a patient's chart by a physician or nurse after a medical screening
  C. i.v. attribute = designation of "M" or "F" on each person's birth certificate
  d.v. attribute = summed total appearing at the bottom of a log on which subjects record number of hours they play videogames each day for a specified number of days
  D. i.v. attribute = Subjects' answers to the question "Are you fraternal or identical twins?"
  d.v. attribute = the number of tally marks recorded by a researcher who marks one tally each time one twin's sentence is completed by the other

1.4. *Many correct answers exist. Examples follow.*
  A. Those with aggressive tendencies may be drawn to violent TV shows.
  B. Violent TV viewed ← Levels of aggression

Analyzing Quantitative Data: An Introduction for Social Researchers, First Edition. Debra Wetcher-Hendricks.
© 2011 John Wiley & Sons, Inc. Published 2011 by John Wiley & Sons, Inc.

1.5. *Many correct answers exist. Examples follow.*

A. A lack of parental supervision may lead to much violent TV viewed and the tendency to behave inappropriately.

B.

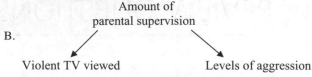

Amount of
parental supervision

Violent TV viewed   Levels of aggression

1.6. A child's desire to read and the amount of time spent reading influence each other. As the desire to read increases, the amount of time spent reading increases. However, an increase in the amount of time spent reading can lead to increased desire to read. The intervening variable of reading level may also play a role in this relationship. Reading level may be directly related to the amount of time spent reading. Spending time reading may cause reading level to increase, or those with high reading levels may spend more time reading than those with low reading levels do. An indirect relationship, involving a second intervening variable, may also exist between these two variables, Reading level may dictate the child's reading class in school, which may influence the amount of time spend reading. In addition, reading level may also relate to the desire to read in that increasing one's reading level leads to an increased desire to read.

1.7. A. quantitative
B. qualitative
C. qualitative
D. quantitative
E. quantitative

1.8. *Many correct answers exist. Examples follow.*

A. The question "For which candidate did you vote?" produces categorical data.
B. The question "In how many general elections have you voted?" produces continuous data.

1.9. *Many correct answers exist. One example follows.*

Income is a continuous variable that is often categorized into groups to indicate economic class.

1.10. A. ratio
B. ordinal
C. interval
D. categorical
E. ordinal
F. categorical

1.11. A. F; an interval level of measurement, allowing for identification of amounts of differences, is used.
B. T; classroom numbers are based on a nominal level of measurement; thus the numbers have no value.
C. T; finishing places are measured ordinarily with increases in numbers indicating decreases in time to finish the race.
D. F; a ratio scale is used. One value cannot be regarded as a part or multiple of another.
E. F; the numbers are dummy variables (nominal level of measurement) and thus have no value.

1.12. A. Not inclusive; response options pertain only to particular types of exercises.
    B. Not mutually exclusive; aerobic and nonaerobic exercise can take place in class or independently.
    C. There is no response option for those who spend time on activities other than exercise

1.13. *Many correct answers exist. Some answers follow.*

Weather: sunny = 1	Mood: happy = 1
cloudy/no precipitation = 2	content = 2
rainy = 3	angry = 3
showy = 4	sad = 4
other = 5	Other = 5

1.14. *Many correct answers exist. One example follows.*
    A. The researcher may wish to consider prices only for those who paid transportation fares.
    B. Those who drove to their destinations would be omitted.

1.15. *Many correct answers exist. One example follows.*

The researcher may wish to obtain information about nights spent at or money spent during vacations for those within each transportation category.

1.16. *Many correct answers exist. One example follows.*
    A. The researcher may wish to determine the amount of money spent per day of vacation.
    B. (total amount of money spent)/(number of nights)

2.1.

Work Status	Frequency	Percent
No job	3	12.0
Full-time	10	40.0
Part-time	7	28.0
Student	2	8.0
Retired	3	12.0
Total	25	100.0

2.2. Mode = 1; more subjects fall into the full-time category than any other category.

2.3.

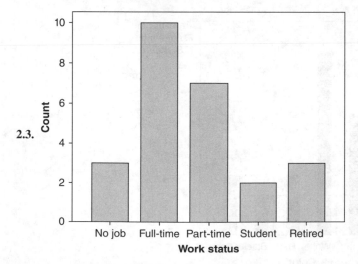

2.4.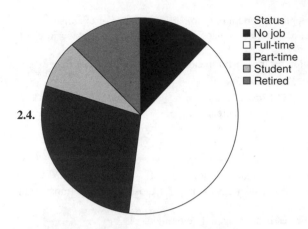

2.5.

Miles Driven per Week	Frequency	Percent
0–20	12	30.0
21–40	11	27.5
41–60	7	17.5
61–80	7	17.5
≥81	3	7.5
Total	40	100.0

2.6.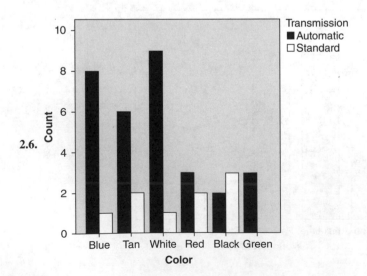

2.7.

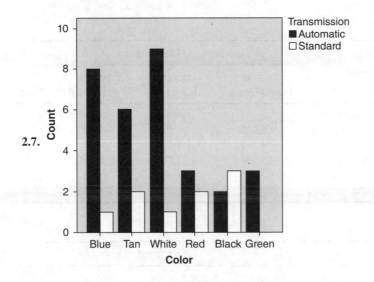

2.8.

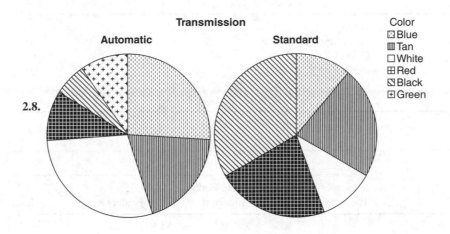

2.9.

Crime		Outcome			
		Suspect Plead Guilty	Suspect Found Innocent	Suspect Found Guilty	Total
Misdemeanor	Count	6	6	5	17
	% of total	24.0%	24.0%	20.0%	68.0%
Felony	Count	3	3	2	8
	% of total	12.0%	12.0%	8.0%	32.0%
Total	Count	9	9	7	25
	% of total	36.0%	36.0%	28.0%	100.0%

2.10.

		Outcome			
Crime		Suspect Pleads Guilty	Suspect Found Innocent	Suspect Found Guilty	Total
Misdemeanor	Count	6	6	5	17
	% within outcome	66.7%	66.7%	71.4%	68.0%
Felony	Count	3	3	2	8
	% within outcome	33.3%	33.3%	28.6%	32.0%
Total	Count	9	9	7	25
	% within outcome	100.0%	100.0%	100.0%	100.0%

2.11.

		Outcome			
Crime		Suspect Pleads Guilty	Suspect Found Innocent	Suspect Found Guilty	Total
Misdemeanor	Count	6	6	5	17
	% within crime	35.3%	35.3%	29.4%	100.0%
Felony	Count	3	3	2	8
	% within crime	37.5%	37.5%	25.0%	100.0%
Total	Count	9	9	7	25
	% within crime	36.0%	36.0%	28.0%	100.0%

2.12.

	Outcome[a]			
Crime	Suspect Pleads Guilty	Suspect Found Innocent	Suspect Found Guilty	Total
Misdemeanor	5	4	2	11
Felony	2	2	2	6
Total	7	6	4	17

[a]Male suspects only.

	Outcome[a]			
Crime	Suspect Pleads Guilty	Suspect Found Innocent	Suspect Found Guilty	Total
Misdemeanor	1	2	3	6
Felony	1	1	0	2
Total	2	3	3	8

[a]Female suspect noly.

2.13.

		Outcome			
Crime	Gender	Suspect Pleads Guilty	Suspect Found Innocent	Suspect Found Guilty	Total
Misdemeanor	Male	5	4	2	11
	Female	1	2	3	6
Felony	Male	2	2	2	6
	Female	1	1	0	2
Total		9	9	7	25

2.14. 44.9%

2.15. 46.2%

2.16. 10.9%

2.17. 5.1%

2.18. 83.3%

2.19. 89.1%

2.20. 9.5%

2.21. 9.8%

3.1.

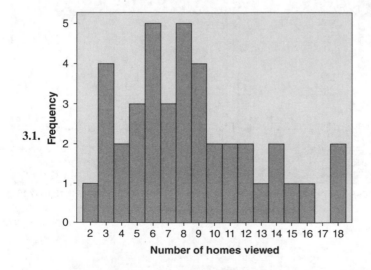

3.2.
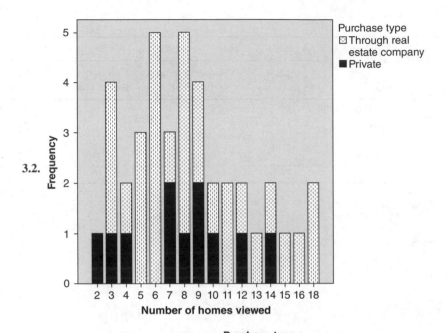

3.3.
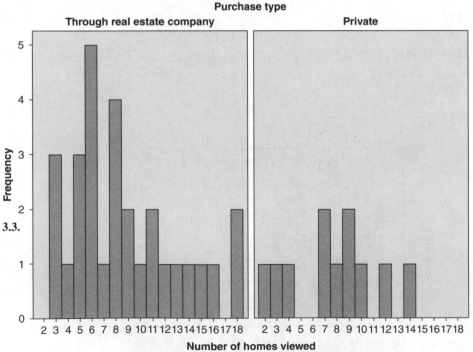

3.4. min = 2; max = 18

3.5. 16

3.6. 8.45

3.7. 6 and 8

3.8. 8

3.9. 1 | 79
  2 | 256
  3 | 22569
  4 | 0124578
  5 | 2468
  6 | 223555788
  7 | 023444
  8 | 357
  9 | 1

3.10. 25th percentile = 40
  50th percentile = 58
  75th percentile = 70

3.11. 30

3.12.

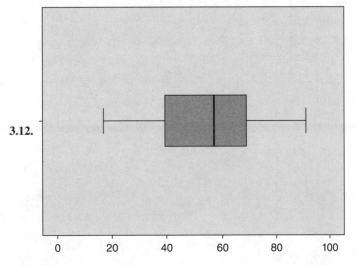

3.13. 1.78

3.14. 1.34

3.15. Raw scores are based on the scale used to measure the variable. However, standard scores identify a data point's position relative to its own mean. With standardized scores, then, one can compare values "placements" within the dataset.

3.16. A standardized score identifies the number of standard deviations between the mean and a raw score.

3.17. A. +1
  B. −3
  C. −0.86
  D. +2.19

3.18. A. 130
  B. 89.26
  C. 29.2

3.19. A. 68.3%
       B. 95.4%
       C. 84%
       D. 47.70%

3.20. A. −0.48
       B. −2.24
       C. 0.33
       D. 1.71

3.21.

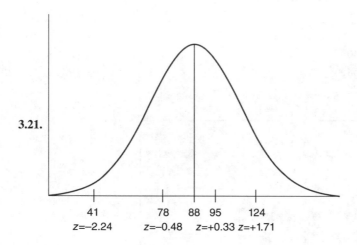

3.22. A.

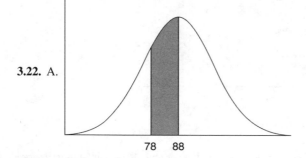

B.

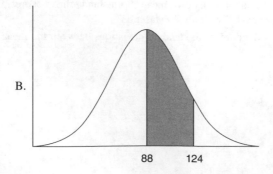

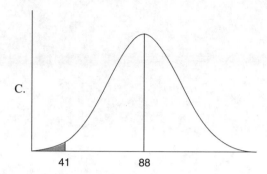

C.

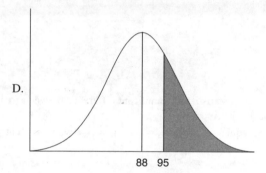

D.

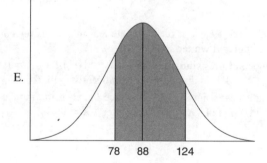

E.

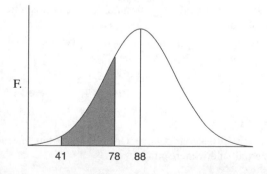

F.

3.23. A. 18.44%

   B. 45.64%

   C. 1.25%

   D. 37.07%

   E. 64.08%

   F. 30.31%

3.24. 48.4%

3.25. 47.7%

3.26. 44.95%

3.27. 49.09%

3.28. 5.05%

3.29. 0.91%

3.30. 94.04%

3.31. 13.09%

 4.1. A. 5

   B. 1

   C. 10

 4.2. The chi-square values that indicate a statistically significant difference between frequencies lie in the right tail area of the distribution.

 4.3. H_0: $f_S = f_F = f_W = f_{SP}$ (where f = frequency) or H_0: $n_S = n_F = n_W = n_{SP}$ (where n = category sample size)

 4.4. 1062

 4.5. 6.60

 4.6. 3

 4.7. $_{.01}\chi_3^2 = 11.34$; $_{.05}\chi_3^2 = 7.81$; $_{.10}\chi_3^2 = 6.25$

 4.8. Do not reject at $\alpha = .01$ and $\alpha = .05$. Reject at $\alpha = .10$. One reason for this rejection is the distinction between summer/fall and winter/spring.

 4.9. For $\alpha = .01$ and $\alpha = .05$, the numbers of arrests during summer ($\bar{X} = 1103$), fall ($\bar{X} = 1096$), winter ($\bar{X} = 998$), and spring ($\bar{X} = 1051$) do not differ significantly ($\chi^2 = 6.60$)

   For $\alpha = .10$, the χ^2 of 6.60 indicates a significiant difference between the numbers of arrests during summer ($\bar{X} = 1103$), fall ($\bar{X} = 1096$), winter ($\bar{X} = 998$), and spring ($\bar{X} = 1051$).

 5.1. A. 5

   B. 1

   C. 10

 5.2. The chi-square values that indicate a statistically significant difference between frequencies lie in the right-tail area of the distribution.

 5.3. H_0: $f_S = f_F = f_W = I_{SP}$ (where f = frequency) or H_0: $n_S = n_F = n_W = n_{SP}$ (where n = category sample size)

 5.4. 1062

 5.5. 6.60

 5.6. 3

 5.7. $_{.01}\chi_3^2 = 11.34$; $_{.05}\chi_3^2 = 7.81$; $_{.10}\chi_3^2 = 6.25$

 5.8. Do not reject at $\alpha = .01$ and $\alpha = .05$. Reject at $\alpha = .10$. One reason for this rejection is the distinction between summer/fall and winter/spring.

5.9. For $\alpha = .01$ and $\alpha = .05$, the numbers of arrests during summer ($n = 1103$), fall ($n = 1096$), winter ($n = 998$), and spring ($n = 1051$) do not differ significantly ($\chi^2 = 6.60$). For $\alpha = .10$, the χ^2 of 6.60 indicates a significant difference between the numbers of arrests during summer ($n = 1103$), fall ($n = 1096$), winter ($n = 998$), and spring ($n = 1051$).

5.10. *Many correct answers exist.* One reason for the significant results is the difference between the frequencies for swings and for monkey bars.

5.11. $\chi^2_{calc} = 3.12$; do not reject H_0.

5.12. Post hoc tests are not necessary because no significant difference exists.

5.13.

Card lype	Diamonds	Hearts	Spades	Clubs	Sum (Σ)
Face	15.78	18.55	19.38	18.28	72
Nonface	41.22	48.45	50.62	47.72	188
Sum (Σ)	57	67	70	66	260

5.14. 4.80

5.15. 3

5.16. $_{.01}\chi^2_3 = 11.34$; $_{.05}\chi^2_3 = 7.81$; $_{10}\chi^2_3 = 6.25$

5.17. Do not reject at $\alpha = .01$, $\alpha = .05$, or $\alpha = .10$.

5.18. For all α levels tested, no significant difference exists between the observed and expected frequencies of face and nonface cards of each suit.

5.19. *Many correct answers exist.* One reason for the rejected null hypothesis is the difference between the frequencies for all those who used no good-luck measure and for all those who used some good-luck ritual.

5.20. A. $\chi^2_{calc} = 75.52$; Reject H_0

B. *Many correct answers exist.* One reason for the rejected null hypothesis is the difference in frequencies for all remedial readers and all on-level readers.

5.21.

Reader level	Type	A	B	C	D	F	Σ (within School Type)	Σ (Total)
Remedial	Public	9.94	21.31	23.62	10.08	7.06	72.01	90
	Private	2.48	5.33	5.90	2.52	1.76	17.99	
On-level	Public	34.22	73.41	81.34	34.72	24.30	247.99	
	Private	8.56	18.35	20.34	8.68	6.08	620.01	
Advanced	Public	11.04	23.68	26.24	11.20	7.84	80	100
	Private	2.76	5.92	6.56	2.80	1.96	20	
Σ (sum)		69	148	164	70	49	500	500

5.22. A. 0–12.59

B. 0–10.64

C. The confidence interval pertains to the area of the distribution that does not fall into the tails. The 90% confidence interval defines the left limit of the distribution's right tail lower than the 95% confidence interval does because a smaller range of values (those in the tail) leads to a rejected H_0 when $\alpha = .05$ than when $\alpha = .10$.

6.1. independent-samples

6.2. one-sample

6.3. paired-samples

6.4. paired-samples

6.5. independent-samples

6.6. H_0: $\mu_{days} = 3$

6.7. .489

6.8. 5

6.9. $_{.01}t_5 = 3.37$; $_{.05}t_5 = 2.02$; $_{.10}t_5 = 1.48$

6.10. no; no; no

6.11. For $\alpha = .01$, $\alpha = .05$, and $\alpha = .10$, the mean number of days needed to sell a home, 35, does not differ significantly from the standard 30-day time period.

6.12. H_0: $\mu_Y = \mu_N$

6.13. −2.35

6.14. 4

6.15. $_{.01}t_4 = 3.75$; $_{05}t_4 = 2.13$; $_{10}t_4 = 1.53$

6.16. no; yes; yes

6.17. For $\alpha = .01$, anxiety levels of the individuals from the roommate pairs who participated in the program ($\bar{X} = 45.50$) and anxiety levels of the individuals from the roommate pairs who did not participate in the program ($\bar{X} = 58.40$) did not differ significantly ($t = 2.354$).

For $\alpha = .05$ and $\alpha = .10$, anxiety levels of the individuals from the roommate pairs who participated in the program ($\bar{X} = 45.50$) and anxiety levels of the individuals from the roommate pairs who did not participate in the program ($\bar{X} = 58.40$) differed significantly ($t = 2.354$).

6.18. H_0: $\mu_W = \mu_C$

6.19. 2.18

6.20. 12

6.21. $_{.01}t_{12} = 2.68$; $_{.05}t_{12} = 2.132$; $_{.10}t_{12} = 1.533$

6.22. no; yes; yes

6.23. For $\alpha = .01$, the t value of 2.18 suggests no significant difference between the mean number of nights spent at vacation destinations warmer (6.71) and cooler (4.14) than their hometowns.

For $\alpha = .05$ and $\alpha = .10$, the t value of 2.18 suggests that subjects spent significantly more nights in vacation destinations warmer than their hometowns ($\bar{X} = 6.71$) than they spent in vacation destinations cooler than their hometowns ($\bar{X} = 4.14$).

7.1. 1.90

7.2. H_0: $\mu_F = \mu_{BA} = \mu_{BR} = \mu_{BU}$

7.3. $\mu_F = 19.32$; $\mu_{BA} = 10.90$; $\mu_{BR} = 19.94$; $\mu_{BU} = 20.30$

7.4. $\sum X_F^2 = 2244.27$; $\sum X_{BA}^2 = 1311.93$; $\sum X_{BR}^2 = 1995.53$; $\sum X_{BU}^2 = 2070.79$

7.5. $(\sum X_F)^2 = 13432.81$; $(\sum X_{BA})^2 = 3931.29$; $(\sum X_{BR})^2 = 9940.09$; $(\sum X_{BU})^2 = 10302.25$

7.6. 7952.00

7.7. A. 30.52

B. 5.70

C. 24.82

7.8. A. 18

B. 3

C. 15

7.9.

Source	SS	df	MS	F
Between	5.70	3	1.90	1.15
Within	24.82	15	1.15	—
Total	30.52	18	—	—

7.10. See table for Answer 7.9.

7.11. A. $_{.01}t_{3,15} = 5.42$; $_{.05}t_{3,15} = 3.29$; $_{.10}t_{3,15} = 2.49$

7.12. no; no; no

7.13. For $\alpha = .10$, $\alpha = .05$, and $\alpha = .10$, the F of 1.15 does not allow for a rejected null hypothesis. Mean times, in seconds, for swimming 25 yards of freestyle (19.32), backstroke (20.9), breaststroke (19.94), and butterfly (20.30) did not differ significantly.

7.14. H_0: $\mu_M = \mu_G = \mu_P$

7.15. 4353.95

7.16. $_{.01}F_{2,87} = 6.94$; $_{.05}F_{2,87} = 3.95$; $_{.10}F_{2,87} = 2.77$

7.17. yes; yes; yes

7.18. For $\alpha = .10$, $\alpha = .05$, and $\alpha = .10$, the percentage that bins for metal ($\overline{X} = 66.5$), glass $\overline{X} = 48.2$), and plastic $\overline{X} = 70.2$) were filled differed significantly (F-4353.95).

7.19. *Many correct answers exist.* One reason for the significant results is the difference between the percentages that bins for metal and glass were filled.

7.20. A. Do not reject H_0 ($F_{calc} = 3.50$; $_{.05}F_{2,9} = 4.26$)
B. No post hoc tests are necessary.

7.21. H_0: $\mu_{BF} = \mu_{BS} = \mu_{BT} = \mu_{WF} = \mu_{WS} = \mu_{WT}$

7.22. $\overline{X}_{BF} = 35$; $\overline{X}_{BS} = 20$; $\overline{X}_{BT} = 30$; $\overline{X}_{WF} = 25$; $\overline{X}_{WS} = 20$; $\overline{X}_{WT} = 27.5$

7.23. 315

7.24. 9275

7.25. A. 49,925
B. 34,025

7.26. 17,225

7.27. A. 8268.75
B. 9275
C. 8320.83
D. 8506.25
E. 8612.50

7.28. A. 1006.25
B. 52.08
C. 237.50
D. 54.17
E. 662.50

7.29. A. 11
B. 1
C. 2
D. 2
E. 6

7.30.

Source	SS	df	MS	F
Row	52.08	1	52.08	0.472
Column	237.50	2	118.75	1.075
$R \times C$	54.17	2	27.09	0.245
S/RC	662.50	6	110.42	—
Total	1006.25	11	—	—

7.31. See table for Answer 7.30.

7.32. $_{.01}F_{1,6} = 13.75$; $_{.05}F_{1,6} = 5.99$; $_{.10}F_{1,6} = 3.78._{.01}F_{2,6} = 10.93$; $_{.05}F_{2,6} = 5.14$; $_{.10}F_{2,6} = 3.46$

7.33. no; no; no

7.34. For $\alpha = .10$, $\alpha = .05$, and $\alpha = .10$, F values of .472 for the type of job effect, 1.075 for shift effect, and .245 for the interaction between job and shift indicate that none of the differences between means qualify as significant.

7.35. It is clear that no interaction effect exists because the lines related to blue-collar and white-collar workers decrease and increase on the same intervals, creating nearly parallel lines.

7.36. $F_{row} = 6.52$; $F_{column} = 54.05$; $F_{R \times C} = .24$

7.37. $_{.01}F_{2,36} = 5.25$; $_{.05}F_{2,36} = 3.26$; $_{.10}F_{3,36} = 2.46._{.01}F_{4,36} = 3.89$; $_{.05}F_{4,36} = 2.63$; $_{.10}F_{4,36} = 2.11$

7.38. yes; yes; yes

7.39. *Many correct answers exist.* One reason for the significant results is the difference between the expenses for all those with moderate and frequent exposure to allergens.

7.40. A. 0–2.04

   B. 0–2.33

   C. The confidence interval pertains to the area of the distribution that does not fall into the tails. The 95% confidence interval defines the left limit of the distribution's right tail lower than the 99% confidence interval does because a smaller range of values (those in the tail) leads to a rejected H_0 when $\alpha = .01$ than when $\alpha = .05$.

8.1. negative

8.2. negative

8.3. neither

8.4. positive

8.5. neither

8.6. $+\frac{1}{3}$

8.7. 50

8.8. $y = 50 + \frac{1}{3}x$

8.9. 83.33 seconds

8.10. As the regression equation's effectiveness in making predictions increases, the absolute value of the correlation coefficient increases.

8.11. moderate negative

8.12. no correlation

8.13. weak positive

8.14. strong positive

8.15. $r = -.41$

8.16. $r^2 = .1681$; 16.81% of changes in one variable's scores can be explained by changes in the other variable's scores.

8.17. negative

8.18. Points are somewhat dispersed, but clearly indicate a downward trend.

8.19. moderate

8.20. 42.25%

8.21. The analysis addressed only linear relationships. A curvilinear relationship may exist. For example, low or high sticker requirements for earning a prize may not encourage children to behave well. Children may earn prizes too easily or may refuse to behave because earning a prize seems unattainable. The most effective sticker requirements may lie in the middle of the range.

8.22. part correlation; i.v.—grade in typing class, d.v.—typographic errors per page, I.V.—typing speed

8.23. multiple correlation; i.v. 1—number of calories consumed for breakfast, i.v. 2—number of calories consumed for lunch, d.v.—number of calories consumed for dinner

8.24. part correlation; i.v.—size of print, d.v.—time needed to complete brain-teaser puzzle, i.v.—subjects' levels of vision

8.25. partial correlation; i.v—air temperature, d.v.—plants' rates of growth, i.v.—humidity level

8.26. A. $r_{XY} = .55$; $r_{XZ} = -.66$; $r_{YZ} = .42$

B. .58

C. The multiple-correlation coefficient of .58 indicates that combination of money spent during a campaign and the weeks spent campaigning has a moderate linear relationship with the percentage of the popular vote that a candidate receives.

8.27. The answer is .34; 34% of differences in the percentage of popular vote received by a candidate can be explained by differences in the combination of money spent during the campaign and weeks spent campaigning.

8.28. A. $-.59$

B. When controlling for subjects' current ages, there is a moderate linear relationship between people's ages at the time of marriage and the number of children that they produce. The partial correlation coefficient of $-.59$ indicates that the number of children people have decreases as age at the time of marriage increases.

8.29. A. $-.59$

B. A part correlation analysis, examining the linear relationship between age at the time of marriage and number of children, regardless of any relationship that subjects' ages may have with the first of these factors, produced a coefficient of $-.59$. This value indicates a moderate tend of a decrease in the number of children as age at the time of marriage increases.

8.30. $-.27$; there is a weak trend for fast-food restaurants to have more children and teenage than adult customers and for the opposite to be true for full-service restaurants.

9.1. ANCOVA; the hypothesis addresses the relationship between hair color (i.v.) and time spent in beauty salons (d.v.) while controlling for hair length (covariate).

9.2. MANOVA; athletic team is the predictor (i.v.) of a canonical variate reflecting strength (d.v._1) and speed (d.v._2).

9.3. Discriminant analysis; the continuous measure of number of students in the class predicts the transportation method, which is categorical.

9.4. Discriminant analysis; the placement of a room into the "lights off" or "lights on" category is predicted by the continuous measure of sunlight level.

9.5. Repeated-measures ANOVA; the same subjects provide data in the morning, afternoon, and evening. Thus, the three means for reaction time (d.v.) compared in the analyses are not independent of one another.

9.6. MANOVA; restaurants' dress code categories (i.v.) predicts the canonical variate score, which reflects the dependent variables of food quality, service, and atmosphere ratings.

9.7. 12.05

9.8. 3

9.9. 6

9.10. 11

9.11. 2

9.12. 19.33

9.13. A. The first post hoc test should compare a combinations of conditions A and B with condition C. Conditions A and B have relatively close means, but condition C's mean is somewhat lower than these are.

B. paired-samples t test

9.14. Testing means of a canonical variate avoids misrepresentation of effects when dependent variables are correlated. The canonical variate values represent a combination of dependent variables while considering any linear relationship between them.

9.15. The SSCP is a MANOVA version of the SS. Calculations for SSCP are based on a canonical variate, not an individual dependent variable, as the SS is.

9.16. A.

Source	SSCP	df	MS	F
Between	112.58	3	37.52	6.85
Within	49.36	91	5.48	6.85
Total	161.94	12	—	—

B. 8.81

C. No; the calculated F value does not exceed the critical F value.

9.17. A.

Source	SSCP	df	MS	F_{calc}
Row (R)	74.89	2	37.45	22.43
Column (C)	61.21	2	30.61	18.33
Interaction ($R \times C$)	122.25	4	30.56	18.30
Within groups (S/RC)	40.05	24	1.67	—
Total	298.39	32	—	—

B. row—19.45; column—19.45; interaction—5.77

C. Yes; no; yes; the calculated F values for the row and interaction effects exceed their respective critical F values, but the calculated F value for the column effect does not.

9.18. A. differences in dependent-variable means for independent-variable groups

B. differences between each subject's dependent-variable score and scores of other subjects in the same independent-variable group

C. differences between each subject's dependent-variable score and scores of all other subjects

D. differences in covariate means for independent-variable groups

E. differences between each subject's covariate score and covariate scores of other subjects in the same independent-variable group

F. differences between each subject's covariate score and covariate scores of all other subjects

9.19. A. university

B. number of months to complete the program

C. years of experience

9.20. 108.90

9.21. A. 16.20; 95.20

B. 111.70

9.22. A. calories in main course

B. type of dessert

9.23. A. x_2; it has the largest coefficient.

B. x_3; it has the smallest coefficient.

10.1. Equal numbers of males have mustaches, beards, and both mustaches and beards (H_0: $F_M = F_B = F_{MB}$).

10.2. The research hypothesis is correct. The research and null hypothesis are identical. The decision about the null hypothesis also applies to the research hypothesis.

10.3. The research hypothesis is not correct. The research and null hypothesis are identical. The decision about the null hypothesis also applies to the research hypothesis.

10.4. Equal numbers of males have mustaches, beards, and both mustaches and beards (H_0: $F_M = F_B = F_{MB}$).

10.5. The research hypothesis is correct. If equality exists, as indicated by a failure to reject the null hypothesis, then the inequality suggested by the research hypothesis cannot be correct.

10.6. The research hypothesis may be correct. The inequality that exists, as indicated by the rejection of the null hypothesis, may be the one predicted by the research hypothesis.

10.7. No; the null hypothesis cannot be rejected, indicating equality between the times.

10.8. No; because subjects took longer to read the sports than the local section, the difference that exists is not the one predicted by the research hypothesis.

10.9. No; the time needed to read the local section may differ significantly from only the time needed to read the local section, but not the time needed to read the sports section.

10.10. Ecological fallacy; characteristics of a category of movies are assumed to exist for a particular move in that category.

10.11. Reductionism; issues other than race are not addressed as possible explanations for the correlation.

10.12. Neither

10.13. Both; issues other than inflation are not addressed as possible explanations for the decline in fresh fruit purchases *and* it is assumed that shoppers now buy frozen or canned fruits and vegetables rather than no fruits and vegetables at all.

10.14. Ecological fallacy; the individuals who are injured are not necessarily children.

Many correct answers exist for Questions 11.1–11.2. Those given below are samples of correct answers.

11.1. For hay fever sufferers, springtime can be frustrating.

11.2. The telephones of those who use email regularly ring less often than do the telephones of those who do not use email regularly.

11.3. Employees are more relaxed when they have flexible schedules than when they have strict workhours.

11.4. When considering all costs, people end up paying just as much in veterinarian bills for their cats as for their dogs.

11.5. There is a positive correlation between a student's numerical grade in a class and how he or she rates the professor of that class on the course evaluation.

11.6. The researcher asked the children to list their favorite and least favorite books.

11.7. Most often, local newspaper reporters obtain information about stories before national newspaper reporters do.

11.8. To avoid subjects giving excessively long responses to interview questions, there will be a time limit for all surveys.

11.9. Students may not use calculators during the test.

11.10. The results of the investigation are clear.

11.11. A new study could investigate a linear relationship between the number of spelling mistakes and the number of grammar mistakes made when writing.

11.12. Cousins share fewer secrets with each other than siblings do.

11.13. C, B, A

11.14. C, B, D, E, A

11.15. C, A, B

11.16. A, C, B, D

Many correct answers exist for Questions 17 and 18. Those given below are samples of correct answers.

11.17. There is a slight tendency ($r = -.27$) for the length of a checkers game (y) to decrease as the age difference between opponents (x) increases. Differences in opponents' ages can explain 7.3% of differences in the lengths of games. Thus, although only a weak relationship exists, the null hypothesis, suggesting no linear relationship between the two, is rejected. The existing linear relationship is represented by the regression equation $y-27.90-.21x$.

11.18. Of those wearing wristwatches, 45.5% were late for their appointments and 61.7% of those not wearing wristwatches were late for their appointments. The χ_1^2 of 10.05 suggests that these percentages differ significantly at $\alpha = .05$. Thus, the null hypothesis is rejected and the research hypothesis is supported.

INDEX

Analyzing Quantitative Data: An Introduction for Social Researchers, First Edition. Debra Wetcher-Hendricks.
© 2011 John Wiley & Sons, Inc. Published 2011 by John Wiley & Sons, Inc.

variable view screen (in SPSS), 21–25, 27,
52, 54
Decimals, 22–23
Label, 22–23
Name, 22–23
Type, 22–23
Values, 22–23
Width, 22
variance, 75–79, 92–93, 107–108, 170–171,
174, 181–182, 215, 242, 247, 250,
257, 275, 283–284
pooled, 170–171, 215
variance, homogeneity of, 284
voice, 329–331
active, 329, 332
passive, 328

Wilks, Samuel S., 281
Wilks' lambda, 289, 293–294, 297–298

x axis, 45–46, 64–65, 68, 82, 107, 164,
189–190, 201, 232, 243, 259

y axis, 45, 47, 64–65, 107, 127, 161, 189,
201, 217, 232, 259, 261
y intercept, 234, 236, 246, 260, 262

z axis, 245
z score, See standardized score
z-score table, 83–84, 355–356